MAIN

Also by
Lynn Peril

PINK THINK

COLLEGE GIRLS

Bluestockings, Sex Kittens, and Coeds, Then and Now

Lynn Peril

W · W · NORTON & COMPANY
NEW YORK · LONDON

For information about permission to reproduce selections from this book, write to
Permissions, W. W. Norton & Company, Inc., 500 Fifth Avenue, New York, NY 10110

Manufacturing by The Haddon Craftsmen, Inc.
Book design by Rubina Yeh
Production manager: Anna Oler

Library of Congress Cataloging-in-Publication Data

Peril, Lynn.
College girls : bluestockings, sex kittens, and coeds, then and now / Lynn Peril.—1st ed.
p. cm.
Includes bibliographical references.
ISBN-13: 978-0-393-32715-1 (pbk.)
ISBN-10: 0-393-32715-9 (pbk.)
1. Women college students—United States—Attitudes. 2. Women—United
States—Identity. 3. Women—Education (Higher)—Unites States. 4. Women college
students—United States—History—20th century. 5. Education, Higher—
United States—History—20th century. I. Title.
LC1756.P47 2006
378.1'9822—dc22   20060188906

W. W. Norton & Company, Inc.
500 Fifth Avenue, New York, N.Y. 10110
www.wwnorton.com

W. W. Norton & Company Ltd.
Castle House, 75/76 Wells Street, London W1T 3QT

1 2 3 4 5 6 7 8 9 0

To my parents, Gene and Alice,
for making sure I became a college girl

CONTENTS

ACKNOWLEDGMENTS

It took almost as long for me to write this book as it did to get my undergraduate degree. I'm not sure who was more patient during that time: my editor, Alane Mason, or my husband, Johnny Bartlett. I couldn't have written this book without either one of them.

Shirley Wajda, Mary Ricci, and Mary Ann Irwin read early, embarrassingly bad drafts, sometimes multiple times—thank you, ladies. Comments from Alessandra Bastagli and Vanessa Levine-Smith were also much appreciated.

Faye Bender has been endlessly enthusiastic. I'm looking forward to our next project.

To everybody at W. W. Norton & Company, thanks from the bottom of my heart for making me look so good in print.

Thanks also go to Michael Beller and Janice Braun at Mills College, Browning Brooks and Lucy Patrick at Florida State University, Diane Cantwell, Karen Finlay, Susan Frankel, Beth S. Harris at Hollins University, the Ladies Lit List, David C. Levy, Miriam Linna, the Mills College Fires of Wisdom Oral History Project (especially Suzette Lalime Davidson and Cecile Caterson), John Marr, Jessica Rudin MacGregor, Sharyn November, Kurt and Karen Ohlen, Mimi Pond, Ron and Maria at Kayo Books in San Francisco, Chip Rowe, Scott Sanders at Antiochiana, Morgan Alberts Smith at Mary Baldwin College, J. Peter Wentz, and Michael Zadoorian. I also thank the helpful librarians and archivists at Cornell University, the Mechanic's Institute Library, San Francisco Public Library (especially in the San Francisco History Room and Photo Collection), Teachers College, Columbia University, and everybody who patted my head when the going got tough.

COLLEGE GIRLS

*A pair of Wellesley students practice poise and posture on
the way to hygiene class, 1936.*

From Bluestockings to Sex Kittens

BLUE STOCKING, a name given to learned and literary ladies, who display their acquirements in a vain and pedantic manner, to the neglect of womanly duties and virtues.

CHAMBERS ENCYCLOPÆDIA, 1872–1873 EDITION

Maybe you know a college freshman like this one: a bright-eyed eighteen-year-old girl who for the past year or so has been caught up in a wealth of glossy brochures and interactive online presentations from giant state universities and small liberal arts colleges. In the 1930s she would have been nicknamed Betty Coed, but we'll call her Jane Doe. Jane's visited a campus or two, or talked to an alumna who lives in her hometown. She has spent countless hours worrying that her admission essay about how her summer job as a coffee-shop barista helped her grow as a human being won't stand out from those of her fellow applicants, all of whom she imagines as having spent their formative years in a combination of volunteerism and philanthropy that would make Mother Teresa look shiftless by comparison. Jane (and her parents) have struggled with financial-aid forms and scholarship applications. The sting of rejection by her first-choice school has been soothed by the balm of fat acceptance packets from numbers two and three. She has carefully considered their degree programs in her intended major, distance from her hometown, tuition costs, and overall reputations for academics versus partying, as well as certain intangible factors—such as whether her brother goes there or how many cute boys or girls she saw when she visited—and come to a decision about which college she will attend.

Then one day in August, she kisses parents, pets, siblings, and perhaps most difficult, boyfriend or girlfriend good-bye, promises to call or e-mail regularly, and heads off to campus—at long last a college girl.

Depending on the rules and facilities at that school, Jane Doe's home for the next year or so may be a 12- x 15-foot dormitory room, furnished with a roommate (whom she's probably never met face to face), bed, desk, chair, and dresser for each of them, and a telephone—though with the ubiquity of cell phones, even that link to the past is becoming obsolete. Jane's room may be located on an all-female or coed floor or one reserved for lesbian, gay, bisexual, and transgender students. She can choose to live on a drug- and alcohol-free floor, one devoted to a particular cultural group or healthy lifestyle (the "wellness" floor), or one with extended quiet hours. Her room may not be much bigger than a hermit's cell, but it is hardly a monastic retreat: it is wired for cable TV and high-speed Internet access, though Jane must rent or purchase a small refrigerator and/or microwave if she wants to have one. At some schools, Jane and her roommate can even order snacks and toiletries, including condoms, from the comfort of their room via Web sites run by enterprising fellow students, who will deliver the items directly to their door.[1] The condoms may come in handy. Depending on where she goes to school, Jane might be entitled to have an overnight guest, free of charge, two nights a month—as long as her roommate approves of the arrangement.

Our girl has a better way to spend her evening hours, for once classes start, Jane carries a full load. Comparative Politics, Perspectives in Engineering, Introduction to Feminist History—Jane has a thirst for knowledge and big plans for her future. She wants to test the waters in as many different subjects as she can before she declares a major. If she didn't bring a laptop with her, the library probably has a twenty-four-hour computer lab, but she might not have to go that far: one may be located in her dormitory. If Jane does have to move around campus after dark, she can call the night escort service to make sure she safely gets where she's going.

For most of her needs, Jane won't have to leave the campus. The student union building provides art galleries and performance spaces, pool tables and arcade games, sometimes even a rathskeller or pub where, as soon as they turn twenty-one, Jane and her friends can drown their academic woes with the golden ale. Many schools have athletic centers where Jane can work out, swim, or play racquetball. If she's not feeling well—physically or mentally—she can stop by the student health center, where she can also get birth control, free or low-cost pregnancy testing, and information about and treatment for STDs (all good reasons to keep a pack of condoms handy, Jane!).

One thing Jane Doe probably won't notice is the number of young women in her classes or, come graduation day, how many of them are crossing the platform to receive their diplomas alongside her. Since the last quarter of the twentieth century, however, more women than men have enrolled in college, and as of 2001, 58 percent of those who graduated were women—a record.[2] Although Jane and her cohort may not yet sign up for engineering or computer science classes in the same numbers as men, those who do don't worry that studying traditionally male subjects will compromise their femininity—or their health.

With the glaring exception of the technology, and some of the social policies, Jane's campus isn't vastly different from the one I spent five years at in the early 1980s—backpacks and paper cups of coffee are still ubiquitous. By personal comparison, however, I was much more of a Jane Don't.

Once upon a time, college seemed so promising. When my friend Ruth and I were ten and eleven years old, we spent slow, sticky Wisconsin summer afternoons playing board games in the basement of her parents' townhouse. Seated on large cushions scattered around the cool comfort of the floor, we took turns sinking each other's battleships and pretending we knew how to play chess. These were cheery enough diversions, but we always came back to the Game of Life.

Based on a nineteenth-century game resurrected by the Milton Bradley company for its centennial in 1960, Life started players out with $2,000 and a tiny plastic car (a solitary pink or blue peg in the driver's seat), then immediately forced them to choose between two different routes along the three-dimensional plastic hills of its game board: one leading "To Business," the other "To College." Depending on the choices made, one ended up—car crammed with pink and blue pegs representing spouse and children accumulated along the way—at either Millionaire Acres or the Poor Farm.

Ruth and I always chose college even though going directly into business made for a quicker payday, and the collegiate route was marked with spaces like the one requiring us to "Pay $500 for raccoon coat"—gibberish to a couple of fifth-graders in 1972. Nevertheless, we trusted that the college experience was going to be a bright part of our future, even the beginning of life itself—the real one, not the Milton Bradley version—leading us to our own personal version of Millionaire Acres.

Of course it didn't turn out that way. One look at the scowling mug on my freshman ID tells the whole story: I did not want to go to college. Not. At. All.

At least part of the attitude I projected was due to a carefully cultivated punk-rock tough-chick persona. Sitting for the school photographer that afternoon in September 1979, I was wearing a purple thrift store T-shirt and black stovepipe jeans from Trash and Vaudeville, a Manhattan store whose mail order department was a godsend to true believers stuck in the flannel shirt and flared jeans wilderness of the Milwaukee suburbs. I was sporting the shortest haircut I'd ever had, a buzz cut anomaly back in the days of Farrah feathering, though twenty-five

The author, September 1979. Bad attitude in a mini-mullet.

years later it looks disconcertingly like a mini-mullet. Lots of black eye-liner completed the look and helped emphasize my sullen glare. If I had to be there, at least I looked hip (though it's questionable whether I would have appreciated any analogy between my punk-rock mufti and the raccoon coats of yore).

Mostly, though, the look on my face reflected turmoil over a bigger problem: I had no idea what I wanted to do with my life. A year earlier—when my classmates had been busy filling out early-decision applications and planning what I imagined were successful futures as doctors, attorneys, and engineers—my mother had asked me again and again what career path I wanted to follow. "But you must want to be something," she finally snapped, exasperated by my silence. I wasn't trying to be difficult. I simply didn't have an answer for her.

In my heart of hearts I knew I wasn't ready for college yet, but in my family there had never been a question about what I would do after high school—and it wasn't taking a year off to do something so nebulous as "find myself." College attendance was mandatory—probably because neither of my parents had been able to enroll because of forces beyond their control. My mother's father died when she was eighteen, and she went to work to help support her mother and five younger siblings. My father spent what would have been his college years on a Navy destroyer fighting World War II in the Pacific. They made sure my brother and I didn't miss the opportunity for higher education that circumstances had denied them, and they worked long and hard to fund our undergraduate degrees.

This bit of knowledge helped me feel extra guilty as I skulked around the Milwaukee campus of the University of Wisconsin in an unrelenting undergraduate haze of doubt, confusion, and depression. It wasn't quite a Midwestern punk-rock take on Sylvia Plath's classic of college girl alienation, *The Bell Jar*, but it certainly wasn't the merry-go-round of proms, parties, and gaiety I read about in books and magazines, or saw at the movies and on television. I wasn't a cheerleader, I never went to a dance, I didn't date the Big Man on Campus. I certainly never crammed myself into a phone booth with twenty other crazed students. I didn't even particularly like the taste of beer. Instead I sulked, stalked into classes late or didn't go at all, and got shockingly poor grades for a former National Merit Scholarship Finalist. Unless it was a class that interested me ("Feminist Film Criticism and the Golden Age of Hollywood," for example); then, of course, I got As. I'm positive my commitment to underachievement frustrated more than one professor.

While such behavior may have been flamboyant, it wasn't anything remotely unusual (except possibly for the part about not liking beer). I was just one of many, many young women (and men, for that matter) on campus struggling with issues of identity and looming adulthood. In other words, I was a normal college girl. I spent little time—OK, no time—thinking about how it came to be, historically speaking, that I was even on campus in the first place. Women always went to college, right?

Despite an almost infallible belief (especially where my parents were concerned) in my intellectual superiority, there was in fact a lot I needed to learn.

Had I only noticed, college-girl history was all around me. That cluster of dark, vaguely Gothic-looking buildings at a northeast corner of the campus, so different from those of 1960s industrial design where I had my classes? This was the site of the all-women Milwaukee-Downer College, born of an 1895 merger between Downer College (originally the Wisconsin Female College, founded in 1855) and the Milwaukee Female College (founded in 1851 as part of domestic educator Catharine Beecher's initiative to train teachers on the western frontier). In 1964, Milwaukee-Downer sold its 43-acre campus to my alma mater, the University of Wisconsin–Milwaukee.[3]

It wasn't until much later that I got interested in the college girl. I was researching a chapter on women and work for my first book, *Pink Think*, when I came across a 1940 *Better Homes & Gardens* article that queried, "If your daughter

A "co-educated girl of the west," circa 1904.

goes to college . . . Will she be a better homemaker? Will college make a spinster of her? Should your daughter go to college to get a husband?"[4] Fascinated as always by the ideas and attitudes surrounding what constitutes proper female behavior, i.e., the "pink think" adhered to by manufacturers, advice experts, and the public at large particularly during the mid-twentieth century, I started to think about just what it meant to be a "college girl"—the monolithic capital-lettered sort beloved of cultural commentators, advice writers, and authors of pulp fiction. Who knew that higher education was once considered, as writer Wainwright Evans suggested, a potential first step toward a lifetime partnership? "Any girl who lets herself forget the fact that one important use of an education is to help her toward achieving a happy marriage, a home, and a family—the things she really wants—is being a very foolish virgin indeed."[5]

Had I been foolish? To me, boy watching was an agreeable by-product of attending class, a pleasing lagniappe provided by a benevolent universe when one made the sacrifice of attending an 8:00 A.M. meeting of Algebra I. It was definitely not an invitation to eternal wedded bliss. I had heard of the fabled MRS. degree, where a girl's college education was crowned by a wedding ring instead of a diploma, but I wrote it off as a fabled and transparent ploy suggested by only the most fear-mongering advice columnists. As it turned out, meeting men was long considered a very legitimate reason for girls to continue their education. "Many parents send their daughters to college with secret or expressed expectation that the latter will be on the lookout for marriageable young men," wrote a Kansas professor in 1910. College was "the greatest matrimonial bureau on earth," where nine out of ten coeds attended classes "only as an aid in securing a husband. . . . Young men, beware," concluded a psychology professor in the mid-1930s. "Do you want to go where there are only women, or do you want your light so to shine among men that you will perhaps get your MRS. as soon as your B.A.?" asked *Calling All Girls*, a magazine for preteens, in 1945.[6]

I was more shocked to discover that "the issue of whether women should stay home or go to college" was the topic debated by the "fellows at Yale and Princeton" as recently as 1961. *Teens Today* magazine reported that one of Princeton's arguments to the negative was the hoary old chestnut "A man wants a woman to fill his pipe, not smoke it!"[7] The whole issue seemingly belonged in a century filled with hoopskirts and tall beaver hats, not in a modern world with its nascent space race, polio vaccine, and miracle fabrics. Yet there it was, in the pages of a popular magazine, more than a hundred years after women started attending college.

It was of course naïve of me to think that college girls were any less subject to the strictures of compulsory femininity (to rephrase from Adrienne Rich) than the rest of us. Indeed, the college-educated woman has always left a high level of cultural

A tight sweater and a prominent bust dominate the cover of this "revealing report," 1964.

anxiety in her wake. From her first appearance in the mid-nineteenth century, the college girl has pressed cultural buttons regarding conflicting ideas about women and education, women and work, women and marriage, and at its very core, questions about the nature of womanhood and femininity itself. As a result, she's been a lightning rod for criticism, advice, and regulation.

This book looks at images of the college girl drawn from a variety of materials: prescriptive literature, fiction, popular works of sociology and guidance, girlie magazines and pulp fiction, as well as student handbooks and the like—a constellation of sources that make up the constant,

under-the-conscious-radar flow of ideas that academics refer to as discourse. The college girl I discuss here is mostly conjured of words, woven
from ideas. As always, the gap between prescriptive literature—or,
heaven forbid, advertising—and human behavior can never be adequately measured. Likewise, the college girls depicted in books, magazines, and movies may or, more likely, may not resemble those who
populated campuses. Obviously, the young women who attended colleges and universities were, from the start, unique individuals with different reasons for pursuing their degrees, who came from different
backgrounds, social classes, races, and religions. Mostly, this book looks
at what we think about when we're asked to think about "the college
girl"—a mass-mediated vision that often has ignored social realities, to
paraphrase historian Mary C. McComb.[8] To that end, I've stuck for the
most part to the locution "girls," for that is usually how the unmarried
young women who attended universities and colleges have been
described in both serious public discussions as well as popular culture
since the mid-nineteenth century and even past the women's liberation
movement of the 1970s.

∞

Perhaps you're wondering just what any of this has to do with you. Maybe
you're currently in college or are a recent graduate, and you say there are
plenty of young women on campus and few of them face discrimination—at least on the basis of gender. It's true that more than half of
today's college graduates are women, but certain attitudes about women
and higher education crop up too frequently to be considered entirely
quaint or anachronistic. For example, in 2002, economists at Northeastern University's Center for Labor Market Studies concluded that the
increased number of female college graduates would lead to a "marriage
gap"—for what woman would want to marry a man with less earning
power than herself? This is a modern spin on long-standing fears that
higher education is a fast track to spinsterhood—for what man wanted to
"marry up" to a women better educated than he?[9]

Along the same lines, when in 2003 CBS's *60 Minutes* television show interviewed three recent female graduates of the Harvard Business School for a story about career women and infertility, they explained something they called "the H bomb": they were reluctant to tell guys, even fellow students, where they attended school because it meant the "kiss of death" for future dates. The young women noted that for male students the opposite was true: "all the girls start[ed] falling onto them" as soon as they mentioned Harvard Business School.[10]

And then there was Harvard president Lawrence H. Summers's maladroit pronouncement in early 2005 that perhaps fewer women had successful math and science careers because "innate sex differences" made them less capable in these areas of study. Summers himself later characterized his words as "a big mistake" (one that may have contributed to his decision to resign the following year), but they carried with them the echo of nineteenth- and twentieth-century debates over how best to educate women, not to mention earlier debates about whether biological differences in male and female brains meant women weren't capable of the type of abstract critical thought integral to a college education. The fall-out from Summers's statement lasted for months, and played out in news articles, editorials, letters to the editor, and Web logs. Clearly, arguments about nature, nurture, and the quality of female intelligence were far from settled.[11]

Hiding one's brains on a date, questioning the very nature of women's intellect, scaremongering over "marriage gaps" based on women's higher education—none of it is new. The question of what makes these ideas so enduring is a bigger one than this book can hope to answer, yet the history recounted here should remind us all not to take women's right to higher education for granted. I like to think that had I taken the time to find out what those dark brick buildings at the edge of campus were, I might have valued my own five years a little more dearly.

Sketching a nearly naked man in art class was just one of many new experiences provided by a college education at the turn of the twentieth century.

The Birth of the College Girl

It has been proposed to establish a "College for Females," in
several of the manufacturing and producing cities of the
Union, in which the following "sciences" are to be taught, by
competent "professors:"
    "Spinology, Weaveology, and Cookology."
    . . . [T]hey will be entitled to receive a regular diploma,
with the honorary degree of "F.F.W.:" "Fit for Wives."

"EDITOR'S DRAWER," *HARPER'S NEW MONTHLY MAGAZINE*
(MARCH 1854)

O n a June day in 1678, before twenty thousand fascinated spectators, Venetian noblewoman Elena Cornaro Piscopia received a
degree in philosophy from the University of Padua, Italy. Other
women had attended or even given lectures in philosophy, law, rhetoric,
and medicine at the Italian universities as early as the twelfth century
(the world's first university, in Bologna, Italy, opened in 1088), and a
woman named Bettisia Gozzadini lectured in law at the University of
Bologna in 1296, but the thirty-two-year-old Piscopia was the first
woman ever to receive a university degree.

Elena Cornaro Piscopia's singular achievement did not mark the start
of new interest and support for the higher education of women. Instead,

immediately after her graduation, the rectors at the University of Padua decided they would admit no more women. It would be a half century before Laura Bassi became the second woman in history to receive a college degree (in 1732, in natural philosophy, from the University of Bologna, where she soon accepted a faculty position).[1]

Bassi, Piscopia, Gozzadini, and the handful of other women who attended European universities prior to the nineteenth century were talented and well-to-do exceptions, who like Piscopia, were probably educated through their fathers' efforts. As for the vast majority of women, however, the universities provided "neither a formal education nor a license to teach," to use the words of historian Phyllis Stock.[2]

When Piscopia received her degree, Harvard had been educating American men for just over four decades. It would be almost another 160 years before an American women stepped over the threshold of a college classroom—closer to two hundred if you count Vassar as the first place for women to get a college education. And it took even longer for attitudes toward women's education and educated women to change.

The Roots of Women's Higher Education in America

In Colonial America, writing was a business skill largely reserved for boys, reflected in statistics which suggested that just prior to the Revolution, 80 percent of men in New England could pen a signature while only half of the women could make the same claim. The dictates of religion, however, necessitated that children of both sexes be taught to read at least a few Bible verses if nothing else. If they happened to be the daughters of traders or other well-placed individuals, girls might be taught to write or otherwise benefit by a brother's education—studying

Latin with him, for example. Historian of women's education Barbara Miller Solomon points out that Bible reading was the wedge by which some young women discovered their intellectual gifts. Yet such study was not meant to lead to independence of thought. When educated, Bible-reading Anne Hutchinson (1591–1643) began holding weekly meetings in her Boston home to discuss sermons as well as her own theological opinions, retribution from the male establishment was swift: she was excommunicated and banished along with her family to the as yet unsettled wilderness, where they were later killed by equally unappreciative Native Americans.[3]

In short, it was reasoned that girls didn't need much more than the most rudimentary education because most of them were going to be wives and mothers. However, the pious education of young men in "good letters and manners," as the founders of the College of William and Mary termed it, was considered an important common goal of the early men's colleges (including Harvard, William and Mary, Yale, the University of Pennsylvania, Princeton, Columbia, Brown, Rutgers, and Dartmouth, all founded before the Revolution).[4] Thus educated, their students would become learned civic leaders and clergymen, neither of which occupation was deemed fit for females. Not that a college education was readily attainable for every young man; a bachelor's degree was a mark of elite status, beyond the social and financial means of most.[5]

If a girl received any education outside her home, it was most likely at a dame school. These were run by older women who brought neighborhood children of both sexes into their homes to teach them a modicum of literacy, as well as simple sewing skills to the girls. So-called French schools expanded the curriculum in the mid-eighteenth century to include fancy needlework and the French language in addition to reading, arithmetic, and possibly much more, depending on the school's location and the woman in charge. The French schools laid the foundation for the "finishing" schools that cropped up in the nineteenth century, and typically offered the ornamental accomplishments (French, English, penmanship, plain and fancy needlework among them) that "finished" aristocratic young ladies for a life in society.

Slowly but surely, the idea took hold that it was all right to educate girls and women if they used that education in furtherance of their traditional roles. The Ursuline order of nuns was founded in sixteenth-century Italy and charged by a papal bull of 1598 with the duty "to remedy the ignorance of the children of the people and the corruption of morals."[6] Despite the order's Italian roots, most Ursuline convents were located in France, and in 1727 the Ursuline Academy of New Orleans opened in what was as yet a French colony. This was probably the first girls' school in the United States—and after almost 280 years of operation, it's definitely the longest lived. The core of its curriculum was the catechism, supplemented by instruction in reading, writing, music, fancy needlework, and etiquette. By 1803 the school had 170 boarding students. Within the next decade, two more Catholic schools for girls, Nazareth and Loretta, had opened in Kentucky.[7] The Catholic interest in girls' education had less to do with a deep-seated belief in female literacy than the belief that an educated mother would in turn instruct her children in both the catechism and secular subjects. This was particularly important in relation to boys who might grow into influential church and secular leaders. Writing much later (in 1867), a French clergyman expounded on this: "[I]t is in relation to sons that maternal ignorance has the most fatal results . . . an intelligent, well-informed mother could . . . point out to him good authors and books worth reading, read with him, teach him to reject dangerous writers and bad books, and stimulate his taste for study, by directing it to noble objects."[8]

Even though Abigail Adams's famous request of her statesman husband, John—that he "remember the ladies" when he and the rest of the Continental Congress hammered out what would become the founding documents of the United States—fell ultimately on deaf ears, women were swept up in the fervor of the Revolution. Along with their husbands and brothers, they debated the ideals of freedom and equality as well as a citizen's duties to the new nation. The concept of what historian Linda Kerber termed "Republican Motherhood" in a seminal 1976 essay charged a mother with the civic duty of instilling these values in her children, and thus required a further commitment to her own education.[9] A wife and mother needed to set the standard for the behavior for both husband and children, especially male children, the heroes and patriots of the future.

Training the mothers of future citizens was important work indeed. Benjamin Rush was a Philadelphia physician who wrote and spoke on the importance of women's education throughout the 1790s. Because budding statesmen learned their first lessons at their mother's knee, basic literacy wasn't enough for girls—nor was the mere instruction of "ornamental accomplishments" taught in the French schools, which Rush deemed decadent and elitist. Rush suggested that girls "be taught the principles of liberty and government," as well as "the obligations of patriotism." When the Young Ladies' Academy of Philadelphia opened in 1787, Rush saw his ideas about female education put into action. Although the Young Ladies' Academy represented a new commitment to the education of women, it more closely resembled a modern high school than what we would consider a college. Until it closed in the early 1800s due to an outbreak of yellow fever, its curriculum included reading, writing, arithmetic, grammar, geography, and religion.[10]

Despite the innovations of the Young Ladies' Academy, as historian Jennifer Manion points out, "it was still widely acceptable for people, including advocates of the formal education of women, to believe in women's fundamental intellectual inferiority."[11] While ideas about female education were changing, it did not mean that the doors of higher education immediately sprang open. In 1783, twelve-year-old Lucinda Foote was found to be "fully qualified, except in regard to sex, to be received as a pupil of the Freshman class of Yale University."[12] Qualified she may have been, but received she wasn't—even though Yale president Ezra Stiles was much impressed by her skill in Latin.[13] Indeed, a young woman in eighteenth-century New England was more likely to have been

A Vindication of the Rights of Woman

 The publication in 1792 of Mary Wollstonecraft's *A Vindication of the Rights of Woman* helped move popular discussion of female education into high gear. Among other things, Wollstonecraft called for better educational and professional opportunities for women, in the belief it would help single women and widows better support themselves, as well as help married women become better wives and mothers. Shortly after *A Vindication*'s appearance in England, excerpts from it appeared in the *Ladies Magazine* and *Massachusetts Magazine* in the United States, and a full American edition soon followed.* Even if people didn't agree with Wollstonecraft's lifestyle (she bore a child out of wedlock and lived openly with its father), her ideas were heady ones in the new republic. With Wollstonecraft's words in front of them and the memory of the Revolution fresh in their minds, people were suddenly talking about woman's *right* to an education, though the form that education should take was the subject of debate for at least the following century. (Freedom and rights were slippery slopes, of course: "It is a curious fact," wrote "A Lady" in 1816, "that a republic which avows equality of right as its first principle, persists in an ungenerous exclusion of the female sex from its executive department."† It remains curious, all these years later.)

* Rosemarie Zagarri, "The Rights of Man and Woman in Post-Revolutionary America," *William and Mary Quarterly*, 3rd ser., vol. 55, no. 2 (April 1998), 206–7.
† Ibid., 227.

taught modern, not classical, languages. As John Adams told his daughter, it was "scarcely reputable for young ladies to understand Latin and Greek—French, my dear, French is the language next to English."[14] Latin and Greek were, along with higher mathematics, the foundation of the men's university curriculum, the purview of church and state. A 1791 poem entitled "To a Lady, Who Expressed a Desire of Seeing an University Established for Women" was blunt in its appraisal of misguided female adventurers like Lucinda who sought educational equity: "Deluded Maid, Thy Claim Forego," read the poem's first line.[15]

"Deluded" or not, women weren't willing to forgo their claims to higher education. Beginning in the 1820s, a trio of women opened schools which, while they didn't rise to the name of "college" just yet, nonetheless offered girls an education above and beyond that offered by other schools, and provided a blueprint for the women's colleges that followed.

Emma Willard, Catharine Beecher, and Mary Lyon: Three Pioneers of Women's Education

Thirty-some years after Lucinda Foote suffered her disappointment at Yale, Emma Willard (1787–1870) was denied permission to sit in on Middlebury College's entrance examinations.[16] But she wasn't interested in becoming a student—Willard was a teacher who wanted to learn how the university evaluated the education of its male applicants. Knowledge of such methods, she reasoned, would help her create standards for female education, which she found sorely lacking in mathematics and the sciences. Willard herself was an autodidact who enjoyed enriching her mind with unfamiliar subjects like geography and algebra, the latter during early morning constitutionals. When her 1819 *Plan for Improving Female Education* (which among other things called for state support of a school for girls) was rejected by the New York legislature, influential citi-

Emma Willard, formidable founder of the
Troy Female Seminary.

zens of the city of Troy promised their financial support if Willard established a school there. The Troy Female Seminary opened in 1821. Calling her school a "seminary" indicated Willard's seriousness of purpose; male seminaries prepared their students for professional futures, just as the new female seminaries prepared students for teaching and educated motherhood. Ironically, because married women could not yet legally rent property in their own right, Willard's husband held the lease.[17]

With a curriculum that boldly included mathematics and science in addition to more familiar weekly lectures on manners, religion, and the "peculiar duties" of women, the school was a resounding success—and remains a highly regarded girls' prep school today. Ninety young women enrolled for its opening session, some coming from as far away as Ohio and Georgia. Although the average student age was seventeen, Willard also welcomed older women, among them teachers who wished to expand their skills and what her biographer referred to as "some young widows who wished to add to their meager education."[18]

In a move that had implications for future college girls, student life at Troy was highly regulated. Housed two each in small rooms rather than en masse in large dormitories as was the current fashion, students were responsible for keeping their rooms neat and orderly. Monitors made hourly rounds, and if they found a careless glove forgotten on the bureau top or a book left on a bed, demerits were given. Bed making received special attention; Willard advised girls that a broomstick was useful for smoothing out a coverlet's most stubborn wrinkles.[19]

Students rose at 6:30 or 7:00, depending on the season, devoted a half hour to study, another half hour to exercise, and took breakfast at 8:00. Classes commenced thereafter with a noon break for dinner. School was dismissed at 4:00 P.M. with a prayer from Willard. Two hours of free time followed. Supper was at 6:00, after which students gathered for an hour of dance, which Willard approved as both relaxation and exercise, before recommencing their studies. Board was $2.50 a week (boarders were asked to "furnish themselves with a table spoon, a tea spoon, and towels" according to an early catalog), whereas the cost of tuition depended on one's course of study. Simple dress was required, so that upper-class students (the governors of Vermont, Michigan, Ohio, and Georgia all sent their daughters to Troy) were nearly indistinguishable from the penniless but ambitious girls who contracted to repay their tuition from wages to be earned when they embarked on their teaching careers.[20] Indeed, most of the students at Troy became teachers, and carried Willard's methods and philosophy with them into the world.

There can be no question that Emma Willard was passionately committed to women's education, but she wasn't a supporter of women's political rights. Before the presidential election of 1824, Willard caught wind of a secret meeting at which some students made fiery speeches in support of incumbent John Quincy Adams, while others championed challenger Andrew Jackson. Willard's response was to lecture her charges on the proper duties of their sex. Men were like oak trees, she explained, while women were like apple trees. Apple trees could never be oak trees (or vice versa), but each was beautiful and useful in its own way. Delving into the world of politics was crossing into oak tree territory, a foreign forest where women didn't belong. As she wrote in her *Plan for Improving Female Education*, women "in particular situations, [were meant] to yield obedience to the other sex." Education did not "mean that our sex should not seek to make themselves agreeable to" men.[21]

Like Willard, Catharine Beecher (1800–1878) believed that the sexes held clearly demarcated social roles (a nineteenth-century worldview referred to as "separate spheres ideology" by modern historians). As mothers and teachers, women were entrusted with the most important task of molding the characters of children: "What is the profession of a woman? Is it not to form immortal minds, and to watch, to nurse, and to rear the bodily system, so fearfully and wonderfully made, and upon the order and regulation of which the health and well-being of the mind so greatly depends?"[22]

How many women, Beecher further asked, devoted time and study in the course of their educations to preparation for these duties? A daughter of one of the most famous families in nineteenth-century America (her father and brothers were ministers, sister Harriet Beecher Stowe wrote *Uncle Tom's Cabin* [1852], and half-sister Isabella Beecher Hooker fought for woman suffrage), Beecher devoted most of her adult life to teaching domesticity. Ironically, nineteenth-century America's answer to Martha Stewart was a childless spinster (to use the terminology of the time). Years of experience raising her seven younger siblings following their mother's death when Catharine was sixteen years old resulted in her theories of domestic economy. In 1823, she and her sister Mary opened the Hartford Female Seminary. Students at Hartford received what Beecher deemed "the most necessary parts of education."[23] In addition to the domestic training she advocated, this meant a rigorous curriculum of English, rhetoric, logic, philosophy (natural and moral), chemistry, history, Latin, and algebra (music and dancing cost extra). Beecher was also an early booster of physical exercise for girls. Students at the Hartford Female Seminary followed Beecher's own system of exercises involving weights and music, which she later shared with the public in *Physiology and Calisthenics for Schools and Families* (1856).

After Beecher left the seminary in 1832, she wrote extensively on the subjects dear to her heart. Her major work, *A Treatise on Domestic Economy* (1841), went through fifteen editions, and royalties from it and her other books helped Beecher fund various projects related to the education of women. She worked to establish colleges where women could be trained as nurses, housekeepers, and teachers (who she believed made the best wives). She helped establish the Board of National Popular Education in 1846 and six years later founded the American Women's Educational Association, organizations that helped recruit and train teachers to serve on the American frontier. This frontier included the wilds of Wisconsin and the Milwaukee Female College, which through a series of mergers and moves became the Milwaukee-Downer College, whose buildings in turn became part of my local campus of the University of Wisconsin—the same buildings I barely noticed as I scurried across campus in the early 1980s. Beecher's advocacy for specialized training for women's duties eventually led to the discipline of domestic science—which paved the way for the twentieth century's home economics.

Willard demanded that the education of girls and women be treated with serious regard, whereas Beecher advocated for a curriculum that particularly emphasized training for women's specific duties (a recurring theme in women's education for years to come). At Mount Holyoke Seminary, Mary Lyon (1797–1849) provided students with what most closely resembled a collegiate education. With its emphasis on academics in a highly regulated yet homelike setting, Mount Holyoke was a model for Vassar and Wellesley as well as for the female departments of numerous coeducational colleges. From its wide white piazza, which gave a residential touch to an otherwise rather industrial facade, to the interior layout, which resembled the floor plan of an oversized house, to the faculty members' motherlike concern for their student-daughters, Mount Holyoke was designed to provided a homelike atmosphere for girls. Discipline was strict. Teachers and students lived on the same floors, lights-out was at 10:00 P.M., and students were required to leave their doors open thereafter. Like Willard and Beecher, Lyon recognized the importance of physical activity; students were required to walk a mile each day in addition to performing calisthenics. By requiring all students to share in housekeeping chores such as cleaning and washing, the expense of hiring maids was avoided and tuition kept low. [24]

An unexpected consequence of this policy (which remained in effect until 1914) was the misconception, noted in an 1897 profile of the college, that Mount Holyoke students were "largely occupied in learning domestic accomplishments."[25] Nothing could have been further from the truth. The entrance requirements (another first) included a rigorous lineup of arithmetic, geography, U.S. history, and English grammar. There had been fears before Mount Holyoke opened in 1837 that not enough girls would be able to pass these stringent requirements, but the inaugural class consisted of 116 eager scholars. The next year four hundred young women were turned away—there simply wasn't enough room for them. From its inception, Mount Holyoke's fixed three-year course of study more closely resembled the regimen of a men's college than that of a female seminary (Emma Willard, for example, admitted pupils at any time during the year provided they attended end-of-term examinations).[26] Nevertheless, Mount Holyoke's curriculum still lacked Latin and Greek and some higher mathematics. With the addition of these courses as well as an extra year of required study, Mount Holyoke became a college in 1888, though the word itself wasn't added to its name for another five years.[27]

The female seminaries at Troy, Hartford, and Mount Holyoke stand out for their rigorous curricula and their lasting influence, both through the training of teachers steeped in the institutes' high educational standards as well as through Beecher's prolific pen. The three educators were aware of and generally supported one another's work. When Mary Lyon solicited contributions to Mount Holyoke's endowment (yet another innovation), she mentioned both Willard and Beecher's successful seminaries. Beecher corresponded with Willard and had unsuccessfully approached a young Mary Lyon to teach at Hartford.[28]

Even as girls were flocking to these seminaries, experiments in collegiate education of women were taking place in other regions of the United States. There was Oberlin, a coeducational school with a history of inclusion: founded by abolitionists in 1833, it was also the first college with an interracial student body. Costs were kept low by requiring daily manual labor from students; men did field work, women did kitchen duty and the male students' laundry. (Nevertheless, when a visitor to the campus in the early 1870s offered $10 to any young woman who could saw a cord of wood, "quite a number" attempted the task, though only one completed it and claimed the prize.) Many historians disparagingly point out that Oberlin offered a special "ladies course" that was less demanding than its collegiate one, but not all women opted for it. Oberlin graduated its first female B.A. from the collegiate course in 1841.[29]

At first, the notion of higher education for women was treated with a mixture of condescension, ridicule, and derision in differing measures. In 1831, the *Raleigh Register* mocked the "Refined Female College" with a curriculum that featured "scolding and fretting" and "running your father into debt for finery, cologne water, pomatum [a hair dressing] and hard soap, dancing and frolicking," among other equally laudatory subjects.[30] More merriment resulted when in the spring of 1835, it was announced that Van Doren's Institution for Young Ladies in Lexington had been granted a charter by the Kentucky legislature and was henceforth to be known as Van Doren's College for Young Ladies. This time the torrent of witticism was released in far-off Connecticut. The school's honorary degree of M.P.L. ("Mistress of Polite Literature"—which, it must be said, strikes the modern ear as rather ludicrous) might stand for "Mistress of Petticoat Literature" advised one newspaper. Not to be outdone, the editor of the *Springfield Republican* in Massachusetts made the following suggestions for degrees, faculty, and facilities:

> M.P.M. (Mistress of Pudding Making), M.D.N. (Mistress of the Darning Needle), M.S.B. (Mistress of the Scrubbing Brush), M.C.S. (Mistress of Common Sense). The Professors should be chosen from farmer's wives and the Laboratory should be a kitchen. Honorary degrees might include H.W. (Happy Wife), H.H. (Happy Husband) and M.W.R.F. (Mother of a Well Regulated Family).[31]

When those mocking words were penned in the mid-1830s, the idea of the college-educated woman was still shockingly new—it wasn't too surprising that the writers couldn't get their minds out of the kitchen.

Even sympathetic observers had difficulty wrapping their minds around both concept and terminology when it came to college women. In the 1870s, a more serious-minded commentator named Alexander Hyde confessed himself "at a loss to indicate" what degree should be given to female graduates—by then a more recognizable though no less controversial figure in the American landscape. He clearly meant well, yet his suggestion still played on a long-standing female stereotype: "The term Bachelor is generally supposed to apply to men alone, but by its etymology it signifies babbler, and as women have tongues we see no reason why they may not write their names with the suffix of A.B., for they can babble about arts as well as men."[32]

Actually, it was Hyde himself who was babbling: a quick look at the *Oxford English Dictionary* shows that the roots of "bachelor" and "babbler" have nothing in common. The graduate degree provided fewer linguistic pitfalls for Hyde; the "M" might stand for "mistress" as well as "master," he said. The confusion extended to some of the new women's colleges, where administrators weren't sure what to call their first-year students. "Fresh*man*" seemed wrong where women were concerned, but the alternatives were worse. Elmira College tried "protomathian," while Rutgers suggested "novian."[33] Luckily, neither term stuck—although another, more pejorative, name did.

Bluestockings

Nowadays mostly restricted to the titles of romance novels and the names of feminist bookstores, "bluestocking" was once an epithet "invariably bestowed upon all women who have read much, and who are able to think and act for themselves," according to a disgruntled young wife in 1850.[34] As originally defined, however, the term was less demeaning and more descriptive.

In late-eighteenth-century London, Mrs. Vesey held a popular salon where men and women met to discuss the literary merits and mistakes of the day. Out walking one day, she encountered Benjamin Stillingfleet, the disinherited son of a bishop and "a failure" according to *The Cambridge History of English and American Literature*. Ne'er-do-well he may have been, but Mrs. Vesey urged him to attend one of her "conversa-tions." Stillingfleet, casually dressed in his worsted wool stockings, begged off, citing a lack of suitable formal garb. Mrs. Vesey, however, was not about to accept such a flimsy excuse. "Don't mind dress. Come in your blue stockings," she implored.[35]

Stillingfleet took her at her word, and he and his unconventional evening wear were such a hit that members of Mrs. Vesey's salon were alleged to have declared "we can do nothing without the blue stockings." In time, the entire group became known as bluestockings, and the term was soon "fixed in playful stigma" to its female members in particular.[36] Helped along by the strong personality of another celebrated salon holder and writer, Elizabeth Montagu, the so-called Queen of the Blues, the term soon applied to all "literary" women.

The members of Mrs. Vesey's salon may have recognized the term as a "playful" one, but "bluestocking" soon packed more opprobrium than endearment. Women who attended literary salons, who expressed their opinions both aloud and in writing, defied long-standing feminine ideals of domesticity and submissiveness. Concurrent with increasing public discussion about the rights and education of women in the mid-nineteenth century, increasingly negative connotations accrued to the word. "Bluestocking" came to represent a certain kind of outspoken or, to use a contemporary and equally negative synonym, "strong-minded" woman. According to a mid-nineteenth-century treatise titled *Piety, the True Ornament and Dignity of Woman*, such women were said to "unsex and degrade themselves, by their boisterous assumption of man's prerog-atives and responsibilities."[37] An 1851 encyclopedia described the blue-stocking as "a pedantic female" who sacrificed "the characteristic excellences of her sex to learning."[38] Thirty years later, magazine articles pinned her as typically "an unfeminine and arrogant Amazon," a "stiff, stilted, queer literary woman of a dubious age."[39] Whereas the salons of Mrs. Vesey and Mrs. Montagu were known for sparkling intellect and witty discussions, a writer in 1875 desultorily described "a purely blue-stocking party, to-day" with its "sponge cake, weak tea, and the dreariest of driveling professional talk."[40]

It wasn't just the "high-toned" nature of female intelligence that allegedly frightened men off. The bluestocking challenged another contemporary (albeit more idealized) image of femininity. As described in both popular and prescriptive literature of the mid-nineteenth to early twentieth centuries, the True Woman was submissive to husband and family and content with her domestic sphere of influence. In proving she could study the heretofore exclusively male liberal arts curriculum, the bluestocking–cum–college girl was sometimes portrayed as a "greasy grind" or "drag" who bored her dates or didn't date at all and was best suited to a future as a spinster or old maid. Woe to the man who dared to marry the "gentleman's horror," as she and her ilk were "not the wives in whom men are very happy."[41] Indeed, the author of an 1872 article on the subject of "old maids" opined that women who "gave themselves up to literature [were] happiest single."[42] Of course, many of the "scribbling women" who took up journalism and fiction writing in the nineteenth century (both were considered acceptable professions for women forced by tragic circumstances and/or shiftless husbands to support themselves) were married—which doesn't necessarily mean they wouldn't have been happier single.

Mrs. Amelia E. Barr didn't actually use the word "bluestocking" in an 1893 essay, but it wasn't difficult to figure out to where her criticism was aimed. She pointed to the "selfishness and self-seeking" at the root of some women's desire to "attend lectures and take lessons," and was especially blunt in her assessment of married women who neglected children and husbands in pursuit of education. The world could "do without learned women, but it cannot do without good wives and mothers." According to Barr, the two were mutually exclusive: female scholars were nothing less than "moral failures, and bad mothers."[43] Barr, an antisuffragist who penned numerous essays and books in the late nineteenth and early twentieth centuries, apparently excluded her own writing for publication from the sort of bluestocking activities that in her opinion rocked the very foundations of family life.

One supporter of women's education framed college as an antidote to bluestockingism. During the ceremonies surrounding the laying of the cornerstone of the women's building at Cornell in 1873, educator Homer

B. Sprague proclaimed that higher education rescued woman "from the possibility of becoming a noisy zealot." Only the superficially educated woman, Sprague argued, engaged in the sort of loudmouthed pedantry that was associated with the bluestocking. "Increase of modesty comes with increase of knowledge," argued Sprague, who later became the president of Mills College in Oakland, California, sometimes called the "Wellesley of the West." Well-educated (and therefore modest) women, he concluded, were unlikely to "parade their intellectual power, or wag their loud sharp tongues."[44]

Sweet Girl Graduates

The bluestocking was the most widely known (and reviled) stereotype associated with the early college girl, but she was not the only popular-culture image available. Where the bluestocking challenged assumed notions of femininity, the "sweet" girl graduate didn't rock the boat. Utterly guileless and innocent in her virginal white commencement gown, the sweet girl graduate from either high school or college accepted her role as nurturer of men and children and used her education for the betterment of her future family. The phrase originated in Alfred, Lord Tennyson's 1847 poem "The Princess," his comment on the au courant topic of higher education for females. Early in the poem, a group of male students and their young lady friends gather at a house party and imagine how a separatist college for women might look:

> And one said smiling "Pretty were the sight
> If our old halls could change their sex, and flaunt
> With prudes for proctors, dowagers for deans,
> And sweet girl-graduates in their golden hair."

The image of the golden-haired sweet girl graduate was a long way from that of the sharp-tongued, high-toned bluestocking. For example, the

"The Bluestocking" and "The Spinster"

 College girls did their best to maintain a sense of humor by reclaiming the terms others used to insult them: *The Bluestocking* (first published in 1900) and *The Spinster* (premiere edition in 1898) were yearbook titles at a pair of Virginia women's schools—Mary Baldwin College (in Staunton) and Hollins College (now Hollins University, in Roanoke), respectively.

An archivist at Mary Baldwin reports that a later volume of *The Bluestocking* defined the term this way: "The name 'Bluestocking' literally means a learned woman of an aristocratic family . . . In olden days the most blue-blooded of all the puritans were also 'Bluestockings' and from that day until this the name has stood for superiority and intelligence."* It's an interesting take—and I don't doubt the grace and smarts of those early college girls—but to date it remains the only source I've seen to reflect this definition of the word.

Jean Holzinger, the editor of *Hollins* magazine, provides several possible explanations for *The Spinster*'s name. The connection between single women and spinning is an ancient one, an affinity so deep that all the bachelorettes in seventeenth-century England

*Correspondence to the author, April 29, 2004.

---

sweet girl graduate preferred clothing to politics. In 1894, the *New York Times* noted that "the sweet girl graduate of this coming June" was as deeply concerned with choosing the appropriate commencement gown "as ever have been any of her predecessors, and even the question of equal suffrage, which has been the theme of school debates the past month, pales before the important one, 'Shall it be muslin or wool?' "[45]

The central character of Mrs. L. T. Meade's late-nineteenth-century were called "spinsters." Indeed, *The Spinster*'s endpapers and cover often featured spinning wheels, and a photo in the first edition shows the yearbook staff seated next to one. Or did the name pay tribute to the fact that for most students, the four years spent at Hollins represented a last period of unfettered pleasure prior to the subordination and drudgery awaiting them after the inevitable marriage? For years, The *Spinster*'s title page bore the motto "Where singleness is bliss, 'tis folly to be wives" (a clever play on Thomas Gray's "Where ignorance is bliss, 'tis folly to be wise").

Hollins students "were well aware that the word *spinster* was pejorative," that a college education not only removed a young woman's focus from the marriage market for its duration but might in itself make her less attractive in the eyes of potential husbands. However, in the words of Hollins history professor Joe Leedom, "you take the criticism and make it your own badge. What is intended to be an explanation of your error becomes an emblem of your superiority."†

The Bluestocking and *The Spinster* continue publication to this day.

† Jean Holzinger, "What's in a Name?" *Hollins*, Spring 2004, 24. This article also supplied all the information regarding the possible origins of *The Spinster*'s name.

novel for girls, *A Sweet Girl Graduate*, exemplified the type. Priscilla Peel is plain featured and poor, but proud. She attends St. Benet's College for Women through the beneficence of a kindly clergyman and the sweat of her terminally ill Aunt Raby's brow. Prissie loves the classics course, but when she (like many a modern student) realizes that a degree in Greek will render her less employable, she readily agrees to drop her studies in order to best "devote herself to modern languages, and to those accom-

plishments which are considered more essentially feminine."[46] When
her devoted friend, the beautiful, moody, and rich Maggie Oliphant,
offers enough money to allow Priscilla to finish her course in Greek and
Latin, as well as to support her sisters and aunt, Prissie turns it down,
preferring an independent life as a schoolteacher to that of a debt-ridden
scholar. Her selfless devotion to family and willingness to self-sacrifice
expose her as a True Woman, willing to "put blessedness before happiness—duty before inclination."[47]

What Was the First Women's College?

Historians are far from agreeing on which institution first granted mean-
ingful baccalaureate degrees to women. Some argue that while there
were many schools that added the fashionable word "college" to their
names in the nineteenth century, the courses of study they offered (and
thus the degrees they granted) were not on a par with those available to
men. Others, particularly Christie Anne Farnham in her study of women's
education in the antebellum South, suggest there is a northeastern bias to
much of the research and that too much emphasis has been placed on
comparisons with the classics-based curriculum taught at men's schools
of the period.[48] Indeed, this seems to be the standard by which modern
historians judge a particular early school for its "college worthiness": did it
offer the rigorous classes in Latin, Greek, and higher mathematics which
formed the core curriculum at the elite men's schools?

By the early nineteenth century, however, the curriculum at the men's
colleges was in flux, in part because of student demands that science and
modern languages be added or offered through parallel courses of study.
In a closely watched experiment in 1824, the University of Virginia,
under the leadership of Thomas Jefferson, allowed students to choose
courses from eight different units or schools: ancient or modern languages, mathematics, natural philosophy, history, anatomy and medicine,
moral philosophy, and law. Three years later, the president of Yale called a

committee of college fellows to consider the elimination of the "dead languages" from the college curriculum. The so-called Yale Report was released in 1828. Among other things, the report argued against adding professional studies to undergraduate education and suggested instead that the "high intellectual culture" provided by the classics would profit all students.[49] Classics remained the benchmark for the time being, and thus became the criterion of contemporary nineteenth-century higher education by which the women's colleges were judged—and to which the elite schools aspired.

To read the curricula or even the entrance-examination requirements of the early colleges for women (or protocolleges, depending on which historian you're reading) is a quick shock to the senses of anyone who attended a typical American college in the twentieth century—certainly to at least one slacker in particular who attended a certain public university in the Midwest in the early 1980s. Consider the hefty program offered in 1857 at North Carolina's Goldsboro Female College. First-year students studied a sophisticated array of courses: arithmetic, English grammar and composition, U.S. history, Latin, French, physiology, and hygiene. The next year they progressed to algebra, natural history, ancient geography, universal history, natural philosophy, botany, and more Latin and French. Upperclassmen added, among other courses, geometry and trigonometry, chemistry, rhetoric, evidences of Christianity, and a class in the U.S. Constitution. Electives included piano, guitar, drawing, and painting.[50]

Even with its wide-ranging catalog of classes, Goldsboro is by no scholar's standards a contender for the bragging rights associated with the title of "first college for women." The Georgia Female College (now Wesleyan College in Macon, Georgia) has long claimed that badge of honor: it opened its doors to ninety students in 1839 and granted its first degrees the following year, thanks to the preparatory work done by former students of the Clinton Female Institute who were admitted as juniors. Despite Wesleyan's claim, many historians argue that the Georgia Female College's course of study was not rigorous enough for it to be considered the first true college for women. According to Barbara Miller

Solomon, the school "resembled a superior academy more than a male college, regularly admitting twelve-year-olds."[51]

Another candidate was founded in Winchester, Tennessee, in 1853. Mary Sharp College (formerly the Tennessee and Alabama Female Institute until a monetary gift inspired a name change) offered the first four-year program for women that required Latin, Greek, and higher mathematics and awarded its first three A.B. degrees in 1855. Between 1856 and the school's closing forty years later (a victim of a financial depression in the 1890s), 4,000 girls attended Mary Sharp College, 350 of whom graduated. Many historians consider Mary Sharp College to be the "nation's best antebellum candidate for the first women's college."[52]

Yet another school often cited as the first college for women was the Elmira Female College, which opened in Elmira, New York, in 1855 and graduated its first class four years later. Elmira College went coed in 1969 and today remains a respected liberal arts college. In September 1909, *Good Housekeeping* magazine published a letter from a reader disappointed that her alma mater was not mentioned in a list of the oldest colleges for women that appeared in a prior issue. "I supposed it was generally known," she wrote somewhat ruefully, "that Elmira College, Elmira, N.Y., was the first college for women chartered to confer degrees for work equivalent to that offered in colleges for men, and is therefore the oldest."[53]

But from its celebrated opening in 1865, Vassar College had two things that Elmira and the other colleges didn't, two things that helped it burn a place in the public memory as the largest, best, and "first": big money and vast publicity.

Mr. Vassar's Memorial

Matthew Vassar (1792–1868) was a self-made man, a brewer by trade, who was born in England but spent most of his life near Poughkeepsie, New York. During the course of his career, he amassed a tremendous personal fortune of over $800,000. Vassar built and later endowed the college that bore his name not because he was a lifelong supporter of women's education, but because he wanted to establish a great public building as a memorial to himself. At the time a women's college was an unusual choice. Vassar had at first leaned toward the idea of a hospital until a new friend, Milo P. Jewett, a Presbyterian minister and proponent of female education, convinced him of the need for a first-rate endowed college for women. Though Vassar originally held no firm convictions as to women's education, once his mind was made up he enthusiastically supported the idea to the tune of over $400,000—almost $9,000,000 in 2005 dollars—and that was just for starters.

Matthew Vassar—beer baron and proponent of higher education for women.

The planned curriculum included the magic trinity of Greek, Latin, and higher mathematics presented in a beautifully designed setting, the college's main building influenced by the Tuileries palace in Paris.[54] Rather than allow young women away from their parents to live among the possibly unsavory characters at local boardinghouses, Vassar proposed to house its students and faculty in the college building itself. "In other words, this university undertakes to be an extensive educational restaurant and lodging house, an elaborate and magnificent literary hotel!" crowed an early supporter.[55]

Even before the ground was broken for what promised to be an extraordinary project, newspapers in New York and Boston followed the

The "magnificent literary hotel" of Poughkeepsie.

story of the man who wanted to endow a women's college. But the individual who did the most to publicize Vassar (man and college) was an indefatigable champion of women's education, Sarah Josepha Hale (1788–1879). Widowed with five children in 1822, Hale first tried unsuccessfully to support her brood with sewing. She then turned to writing, and in the best rags-to-riches tradition her novel *Northwood* (1827) became an instant sensation on both sides of the Atlantic. Within a month of its publication, Hale was asked to edit a new periodical for women, the *Ladies' Magazine.* Then, in 1837, publisher Louis Antoine Godey hired Hale to edit his *Godey's Lady's Book,* a position Hale wielded with authority for the next forty years.

As "Lady Editor," Hale didn't hesitate to promote her pet causes in the pages of the *Lady's Book,* chief among them women's education. She herself owed her knowledge of Latin and higher mathematics purely to the kindness of her brother, Horatio, who used his vacations from Dartmouth to tutor his younger sister. "He often regretted," she remembered, "that I could not, like himself, have the privilege of a college education."[56] She sent her own daughters to Emma Willard's school in Troy. Over the years, Hale wrote countless articles and editorials in both the *Ladies' Magazine* and *Godey's Lady's Book* supporting the education of girls and women. When she got word of Vassar's project in 1860, she immediately wrote him for further information about his great "plan in order to make it known to the readers of the *Lady's Book*."[57] This was a gift indeed, for around that time the magazine reached a peak of 150,000 subscribers— Godey himself estimated readership at half a million. The first article about Vassar's proposed college appeared in the *Lady's Book* in 1861.[58]

A friendly correspondence thereafter bloomed between Hale and Vassar, who consulted her on all sorts of details. Should there be a student costume, perhaps along the lines of the Bloomer suit, which would blur distinctions between richer and poorer students? Hale quickly disabused him of that idea: "Would it be well to enforce an equality of personal appearance . . . which cannot be found in life?" Besides, dressing students in the mercilessly ridiculed modified skirts would "be a serious injury to the college."[59] It would be better to merely counsel simplicity in dress. Meanwhile, Hale's editorials in the *Lady's Book* publicly prodded Vassar and the board of trustees to take actions they otherwise might not have—in particular, to hire women teachers.

Hale even talked Vassar into changing the very name of the institution. Vassar Female College opened its doors to some three hundred students in September 1865. But the word "female" rankled Sarah Hale. "Female! What female do you mean?" she asked in a sharply worded letter to Vassar. "Not a female donkey? Must not your reply be, 'I mean a female woman'? Then . . . why degrade the feminine sex to the level of animals?"[60] The offending word was dropped two years after the college opened, thereby setting a standard followed by other "female" academies making the transition to collegiate status.

Vassar was a stunning success, and set the pattern for the large women's colleges that followed fairly quickly in its wake: Smith (1875), Wellesley (1875), the Harvard Annex (1879; it became Radcliffe College in 1894), Bryn Mawr (1885), and Barnard (1889). (Along with Mount Holyoke, which attained collegiate status in 1888, these rounded out the so-called Seven Sisters.) Matthew Vassar vigorously supported the school until his death at age seventy-seven, when he collapsed while addressing the trustees during their annual meeting. In what might be seen as the last unstinting act of an exceedingly generous man (an obituary termed it "a singular coincidence"), he was wearing a new black suit—the one his family laid him to rest in.[61] It is said that he once received a letter from an ungrateful scholarship alumna stating that "A college foundation which is laid in beer will never prosper." Upon reading this, Vassar startled several student onlookers by shouting, "Well, it was good beer, wasn't it?" before dissolving in laughter.[62]

The First Black Women's College

Around the time of Vassar's inception, the first historically black colleges and universities were opening in the South. Before the Civil War, it was extremely difficult (to say the least) for an African American to get any education. Slaveholders viewed black literacy as a sure route to insurrection, and many southern states made it illegal to teach slaves to read and write. For those African Americans who lived in free states, opportunities remained limited; by one historian's estimate, only fifteen black men (and no women) attended institutes of higher education prior to 1840.[63] Among them were the first two black college graduates in the United States, Edward Jones (Amherst) and John Russwurm (Bowdoin), both of whom graduated in 1826. In 1850, Lucy Ann Stanton became the first black woman to graduate from college (she attended Oberlin's literary course). The first black woman to receive a bachelor's degree was Mary Jane Patterson, who graduated from Oberlin's collegiate program in 1862—three years before Vassar opened.[64] Another African-American graduate from Oberlin, Helen Morgan, became a Latin professor at Fisk University in 1869—a post she held for the next thirty-eight years, becoming one of the first women to attain full professorship at a coeducational institution. (It took substantially longer for black women to become faculty members at the nation's top-ranked and predominantly white universities. Harvard, for example, did not appoint a black woman to a full professorship with tenure until 1975.)[65]

After the Civil War, white missionaries from the north—members of the American Missionary Association and American Baptist Home Mission Society foremost among them—worked along with black churches and the Freedman's Bureau to establish colleges for newly liberated slaves in the South. By the late nineteenth century, white benefactors in the north helped fund Fisk (1865), Howard (1867), Atlanta (1867), Tougaloo (1869), and other historically black colleges, in an effort to train teachers.

While the question of coeducation remained a controversial one in white communities, the majority of institutions that became known as the historically black colleges and universities accepted female as well as male students from the start. For one reason, the historically black colleges simply didn't have the resources to create parallel systems for men and women—coeducation was more economical. Furthermore, while white women were still largely bound by ideals of True Womanhood that made homebound domesticity a woman's highest achievement, the black community recognized that marriage and work were not incompatible, and that its married women often needed to earn a living. Higher education not only increased a black woman's income-earning potential, it helped her "uplift" the race, a widespread concern at the time.[66]

At first, these schools operated under the most primitive conditions. Fisk University was born in an abandoned army barracks in Nashville, Tennessee, in 1866, and other institutions operated out of whatever space was available. There was always the threat of physical violence from the nascent Ku Klux Klan or other whites ill-disposed to the idea of an educated black citizenry. "The higher education of the Negro unfits him for the work that it is intended that he shall do, and cultivates ambitions that can never be realized," editorialized *The New*

Orleans Times-Democrat at the turn of the century.[67] (Similar charges were made by opponents of higher education for white women, who proclaimed that college "unfit" women for their domestic duties.) The need for basic education was great; in the words of historians Susan L. Poulson and Leslie Miller-Bernal, "many of the 'colleges' represented their founders' hopes for the future more than actual institutions of higher education."[68]

In 1881, Sophia B. Packard and Harriet E. Giles, two white teachers from the eastern seaboard, founded the Atlanta Baptist Female Seminary under the auspices of the Woman's American Baptist Home Mission Society. The school held its inaugural classes in a "dark and damp" church basement in Atlanta, Georgia, where the "glass [was] broken from the windows" and "the floor laid right upon the bare earth." When it rained, Giles and Packard stood in puddles. Sitting on the "hard seats" (there were no desks) were eleven pupils "of all ages and attainments," though a decision was quickly made to restrict the student body to those over the age of fifteen.[69] Two years later, the seminary moved to a converted Union Army barracks, its original eleven students having multiplied to two hundred. Compared with Vassar (where an early observer noted that the dormitories were heated "even in the severest weather by over 14 miles of steam pipe" and the kitchen supported by "an ice-house of generous capacity"), the environment at the converted barracks was notably less posh: a central room in each dormitory was heated by one stove to save expense, buttermilk was stored in a backyard pit, and white deliverymen refused to deliver groceries to the buildings and threw them over the fence instead.[70]

None of this stopped the students from coming, but when Packard and Giles met John D. Rockefeller in 1882, the rugged conditions began to change. Rockefeller's ongoing beneficence eventually led to an 1884 name change to Spelman Seminary in honor of his wife, Laura Spelman Rockefeller, and her abolitionist parents (eventually there was a Rockefeller Hall on campus too). In 1897 the college department opened and four years later Spelman granted its first two degrees. The name was officially changed to Spelman College in 1924.[71]

Here Come the Coeds!

The idea of young women attending single-sex institutions was bad enough to some conservative minds, but the opponents of female higher education saved much of their vitriol for the specter of coeducation, taking place at progressive white schools such as Oberlin, Antioch (1853), and the Universities of Iowa (1855), Wisconsin (1863), and Michigan (1870). Perhaps the most popular argument against coeducation was medical in nature. Some doctors, most notably Edward H. Clarke in his best-selling *Sex in Education, or A Fair Chance for the Girls* (1873), claimed that the rigors of study during the menstrual period would destroy a woman's reproductive health. Of course, this could also happen on a single-sex campus, but Clarke suggested it was more likely to happen where women tried to compete with men. Competition between the sexes was a further blow to the separate spheres, already threatened by college women's encroachment into the professions.

Another "objection to coeducation to be considered," wrote an observer in 1905, was "summed up in the word 'love-making.' "[72] This was distasteful from several angles. Parents worried that a daughter away at college might make an unsuitable match with a young man she met on campus. Writing shortly after the turn of the twentieth century, a professor at the Kansas State Agricultural College took a realistic approach to the issue. He recognized that a coeducational college was "necessarily a place of much courting and match-making." It only became "a matter of serious concern" when girls threw "themselves carelessly into the company of young men of questionable morals in places of doubtful propriety" or when romance crowded out "attention to lessons." He recommended that schools build enough dormitory space for all women students, so as to keep them out of rooming houses and under direct college supervision, and engage strict matrons to regulate their behavior (or, in his words, "mature mentor[s] . . . to observe the girl's conduct at close range . . . and give motherly advice").[73] Opponents of women's education argued that husband-hunting coeds who dropped out to marry before graduation as well as those who married soon after commencement usurped resources needed by men who would go on to head households. Indeed, many early coeds chafed at the oft-made suggestion that their interest in higher education was merely a frivolous attempt to meet men.

The University of Iowa became the first public coeducational college in 1855, when it admitted forty-one women—almost exactly a third of the student body. Iowa was quite the trailblazer when it came to educating women and men together. It opened the first coed medical school in 1870, and its law department granted a J.D. to a woman in 1873. Coeducation really took hold when the Morrill Land Grant Acts of 1862 and 1890 opened up funding for the creation of state universities in the west offering agricultural and mechanical arts; the second act specified that the funds be "fairly divided by Negroes and Whites," which led to interracial student bodies—in theory, at any rate. The acts didn't specifically refer to women, but because the western states were so sparsely populated, coeducation at the collegiate level was attractive from an economic standpoint. The west also lacked the eastern seaboard's century-old tradition of private single-sex colleges.

Like several other schools, my own alma mater, the University of Wisconsin, showed its ambivalence to coeducation via a series of fits and starts over the first several decades of women's attendance. In 1863, thirty women were admitted to the Normal Department (i.e., the teacher training program). With male enrollment down because of the Civil War, the coeds were allowed to attend other classes as well—though they weren't permitted to sit down until all the men had seats. Four years later, under the auspices of university president Paul A. Chadbourne, segregation by sex was reinstated and a separate Female College opened. During Chadbourne's administration, men and women took the same courses but recited separately—a philosophy professor, for example, would meet his male students at 1:00 P.M. in Room 203, then go next-door to teach women the following hour. Full coeducation began in 1874 when the previous system "broke down under the weight of its own absurdity," as a contemporary observer noted. A reactionary rumbling of concern regarding the effect of study on female health was heard in 1877, but this was countered by the university's new president, John A. Bascom, a strong supporter of coeducation.[74]

One might imagine that decades of successfully educating men and women together would be the end of the controversy, but this was not the case. Thirty years later, when coeds accounted for 50 percent of the student population and male students showed a 10 percent decline, President Charles Richard Van Hise blamed the seemingly overwhelming numbers of women for "undoubtedly pushing the men out" of the liberal arts. Van Hise's theory of "sex repulsion" suggested that as soon as one sex tipped the numeric balance in the coed classroom, the other fled in fear of competition (this was reported to occur at other coeducational institutions as well). He advocated a limited return to segregated classes in several disciplines, including psychology and hygiene. The alumni rallied in opposition, however, and with support from Senator Robert "Fighting Bob" La Follette (class of 1879), coeducation prevailed.

Wisconsin was not the only state where coeds' enthusiastic response to the prospect of a college education caused problems. At the first meeting of Stanford University's board of trustees in 1885, founder Leland Stanford, Sr. "deem[ed] it of the first importance that the education of both sexes be equally full and complete." Ten years later, there were fifty-one women for every hundred men students, and one commentator proudly wondered whether the university was on its way to becoming "the Vassar of the Pacific Coast."[75] But not everyone shared that enthusiasm. Some grumbled that a series of gridiron losses to the rival University of California might be due to the number of pretty women on campus, who distracted athletes from practice. Others worried about "the increase of power among the women" on campus:

> They are voting themselves into all the offices and thereby rendering the institution less desirable to male students than it otherwise would be. A woman edits the Junior annual, another brings out the weekly paper, and

still another leads the inter-collegiate debate. Thus there is an alarming tendency apparent toward reducing the University to the level of a "woman's seminary," which Mrs. Stanford very much dreads.[76]

That was Mrs. Leland Stanford, of course, widow of the prominent industrialist, cofounder of the Central Pacific Railroad, and governor of California, and mother of the deceased Leland Stanford, Jr., in whose memory the university was founded. When women reached 40 percent of the student body in the late 1890s, Mrs. Stanford made a decision. Without consulting anyone at the university, she amended its charter to limit the number of female students to five hundred at any given time. It wasn't that she disliked the presence of women on campus, she told reporters. She confirmed that they received as many honors as the men and noted that "the refining influence of the girls is wonderful." But she did not want the public to regard Stanford as a university for women. "This was not my husband's wish, nor is it mine, nor would it have been my son's," Mrs. Stanford told the board of trustees in 1899. Flummoxed by the arbitrary limit, university president David Starr Jordan suggested a more flexible interpretation of the quota or the substitution of a percent-age system, but his pleas were met with a deaf ear by Mrs. Stanford (who had also considered, but rejected, eliminating the women entirely). The limit was reached in 1903, though four or more times as many women continued to apply. Despite this interest, the five-hundred rule remained in effect for another thirty years—until Depression-era economics sud-denly made the prospect of additional tuition-paying women students much more interesting to the trustees.[77]

Mrs. Stanford was not the only person to comment on the "refining" nature of the female presence on rough-and-tumble male manners. This was frequently mentioned as an advantage of schooling men and women together, as here in an 1871 article on "The Co-Education of the Sexes":

Boys accustomed to the use of profane and obscene language among themselves, will never swear in the presence of young ladies, nor indulge in ribaldry. . . . Let a few tidy, genteel young ladies become members of the school, and the effect on dress and manners of boys is magical.[78]

In real life, however, the magic was less immediately apparent. The first time the University of Michigan's only coed was called on to read aloud in her Greek class in 1870, she was pointedly given the following passage from Sophocles's *Antigone*: "It behooves us in the first place to consider this, that we are by nature women, so not able to contend with men; and in the next place, since we are governed by those stronger than we, it behooves us to admit these things and others still more grievous."

Evincing much generosity of spirit, Madelon Stockwell always contended the choice of reading matter was an accident, not maliciousness on the part of the professor or her classmates—the same ones who later that day lined up on either side of the campus's Diagonal Walk to stare at the "She-sophomore" as she passed.[79]

Olive San Louie Anderson was another pioneering coed at the University of Michigan. Four years after her graduation, she published a thinly fictionalized novel about her undergraduate experiences titled *An American Girl and Her Four Years in a Boys' College* (1878). It is the story of Wilhelmine Elliott—called "Will" by friends and family, just as the author was "Louie" to hers—who attends the University of Ortonville as one of nine girls in the freshman class. A plucky tomboy in the mold of Louisa May Alcott's Jo March, Will faces opposition to her education at a "boys' school" from her mother, boardinghouse operators, and some professors and administrators, as well as her fellow students. None of it can dampen Will's desire to get a degree, even when caught in the midst of frenzied freshman-sophomore hazing battles. She is hit in the eye with an apple core while gathered with the rest of the female students before a chapel service, and her nose is bloodied when she is pushed into a stair railing during a bout of rushing (a custom at men's schools where sophomores and freshmen tried en masse to push the others off a stairway or path). When a male classmate entreats the others to wait until the girls are out of the way, the only response is a hearty "Damn 'em, they have no business here anyway." Will resolves to laugh at her bruises and to bear them "bravely, feeling something of that rapture the old martyrs must have felt—for was I not suffering in the cause of co-education?"[80] Despite such manhandling, she vastly prefers coeducation and asks a friend who attends Vassar how she can prefer that "old boarding-school, where you don't see a fellow once a month, and are always watched by some old corridor-spy . . ." to the relative freedoms afforded by coeducation.[81]

Catholic and Other Denominational Colleges

The old corridor-spy was exactly the sort of strict moral arbiter some parents looked for when it came to sending their beloved daughters away to college. In fact, most of the founders and organizers of the women's colleges were religious men or organizations. Matthew Vassar was a devout Baptist, Bryn Mawr had ties to the Quaker religion. At Wellesley, Henry Fowle Durant was a lay preacher who made it clear the instruction given there would be "Christian in its influence, discipline, and course of instruction."[82] Spelman and the rest of the historically black colleges and universities were associated with white Christian missionaries. These schools and others turned to the Christian gentlewoman as a model for their graduates, an ideal that made a daughter's college education more palatable to many parents.

For others, only the imprimatur of the Church itself would do. There were 115 Catholic girls' schools in operation in the United States by 1852, all but three of them directed by religious communities, even though there was a strong resistance to the idea of higher education for Catholic women.[83] This was due in part to the church hierarchy's "traditional but unofficial" belief in the natural inferiority of women. When it came to the question of whether a college education would make women better wives and mothers, historian Edward J. Power pointed out that "to the Catholic priest-professor who could proclaim without any sign of mirth that the best diploma for a woman was always a large family and a happy husband, the answer . . . was unequivocally 'no.' "[84]

The church's refusal to countenance collegiate education for women became problematic, however. In 1884, church leaders responded to the rapid development of Protestant-based public schools, and their threat of luring Catholic children away from the true church, by legislating the system of parochial schools that generations of Catholic schoolchildren came to know and love—or hate. Who would fill many of the teaching slots in the proposed schools but laywomen and nuns? Where would they get their training? The established Catholic men's colleges—of which there were eighty-four by 1860—didn't exactly rush into action producing elementary schoolteachers. According to Power, they simply pretended that the legislation of 1884 "was unreal" or otherwise ignored it.[85]

Yet another decade passed before the first (and historians seem to agree about this) institute of higher learning for Catholic women, the College of Notre Dame of Maryland, finally opened in 1896—a full thirty years after Vassar, fifteen after Spelman. It was followed by the College of Saint Elizabeth (Convent Station, New Jersey), Trinity College (Washington, D.C.), St. Joseph's College (Emmitsburg, Maryland), and the College of New Rochelle (New Rochelle, New York), all of which opened prior to 1905.[86]

Of these, only Trinity College (1900) was planned from the start as a women's college (for example, the College of Notre Dame began as a girls' institute in 1863).[87] Its prospectus of 1899 promised an education on a par with the best secular colleges for women, with additional training in

> the science of Religion, Domestic Economy, and other branches deemed useful in fitting a woman for her proper sphere in Home and Society. Together with science and religion—knowledge and love of God—love of country will be instilled; a laudable pride in its glorious history and fidelity to its Constitution and laws inculcated at all times.[88]

Womanhood, citizenship, and religion were thus bound up in one glorious package.

A Priestly View of Higher Education for Catholic Women

 Not all members of the church welcomed the opening of the first Catholic women's colleges. *The Catholic Girl's Guide* (1905) was a book of "Counsels and Devotions for Girls" written by a priest. Father Francis X. Lasance warned that the majority of young women stood in danger of becoming "muddled-headed" if forced into higher education by well-meaning parents, with "the baneful results that other more necessary and useful studies" would fall by the wayside. These included housekeeping and household accounting, though the study of language and literature was acceptable in order to "take part in conversation with husband, father, son or brother who takes an interest in and likes to discuss such topics." The serious study of theology, however, was a no-no (shades of Anne Hutchinson, at the remove of centuries and Protestantism). Women made "downright poor theologians . . . because not intended or gifted by God for such a study." A solid knowledge of the catechism was all that was necessary for girls. The future housewife in particular needed practical religious knowledge, not higher education, "to accomplish her lofty task, namely, to cultivate religion in her family, to instruct her children in its truths, and thus to become the priestess of the domestic shrine."*

* Rev. Francis X. Lasance, *The Catholic Girl's Guide* (New York: Benziger Brothers, 1905), 394, 389, 394, 403.

In 1909, an eight-week summer school for nuns and laywomen was held at all-male Marquette University in Milwaukee, Wisconsin; this is considered the first experiment in coeducation in the Catholic colleges. Five years later, DePaul University in Chicago became the first fully coeducational Catholic college.[89]

∽

Thus for both religious and secular, black and white, the trends all led in one direction—toward greater educational opportunities for women. Despite slurs and stereotypes, questions about her physical and mental abilities, a teenage girl in the late nineteenth century had more hope than ever before of achieving a higher education. By 1870, approximately 70 women's colleges and 170 coeducational schools enrolled 11,000 young women, who accounted for 21 percent of all college students. By the turn of the twentieth century, 85,000 women made up 36.8 percent of the student population.[90] The College Girl had arrived.

Students roll for glory at Bryn Mawr in 1943.

New Girl on Campus

No one cared whether or not I knew anything. Every one asked if I were interested in debating, class banners, class meetings, self-government, sunrise hikes, crew tests, college songs, humorous stunts, the Bird Club, St. Hilda's Guild.

FRANCES WARFIELD,
REMINISCING ABOUT HER TIME AS A
COLLEGE GIRL IN THE 1920S[1]

There is at least one experience that both the pioneering college girls of the 1860s and Jane Doe of today would recognize as largely unadulterated by changes in technology, fashion, and the social status of women. This is the moment when after all the planning, test taking, and nail-biting expectation you find yourself alone on campus—your college campus!—for the very first time. Excitement and apprehension, anticipation and fear are all mixed up with the tantalizing realization that you are at last on your own. At long last, there is no one to tell you to go to bed before 2:00 A.M. or even to go to class the next morning. It's a heady moment.

For me back in 1979, the exhilaration was muted by raw terror. I yearned to be sophisticated, urbane, and witty. In reality, I was too shy to call the pizza delivery place let alone raise my hand in class. Even offers of friendship scared me. During my first week as a bona fide coed, I walked into the first meeting of French II, sat down, and found myself sitting next to Robby Thayer. I barely recognized him—he was so much older and his voice discernibly lower since the last time I'd seen him when we were eleven. After making small talk, his dark eyes sparkling, he teasingly promised to help me with my homework.

I panicked. Hadn't he and Candi Baker had what passed for a torrid affair in Mr. Siegel's sixth-grade class? Everyone knew they spent time alone together in the bushes at the park across the street from the play-ground. At the time I hadn't a clue what they might have been doing. Now I had some ideas—and they frightened me. Clearly, there was only one course of action open to me. I immediately dropped the class, never to return to Robby and his teasing brown eyes, never to speak French beyond the first-person present.

Had I only read any of the college girl guidebooks written over the decades, I would have known that a good first impression was the social equivalent of going Phi Beta Kappa. "The coed's first days at college are full of Opportunities," counseled a 1949 guide for brand-new college girls. "This is no time to be an ice cube."[2]

Getting to Know You: Freshman Initiations

Freshman shyness was nothing new. Most schools did their best to help new students out of their shells and into the swing of college life with special activities before or during the first weeks of the semester. Begin-ning in the nineteenth century, the women's colleges often paired classes off with one another (freshman with juniors, sophomores with seniors);

at most schools, each had traditional responsibilities to perform—be it for their "sister" class or another. These duties usually consisted of hosting dances, receptions, or teas or otherwise providing some sort of service to members of the other class. In 1895, *The Century* magazine described Smith College's annual "Freshman Frolic," the dance by which the sophomore class welcomed incoming freshmen:

> Men are not missed, so well are their places filled by the assiduous sophomores. Each new girl is escorted to the gymnasium by her partner, who, in addition to filling out her dancing-card and sending her flowers . . . sees that she meets the right person for each dance, entertains her during refreshments, and escorts her home. . . . You cannot treat it all as a joke when you see the scrupulous politeness of your partner, and the responsible air with which she makes conversation.[3]

The effect of "seven or eight hundred girls dancing together" was noted to be striking. A similar affair was held at the fictional Gale College in *Her College Days* (1896). "Oh! Won't there be any men there?" exclaims a freshman upon hearing of the sophomores' welcoming reception:

> "Men!" said Miss Hewitt, a Sophomore, and therefore an authority on all college matters. "Put aside the thought of men, Miss Arden, until you are a Junior. Juniors and Seniors may invite men to their dances but nobody else."
> "Then I don't see how you can have any fun," said Miss Arden, frankly.[4]

Miss Arden remains incredulous—until she's had a lovely time at the dance, of course. Contemporary observers often noted that such welcoming dances were a feminine alternative to the often brutal hazing that led to black eyes and broken bones on men's campuses. Miss Hewitt makes the same observation to her freshman tablemates, noting that the dances were "one of the ways we Sophomores have of rushing you Freshmen . . . a far better way than cane fights and hazing."[5]

In place of violence, the nineteenth-century women's colleges initiated new freshmen with pomp and circumstance—sometimes along with a wee bit of what might be considered gentle hazing. At Bryn Mawr in the 1890s, sophomores presented each new freshman with "a lantern to light her steps through the unknown ways of college life" in a beautiful ceremony which takes place to this day.[6] Once the freshmen were officially welcomed, however, the sophomores spent the rest of the evening trying to steal their caps and gowns—which the frosh were required to wear to chapel the following morning. At Wellesley, upperclassmen did their best to uncover the freshman class's motto, flower, and song before they were officially revealed on Tree Day (another ongoing tradition), when the campus was closed to outsiders and the freshmen planted their class tree. In the nineteenth century, Vassar had a similar tradition of planting class trees, except it was done during sophomore year and it was the freshmen who tried to ferret out the secret information—only to have the wily sophs send them on wild goose chases for their troubles.[7]

In the twentieth century, the freshman beanie was a popular way to initiate the newcomers at both coed and women's campuses. Each member of the entering class was expected to wear a beanie in school or class colors for the first week or so on campus. If a girl was caught without the little hat, she had to do the bidding of the upperclassman who apprehended her. Class headwear took on added significance at Mills College, where from the 1930s through the 1960s the cap hunt was an annual fall event. The freshmen hid a box of their class caps somewhere on campus, and the sophomores searched for them. If the sophs didn't find them by the deadline, freshmen were allowed to keep their caps. Otherwise, they might not receive them until later in the semester. A later twist gave the winners of the traditional pushball contest between the two classes additional rights to withhold or secure the class caps.

Traditions and ceremonies varied in time and from place to place, but they all served to bond new students with their alma mater. Classes took their traditional responsibilities to one another seriously. At Mills in 1933, the round of obligations meant that the freshmen gave a formal dance in honor of the juniors, and put on a wienie roast for the same sophomore class that bedeviled them over their beanies. "In a kinder frame of mind," the sophomores gave a "Bowery Party" for the freshmen.

They also serenaded the seniors at the Pin Dinner, gave a picnic in their honor, and served at the Junior-Senior Breakfast. The junior class was in charge of Freshman Days, gave a campuswide Halloween dance, and put out the yearbook. Seniors were the big dames on campus: they had the fewest responsibilities to other classes, caught up as they were in the drama of their last year of college, but they still found time to meet the freshmen at a special dinner.[8]

It was all very organized, but tensions could erupt if a particular class was judged to be shirking its duties. A member of Hood College's class of 1929 chided incoming freshmen for their "general lack of courtesy and respect for the faculty and upperclassmen" in an anonymous letter to the student newspaper:

> It seems to be a great burden to you to even so much as hold the door for those in classes above yours. . . .
>
> The table manners of some of you are disrespectful. . . . You have all been told that you are not to leave the table at dinner time before everyone at that table is ready to leave and the hostess dismisses you. We also think it a matter of courtesy for you to pass the vegetable and other dishes to the head of the table before helping yourself. At noon, you should ask to be excused before rushing off to a class.
>
> Also, when a member of the faculty, a hostess, or an upperclassman speaks to you or enters your room, it would do you no harm to respect them by standing up at least until they are seated.[9]

Was the freshman class really a bunch of oafs or was the Class of '29 just feeling their sophomore oats? Ceremonies and traditions designed to bond individuals with class, and classes with alma mater, did occasionally backfire. A 1942 Mills graduate remembered how a tremendously long receiving line of faculty members at the college president's orientation tea turned introductions into a child's game of telephone: "I started the receiving line as Jane Cudlip. And in the noise and confusion . . . When I came out the other end, my name was Meredith Appleby."[10] If there was ever a moment for a lonely girl to feel overwhelmed by the size and anonymity of both class and campus, a malfunctioning assembly line of freshmen was surely it. Indeed, all the welcoming dances, orientation teas, wienie roasts, and candlelight ceremonies couldn't obscure the fact that for most girls, going to college meant leaving home for the very first time.

Homesickness: The Freshman Scourge

"I had no idea how hard it was to go away and leave 'em all. It's terrible," wrote fifteen-year-old M. Carey Thomas in an 1872 letter to a beloved aunt.[11] The future president of Bryn Mawr was then a student at a Quaker academy for girls. As a freshman at Cornell three years later, she was an old hand at living away from home. For those without her boarding-school experience, however, the homesickness experienced during the first weeks or months on campus could be crushing. Nor did the freshman's feelings of loneliness and longing for home's familiarity change much over the generations. "The first days at college are almost sure to be a time of great anxiety and strain" advised *The Freshman Girl* (1925).[12]

For some girls, the loneliness and longing for home were assuaged by a familiar presence—that of their mother. Vida Scudder's mother accompanied her to Smith in the nineteenth century, where she helped set her daughter's hair every day. Finally her mother realized Vida needed to be thrown on her own hairstyling resources and went home. A 1920s-era college guidebook suggested that the moment of parting between parent and child should be similar to removing a Band-Aid from a scabby knee: quick and clean. The well-meaning mother who accompanied her daughter to school, stayed in her dorm room, and helped her unpack set her up for "an attack of homesickness" after the mother's departure. It was better for parents to keep their distance until at least Thanksgiving, by which time their child would have become "a real personage, instead of the dazed, uncertain newcomer of a few weeks before. It is more pleasant for all concerned."[13]

Homesickness in action at Florida State College for Women, 1941.

College Girl Bookshelf: "Her College Days" (1896), by Mrs. Clark Johnson

Unlike the average freshman away from home for the first time, sweet and innocent Lois Darcy isn't plagued by homesickness thanks to one simple expedient: she's brought her widowed mother to college with her. Therein lies the conflict in *Her College Days*. For, as one of Lois's well-meaning friends puts it, "A girl can't get the benefit of being away from home if she has to be hampered with a mother."* Lois, who at sixteen is a little younger than her classmates and really doesn't mind living off campus with her unusual roommate, overhears her friends' conversation and repeats it to Mrs. Darcy. The seeds of doubt are thus sown in her mother's mind. Meanwhile, Lois meets Mr. Hamilton, a star athlete at Houghton College. Mrs. Darcy acts as an approving chaperone, and the three of them spend many lovely times together.

Despite the whirl of gaiety, Mrs. Darcy worries that Lois would be happier without her cramping presence. She decides she must move back to their hometown of St. Mark's. Lois is guilt-stricken and tearful at the news, worried that her class schedule and active

---

* Mrs. Clark Johnson, *Her College Days* (Philadelphia: Penn Publishing Co., 1896), 35.

social life have left her mother lonely. It is a difficult parting, and neither reveals her true thoughts to the other.

Lois keeps her chin up and throws herself into even more campus activities. Meanwhile, back at St. Mark's, Mrs. Darcy wastes away from illness but refuses to let her friends contact Lois until it is almost too late. Then Lois races back to St. Mark's—for a short while in the unchaperoned presence of Mr. Hamilton! Of course, Lois's arrival at home recalls her mother from the brink of death. This is because, as the fully recovered Mrs. Darcy later confesses to her daughter, "it was the idea that you could be happy without me, perhaps happier than with me, that almost killed me."† Oy.

Despite the copious amount of campus details, *Her College Days* ends like a typical romance. The doctor prescribes a complete change of air and scene for the convalescent Mrs. Darcy, so she and Lois head to Europe. Gale College is forgotten, mentioned not at all in the last chapter. When Mr. Hamilton, fresh from the Houghton Glee Club's English tour, shows up on their doorstep, Lois's fate is sealed: marriage, not a diploma, will be her future.

† Ibid., 332.

The mother who came to college continued to be a leitmotiv for years to come. "The mother who packs all her daughter's clothes, selects drapes and bedspread . . . and even arranges her dormitory room, is going too far," reported the *New York Times* in 1955. "In fact, this mother may be trying to enjoy again through her daughter her own college days" or the ones she never had, the paper suggested in a fit of armchair psychoanalysis. Even in what we like to think of as our own enlightened era, some mothers can't quite say good-bye. "Dear Abby: I am a 21-year-old college student," began a letter to the venerable advice columnist in 2002. "This year I'm living with three sorority sisters in a house off campus. We get along fine except for one thing"—that being the mother of one of the roommates who spent "every single weekend" with her daughter. Not only was she "always underfoot," but she committed the ultimate roommate sin: she never replaced the toilet paper after using the last of it.[14]

For those who arrived alone on campus, most twentieth-century college advice guides recommended keeping busy as a remedy for homesickness. Partaking of myriad campus activities for freshmen held loneliness at bay and helped a girl forge new relationships. "At home people know that you don't like onions in your potato salad, and how talented you really are, and how you need to be given lots of encouragement," commiserated the author of *You Can Always Tell a Freshman* (1949):

> Lock the stable before the horse runs away. . . . If you are the type who waxes sentimental over mood music, guard yourself! Do not linger in the bathtub. Do not take up embroidery. Keep occupied with lots of people. Cultivate the ability to laugh at yourself. Need I say more?[15]

Needlecrafts and long, relaxing baths were solitary activities that gave girls time to brood over the folks back home. For instead of darling Mom, Dad, and Sis, who knew a girl's taste in potato salad and other things, there was a roommate, a complete stranger who may or may not have been the sort to give a pat on the head when a girl needed it.

Roommates and Others

Meeting one's roommate *was* a stressful moment, and guidebooks offered advice on how to act. *You Can Always Tell a Freshman* suggested taking a proactive role:

> Break the ice with a homely gesture. Make some cocoa together the very first night. It is simply amazing what a little "prepared" cocoa, mixed with some hot water from the bathroom spigot, will do to promote comradery. The girl who does not shed her reserve under the influence of such elementary hospitality belongs at Harvard in a bottle, and sooner or later she will find her way there.[16]

In addition to the somewhat disturbing suggestion that one's roommate-to-be might better belong in a scientific specimen jar than a college dormitory, the last sentence implied the possibility of a painful truth: despite cocoa's convivial powers, some roommates were not destined to be friends. "Socially, my first experiences with college were mostly unpleasant," reported a freshman in the mid-1950s: "My roommates were quite a group the first semester. One was a genius, I think, but partly neurotic (always crying). Another was failing, a third was foreign and understood very little English, and the fourth had insomnia . . ."[17]

She certainly didn't appreciate them at the time, but this student probably still entertains at cocktail parties with stories about the eccentric bunch she lived with freshman year. And she got off easy. An insomniac and someone who cried all the time paled in comparison with the student at the Florida State College for Women who, it was reported by the *Florida Flambeau* student newspaper in 1942, kept an "extraordinary" collection in her room. Asked by "a pre-med friend of hers" if he could bring her anything on an upcoming visit, the puckish girl responded "Just bring me a finger or an ear"—knowing he was a dental student. "Imagine Jean's surprise and horror," the paper blithely continued, "when he took out of his pocket and gave to her there in the parlor a bottle with two pre-

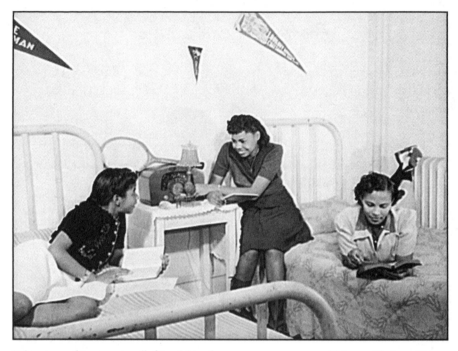

When everything went well, friendships between roommates could last a lifetime. Here, at Bethune-Cookman College, 1943.

served human ears in it—one black, and one white." These were reported to be "perfectly formed" and floating in formaldehyde. Not only did Jean receive her unusual gift with aplomb, she was reported to very much want "a hand or a leg to hang on the light cord in her room."[18] There was no word on what her roommate had to say about such an unusual decorating scheme.

As uncomfortable as it could be, meeting people with different viewpoints and habits was (and remains) an important part of the college experience. This was especially true for college girls in the nineteenth century and much of the twentieth, when travel was less frequent and local customs hadn't been all but obliterated by the ubiquity of chain stores and mega-malls. Ideally, the result was a positive one: exposure to a roommate's thoughts and habits resulted in an expanded worldview while the diminutive dimensions of most dorm rooms ensured a crash course in cooperation. This might have more personal benefits in the future. "A girl who has lived successfully in a dormitory or sorority house should make a better wife some day because of her training," wrote the author of *CO-EDiquette: Poise and Popularity for Every Girl* (1936). "For if college teaches her nothing else, it does teach her how to live congenially with somebody else." The penalty for not making the "fundamental adjustments required for peaceful living with another person" was heavy. "Such failure will lead her [the unsuccessful roommate], when married, to the divorce courts," reported the dean of Guilford College, Guilford, North Carolina.[19]

Sometimes the differences were too great. This was frequently the case when roommates or classmates were "others," foreigners with poor English skills, Jews, or nonwhite students. Racism and anti-Semitism lurked at all the colleges. It took a forward-thinking, open-minded administration to accept nonwhites or Jews, and the same and more from the student body to make black or Jewish girls really feel at home. While *Florida Flambeau* didn't theorize on the presence of the black ear in that jar of formaldehyde, it certainly carried a different cultural punch than that of the white one—especially since there were few, it any, black students at the Florida State College for Women in 1942.

Even at abolitionist Oberlin, race was an issue among the student body. When the college first considered admitting black students two years after its opening in 1833, the white women on campus were "not prepared to embrace it at once," recalled President James H. Fairchild, in an address before the alumni in 1860:

> Young ladies who had come from New England to the school in the wilderness—young ladies of unquestioned refinement and goodness, declared that if colored students were admitted to equal privileges in the Institution, they would return to their homes, if they had to "wade Lake Erie" to accomplish it.[20]

According to Fairchild, the experience of integrated dorms, dining facilities, and classes changed its white students' attitudes toward African Americans (who never made up more than 4 or 5 percent of the

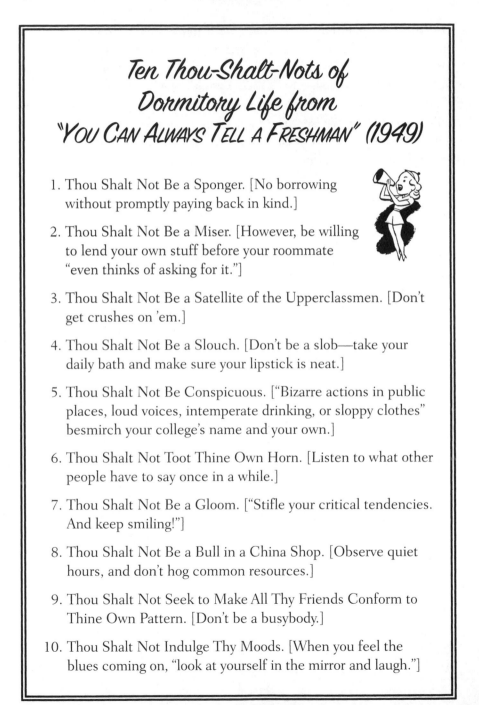

Ten Thou-Shalt-Nots of Dormitory Life from "You Can Always Tell a Freshman" (1949)

1. Thou Shalt Not Be a Sponger. [No borrowing without promptly paying back in kind.]

2. Thou Shalt Not Be a Miser. [However, be willing to lend your own stuff before your roommate "even thinks of asking for it."]

3. Thou Shalt Not Be a Satellite of the Upperclassmen. [Don't get crushes on 'em.]

4. Thou Shalt Not Be a Slouch. [Don't be a slob—take your daily bath and make sure your lipstick is neat.]

5. Thou Shalt Not Be Conspicuous. ["Bizarre actions in public places, loud voices, intemperate drinking, or sloppy clothes" besmirch your college's name and your own.]

6. Thou Shalt Not Toot Thine Own Horn. [Listen to what other people have to say once in a while.]

7. Thou Shalt Not Be a Gloom. ["Stifle your critical tendencies. And keep smiling!"]

8. Thou Shalt Not Be a Bull in a China Shop. [Observe quiet hours, and don't hog common resources.]

9. Thou Shalt Not Seek to Make All Thy Friends Conform to Thine Own Pattern. [Don't be a busybody.]

10. Thou Shalt Not Indulge Thy Moods. [When you feel the blues coming on, "look at yourself in the mirror and laugh."]

student body between 1840 and 1860, or for much of the following century). He described how these same young ladies later faced "torrent[s] of abuse and reproach" for their "fearless advocacy of their cause of the oppressed."[21] Fairchild may have been overly optimistic. As abolitionist influences at Oberlin and elsewhere faded in the late nineteenth century, tensions rose between white and black students. In 1882 (while Fairchild was still president), a professor objected to plans for a black student and a white student to share a dormitory room, and despite a committee of six African-American students who pointed out the discrimination to the faculty, they were not allowed to do so. Also during the 1882 school year, white women students living at Ladies Hall refused to eat at the same table with black residents, as had previously been the custom. White student complaints became so numerous that a separate table was established for the black girls. News of this segregated dining brought a flood of protests from black and white alumni, but it was only through "much persuasion" that President Fairchild and the principal of the Women's Department were able to convince white students to once again sit at dinner with their black counterparts.[22]

Racial tensions also erupted at Cornell when in 1911 two black students, Pauline A. Ray and Rosa A. Vassar, tried to move into Sage College, the women's dormitory. After an article (penned by a black male student) appeared in the student newspaper describing how the girls had been denied rooms and demanding an official explanation for it, a petition protesting their admission was circulated among the dormitory residents. Two hundred coeds signed, though some of these were what the *New York Times* called "outsiders" who didn't actually live in the dorm themselves. Ray and Vassar maintained they were not agitators "seeking social equality," merely students who desired the convenience of living on campus. They promised that if they moved into the dorm, they would not take part in their less-than-welcoming neighbors' social life but would remain "as separate as two fingers on one hand."[23] In the end, Cornell president Jacob Gould Schurman ruled that Sage College had to admit the young women.

It is impossible to know how many light-skinned African-American

students tried to avoid the demeaning facts of racial prejudice by "passing" themselves as white, but at least one was turned in by her roommate. When Anita Florence Hemmings applied to Vassar in 1893, she
listed her ancestry as French and English. Her classmates described her
as an "exotic beauty," and a Boston newspaper later noted that Anita
"could pass anywhere simply as a pronounced brunette of the white
race." Unfortunately, Anita's roommate had a different assessment of
Anita's appearance, and revealed her suspicions to her father just before
graduation in 1897. The father then hired a private investigator to track
down Anita's parents in Boston. "We know our daughter went to Vassar as
a white girl and stayed there as such," Anita's janitor father told the newspapers. "As long as she conducted herself as a lady she never thought it
necessary to proclaim the fact that her parents were mulattoes." In the
end, a "crestfallen" Anita—an excellent student and a soloist in the college choir—appealed to Vassar president James Monroe Taylor to be
allowed to graduate with her class. Her request was granted, but it would
be another forty years before Vassar knowingly accepted another African-
American student.[24]

A somewhat similar issue arose in 1913, when Smith unknowingly
accepted the application of a young black woman. Carrie Lee did not try
to pass as white—she simply did not list herself as black. When she met
her new roommate from Tennessee, the result was not a harmonious
expectation-defying friendship. Instead, Lee was barred from student
housing after the roommate complained. She turned to the college-
approved boardinghouses but was told she would have to enter and exit
by the backdoor along with the servants. After the NAACP intervened,
she lived with a sympathetic professor. During the fracas, Smith polled
its Seven Sisters about their racial policies. Among them, only Wellesley
stated that it did not discriminate against African Americans when it
came to admissions and housing. However enlightened the college's
administrative practices, its white students still "parodied Negro dialect
and sang 'Coon songs' on their mandolins and banjos."[25]

In 1926, activist and educator W. E. B. DuBois summed up the situation at the women's colleges: "Vassar has graduated but one Negro stu-

dent and did not know it at the time. Bryn Mawr and Barnard have tried desperately to exclude them. Radcliffe, Wellesley, and Smith have treated them with tolerance and even cordiality. Many small institutions or institutions with one or two Negro students have been gracious and kind toward them, particularly in the Middle West. But on the whole, the attitude of northern institutions is one which varies from tolerance to active hostility."[26]

This could also be said of the attitude toward Jews. In addition to being almost entirely white during the nineteenth century, colleges were also almost entirely Protestant. Catholic and Jewish girls were allowed to enter the women's colleges "by ones and twos" later in the century, as long as they didn't rock the boat.[27] When in 1898 a Bryn Mawr student and her mother complained that the girl's roommate was Jewish, M. Carey Thomas's response was unequivocal. She wrote the student's mother and told her that her daughter's roommate would not be asked to move. Rather than take part in a "religious controversy," Thomas expressed the college's "great desire . . . to show the strictest impartiality" among students. She then moved them both. Tolerance was the official policy at Bryn Mawr, but Thomas's private feelings were less laudatory. The president of Bryn Mawr was a remarkable woman, ahead of her time in many respects, yet even she was unable to fully rise above the anti-Semitism and racism of her times. In a letter to a close friend, she vowed that "Never again shall we put a Jew and Christian together" as roommates. Despite having hired a German Jewish physiology professor in 1891—a daring move—Thomas later worked behind the scenes to prevent other Jews from joining the faculty. "It is much more satisfactory to have a faculty made up as far as possible of our own good Anglo-Saxon stock," she wrote to a professor who recommended a candidate in 1906.[28]

During the nineteenth century and first decades of the twentieth, Jews formed only a small part of the student population, but in the 1920s, the children of those who arrived in the big waves of Jewish immigration from eastern Europe at and just before the turn of the century began applying to college. Many schools responded with quota systems.

These were rarely made public, though applicants and students long had their suspicions. An application form question like "What change, if any, has been made since birth in your own name or that of your father?" weeded out Browns who entered Ellis Island as Brownsteins. Some schools employed "psychological tests." As part of one such procedure, a student who applied to the medical school at New York University in the early 1920s appeared before a faculty panel and "among the many questions asked him were how often he attended synagogue, was he very religious, etc. He was not admitted."[29]

As part of her research on the history of women's higher education in the United States, historian Barbara Miller Solomon came across a file folder in Radcliffe's archives labeled "Admissions, the Jewish Problem." It showed that, in the fall of 1937, five of the Seven Sisters exchanged information on the number of Jewish students admitted over the past several years. Bryn Mawr bluntly stated it had "no Jewish problem—of this year's freshman class, 6.0 percent are Jewish." Not coincidentally this was the lowest percentage given by the five reporting institutions for 1937–1938 (Radcliffe had the highest at 16.5 percent). More than a decade later, the president of Sarah Lawrence assailed both higher and elementary education for catering to the "white, gentile, and wealthy"—even though an alumna writing in the 1980s suggested that the school maintained its own quotas into the mid-1950s (a charge the school denied).[30]

The rise of Hitler and his anti-Semitic policies in Nazi Germany, as well as America's entry into World War II, helped students (if not administrators) on some campuses accept their Jewish classmates more fully. It was "only fair and democratic," suggested a 1942 editorial in the *Florida Flambeau*, that the Jewish and Catholic faiths be included in the school's upcoming "Religious Emphasis" week (just after a Christian Youth Conference was held on campus). The editorial even advocated inviting the occasional non-Protestant speaker. There was more: the editorialist noted how her Jewish classmates had to take cuts for classes missed during the high holidays of Rosh Hashanah and Yom Kippur, whereas Christians enjoyed holidays at Easter and Christmas. It was, she concluded, "another way the rights of a religious minority on our campus have been ignored."[31]

The Spread:
Making Friends in the Midnight Hour

Few things assuaged homesickness better than letters and packages from home, but most early colleges and prep schools requested that parents refrain from including foodstuffs in those packages. The Connecticut Literary Institution, a coed academy located in Suffield, laid down the law in its 1870–1871 catalog:

> Boxes of confectionary, cake, etc., sent to students, so far from being the kindness intended, are a positive source of evil. Their contents, eaten, as is generally the case, irregularly and late at night, produce sickness and impair scholarship, perhaps more than any other single cause. Unless parents and friends heed this remark, we shall be obliged to make the reception of such boxes and parcels by the pupils ground for animadversion.[32]

"Animadversion" was just the sort of word to put the fear of God into parents and students caught without a dictionary at the ready. In reality, it merely meant that an "adverse comment" might be made—in other words, receiving a forbidden box of cookies from home might go down on one's permanent record.

Between-meal and midnight snacking was problematic in light of contemporary wisdom regarding how the human body worked. Influenced in the 1840s by new developments in physics, specifically theories concerning the conservation of energy, the medical establishment viewed the human body (male or female) as a closed system with a limited amount of resources to devote to any particular function at a given time. "Brain-work and stomach-work," for example, interfered with one another and made an after-dinner nap a foolhardy venture. "The experiment of trying to digest a hearty supper, and to sleep during the process," reported a medical man, "has sometimes cost the careless experimenter his life."[33] These arguments were long lasting. A 1925 essay titled "How to Study" warned college girls against hitting the books after a hearty meal "since

Chafing Dish Dainties

The chafing dish was useful for whipping up all sorts of late-night delicacies, though a purloined Bunsen burner worked well in a pinch too. Omelets, custards, and Welsh rarebit—a creamy cheese sauce served on toast or crackers—were reliable standards in the college girl's repertoire. At eastern colleges, oysters and lobster Newberg were also popular. Cocoa was both inexpensive and easy to make, qualities that made it a prized recipe in dormitories the country over. (One didn't even need the chafing dish: a recipe from 1904 called for one heaping teaspoon of cocoa and one generous tablespoon of condensed milk to be mixed to a paste in a cup; boiling water was added and stirred "until the unseemly mess is transformed into a cupful of fragrant, creamy chocolate.")*

The undisputed favorite snack among college girls, however, was fudge. Whereas cooking a rarebit required little more culinary skill than the ability to melt cheese, making fudge in a chafing dish was an undertaking that required luck as well as kitchen finesse. It wasn't easy to gauge the exact moment to remove the candy from the heat—most college cooks were familiar with what *Mademoiselle*

* May Norton, "Chocolates and Secrets," *Ladies Home Journal*, November 1904, 30.

there cannot be a proper supply of blood in both places at the same time." The explanation was the same as in the previous century: either digestive organs or brain would suffer—though the modern consequences were held to be merely indigestion or poor schoolwork, not sudden death.[34]

A champion of "scientific" cooking with its emphasis on nutrition and sanitation, Sarah Tyson Rorer described the link between college break-

called "the dormitory horrors of fudge that turns to sugar or goo."†
Some factors were beyond the cook's control: atmospheric humidity
also played a role in the success or failure of a particular batch.

For intrepid individuals who would like to try to re-create the
taste of spreads gone by, fire up your chafing dish and try this old-
fashioned caramel-like recipe for fudge from *Midnight Feasts*:

> Put into the blazer two tablespoonfuls of butter, one cupful of dark
> brown sugar, half a cupful of milk, two cupfuls of New Orleans
> molasses and four squares of grated chocolate. Light the lamps and
> stir the mixture constantly, until it will form a rather hard ball
> when dropped in to ice water. [A candy thermometer will register
> 242–248° F.] Put out the light; add a teaspoonful of vanilla [be
> careful, it may splatter], pour into a buttered pan and check off in
> even squares while soft.‡

If you don't have a chafing dish at hand, a heavy saucepan will
work just fine.

† "Eat and Run," *Mademoiselle*, August 1940, 82.
‡ May E. Southworth, *Midnight Feasts: Two Hundred and Two Salads and Chafing Dish
Recipes* (San Francisco: Paul Elder & Co., 1914), 134.

downs and snack foods in an anti-pastry diatribe entitled "Why I Am
Opposed to Pies" (1900):

> Who does not look pityingly upon the boy or girl who, under brilliant aus-
> pices, enters college, and at the end of the first or second year is returned
> home a broken-down wreck with nervous prostration—not because of

overwork, but . . . over-feeding as far as bulk is concerned and under-feeding from true food standpoint? They have consumed all the blood necessary for good brain work in the digestion of their food.[35]

The biggest enemies of good brain work were just the sort of sweet, heavy treats that came in food boxes from home. The founder of Welles-ley, Henry Fowle Durant, promised that "pies, lies, and doughnuts" would never find a place at his school and forbade students from having any foodstuffs other than fresh fruit in their rooms.[36] The administration of Mills College concurred. Parents might send fruit to their daughters, but a table "abundantly supplied with good food renders [other] such additions unnecessary," its 1908 catalog firmly suggested.[37] (Of course, school food could prove unappetizing. The anonymous author of the waggish "Sonnet to a Turkey" that appeared in the 1904 *Vassarion* year-book penned its first line with the authority that came from sad experi-ence: "Oh! Bird of Strange and Undetermined Parts.")

On most campuses, however, the rules against food boxes were noted only in the breach. "Boxes from home are welcomed with joy," the *New York Times* observed in 1903. Indeed, the arrival of delicacies from home often signaled the opportunity for a girl to put on a "spread"—a picnic-like dorm room feast. The lucky recipient of a package from home invited friends to sample the goodies, and perhaps bring their own recently received treats. Certainly not all spreads took place under the cover of darkness, but breaking dormitory lights-out rules by meeting at midnight added an extra fillip of excitement and provided a way for well-bred col-lege women to flout authority.

"There are few social relaxations that are pleasanter than midnight suppers," wrote the author of *Midnight Feasts: Two Hundred and Two Sal-ads and Chafing Dish Recipes* (1914).[38] In addition to sharing cakes and cookies sent from home at these clandestine gatherings, girls did their fair share of in-room cooking at spreads. This was made possible by the use of a chafing dish—a forerunner of the fondue pot that consisted of an alcohol-fueled burner and two shallow pans, a configuration that allowed the dormitory chef to use the chafing dish as a double boiler by

Whether it held fudge or Welsh rarebit, the chafing dish stood at the center of the spread (circa 1904).

filling the bottom pan with water or to place a single pan directly over the heat of the flame. Popularized by Boston Cooking School doyenne Fannie Farmer in her *Chafing Dish Possibilities* (1898), the "blue flame and copper kettle" was shortly thereafter a popular "departing gift" to girls headed off to college.[39]

Spreads cemented peer culture at the turn of the century, and for decades thereafter they were a reliable source of fun and friendship. The late-night repast was "the very soul" of college girls' "good fellowship," an occasion on which they lavished not only "the very best of their friendship, but the very best of their wit and brains," according to cookbook author May Southworth. Spreads shared the fascinating allure of all forbidden pastimes and were tailor-made for young women "fond of fun, laughter and a good deal of nonsense," especially "those whose digestions are in good working order . . ."[40]

The *Ladies Home Journal* frequently described the fun and danger of midnight feasts. "I remember while at college receiving a box of home goodies, the chief dainty being a large molasses cake carefully packed in wax paper," began an anecdote from 1900. The invitation goes out for a get-together after lights-out. Just as the supper is set, there is a knock at the door. The pickles go under the bed, the girls into the closet. But what to do with the cake? It is safely hidden away under a pile of cushions on the couch when a professor in search of a toothache remedy enters the room. But the toothache drops are in the closet with the hidden girls! Comedy ensues when—you guessed it—the prof sits on the buried pastry. When she is hastened out the door, the giggling girls emerge from hiding and hold "an autopsy on the molasses cake. They find it to have forever lost its form and comeliness, but by no means its entire charm, as evinced by the few crumbs that were smuggled out with the pickle-bottle in the morning."[41]

Despite their basic rule-breaking nature, spreads could bring students and faculty closer together. At least that was the contention of the award-winning Christmas-related prank chosen by the *Ladies Home Journal* in 1906. A group of students sequestered over the holidays at a "small Eastern sectarian" college planned a dazzling spread for December 24. Boldly, a senior suggests they invite the remaining faculty, even though "spreads were forbidden and the halls were vigorously patrolled for the suppression of them." A little shyly, given the prohibition against midnight feasts, the dean and the faculty arrive at the designated dorm room. The "laughter was a little quavering and the jokes a little forced," but a good time is had by all until, just as the singing begins, "there was a sharp knock at the door and a sternly familiar voice called, 'Young ladies, lights are out.'" It is the maid, who is usually accompanied by the junior professor—who at this precise moment is enjoying a moment of role reversal:

> From sheer force of habit, with smothered exclamations, the girls dashed for their accustomed cover. Into the closet, under the bed, they disappeared like rats into their holes, and the Senior with one practiced hand upon the gas-jet was about to reduce all to darkness when she realized

that the dreaded Junior professor was rocking to and fro on her sofa-pillow in helpless laughter, an olive held aloft impaled upon a hatpin.

Even the Dean was laughing . . .[42]

An even happier ending comes the following day, when girls and teachers enjoy "a real Christmas of plum pudding and friendly gifts."

With the great influx of students in the 1920s, the authority-flouting nature of spreads was diluted when they became less spontaneous and more codified. *Etiquette at College* (1925) explained the ins and outs of spreads in a manner previously unthinkable:

> Girls usually wear their best lounging robes to a spread of any importance. Lingerie and night-clothes without a heavier covering are not only rather unpleasant apparel for a gathering, but are too apt to catch fire from candles or the flame of a chafing-dish, if it burns alcohol.
>
> It is high treason to interfere with cooking candy or a dish that the hostess is preparing from her own recipe, unless one is asked to stir it or pour it out.
>
> One may make remarks on the implements used in cooking and eating, but it is not good form to show aversion when one maiden eats tomato soup out of a powder dish and while another marks the fudge into luscious squares with a nail-file.[43]

Who (other than presumably middle-aged advice writers) complained about divvying up a pan of fudge with a nail file, when such freewheeling spontaneity was exactly what traditionally made spreads so appealing— especially to generations of college girls beset by regulations and restrictions on almost their every movement?

Historian Margaret Lowe suggests that during the 1910s–1930s the spread—a girls-only event with homemade food that took place within dormitory walls—began to be replaced by "largely mixed-sex off-campus gatherings," i.e., group dating with a focus on commercially prepared victuals. At Smith, "batting" became the rage: students and their boyfriends picnicked together in the countryside. (According to Lowe, at Smith in the 1910s "batting" was popular slang for an outdoor picnic. It stemmed from an early definition of "bat": "to go or move; to wander, to potter.")[44]

The spread didn't up and die out, of course. "Remember all the *mid nite* feasts? (Mum's the word, eh?)" read a sassy inscription in a 1928 copy of the Westmoorland College *Wand* yearbook. But the heyday of the spread was clearly over. Snacking was still "considered one of the major activities at all accredited seats of learning," *Mademoiselle* observed in 1940, but the new processed foods it introduced to readers in its "Eat and Run" column took the tradition out of an old favorite: "Human nature being what it is, a freshman is a lot more likely to succeed if she comes to college knowing about such things as a 4-minute Prepared Fudge Mix, and how to grill a divine cheeseburger."[45]

Fudge from a box? What about ye olde chafing dish? You certainly couldn't grill a cheeseburger in one of those. But this was just one sign of the spread's slide into decrepitude. The 1947 edition of Stephens College's *Within the Ivy* student handbook called the spread "one of the joys of college life," then proved without a doubt that its authority-flouting nature was deader than a doorknob: "Special permissions for spreads are obtained from the hall counselor."[46] Special permission? Had those larking turn-of-the-century College Girls asked for permission before breaking out the chafing dish and fudge pan? Not on your life!

Sororities and Clubs

There were other, officially organized ways for girls to make friends on campus. When coeds first arrived on the scene at the state universities, there were no women's dormitories. Girls turned to boardinghouses and private families who rented rooms to students, although this too could be a tricky proposition. At first, coeds looking for rooms were viewed with suspicion. In *An American Girl and Her Four Years in a Boy's College*, Will is turned away from several boardinghouses by proprietors who "could not think of taking a lady-student, it's so odd." (The coeds have the last laugh; a year later, Will notes that some of the same houses are advertising for girls, having heard that they don't smoke, drink, or "spit tobacco-juice on the furniture" as did male boarders.)[47]

Boardinghouse proprietors weren't the only ones to look down their noses at the coeds. Male students viewed them with what president of Smith College from 1875 to 1910, L. Clark Seelye, aptly referred to in 1907 as "suspicious jealousy."[48] Depending on the college, official attitudes were little better: some faculty members and administrators did their best to ignore the coeds altogether and provided few extracurricular activities for them. It's not surprising that these young women looked at the men's fraternities, comfortably ensconced in their well-appointed chapter houses, and decided to organize their own Greek-letter societies. Sororities thus provided badly needed housing as well as a place for outnumbered and often unwelcome coeds to band together for friendship and support.

There are two contenders for the title of first women's Greek-letter fraternity (the word "sorority" didn't exist until 1882 when a Latin professor at Syracuse University suggested it to the women who founded Gamma Phi Beta as a parallel for "fraternity"; Smith's antisorority President Seelye, a stickler for correct Latin, found the fabricated word "barbarous").[49] The first claimant, Kappa Alpha Theta, was founded in 1870 at Asbury College (now DePauw University) in Greencastle, Indiana. The other candidate is Alpha Delta Pi, which grew out of the literary Adelphian Society, which was founded in 1851 at what was then still Wesleyan Female College in Macon, Georgia. It became Alpha Delta Pi in 1905 (after it was discovered that the original choice of names, Alpha Delta Phi, already belonged to a men's fraternity).[50] The controversy arises over Alpha Delta Pi's prior incarnation as the Adelphian Society. Alpha Delta Pi partisans count the sorority's birthday as May 15, 1851, the Adelphian Society's first meeting date. Kappa Alpha Theta fans suggest that Alpha Delta Pi remained a mere literary society until the name change in 1905, making theirs the first sorority by

In April 1959, twenty-seven members of Alpha Delta Pi and Delta Zeta did their best to set a new record for the number of women packed in a car.

thirty-five years. Which is the first women's Greek-letter fraternity? Never having belonged to a sorority myself, and not wanting to plunge myself into the roiling waters of controversy, I leave the decision to you, dear reader.

Not that there hasn't always been plenty of controversy to go around. Long-standing and heated debate has always surrounded the nature and influence of the Greek-letter societies. Sororities were not democratic, detractors claimed; they admitted girls based on social position and wealth, excluded others because of racial and religious prejudices, while the rushing procedure itself made for hurt feelings. Supporters pointed to lifelong friendships made, the way sisters banded together to boost underachieving members' academic performances, and the community service performed by various houses. These pro- and antisorority arguments remained surprisingly unchanged over the decades. Smith's L.

Clark Seelye claimed that the clannish nature of sororities prevented members from taking full part in college life, given that their first allegiance was to sorority, not school. He also despised what he saw as their manipulation of student elections:

> In their "rushes" to secure the most desirable candidates, in their combinations to monopolize college honors, to put in office those whose eligibility is determined not by personal fitness but by society membership, the societies give rise to the most disturbing and belittling factions of college life.[51]

Friendships were "more readily and naturally" made in the congenial atmosphere of the college community at large, Seelye argued, whereas the sorority cast "a coarse and vulgar influence" over members that was all the "more pernicious" because of the "confined atmosphere in which it is exerted." Seelye claimed there were no Greek-letter fraternities at Smith, but a group of students living off campus at the turn of the century rented their own "Invitation House," hired a matron, and chose the next year's occupants through a formal vote. Historian Helen Lefkowitz Horowitz points out that White Lodge and Delta Sigma weren't called sororities, but they "linked residence and social selection" in a manner similar to that of the Greek-letter organizations.[52]

The controversy continued into the twentieth century, and the rhetoric was almost always at a fever pitch. "What a pity if the girl with the cleverest and richest mind in the Freshman class, in her anxiety to bow to a man with a Greek pin, misses knowing a man with a Greek mind!" lamented the women's dean at the University of Wisconsin in a 1925 guidebook.[53] Did acceptance or rejection from a sorority truly influence a college girl's "happiness all through college" as *Life* magazine alleged in 1945? Most girls who didn't make the cut went on to full and happy lives, once past the initial sting of rejection. For some girls, however, the rejection was more than they could bear. Antisorority forces pointed to the 1942 suicide of an eighteen-year-old girl from White Plains, New York, who shot herself when her younger sisters were blackballed from her high-school sorority. Her grieving parents understandably went on a crusade against Greek-letter societies at the high school level. Ironically, they were already banned at the young woman's school and forbidden to advertise in the student newspaper or march on the football field, but continued to function off school grounds.[54]

It was the rushing procedure by which Greek-letter societies chose their members that caused the most hurt feelings and thereby came in for the most criticism. Although they shared a name, this isn't to be confused with the mid- to late-nineteenth-century hazing practice at men's schools, wherein groups of freshmen and sophomores fought with fists and canes, trying to push each other off paths and stairways. "Rushing" prospective fraternity members was a more benign practice. Rush week took place (and continues to do so) during the first weeks of the fall semester. Girls who wanted to join sororities visited the various houses for a series of parties during which current and potential members sized one another up. The sororities then held house meetings and decided which girls they wanted to pledge. Negative votes blackballed girls based on appearance, religion, wealth, and any number of intangibles. At the end of the week (which may have been longer than seven days depending on the campus), the sororities extended bids to the chosen few. Meanwhile, the would-be sorority girls submitted the names of the sororities they would most like to join to the school's Panhellenic council, which kept a tight rein over the whole proceeding. Ideally, every rushee received a bid from the house of her choice—but logistics made this impossible. In 1945, *Life* magazine reported that most of the 802 female freshmen at the University of Colorado that year wanted to join sororities, but only 259 made the grade.[55]

During the mid-twentieth century, the pros and cons of sorority membership were topics of perennial interest in the pages of *Seventeen*. While the magazine's editorial stance was generally antisorority, for the most part it attempted to present a balanced portrait in its articles. No matter how fair an article seemed, however, the letters column in the following issue exploded with correspondents describing their own experiences, good and bad. "I have just finished reading 'Why Sororities Survive' and my reaction was one of complete disappointment. I have been black-balled from three sororities because I am Jewish," wrote R. B. of New York, New York, in response to a 1953 article. Another reader suggested that if the author really believed "that any girl can belong to a sorority who wants to, she is either terrifically naïve or utterly blind. One girl in my dorm (a freshman) quit school because none of the four sororities on our campus would accept her."[56]

The letters following a 1950 story called "Initiation Fee" were mostly from the prosorority faction. "[W]e do not pity those who do not belong to Greek organizations," wrote a self-described sorority girl from Oregon. "We realize that not everyone can afford to join or even wants to. Independents have just as much chance in activities, and no one cares if you have a pin or not!" "Why label *all* sororities snobbish?" asked another reader. "I joined one to be with the girls I really like and to have contact with them after I leave school. We definitely don't give a hoot about how much money our members have or what boys they date." This time, the magazine made its stance clear in a reply to the letter writer. "If your group has a real purpose, good luck to you! Many sororities, we feel, are guilty of undemocratic practices in a world where democracy is facing its most serious challenge."[57] Coming as it did in the cold war year of 1951, *Seventeen's* criticism seemed to suggest that sorority membership might well have been another front for the "red menace" of communism.

Over the years, "undemocractic" was perhaps the most frequent charge lobbed against Greek-letter organizations. The decidedly pro-Greek *CO-EDiquette* (1936) described how the charge came to be:

Of course, the fraternity system did not escape attack by radical members of the student body. Sometimes, they were sincere thinkers; sometimes they were hurt rushees who had not received bids. They gathered in the back room of the college joint and drank beer and discussed Life

earnestly. They agreed that marriage was a moth-eaten institution and
football the curse of the American college. They believed in Socialism
and the style of Ernest Hemingway. And they railed against the fraternity
system because it was undemocratic. It glorified money above brains. It
preferred a man whose father was born on the right side of the tracks and
who dressed well and danced correctly, to one who hashed [i.e., waited
tables at the dining hall] his way to Phi Beta Kappa.[58]

In other words, the people who dared castigate the Greeks were the
passed over dregs who were antifrat, antimarriage, antifootball socialists.

Frankly, many of the accusations of undemocratic behavior and bias
were based in fact. In 1951, a coed at the University of Oregon was told
to move out of the Gamma Phi Beta house when she refused to stop dating a black student. She also reported that a cross had been burned on
the sorority's lawn.[59] This isn't to say that all sororities on all campuses
shared such reprehensible attitudes. Occasionally, an individual sorority
chapter had a more liberal attitude about race than the national organization to which it ultimately had to answer. In 1956, the local Sigma Kappa
chapter at Cornell University offered membership to a black woman,
Barbara Collier Delany. "The girls in the sorority were very nice to me,"
remembered Delany, "but the officials at the national headquarters were
furious" and told the students to reject the new pledge or they would
shut down the Cornell chapter. When the white students refused to kick
out Delany, the national organization made good on their threat and shut
down the sorority. The same thing happened to the Sigma Kappa chapter
at Tufts University, which had two black pledges that same spring of
1956. Along with Delany, these were the first black women to be pledged
to a white national college sorority.[60]

Intergenerational differences of opinion between national and local
chapters in matters small and large were an ongoing fact of sorority life.
In the wake of the Civil Rights movement, schools required Greek-letter
organizations to sign statements revoking discrimination clauses in their
charters or constitutions. These were usually signed by the local chapter.
In 1966, the University of Wisconsin required additional signatures from

the national president. All of Kappa Delta's local chapter signed, but when the national president refused to do so, the university threatened to suspend the local chapter.[61] The same year *Seventeen* counseled prospective rushes to "Examine your own prejudices . . . Do you avoid people who come from social, economic, intellectual, cultural, religious or racial backgrounds different from your own?" The magazine reported on an attempt by Pat Popkin of Alpha Omicron Pi to start a "Greeks Against Discrimination" movement at Northwestern University. "We tried to get people excited about how free they were to pledge anyone they wanted," she explained. "We tried to compose a list of alumnae, not only ours but also from other sororities, who were willing to write recommendations (required by all sororities) for girls regardless of race or creed. We got a good response from the alums and gave the list to various sororities. No action." Pat graduated that fall, but Northwestern's chapter of Alpha Omicron Pi pledged its first black member the following year, as did another sorority on campus.[62]

∞

For those who weren't inclined to Greek life, there were plenty of social clubs and honorary societies. "No girl should refrain from this club life," said the authors of *She's Off to College* (1940). Joining clubs helped a girl adjust socially to both campus and cohort, and gave her a chance to "learn the art of co-operation, the art of admiration, corporate enjoyment, and group success."[63] Club participation could also lead to success in a more personal realm. The college men who penned *Lady Lore* (1939), an advice book for young women, told readers that clubs were a great way for college girls to meet men—directly if you were on a coed campus, or via the conduit of friends for those sequestered at the women's colleges. In the scheme of things presented by *Lady Lore*, dating and extracurricular activities competed for the brunt of the coed's time, while study limped in a distant third. "After all," they wrote, ". . . your most important outside activity is dating." It was even better if a girl held office: "Men like to date presidents and chairmen, of course.

And on the morning after it make[s] the old chest swell to say in reply to who 'she' was, 'Why, she is the president of so and so.' And it advertises you in the right way."[64]

Leaders couldn't get too tied up in their responsibilities—*Lady Lore* warned against letting club or committee take too much time away from one's dating life.

In addition to school-sanctioned clubs and honorary societies, each campus had a plethora of organizations devoted to a wide range of interests. Some, like the National College Equal Suffrage League (founded in 1908) and the national honor sorority Mortar Board (founded in 1918), were serious in intent. Other, mostly local, alliances were decidedly less so. A proposed "man-haters' club" never got off the ground at the University of Chicago in 1924 ("I never heard of such asininity as the organization of a man-haters' club. The idea is terrible," said the prom queen when asked about it). Hood College's *Blue and Grey* newspaper reported in 1927 that William and Mary had a new club open only to girls who had been engaged and jilted—the Muffet Club.[65] In addition to a chapter of Mortar Board, the Florida State College for Women had its very own "dishonor" group, "Mortified":

> Mortified is a very ancient organization which was founded at Florida State college for women in 1936 by campus leaders who were not tapped for Mortar Board because of their grades. It stresses leadership, service, and active personalities (so active that they cannot make a 1.7 average). Their yell is "Leadership, service and scholarship"—scholarship being a long drawn-out groan.[66]

With "frequent meetings which none of the members attend" and club colors of "blush pink and envy green," Mortified followed the tongue-in-cheek tradition in some men's colleges of honoring the students with the lowest grades. In a tradition that still holds at West Point, for example, the student who finishes last in the class is termed the "goat" and collects a dollar from each of his or her classmates at graduation.

Crushes, or Making the Appropriate Adjustments

The friendships made at school, be it in class, at a spread, or in a club or sorority, were in many cases deep, true, and long lasting. But one particular kind of friendship long ago entered the annals of women's college lore: the crush. Crushes were "an epidemic peculiar to college girls," according to Barnard's 1907 yearbook, "caused by a Junior or Senior microbe and . . . characterized by a lump in the throat, a feeling of heat in the face and an inability to speak." Four years later, the freshman show included a "Crush Chorus" that further described the symptoms:

> When your heart goes pitter-patter
> Just to meet her on the stairs,
> When she smiles upon you kindly
> Tho to speak you do not dare
> When you jealously, when you jealously
> Look upon a rival claim
> That's a crush, that's a crush,
> Yes, that's a crush.[67]

The Class of 1911 may have been just discovering hitherto unexpected twists and turns of female friendship, but crushes were nothing new. In 1873, a letter to the Yale student newspaper detailed the "regular course" of bouquets, notes, "mysterious packages of 'Ridley's Mixed Candies,' locks of hair perhaps, and many other tender tokens" that might be sent by one besotted Vassar student to another until her affections were noticed and hopefully reciprocated. The aggressor was then officially considered "smashed."[68]

Paging through turn-of-the-century yearbooks for women's colleges, it seems every school had at least one campus flirt. The Maryland College for Women's *Oriole* yearbook listed the following "Census Return" for a

particularly butch member of the class of 1898, whose crush on a classmate was subjected to gentle ridicule:

> KNOWN AS. Mikey. . . .
> MARRIAGE PROSPECTS. Doomed.
> REASONS FOR COMING TO COLLEGE. To wait on Nannie.
> CHIEF OCCUPATION. General smasher.

In all likelihood, "Mikey" probably went on to marry a nice boy and
raise a flock of children, perhaps a girl named "Nannie" among them. In
general, whether local slang termed it a smash, a crush, or a "spoon,"
such relationships were considered a common form of adolescent behavior that would eventually be abandoned once a young woman matured,
i.e., discovered boys. As theorized by one 1880s commentator, crushes
sprang from the "massing of hundreds of nervous young girls together" on
remote college campuses. These girls were "just at the romantic age"
with no other outlet for their sentimentality, hence they turned to one
another.[69] While this may have explained the practice in the remote hin-
terlands of Poughkeepsie at Vassar, as historian Rona M. Wilk points out,
it doesn't account for the flourishing of female relationships on urban
campuses like Barnard, located just a short trip across the street from the
all-male Columbia University in New York City. Despite the convenient
pool of eligible men nearby, Wilk nevertheless unearthed a wealth of
crush-related material from Barnard's archives. Helen Lefkowitz Horowitz suggests that the "dominance and subordination" at "the heart of the
collegiate experience," played out in such traditions as pairing off "sister"
classes and the ritualized respect with which freshmen were supposed to
treat upperclassmen, helped lead to the crush.[70] "Some gals get an exaggerated sense of importance from being familiar with the Big Names on
Campus. There is no surer way of getting a Little Name for yourself,"
warned a 1949 guidebook for freshmen.[71]

Peer pressure probably kept many crushes from going further than
what was deemed socially acceptable. In 1900, the *Ladies Home Journal*
provided a glimpse of how one community of girls reacted to such a rela-

tionship in their midst. "Now it happened that a girl in A—— building had a most overgrown 'crush' on a girl in B—— building. It happened, too, that these two hearts, which beat as one over Latin verbs and conic sections, one day yearned to be together at an early service at the church near by."[72]

The crushees, surely thinking only of convenience the next morning, decide to spend the night together. Their classmates decide to pull a prank. Six alarm clocks, set to go off every hour beginning at 1:00 A.M., are hidden in the room the girls are to occupy, ensuring a wakeful night. The sleepy girls make an appearance at church the next morning, but "in no very Christian spirit." To add insult to injury, they later receive a bill for the clocks. Their relationship is unbroken, but their classmates have effectively registered their feelings on the matter. The gist of the story, it should be pointed out, is not that crushes are bad, but that nobody likes public displays of affection.

The ubiquity of campus crushes, and the tolerance with which they were accepted by both campus authorities and such a bulwark of middle-class morals as the *Ladies Home Journal*, may have been due in part to the long-accepted ideal of romantic friendships among women. In a seminal essay, historian Carroll Smith-Rosenberg described the "female world of love and ritual" that resulted from the mid-nineteenth-century's strict division of male and female spheres and "severe social restrictions on intimacy" between young people of the opposite sex.[73] Women filled in the empty emotional spaces in each others' lives, even after marriage and motherhood. Thus, when young M. Carey Thomas wrote home from boarding school about a girl she was "smashed" on, her mother reacted not with fear or disgust but nostalgia: "I guess thy feeling for Libbie is quite natural. I used to have the same romantic love for my friends. It is a *real* pleasure."[74]

As author Lillian Faderman points out, college girls often had close at hand the example of female couples living in so-called "Boston marriages" (because so many were said to occur there). Faculty members were often required to live on campus, and many female professors did so in pairs.[75] The relationship between the women who founded Spelman reflects the sort of genteel, loving life partnership that caused nary a raised eyebrow in the nineteenth century. In the mid-1850s, Sophia B. Packard was a thirty-year-old "preceptress" and teacher at the New Salem Academy in Salem, Massachusetts. There she met Harriet E. Giles, a senior student and "assistant pupil . . . who was destined to share with Sophia those dreams and visions of their later life."[76] The *History of Oread Collegiate Institute*, a Worcester, Massachusetts, protocollege for women (headquartered in a replica of a medieval castle) where Packard served as head beginning in 1864, described the women's close relationship:

> Miss Packard was ably assisted in her duties of instruction and discipline by Harriet E. Giles, her devoted friend, with whom she had been constantly associated in all that she had done for ten years . . . It would have been impossible for a school girl of those days to speak or think of one without the other. They dressed alike and in leisure hours were nearly always together.[77]

They lived together, worked together, and when they died (Packard in 1891, Giles in 1909), they were buried side by side. Packard's diary referenced "my darling Hattie" and Giles's "my dear Sophia"—but it's impossible to know what more, if anything, there was to their relationship other than a long-standing, deep-seated affection.[78] Also at the turn of the twentieth century, Bryn Mawr's redoubtable M. Carey Thomas lived on campus with her "devoted companion," Mamie Gwynn, at least until 1904, when Mamie "mysteriously altered her powerful animosity towards males" and absconded with a married philosophy professor.[79] Mamie's place was soon filled by millionaire philanthropist Mary Garrett, who along with Mamie had long been part of a triangular relationship with Thomas (an affair that the young Gertrude Stein made the focal point of "Fernhurst," a story that remained unpublished until 1971).

Despite the acceptance of crushes on college campuses, advice writers in the nineteenth and early twentieth centuries recognized them as potentially unwholesome. In *What a Young Woman Ought to Know* (1898), author Mrs. Mary Wood-Allen, M.D. provided a less-than-complimentary description of gushing friendships between adolescent girls: "They go about with their arms around each other, they loll against each other, and sit with clasped hands by the hour. They fondle and kiss until beholders are fairly nauseated." At best, Wood-Allen wrote, such relationships were mawkish. At worst, girls who acted "like silly lovers" in each other's company and wept in "uncontrollable agony" when separated, might be in the throes of "a sort of perversion, a sex mania, needing immediate and perhaps severe measures," the grimmest of which was female circumcision.[80]

What Wood-Allen hinted at, however, had yet to be identified. The stigma of lesbianism only arose after "certain feelings and preferences that had before been within the spectrum of 'normal' female experiences" were recast by Freud and the early sexologists as outside the pale of acceptable feminine behavior. Havelock Ellis described the women's colleges as "the great breeding ground" of same-sex relationships as early as 1902, but it wasn't until after World War I that "lesbian," the word and the concept, filtered down to most Americans.[81] In her history of lesbian life in twentieth-century America, Lillian Faderman describes how this affected the college crush, using as an example a 1928 novel about Vassar, *We Sing Diana*. On the campus of 1913, crushes were so common as to be considered "the Freshman disease," but when the protagonist returns seven years later as a teacher, all has changed. "Intimacy between two girls was watched with keen distrustful eyes. Among one's classmates, one looked for the bisexual type, the masculine girl searching for a feminine counterpart, and one ridiculed their devotions."[82]

The essential innocence surrounding the crush was gone, although as Faderman points out, "the luxury of naiveté regarding lesbianism" sheltered many middle-class college girls well into the 1920s.[83] The Oberlin Lesbian Society of poetry-loving girls flourished in the early 1920s, as did a similar organization founded at Hood in 1893. Members of Hood's society sought "to imitate intellectually the sweet Lesbian singer, Sappho, who was the wisest and most highly cultured woman of her age."[84] And in 1928, a lovesick student at Westmoorland College in San Antonio, Texas, memorialized her feelings in the *Wand* yearbook. "Roommate, darling, how I love you. Oh what a lump it makes in my throat at the thought of telling you good-bye," begins a long message written on the book's very first page. Was it a romantic friendship of a sort harkening back to the previous century? "Roomie, I just can't write all I feel about you cause I love you *so much*. . . . you know I think you are the sweetest, cutest, darlingest, most adorable roommate a girl could have!" Was this mere mawkishness or something more erotic? "But, *I love you* and *how*!!!" was the passionate ending of another missive on another page, the word "you" triple underlined for emphasis. At the remove of decades, it's impossible to know anything other than at least one girl on the campus of the all-women's school had some very deep feelings for her roommate.

Authorities began to recognize a difference between the crush, in which two girls reveled "in emotion for emotion's sake" and the "failure to develop the heterosexual interests which are natural" in adolescent girls. The female author of *Counseling the College Student* (1929) suggested that deans of women and other counselors keep an eye out for the "exaggerated athletic bent" and "over-boisterousness which really belongs in the tomboy age" as potential markers of the latter.[85] A 1940 guidebook described a fictional athletics chairman, Margaret Clinton, who filled this bill: she was "quite a different type, with broad shoulders, a good tan, and a very short bob."[86] Students bolstered the dangerous tomboy stereotype as well. The 1928 Westmoorland *Wand* yearbook included a cartoon poking fun at students and their hairstyles. One crude drawing of a girl in a masculine collar and boyish haircut was labeled with both her name and the legend "The Campus Flirt." Her class photo showed a young woman whose personal style distinctly contrasted with that of the stylishly feminine flappers who surrounded her, and was accompanied by the insinuating words, "May she obtain great recognition in the athletic world."[87]

The Importance of Popularity

After the turn of the twentieth century, students of both sexes flocked to campuses across the United States in unprecedented numbers. College attendance jumped threefold in the years between 1900 and 1930, with the 1920s seeing the most rapid rise. Enrollments doubled at the University of Illinois, from three thousand in 1919 to six thousand in 1922; the same thing happened at Ohio state, where the numbers went from four thousand to eight thousand in the same period.[88] For many new students, college was less an academic experience than a social one. These "college tourists," as one 1920s guidebook referred to them, were not an entirely new phenomenon. They had been recognized as far back as the 1890s, when one essayist referred to the social student as one who in another era might more "naturally find her proper place in the fashionable finishing school," but was now desirous of a college education alongside her more scholarly sisters.[89] Whereas the first generations of college girls stood out from their friends by their unusual choice to pursue higher education, by the 1920s college was an increasingly acceptable path for a young woman to take after high school. This was due in part to the numerous articles in women's magazines and elsewhere that portrayed college as a wholesome experience, as well as firsthand knowledge from female friends and relatives who benefited from higher education with no ill effects.

Once on campus, the search for popularity became as important as schoolwork—at least according to prescriptive literature and magazine articles. As defined in a sociological study in the late 1930s, male popularity required the trappings of the Big Man on Campus (BMOC) lifestyle: fraternity membership, a car, the right clothing, and the money to buy it all. For women, popularity was defined by their reputation for being popular. In the words of historian Beth Bailey, "They had to *be seen* with popular men in the 'right' places, indignantly turn down requests for dates made at the 'last minute' (which could be weeks in advance), and cultivate the impression they were greatly in demand."[90] In relation to the opposite sex, this meant "dating and rating," a phenomenon that started on college campuses in the 1920s but eventually spread beyond its environs, and remained the dominant form of dating until it was replaced after World War II by "going steady."

Simply put, according to the strictures of dating and rating, female popularity was measured by the number of dates a girl had, ideally with as many different, high-status men as she could. It's useful to remember that despite the prevalence of petting, these casual dates were largely nonsexual in nature—the point was to be seen with as many different men as possible, not to sleep with as many different men as possible. At the University of Michigan in 1936, a group of coeds assembled a list rating the BMOCs (they had to have dated several women or they didn't make the list): "A—smooth; B—OK; C—pass in a crowd; D—semigoon; or E—spook." Copies of the list were left around campus, and the Michigan *Daily* reported that women used them "quite extensively" before blind dates. As Beth Bailey points out, under the dating and rating system it was better to date an E-rated boy than sit home on Saturday night. The list helped women conform to their peers' notions of popularity (and gave the women a modicum of power, however baseless, over the highest-status men).[91]

Popularity extended beyond the bounds of boy-girl relationships and continued to be important long after dating and rating ceased to be important as a dating style. Because the competition was so intense, if a freshman wanted to be popular, she had to begin the campaign the moment she set foot on campus. The aloof, standoffish girl who withdrew from dormitory get-togethers or campuswide dances endangered "the wholeness of her college opportunity," according to the authors of *She's Off to College* (1940). Forgetting for a moment that college's purpose was supposed to be academic, they suggested that a girl who ignored social opportunities "might just as well never have come to college at all."[92]

Instead, *She's Off to College* promoted enthusiastic social participation on coed campuses as an expressway to popularity with the opposite sex. All one had to do was "Go to all the house meetings that are posted, eat all your dinners with your group in the dining room, go to all the faculty teas, and there will be no trouble about the dances."[93] Of course, this assumed that the boys were equally interested in house meetings and faculty teas.

While the blot of a less than stellar high-school social career could be expunged by virtue of the anonymity provided by the crowds at a big university, a freshman still needed to exercise extreme caution when it came to how others viewed her. A girl "might be a Personality Kid from way back, and/or . . . have a heart of gold," but all fellow students would know "is what they see," warned one of *Mademoiselle*'s college-issue guest editors in 1945.[94] The campus was a tabula rasa—a blank slate on which a teenage girl might write herself a whole new persona. Traditionally, this is just what parents have worried about when they sent their darling daughters off to college.

Acting the Part: Guidebooks and Etiquette Manuals

There were other ways for girls to learn the ins and outs of campus life besides the August issues of *Mademoiselle* and *Glamour* or college novels and stories in *Seventeen*. By at least the early 1900s, etiquette books had begun adding chapters on how to behave at college. *The Correct Thing in Good Society* (1902) included dos and don'ts for students at both women's and coeducational colleges. Its author, Florence Howe Hall, was the daughter of Julia Ward Howe, a passionate supporter of women's education (though best known today for her stirring Civil War anthem "The Battle Hymn of the Republic"). Hall shared her mother's views, and planted a defense of college education for women among the lists of "Correct" and "Not Correct" things to do.

> It is the Correct Thing . . . For critics to remember that women's colleges are new, while behind the older universities stands the culture of centuries.

> It is not the Correct Thing . . . For critics to expect at once in women's colleges, the ripeness and perfection of long-established universities.[95]

But Hall's political moment passed just like that, and much of the rest of her advice to college girls concerned the social niceties: when to enclose visiting cards with invitations, the need for chaperons, and the importance of remaining ladylike on both coed and women's college campuses.

By the 1920s, with so many more young people pursuing higher education, etiquette books specifically for college students began to appear. A book like *Etiquette at College* (1925; also called *The Campus Blue Book*) explained the ins and outs of social behavior to young men and women still in the uncertain blush of adolescence, and away from parents who might otherwise guide them. "Half of the situations in which a student is placed are perplexing because they develop suddenly and without warning at a time when he is intent upon learning new people, and new customs. To put him on his guard, and help him know the formalities and informalities of college life as it is likely to present itself" was the stated intent of *Etiquette at College*, and pretty much every other college guidebook as well.[96]

All etiquette books mirrored the social concerns of their times. Written in 1925, the essays that comprised *The Freshman Girl* reflected a defiant last gasp of True Womanhood with its ideals of purity, piety, domesticity, and submissiveness in the face of recently obtained woman suffrage and the arrival on campus of the cigarette-smoking, sexually curious flapper. An essay on good health that took the format of a "Letter from a Medical Man to His Niece" warned of modern dangers: "Jazz, alcohol, and sexual immorality are sapping the strength of the race; we are nearing the precipice over which all previous civilizations have plunged . . ."[97] Higher education was all very well and good, he suggested, but college girls had a duty to produce healthy future generations. Le Baron Russell Briggs, the recently retired president of Radcliffe College, lauded sensitivity, empathy, "instantaneous and practical sympathy with grief, reckless devotion beside the sick bed" as the qualities which made up "the essence of woman's power." In a direct invocation of True Womanhood, Briggs reminded his audience that what was highest in women was "what is highest in all human creatures—the power of transfiguring this daily drudging life of ours" into something soulful and

The Correct Thing to Do ... in 1902

The 1902 edition of *The Correct Thing in Good Society* included the following dos and don'ts for college girls.

IT IS THE CORRECT THING...	IT IS NOT THE CORRECT THING...
To behave so as to refute the statement that women deteriorate in manners at college, while men improve.	To ape the manners or behavior of men, since a woman can make but a poor copy of a man, and that copy not a pleasing one.
To moderate so far as possible the conceit sometimes attendant upon the acquisition of information, especially during the sophomore year.	To look down upon your parents, because they know less Latin and Greek than you, or are ignorant of modern science . . .
To be ever womanly, however merry and full of spirits.	To let the athletic girl degenerate into the tomboy.
To be moderate in your demands for remittances from home.	To write home only when you need money.

shining for all those who came into contact with her.[98] Yet this high-mindedness would seem increasingly out of step with the priorities of modern college girls.

In fact, by the following decade, the "tourists" who, according to one of the essays in *The Freshman Girl*, "marred" college had inherited the

"This book begins where classes end."
CO-EDiquette, 1936.

campus. Elizabeth Eldridge's *CO-EDiquette* (1936) made no pretense to being anything other than it was: a guide for the ambitious would-be campus queen. Too many other books explained how to study and the best way to budget's one time. *CO-EDiquette* filled an empty spot on the college girl's bookshelf. Eldridge didn't care if a girl entered college "to study, to date or just to pass the time," but she was highly concerned about "the world of the sorority house and the dormitory, the formal and the prom, the Union, the evening date, and the big game." In short, she wrote almost exclusively for the much-belittled social student:

> No book of etiquette has yet been written that explained adequately how a girl should conduct herself at a football game or that told her what to do at a rush tea. No Lovelorn column describes a bull session or tells a co-ed whether she should accept a man's fraternity pin. Yet a girl who wants to go through college and be successful must have this information.[99]

Like some other etiquette books written in the depths of the Depression, *CO-EDiquette* described a fantasy world of privilege and popularity that may well have been out of reach of most of its readers. Most guidebooks had a more pragmatic bent and, assuming their readers had both academic and social lives, divided their advice accordingly, explaining the best methods of study on one page and what to wear on a date on another.

Still, learning the "elemental rules of social intercourse" (as the Massachusetts State College freshman handbook put it in the mid-1930s) stood students in good stead on campus and in later life.[100] Emphasis on ladylike good manners at the early women's colleges helped counter arguments that higher education masculinized young women. One semester at Wellesley was all it took to turn a pig's ear into a silk purse in a possibly apocryphal story from *The College Girl of America* (1905). Florence Gray had a good mind but bad manners. At the dinner table, she was "horribly noisy, voraciously hungry,—a thing all waist and elbows and giggles":

> But that was before she went to college. When she came home for her first Christmas vacation, she was so changed that I scarcely could believe my eyes! Her voice was quiet, her manners deferential, her elbows at her sides instead of on the table, and she had learned that a lady does not display, even if she possesses, the appetite of a tramp.[101]

Florence's home "lacked refinement," but at college she came into daily contact with better-mannered fellow students and was thus rescued from her "heritage of vulgarity."[102]

As part of her larger, fascinating study of the college girl and body image at the turn of the twentieth century, historian Margaret A. Lowe described how the complex dinner etiquette employed at the all-black Spelman College in Atlanta, Georgia, helped rescue its students from a heritage of racism. Consisting of eleven sections with three to four rules in each, Spelman's turn-of-the-century "Rules for Table Etiquette" involved a virtual ballet of standing, sitting, and positioning one's chair in relation to the table. For young African-American women, table manners and restrained eating signaled to the culture at large that they had "mastered their physical desires and thus deserved social respect."[103] "When a girl comes to Spelman and returns home," wrote a student, "everybody can see great improvement in her manners, housekeeping, and in fact in every respect. . . . One special thing Miss Giles [the school's head administrator] requires of her girls is quietness, which always showed the mark of a lady."[104]

Courtesy rules presented an idealized form of adolescent behavior

College Girl Bookshelf: "Unforbidden Fruit" (1928), by Warner Fabian

The undergraduate flapper antiheroines of the sensationalistic *Unforbidden Fruit* were just the sort of flaming youth that made educators and advice mavens tremble with loathing in the 1920s. Roommates Sylvia Hartnett and Starr Mowbray are students at the fictional Sperry College for Women who call themselves the H.B.V.s— Hard Boiled Virgins. They are girls of the "modern, restless, experimental-minded, keen, cynical, adventurous and slightly neurotic type" who smoke cigarettes and visit the bootlegger.* Together with their third roommate, the decidedly soft-boiled Verity Clarke, they discuss the best way to cure the "red devils" (sexual desire) and poll their dormitory neighbors to see who still belongs to "Class V" for virgin (despite a lot of big talk, it's most of them). They watch their friends go "thicketing"—spending the

---

* Warner Fabian [Samuel Hopkins Adams], *Unforbidden Fruit* (Cleveland: International Fiction Library, 1928), v.

---

deemed "appropriate" by the adults in charge. Almost every college handbook included at least some rules for proper social behavior in addition to campus rules. For example, a small section on "Good Form" in the 1935–1936 freshman handbook at the coed Massachusetts State College presented general rules of etiquette, such as the necessity of replying to invitations, the proper way to make introductions, and that dinner night in the woods alone with bedding and boyfriend—and cagily note that, unless the girls are careful, sooner or later "Old Lady Trouble" will knock them "for a row of triplets." Despite this wise observation, Sylvia calmly enters into a secret affair with her married English professor. But even she is shocked when the hot-to-trot chemistry whiz Elsie "Nixie" Nichols leaves school after contracting syphilis (obliquely referred to as "an infectious or contagious disease") from the big man on a neighboring campus.† In other words, it's just another semester at Sperry.

Unforbidden Fruit is miles away in concept from books like *Her College Days* (1896) or *When Patty Went to College* (1903). These were aimed at young readers, for one thing, who were expected to identify with a bright-eyed freshman protagonist's experiences with school and social life. Fabian offered a less innocent voyeurism to adult readers seeking a titillating look at the collegiate flapper and her bold new sexuality.

† Ibid., 146, 29, 28.

invitations required prompt arrival. Further fine points of on-campus etiquette pervaded the Student Council Regulations: coats and neckties were to be worn at assemblies held in the auditorium, freshmen were to use only the left-hand door when entering Stockbridge Hall, etc. Given that the Student Religious Council edited the handbook, it must have been the deadly combination of poor grammar and a lazy copyeditor rather than an upperclassman's prank on the frosh that one of the Student Council Regulations implored, "All senior men shall remain seated until senior women pass out."[105]

Students themselves seemed to crave information on how to behave. In 1940, coeds at the University of Maryland published their own guide to appropriate feminine behavior, *That Is the Question, A Social Blue Book of Campus Etiquette*. Rather than discussing how to use the library in furtherance of study habits, it reminded girls to do their date making elsewhere. "What of the student who actually goes to the library to study?" it asked. Not that this guide was terribly concerned with a grind like her, for as *Life* magazine reported, Maryland's 1,176 coeds were acutely aware of "the necessity of being popular." Hence the boy-savvy advice proffered within *That Is the Question*'s pages: "Don't come to an 8:20 with your eyelashes dripping mascara"; "Don't sit around and giggle" in the library; and when you get up the nerve to smile at the cute guy in English, "Let him have it right between the eyes."[106]

The University of Maryland was not the only college to publish its own etiquette guide. During the mid-twentieth century, students at the University of Illinois brought their social anxieties to Irene Pierson, the social director of the Illini Union. She later compiled these into *Campus Cues*, an etiquette guide for UI students that went into several editions beginning in the late 1940s. It too offered advice on dating, what to wear, and how to interact with the opposite sex—for men as well as women— but it also included a helpful section called "Let's Get Employed." ("Girls should wear a suit or tailored dress and comfortable shoes" to an interview. "A conservative hat, an efficient looking hairdo, and clean gloves are a must.")[107] Then again, this took up a mere 5 pages out of a total of 192, half the number devoted to sections on engagements and weddings. Which was, after all, where all the advice on being popular was headed.

*Four fashion plates strut their stuff at Syracuse
University, 1955.*

The Collegiate Look

*Advanced mathematics, Virgil and Oedipus, do not stifle a
knowledge that is instinctive of the width of a hem or the
depth of a ruffle, and the problems of Calculus are still
uninteresting beside the estimate of a twenty-dollar gown
evolved from a ten-dollar bill.*

"GOWNS FOR COMMENCEMENT,"
NEW YORK TIMES (MAY 6, 1894)

Strolling along the edge of campus on a sunny day, I wore a dress
of pink and black horizontal stripes and an army green bomber-
style jacket. A pink vinyl tote bag was slung over my shoulder. I
find it hard to remember what I had on my feet: was it the blue vinyl
high-heeled boots or perhaps the brocade T-straps with rhinestone buck-
les? There's nothing else to the memory—there were neither wolf whis-
tles nor catcalls (the latter much more likely; fashion-forward punkettes
were not especially appreciated that year), no coincidental meetings with
people who would play important roles in my future. There is just the
strong bright picture of that particular dress, that particular moment in

time, when perhaps a hint of adult identity to come flashed through my brain and permanently fixed the moment there.

Clothes Make the College Girl

Given that clothing is such an important marker between college and high school, it's not all that surprising that my pink and black dress stands out so clearly in my memory. Clothing marks the passage from schoolgirl to adult, when we don the ritual outfit of graduate's gown and cap. Long before manufacturers sold a ready-to-wear college-girl look, new clothing and new endeavors were firmly entwined.

In *Little Town on the Prairie* (1941), Laura Ingalls Wilder described the dress her mother made in the 1880s for Laura's sister Mary to wear during her first semester at the blind college in Vinton, Iowa. The following is a mere dollop of the loving, almost fetishistic detail from the seven pages it took Ingalls to describe the dress and its creation:

> It was brown cashmere, lined with brown cambric. Small brown buttons buttoned it down the front, and on either side of the buttons and around the bottom Ma had trimmed it with a narrow, shirred strip of brown-and-blue plaid, with red threads and golden threads running through it. A high collar of the plaid was sewed on, and . . . a gathered length of white machine-made lace . . . was to be fitted inside the collar, so that it would fall a little over the top.[1]

Ma Ingalls's ordeal of pattern making, cutting, fitting, and sewing was par for the course. The earliest college girls didn't pop out to the mall with their mothers for an orgy of buying—ready-to-wear clothing wasn't available until the last quarter of the nineteenth century. Nor did store-bought clothing immediately conquer the marketplace: when in 1900 the *Ladies Home Journal* showed illustrations of clothing for "The Girl Who Is Going to College," the designs were for seamstresses to copy—

extremely talented, pattern-making seamstresses like Ma. As with *Godey's Lady's Book*, the nineteenth-century fashion bible at which Mrs. Ingalls so longed to take a peek before sewing Mary's frock, instructions were not included. Change was creeping in, however: ads for ready-made shirtwaists, underclothing, and corsets sat cheek by jowl with the fashion plates in *Ladies Home Journal*.

Lacking the guidance of mid-twentieth-century teen magazines and their back-to-school issues stuffed with copious pages of fashion advertising and editorial, the best way for the turn-of-the-century college girl to find out the clothing fads and necessities at her campus of choice was to simply write ahead and ask. "Be sure to write such a letter of inquiry before purchasing your fabrics unless you are perfectly certain of what to wear and when and how to wear it," advised the *New York Times* in a 1906 article on "What Should Go in the Freshman Trunk." Making a good first impression on campus was extremely important, and a girl's clothing needed to be up to the task. After all, a newly arrived freshman wanted to look like she fit right into campus life, not like a scared greenhorn. She wanted, above all, to look collegiate. Thus, while packing the freshman trunk was "one of the rarest delights of the girl who is anticipating life at college," it was also fraught with anxiety:

> . . . for the contents of this trunk more than of any other must be "just right," or the blush that comes through the knowledge of wearing clothes that are not in good taste must dye the cheek many, many times in that critical first year among associates who are destined to become acquainted with a girl's every trait of character, whether it be blameworthy or praiseworthy.[2]

Sharp eyes and wagging tongues, it was suggested, awaited the girl who showed up with the wrong clothing. To avoid this fate, the *Times* writer prescribed girlish styles of "the utmost simplicity," preferably in virginal white, down to sweater, tam-o'-shanter, and wool gloves for winter sports. "At college everything is so scrupulously clean that white gowns are in little danger of soiling," the writer reassured readers who with good reason questioned the day-to-day practicality of a pale-hued wardrobe when all laundering was done by hand.[3]

Despite fears that college might make girls more masculine, it turned out that, as the *New York Times* felt compelled to report to its readers in 1894, "the higher education of women has not robbed her of her fondness for feminine fripperies and furbelows."[4] Fashion and clothing concerns took up a good deal of the nineteenth-century college girl's time. Historian Margaret A. Lowe showed that college girls at Smith and Cornell wrote chatty letters to the folks at home about shopping trips made, new hairstyles tried and adopted, and what outfits they wore to campus events. Girls frequently described desired garments, and asked for both permission and money to purchase them or have them made. "I still think you had better not try to make our dress skirts yourself before we come. We want them made in the latest style and would rather wait and decide ourselves how we want them made," wrote Cornell student Ruth Nelson on behalf of herself and her sister Gertrude to their "Momsie and Popsie" in 1893, evidencing perhaps just the slightest lack of faith in Momsie's fashion sense. Girls who didn't want to wait until their next visit home to have a new skirt or suit fitted often had closer options. Local dressmakers did a land-office business: in the early 1890s, more than two hundred seamstresses made their living in just one town near Smith College. One reported getting "orders for as many as 4 or 5 suits at a time" when the girls returned from vacation.[5]

Simplicity in dress was not always uppermost in the college girl's mind. In early December 1893, just a month after they requested their mother to hold off making their dress skirts, sisters Ruth and Gertrude Nelson submitted their joint Christmas list, which included: "handkerchiefs, purse (very necessary), an evening dress, an otter muff, silver hairpins, iced-wool fascinator [a type of scarf], a tray with set of manicure articles, mink muff, and a shell hairpiece." Five weeks later, Ruth was at it again; this time she needed "slippers and stockings for a ball," preferably satin.[6]

Taking the Nelson sisters' taste for little luxuries as an example, perhaps it's not surprising that the extent and nature of the average college girl's wardrobe came in for criticism. "Extravagance in . . . dress" was one of the "College Girl Follies" identified by an anonymous "Mother" writing in *Good Housekeeping* magazine in 1909. "Once one jacket, to be worn with her street suit in winter and one for spring would have been enough," sighed the mother, clearly longing for the good old days.

> Today she needs not only those two to begin with, but a long coat to wear over dresses without jackets, a sweater to run about in, a white coat to go with white skirts and one of colored linen to match a skirt of the same, an evening coat for winter and another for spring and fall and an ulster [a type of overcoat] for extreme winter days. All these are in addition to the mackintosh, which is a necessity, and the fur coat, which is a luxury.[7]

Part of the friction between Mother's generation and that of her daughter was a decided change in how women behaved. The college girl of the late nineteenth and early twentieth centuries took part in vigorous activities that required special clothing: calisthenics, for example, or bicycle riding. She needed "a sweater to run about in" because she, well, ran about in a way alien to a mother raised on the belief that a woman's place was in the home, first her father's and then her husband's, without the luxury of the worldly four-year interval enjoyed by her daughter.

A trunk packed under Mother's watchful eye was less likely to contain items of which she disapproved, a low-necked evening gown, for example. Even so, a girl at college had the freedom to wear what she wanted when she wanted to—and the resulting combinations could be disconcerting to parents. The following comes from the same exasperated "Mother" of 1909, but timeless is the scene described therein:

> A mother arrived on a visit to her college daughter on a bitter winter's day and was met by the girl at the train in low shoes with transparent stockings, a delicate lingerie blouse showing that no warm underwear was beneath, no hat and a light jacket flying open at the throat. "I just cried," said the mother simply.[8]

Clearly, not only did college girls ignore their health (a frosty day and no long underwear meant catching one's death of cold and perhaps killing one's mother in the process), but they were shameless when it came to confronting their devoted parents with the fashion independence gained on campus. Then, as now, campus clothing fads played an important role in changing a girl into a college girl: depending on the era, bobbed hair, miniskirts, bralessness, crazy-colored hair, tattoos, and/or facial and body piercings have marked an adolescent's new identity and driven parents to tears of despair or anger. If girls at a particular school considered low shoes and transparent stockings "the thing," it branded them as college girls both on and off campus.

Keeping up with evolving campus fads, let alone the need for an expanded basic wardrobe, cost money. In 1922, the *Ladies Home Journal* remarked on "sub-freshmen" whose clothing demands before heading off to campus stressed a father's already "overstrained pocketbook." In fact, the *Journal* noted, a college girl only needed four dresses "to be well and appropriately dressed from registration day till Easter vacation." Supplemented by a skirt, blouses, sweaters, and "one's leftover summer dresses," the suggested quartet comprised:

> A simple cloth dress for classroom and general wear; a dark-colored frock . . . smart enough to wear to an occasional matinee and "tea-drinking," yet sufficiently conservative for church; a lighter georgette crepe or crepe de chine for the evenings when "dressing for dinner" is required and for informal dancing in the gym, college plays and the like; and lastly, a dancing frock . . . not too sophisticated . . .[9]

If this mandate against extravagance and sophistication wasn't a bucket of cold water on the soon-to-be college girl's dreams of a new wardrobe, then the *Journal*'s suggestion that these dresses be made over from "old clothes and remnants" surely drove a stake through sartorial aspirations.

Dress Codes and Uniforms

Even where parents were willing and able to gratify a stylish daughter's clothing demands, she often still faced campus regulations concerning clothing. A student's wardrobe clearly indicated her class status, and on campuses where scholarship girls and those who worked their way along mingled with daughters of the wealthy, reminding students of the need for simplicity was a way in which administrators tried to keep things on an even keel. "We may beg that *expensive trimmings* should be entirely laid aside, and may *suggest* that the skirts of dresses be left plain, unless in remaking some fold is needed to hide a defect," read a letter sent by Vassar's first "lady principal," Hannah Lyman, to the parents of early Vassarions.[10] While Lyman's policy against decorative folds seems particularly restrictive, the request that girls bring an austere wardrobe was a common one. In 1908, Mills College found it "especially desirable that the dress be simple and plain" and also hoped that student wardrobes would be "so complete at the outset as to avoid the necessity for frequent purchases during term time," an administrative strategy perhaps calculated to help keep conspicuous consumption at bay. The *Ladies Home Journal* suggested in 1912 that if a girl's wardrobe was carefully planned and purchased in advance, "the subject of clothes need not in any way interfere with her studies and other activities" during the school year.[11]

Sometimes administrators, notably those in Catholic schools and historically black colleges, took the bull by the horns and mandated simplicity in dress by requiring students to wear uniforms or conform to strict dress codes. From an administrative viewpoint, uniforms and dress codes had an added advantage of reinforcing discipline by visually underscoring the difference between student and faculty as well as keeping students' potentially troublesome individuality at bay.

During the 1923–1924 academic year, while the short-skirted flapper reigned supreme at other campuses, students at the all-female College of

Notre Dame of Maryland were required to wear blue or black dresses with white collars and hemlines that measured no more than ten inches from the floor. Sleeveless dresses, low-cut evening gowns, and even the seemingly innocent sweater were forbidden. "The College desires to occupy students with the acquisition of virtue, knowledge and usefulness in general, rather than to excite emulation in following fashions or grati-fying inclinations to vanity," the catalog dourly noted.[12]

For the faculty at Spelman Seminary, student dress meant more than merely being fashionable or gratifying vanity. From 1910 to 1927, Spel-man's president was a formidable character named Lucy Hale Tapley. Tall and broad-shouldered, Tapley more closely resembled a sea captain than a schoolteacher—or at least that's what one faculty member remembered about her. Not surprisingly, Tapley was a stickler for rules. Under her care, students were required to don long underwear on a spe-cific calendar date in the fall and to remove it on another in the spring, no matter the actual weather conditions at the time. Graduates gleefully recalled Tapley's springtime announcement to students gathered in the dining hall: "Good morning, girls. I have good news for you. Tomorrow you may leave off your woolies!" Of course, by this time enterprising stu-dents had long ago substituted "a wide armlet or half-sleeve" under their dress or blouse which, when pinched by a suspicious teacher, gave the impression of a full set of long johns.[13]

The seasonal donning of long johns was but one of several dress man-dates adopted under Tapley's tenure. White shirtwaists and dark skirts became required wear in 1912, and the 1916 catalog forbade students from bringing "silk, net, chiffon, velvet, or any of the fancy dresses, as they will not be allowed to wear them." A circular distributed to incoming students in 1918 explained that well-dressed women looked for "becom-ingness and propriety" when selecting clothing and avoided the "loud, inharmonious colors, extreme styles, and inappropriate materials" that were "always in poor taste."[14] When students at the nearby Atlanta Uni-versity were allowed to go into town without gloves, Spelman students could still be identified by their white ones.

Neckties and Boaters: A Menswear Fad at the Turn of the Century

In a letter home to her parents in December 1880, Wellesley student Charlotte Conant wrote of her need to keep up with the latest campus fads:

> Three things I ought to have at once if I am to keep anywhere near the style; these things are a pair of blue eyeglasses, a baby elephant necktie and some dark blue stockings. Now, nothing is the matter with my eyes, but it is quite the thing for all *collegians* to wear eyeglasses . . .[15]

According to fashion historian Diana Crane, Charlotte's request for a necktie represented more than a simple desire to be in with the in-crowd. Crane suggests that during the latter half of the nineteenth century a women's "alternative dress" style coexisted alongside the fashionable one.[16] This alternative style incorporated highly symbolic items of men's clothing such as ties, jackets and vests—but never trousers, which would have been perceived as going beyond the pale—worn in combination with a woman's regular wardrobe of dresses, skirts, and blouses. Paging through yearbooks from the first few decades of the twentieth century, one almost always sees a few girls wearing neckties, with or without boyish jackets. Not that all the college girls who slipped on a necktie, boyish vest and jacket, or jaunty straw boater ever looked in the mirror and thought, "I have appropriated the power of men via this symbolic vestment." Most, like Charlotte, merely wanted to be considered "quite the thing" as they strode across campus.

Yet there is no doubt that to some girls, the appropriation of menswear meant much more than merely following a fad in the quest for campus popularity. In 1891, novelist Willa Cather entered the University of Nebraska dressed as a boyish twin of her female self. She further emphasized her new identity by introducing herself as William

"Quite the thing" in ties at the Maryland College for Women, 1898.

Cather, Jr. Following her youthful ambition to be a surgeon, she took science courses and signed her letters home with a hopeful "William Cather, M.D." She maintained the fiction, wearing a crew cut and men's suits and ties, for her first two years on campus. A fellow classmate recalled how students were awaiting the instructor's arrival when "the door opened and a head appeared with short hair and a straw hat," and a masculine voice inquired whether they were the beginning Greek class. Upon being informed she had found the right place, Cather entered the room and the class laughed to see that her "masculine head and voice were attached to a girl's body and skirts."[17]

Laughter seemed benevolent next to the involuntary "makeover" inflicted on a classmate deemed too masculine by the denizens of a women's college almost a decade after Cather's experience. "How a Case of 'Mannishness' Was Cured" appeared as part of the *Ladies Home Journal's* series on "College Girls' Larks and Pranks" in 1900:

> The "Freak" was enough to handicap any self-respecting Freshman class.
> What were the girls to do with a girl who set about in bloomers, had her

hair cut short, and who doffed her fore-and-aft cap like a man when she met her classmates?

"Something must be done," said the President of the Freshmen.[18]

This tactic will be recognized by anyone who lived through junior high school. First the popular-but-mean girls call the Freak by an awful name, then they set her up in a nasty prank—but they're only trying to help, of course. The freshman class president invites the Freak, who lives in the village, to her dorm room for a visit. When the Freak gets ready to leave, the class president warns her that it's too late to walk back home alone. "There were college men about, who might think it queer."[19] The Freak fears no man, however, and begins her trip across the dark campus. Along the way, she is beset by several young men, none of whom threaten her with sexual violence, but all of whom mistake her for a man. The deeply embarrassed Freak is left in tears. This is the psychological punishment devised by her classmates, for of course the "men" are only girls dressed in their brothers' clothing. The shaming cure is pronounced a success: "I think she'll be more like a girl now," says one of them, "at least she means to be."[20]

Most turn-of-the-century college girls didn't take male drag or behavior as far as Willa Cather or the Freak. Instead, they appropriated only an article or two of male clothing for their own closets: straw hats, vests, and neckties were all popular counterpoints to an otherwise feminine toilette. They provided a piquant touch of boyishness that served, in many cases, to reinforce the wearer's femininity. The alternative dress style faded away after World War I, when the boyishly athletic and sexually aggressive flapper replaced the "voluptuous matron" as the idealized woman.[21] Not coincidentally, women received the vote in 1920—perhaps they needed less power from men's clothing once they had more from the political process.

Hollywood Coeds: Selling the Look to the Noncollegiate Crowd

During the 1920s, popular culture latched on to the collegiate ideal. A fashionable novel of the day referred to "Flaming Youth," and the name stuck in the public's imagination along with the suggestion that the younger set was running wild both socially and sexually.[22] Movies, general interest magazines, and advertising helped turn that image into an easily sold commodity.[23] Historian Paula Fass quoted the disgruntled editor of the *UCLA Daily* in 1925: "No longer can you tell a college man by his clothes . . . 'Collegiate, collegiate,' everything is being collegiate."[24] By giving consumer items names like "campus" or "coed," manufacturers hoped that nonstudents would associate the college girl's youth and freshness—or her sexuality—with such products, and thereby profited from a national obsession with youth and youthfulness that continues to this day. Of course, manufacturers used male college students the same way.

"Colorful—chic—charming—Co-ed," circa 1920s.

For example, a 1920s catalog described the "colorful—chic—charming—Co-ed" brand frocks within as " 'smart' dresses for the youthful and 'those who would stay young' " and used a girl in a mortarboard as its logo. The dresses were made of fabrics such as crepe de chine and georgette, and featured details such as hand-embroidery and pearl buttons. The price of $16.75 (close to $200 in 2005 dollars) marked them as luxury items—though within the reach of a lucky middle-class college girl's parents for a special occasion.[25] Clearly, simplicity in dress was the sort of puritan value that was rapidly being replaced by the consumerism we all know so well.

Hair nets were definitely not luxury items; to women who hadn't yet taken the plunge and bobbed their hair, they were an inexpensive necessity. A line of hair nets sold in the 1920s under the brand name "The College Girl" featured an illustration of an attractive young woman with fashionably bobbed hair on the package, but left it to the consumer to divine the implied connotations of youth and hair-net usage.

Nor did this marketing phenomenon end with the 1920s. The September 1944 issue of *Ladies*

Why college girl hairnets? Why not? (circa 1920s)

Home Journal included an ad for Campus Make-up, "created in Hollywood for coeds, for the stars . . . and for YOU!" This language suggests that the targeted consumer of Campus Make-up was neither coed nor starlet, just an average woman looking for "the clear, fresh loveliness of Youth . . . the glamour of Hollywood!" Both of which Campus Make-up promised to deliver, of course.

If referencing one idealized version of femininity was good for sales, then name checking two had to have been better, or so one imagines the thinking behind a World War II–era mail-order house called "Betty Co-Ed of Hollywood." Not a college girl or starlet? Then look just like one! The Betty Co-Ed catalog featured at least one genuine campus fad in its pages. The oversized "Sloppy Joe" sweater and skirt set was a casual combination beloved by college girls in the 1940s and 1950s. Betty Co-Ed touted its version as the "Pride of the Campus Cuties!"

Mostly, though, Betty Co-Ed made more of its West Coast connections and featured Hollywood starlets modeling "California styles."

The Betty Co-ed catalog also showed models wearing pants, a newly popular item for women during the war years. While divided skirts and bloomers had been accepted in varying degrees as female sportswear since the 1890s or so (as long as they were worn in the gymnasium), the sight of a woman dressed in trousers in public was unusual enough to shock well into the 1930s. Pants-wearing pioneer Marlene Dietrich helped make trousers for women stylish, and in the 1940s they began to appear with regularity in fashion magazines and catalogs. Hollywood stars notwithstanding, for the ordinary woman slacks were loungewear to be worn at home or workwear to be worn in the garden, much too informal to wear to school, church, or even on shopping trips downtown. Campus was another matter, albeit one on which girls and administrators disagreed.

In 1944, Campus Make-up promised both youthful good looks and Hollywood glamour.

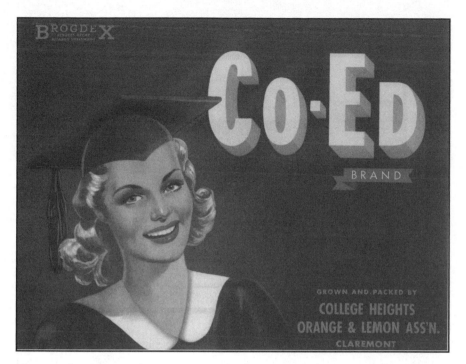

No matter how tenuous the connection, it made some kind of sense to associate beauty products and dresses with college girl iconography—but produce? The blue-eyed blonde wearing graduation robes and mortarboard pictured on the Co-Ed brand citrus fruit crate label seemed to have little in common with the oranges and lemons packed within. Perhaps it was a subliminal association with youthful freshness and a suggestion that buying fruit was a "smart" thing to do—or maybe it was the illustration's simple "good girl" sex appeal, though one can't overlook the fact that the fruit came from the College Heights Orange & Lemon Association.

Tweed Blazers:
The Menswear Fad of the 1940s

The alternative style that had faded by the 1920s rebounded to become a bona fide fashion fad in the 1940s. It was such a rage on college campuses that some girls pillaged their boyfriends' and brothers' closets for newly fashionable togs. The cover of *Mademoiselle*'s 1940 college issue

Skirts and "Sloppy Joe" sweaters were de rigueur on campuses nationwide in the 1940s and 1950s.

featured a smiling Smith graduate posed "in an outfit swiped from a man's world" which featured a broad-shouldered jacket that "buttoned the 'wrong way' like a boy's." The outfit was completed with a matching skirt, kneesocks, and "boys' brogues."[26] Advertisements for fashions that mimicked menswear appeared throughout the issue. One began "You wanted a man's tweed jacket . . . bulky, casual, and sturdy enough for campus wear." Another referenced "mannishly smart" designs, and yet another pitched "tweeds tailored like your brothers.' "[27]

Adults suggested that the menswear fad was at least in part a reaction to World War II. Early in the conflict, even before the United States was attacked at Pearl Harbor, newspaper analysts pointed to the "deep girlish instinct" that led college girls in a war-torn world to replace feminine "frills and gadgets" with "sturdy masculine common sense" dressing.[28] Some girls borrowed overcoats from boyfriends who went off to fight, while others filched pieces of their military outfits. "Pilots' helmets, pea-jackets, and numberless wings, pins and insignia" were not only stylish, but they connected college girls "in some vague, abstract way with the war effort," reflected the *New York Times* in 1946. Some girls went far-ther, borrowing entire uniforms from returning males. After a visiting general caught sight of "captains in pigtails and sailors in page-boy hairdo's" strolling around campus, an unnamed women's college posted signs in the dormitories "reminding students of the penalty for imperson-ating service men."[29]

The postwar era saw a return to more traditional dress—along with an influx of men attending college on the GI bill. Indeed, "with hundreds of veterans returning to the campuses," *Mademoiselle* predicted with emphasis in August 1945 that "after-dark costumes will be bare-armed, **feminine**, romantic."[30] But college girls never entirely gave up military looks (the combination of flak jacket and jeans was a time-tested winner by the time I got to college in 1979), and the menswear fad begat one lasting campus fashion: that great scourge of the arbiters of ladylike dress and deportment otherwise known as blue jeans.

Slobs on Campus

American fashion in general became more informal as the twentieth century progressed, and campus styles were no exception to the trend. Blue jeans began their inexorable march to campus fashion domination in the early 1940s, but they did not reach ubiquity without a fight. The first college girls to don the denim were the "farmerettes" who did their part for the World War I effort by working in campus victory gardens. Recalling her days at Smith from the vantage point of 1945, Mina Curtiss (class of 1918) suggested that the blue jeans and overalls she wore as a farmerette were something completely different from those worn by the younger generation as a disgraceful fashion fad: "They were pants, but they didn't cause us to resemble a cross between an untidy boy and an *opéra comique* guttersnipe as does today's college uniform of rolled-up dungarees, flying shirttails and dirty saddle shoes."[31]

Ah, yes: *we* were cute; *you* are slobs. In fact, Curtiss's gripe was nothing new; the charge of sloppiness had long been leveled at those who attended the women's colleges. In 1911, the Wellesley *College News* complained about students' lackadaisical attention to such telling details as hairpins and well-fastened belts. "Do we enjoy hearing it said that . . . Wellesley girls do not look so well as other college girls, Vassar people, for instance?" queried the article, which was reprinted in the *New York Times* under the singular title "Wellesley Lacks Prinking."[32] The women of Lake Waban apparently weren't prinking any better three years later, when they were accused of stooping, walking badly, and being "very free with provincialism and slang" in a report made to the Graduate Council of Wellesley College by "prominent educator" and alumna Bertha Bailey. These defects could be remedied, she suggested, if seniors showed "by word and example their disapproval" of the same to the underclassmen.[33]

By the following decade, however, the tide was clearly turning on campus and elsewhere in favor of more casual dress. Old-fashioned beliefs about what "respectable" ladies wore in public collided with new ideas about informality. In the early 1920s, for example, a student at

Barnard still needed permission from the dean to go hatless when walking around campus or in Riverside Park, while girls at Syracuse were forbidden from wearing "army breeches, flannel shirts or V-shaped sweaters downtown." Crafty coeds planned to establish a "dressing station" at the edge of campus so they could "costume themselves for hiking" without running afoul of the latest blue law to hit their campus (they had recently been criticized for smoking). A few years later, Mills College students were enjoined from wearing "middies [loose blouses fashioned after those worn by sailors], riding habits or athletic sweaters" to dinner, and couldn't wear their "gymnasium suits" on campus "unless covered by a long coat."[34]

At the women's colleges in particular, the relaxed attitude toward clothing had solidified into a distinctly recognizable student style by the 1930s. "[Y]ou could lead a person blindfolded into a girls' dormitory anywhere and, as soon as you removed the bandage, she could tell by a glance at the first six girls she met whether she was in a co-educational or women's college," noted the president of the student government at a single-sex school. "The fluffy ruffles that are admired in the classrooms at Northwestern and Michigan would seem ridiculous at Vassar and Smith. They think we're sloppy. We think they're overdressed."[35] Students continued to see dressing for comfort and not to impress male classmates as one of the perks of attending a women's college. Marilyn Moreland was an eighteen-year-old from Aloha, Oregon, who chose Vassar sight unseen after winning a scholarship. "I must say that I love the casual dress and it is beneficial to have no clothes or date competition during the week," she told *Seventeen* in 1961.[36]

Still, jeans and other pants remained taboo for public consumption except under very certain circumstances. *She's Off to College* (1940) included a grasshopper/ant story about the perils of too much play and not enough work, which also subtly illustrated the division between public/private modes of dress. One night, party-hearty grasshopper Claribel, who is "dressed to go out," knocks on academic ant Dorothy's door: "Dorothy was studying. She had on her study slacks, and her papers were all over the room."[37] Her pants were an immediate cue that Dorothy was not ready to leave her dorm—at least before putting on a skirt. *She's Off to College* also recommended skirts for outdoor activities where slacks or jeans would have been eminently more practical. Girls going on a hike and picnic were told to wear "heavy, flat-soled shoes, [and] a full flannel skirt."

When a photograph of two Wellesley students dressed in baggy blue jeans and men's shirts appeared in *Life* in 1944, it set tongues wagging. "Why do college girls dress the way they do?" asked the *New York Times* shortly thereafter. Comfort seemed to be the primary reason, though "an unashamed desire to be 'different' and to slap at convention" also played a role in the popularity of blue jeans on campus, as did paradoxically a desire to fit in. Freshman in particular liked to "look like college girls," noted a representative from Smith College, "and if blue jeans are the current academic badge, they will be worn."[38]

Two years later, the idea of jeans as a badge of safe rebellion was further explored by the *New York Times*. Fashion writer Patricia Blake described "the campus spring outfit of frayed and faded blue jeans rolled to the knee, men's shirts with flapping tails and moccasins, run down at the heel, broken and gaping, with toes protruding." She concluded that in addition to comfort and conformity, "campus sloppiness" as exemplified by blue jeans offered the college girl a chance to play at being a bohemian "before settling down" to housewifery: "It's fun to look like an intellectual, like an artist, or like a pauper—particularly when you're none of these things. After graduation college girls can cozily settle down to marriage and babies, thinking they've run the gamut, lived the full life."[39]

It was a rather pathetic suggestion. One would hope that most young women were bright enough to appreciate the difference between wearing a pair of jeans and drinking the cup of life to its dregs. (However, this is just the sort of "lifestyle" branding that manufacturers depend on these days: wear our jeans and you can live the life of a supermodel!)

Alas, many students didn't have the opportunity for this form of make-believe bohemianism because of campus restrictions on slacks and shorts. In the early 1940s one could wear slacks or shorts to breakfast at

Pomona College in Claremont, California, but girls who did so were requested to use the dining hall's side doors. "Informal afternoon dresses" were expected at dinner.[40] In 1947, the "Standards of Dress" listed in Stephens College's student handbook included a prohibition on pants at dinner as well as a throwback requirement that skirts be worn over gym suits:

4. Girls are expected to dress for dinner in tailored afternoon clothes with heels, except on Saturday and Sunday when campus clothes may be worn.

5. . . . Slacks are not to be worn in the parlors after 5:30 P.M. nor in classes or blue rooms [the smoking rooms] unless a girl is taking flight or another class that requires slacks. . . .

7. Shorts may be worn in gym classes and for certain sports. Skirts must be worn over shorts or gym suits.[41]

At Stephens, "taking flight" meant taking a class in aviation, not running way from the campus and its litany of rules—at least in this context. While the rules didn't explicitly state one couldn't wear pants to dinner, in the mid-1940s one only wore heels with skirts or dresses. *Within the Ivy* had a curious phobia regarding sweaters: girls were told they were acceptable with a skirt for classroom wear but were prohibited from wear at dinner and church services—one can only assume that tight sweaters were too sexy in some circumstances, while loose ones were too sloppy in others.

The handwriting was on the wall, however. The young author of the advice guide *You Can Always Tell a Freshman* (1949) took a long and practical view:

My last word to you before we emerge from the clothes closet is that blue jeans—no matter what the deans of glamour say—are here to stay, so pack yours in a safe and handy spot. Never, oh never will they be fetching with white shirttails flapping like a distress signal in the breeze. But . . . tucked in and anchored with a wide leather belt, they take study duty like veterans. And they are completely at home on the cozy edges of campus where a weenie roast is in session. Jeans in the classroom or on the streets of town, however, are too much of a good thing.[42]

In the early 1960s, slacks and shorts were still considered suitable for wear only in the privacy of one's dorm room or on hayrides, at picnics, or other outdoor parties. Slacks and blue jeans were problematic when one "inflict[ed] them on other people, in business offices, or when someone is entertaining guests," noted the author of a campus etiquette book. Wearing pants was "horrible" and evidenced "bad manners" in the wearer, who showed disrespect for others by failing to pay them the "simple compliment of being clean and well groomed" in their presence.[43] But they were so darn comfortable! In the late 1960s, students at the Colorado College for Women were required to wear skirts for Sunday dinner, a rule clever girls circumvented by gathering a swatch of fabric on an elastic waistband and wearing the improvised garment over their jeans. It was a stopgap measure at best: in 1969, students at Mount Holyoke voted to do away with "the gracious living rule whereby skirts were mandatory for dinner twice a week, followed by demitasse in the living room."[44]

The word "sloppy" may well have been a badge of honor on many women's campuses, but outside criticism of dress standards nonetheless sometimes stung. In 1940, the same year it ushered in the "boyish" look with such great fanfare, *Mademoiselle* reported that the undergraduates at what was then the all-female Skidmore College in Saratoga Springs, New York, had undertaken a campaign to reverse their status as the "worst-dressed college in the East" (the judges of this pageant weren't revealed). The following semester students "concentrated" on clothing and appearance, and the campus Costume Club elected the school's best-groomed girl.[45]

Skidmore was not alone in its war against the stereotype of the intelligent-but-unattractive woman, and not alone in offering lessons in dress, deportment, and good grooming to its female students. Of course, by suggesting that personal attractiveness was "a requisite of success, be it with the bridge club, the boy friend or the boss," these programs reaffirmed that it wasn't enough for a woman to be smart—she needed beauty too. Stephens College's midcentury grooming and clothing clinics provided interested students with individualized makeovers: a girl might receive a new dress designed specifically for her, while professionals helped her choose the most flattering makeup colors and hairstyle.[46] (Later, after Stephens had been taken to task in *The Feminine Mystique* and elsewhere, a school history noted that the purpose of the clinics, "which evolved some unflattering criticism," was "not to produce glamour girls but to improve mental health by helping the Cinderella-type student overcome feelings of inadequacy or inferiority. . . .")[47]

Appearance even played a role in whether a girl got into school or not. Girls were instructed to "make sure your nails, hair and complexion" reflected good grooming at their college interviews. "Good grooming and good taste—not great beauty and expensive clothes—are an interviewer's criteria in judging your appearance," stated the "Dean of Women" at an unnamed "small eastern college" in a 1961 article in *Seventeen*.[48]

Attention to appearance was seen as a positive step away from the negative stereotype of the college girl as a horn-rimmed-glasses-wearing spinster-to-be, a modern improvement that showed just how far the college girl had come. The authors of *She's Off to College* described attention to appearance as a mark of the modern college girl:

> Colleges are not the isolated scholastic retreats they were in the [eighteen-] nineties. Then a girl who went to college was almost by that very fact labeled a little queer, or at least considered the "studious type" not attractive to men, and she probably went in for the bookish life and the teaching profession later. . . . Culture and knowledge have come out of hiding, and everyone realizes that an educated woman is more attractive and exerts more influence than an uneducated one.[49]

A college girl therefore owed it to herself and those around her to pick up a lipstick along with her Latin textbooks.

Brains into Bombshells

In an odd little December 1958 essay in *Seventeen*'s "From a Boy's Point of View" column, the token boy on staff, Jimmy Wescott, derided girls who came home from their first semester of college at the holidays with brand-new personalities. There was, for example, "the Duchess," who after being "hazed, snubbed, insulted" at school came home all high-toned, and ditched rock 'n' roll in favor of classical music. "Worse than the Duchess," however, was "the Brain" who was easily identified "by any number of attractive things—sneakers, black worsted stockings, thick glasses."[50]

It was but a short linguistic hop from "brain-buster" to "brain," per-haps the most popular mid-twentieth-century slang terms for the overly smart student. "Brain" had positive and negative connotations: being smart was good, of course, while being "too smart" was bad—especially for women. Even worse than being too smart was *looking* too smart. *Glamour* magazine expanded on this idea in a 1961 article entitled "Brains Are Not Enough." According to writer Mary Ellin Barrett, the intellectual life was a "booby trap" for smart young women who failed to embrace the beauty culture along with their mental gifts. She traced the evolution of the unattractive smart girl from her bluestocking roots to her contemporary incarnation as a "bohemian," whose sloppy jeans and ponytail proclaimed her allegiance to books over boys. A wasted mind betrayed one's complete fulfillment as a human being, but more impor-tantly to Barrett, "wasted looks [were] a betrayal of yourself as a woman." Barrett bolstered her argument with a quote from the assistant dean of women undergraduates at the University of Chicago, who noted that the "really bright person cares about how she looks." As for those most extreme bohemians—beatniks!—whose uniform of black tights and pale makeup proclaimed their difference from the pack, Barrett noted that, for a woman, "the pursuit of beauty is as much a part of her individuality as the pursuit of knowledge." Indeed, the two went hand in hand: Barrett pointed out such babelicious brains as Virginia Woolf ("exquisitely

"*The Brain* 🎓 learns an angle not in the 📖 geometry book.

Carol is our Valedictorian and a math shark, but as my brother Boz remarked—"too bad she dresses like the square root of pi."

The awful part was she heard him. And later on, at my house, she was almost in tears.

"I know I'm terrible at picking clothes," she said. "And I never have enough money. Mother will probably hunt the sales for my graduation dress—and I'll look like a creep."

"Listen, Genius!" I said. "Why don't you get <u>really</u> smart and take the Teen-Age Sewing Course at the Singer Sewing Center? You'll save about <u>half</u> on your clothes, and you make a dress while you learn!"

Well—at graduation when Carol got up to make her speech, everybody goggled. Her dress really took the honors—sweet as an angel's, with simply super lines.

Afterwards, I saw Boz bee-lining it for a date, and did <u>I</u> get a laugh—because two other guys got there first.

Have More...and Prettier Clothes!

Take Singer's Teen-Age Sewing Lessons on Saturdays or after school. Special low rates for girls 12 to 17. Ask your Singer Sewing Center (listed in the phone book under Singer Sewing Machine Company) for details.

S SEWING CENTERS EVERYWHERE

SINGER SEWING MACHINE COMPANY

Junior Vogue Pattern No. 3091. 2¾ yds. (39")

37

" 'Listen, Genius!' I said. 'Why don't you get really smart . . . ?' " *Singer Sewing Machines, 1946.*

groomed") and Collette ("immaculate sense of style"). Interestingly, Barrett went on to argue that the original members of the bluestocking circle "flashed looks as well as wits," never mind what slurs went on to be cast against lady intellectuals in their name.[51]

The female brain was a frequently used image in both pop culture and advertising, where she sometimes needed a makeover, and sometimes didn't. In a common scenario, a brain who hadn't seen the light of good grooming was redeemed when she was taken under the wing of her more with-it friends and classmates. In 1946, the makeover from brain to "regular girl" was illustrated with cheerful cartoons in an ad for sewing lessons. Carol is valedictorian and "a math shark," but as the narrator's brother Boz notes, "she dresses like the square root of pi." A few sewing lessons and the resultant updated wardrobe are all that are needed to change Carol from square to swinger. That the makeover was successful is without doubt: when the repentant Boz

Fashion forward with a stocking on her head in 1959.

makes a beeline for her side, the newly glamorous Carol is so mobbed that "two other guys got there first."[52] That'll teach him!

With no makeover needed, an adorable brain modeled hoisery in 1959. A charming line drawing of a big-eyed girl with her nose in an algebra book accompanied copy reading "All the brains wear Hanes seamless stockings." True, the math-loving girl was depicted wearing a stocking on her head, but this seemed cute and madcap—and not the result of brainy absentmindedness.

Despite the makeover myths, it seemed that intelligent girls could be popular ones too. In 1959, "four brainy girls" from Barnard comprised the first all-girl team to compete on CBS TV's *College Bowl* quiz show, where they answered questions like "How do you say 'I love you' in Latin, French, Spanish, German, and Italian?" and "Would a good whiff of $CHCl^3$ make a boy more apt to try to date a beauty queen or take a nap?" (The correct answer is "take a nap"—$CHCl^3$ is chloroform.) The girls beat men's teams from Notre Dame and USC before losing to the University of Minnesota. One of the team members noted that while "winning was grand," when the team finally lost to the University of Minnesota, they "stopped getting proposals by mail."[53]

Campus Queens of Commerce: Conformity for Sale

Just as the college girl was used as a saleswoman, she was also a heavily desired consumer: the annual college issues of magazines like *Mademoiselle* and *Glamour* were gravid with advertisements for clothing, jewelry, luggage, and shoes, all with a collegiate slant. Then, as now, the end of summer saw a selling frenzy in back-to-campus goods.

College-girl imagery may have been catnip to manufacturers of clothing and makeup who used youthful beauty and fresh sexuality as a selling point to an adult audience, but college girls were used to sell to their peers on campus as well. Pictured peering over her shoulder with a rather haughty stare and a load of books in her arms, a "vivacious University of Michigan coed" promoted Laco Genuine Castile Shampoo in 1946. Described as "a junior, a member of Tri Delt sorority, and the night editor on the staff of the Daily University newspaper," she was clearly the type others should want to emulate.[54]

It helped that the girls who appeared in ads were often described as "campus queens." A campus queen was the female equivalent of a Big Man on Campus, whose affiliation with a Greek-letter society and a full load of extracurricular activities propelled her to the top of the social heap.

Midcentury bra manufacturers were particularly fond of "campus queen" imagery. A 1948 ad for Marja's Hi-A brassiere featured "Norma Peterson, of Dallas, recently chosen most beautiful girl at Southern Methodist University, snapped on the SMU campus." In the accompanying photo, sweater-clad Norma presumably modeled the Hi-A as she leaned—perkily— against a tree. Like the girl, the bra was "in every way . . . a true 'queen of the campus.' "[55]

Another ad directly suggested that all that stood between Susie Sadsack and Polly Popular was the proper foundation garment. "Do You Know This Woman?" began a 1956 ad for the Peter Pan Show-piece bra. "She's the co-ed who sat out every dance with the house-mother. Then she discovered the PETER PAN Showpiece. Now she staggers the stag line . . . and figures to be the next Campus Queen."[56]

Also advertised to young women in the late 1950s—though

"It takes a good head to make the grade."
Laco Genuine Castile Shampoo, 1946.

they didn't use campus queen imagery—Graduate bras by Lovable were described as a "Required course for young blossoming beauties . . . they major in glamour, they're minor in price!" The text was accompanied by a photo of three teens in bras and mortarboards holding an oversized "diploma" reading "Lovable."[57] The advertisement played not too subtly on the association between graduating from school and "graduating" to an adult brassiere. Given the product's brand name, it also suggested that smart girls were lovable ones too.

One hopes no one really expected a bra to boost a girl's popularity or her grades (other attributes were a different matter, of course). But the latter is exactly what one midcentury manufacturer promised if only one wore their dresses. "Do you rate A in the classroom?" asked the 1948 ad for Gray Gibson Juniors. "With this dress you'll pass every test like a quiz kid." Another ad from the same issue of *Seventeen* touted the benefits of wearing a "Millers Coed-Charmer" suit: "Keep your fashion I.Q. high! Be the Queen of your campus in these two-piece charmers." Millers covered all the bases, just in case people weren't coordinating their dresses with their blue books after all. The names of the two styles shown cut right to the chase: "Date-Baiter" and "Beau-Rater."[58]

College Shops

"Clothes are very important to a girl," noted a girl named Judy in *So This Is College* (1954), a guidebook written by a sociology professor who over the years asked his students to "analyze the development of their personalities" in a final term paper, then compiled and published the results. Judy's parents didn't understand how much clothing meant to her, and so she arrived at school with "only three different outfits to wear." After a freshman semester of rotating her clothing and casting envious glances at her better-dressed peers, Judy convinced her parents of her need for a fuller wardrobe. "[A]fter I had gotten the clothes I became more self-confident and my sarcasm and inferiority feeling soon vanished."[59] This no doubt was much to the relief of Mom and Dad, who probably bore the brunt of that sarcasm until their darling's clothing demands were met.

Like the girl who packed her freshman trunk at the turn of the cen-

tury, Judy wanted her college wardrobe to be "just right." As a 1946 article in *Seventeen* explained, conformity, not innovation, was the key to
campus acceptance where clothing was concerned:

> As Susie, the sought-after senior, you may have been a fashion-starter—
> the first with your thumb cut out of your glove, the first to paste pink
> hearts on your blue sweater, the first to wear anklets glued to your tanned
> legs. But as Susan-the-newcomer, be a follower, a wearer of the tried-
> and-true, the accepted.[60]

The happy outcome of knowing what to wear was described in *She's Off
to College* (1940). When Rhoda Palmer arrives at school for the first time,
she is "dressed in a dashing Fall style, a tilted hat on her forehead, a short,
kilted plaid skirt." As she makes her way up the path to her dormitory, she
is greeted by "a girl in another plaid kilted dress," and as her parents pull
away they see "two girls talking on the steps . . . , gay in their short skirts
and flat soled shoes . . ." Rhoda has chosen the appropriate uniform, con-
forming to campus standards. She fits right in, her plaid kiltie announcing
her arrival as loudly as a shout of recognition. (Even so, when Rhoda meets
her roommate, Anne Benedict, she is secretly thankful Anne is not wearing
a plaid skirt, for "some of the thrill would be gone if every girl in college had
one just like it—or at least so she thought for the moment. By-and-by she
found it was almost a college uniform for the year.")[61]

Of course, retailers were always happy to help a girl choose that uniform. During the mid-twentieth century, both large and small department stores operated seasonal "college shops"—usually a special floor or
area devoted to campus fashions and accessories. In 1930, Stern Brothers, a New York clothing store, advertised what was probably the first college shop along with a "college board" comprising what it called "seven
prominent [female] students" from Smith, Vassar, Cornell, and other
elite schools. The college board was a revolutionary idea—members were
glorified salesgirls who offered fashion advice and modeled clothing in
addition to their retail obligations. In some establishments, they were
also given a chance to learn about the business end of merchandising.

The lure was great: instead of having her loving-but-square mother choose her clothing with the advice of an adult (i.e., square) saleswoman, a young woman could consult with girls her own age, who theoretically knew what was hip on campus. In its first advertisement, Stern's College Shop promised "Real knowledge given firsthand by girls who have been there themselves . . . and everything is college right, for every dress, coat, hat, shoe and pajama has been 'Passed by the College Board!' "[62]

Soon nearly every major department store in the United States offered its own version of the college shop. While not every store assembled a college board, most understood the sales power of pure peer pressure. As *Life* magazine reported in 1941, "gushing freshmen will buy anything if the right upper classmate is wearing it." In addition to a board of peers, some 1940s-era college shops offered customers soft drinks, jukeboxes, and rumba and conga lessons—all free of charge. Even if she came through the door for a free soda and a dance or two, a girl was unlikely to leave empty-handed: in 1941, a "smallish store in Texas" sold almost $4,000 worth of merchandise during the first three days its college shop was open.[63]

Retailers tried to keep up with the times. In 1970, a Manhattan Lord & Taylor store offered visitors to its sixth floor "Campus Life" shop an "Ecology Walk" with the "sounds of wind, water and wild birds," along with a "resident folksinger" and a coed college board ("yes, young men, too, to help you").[64] It was a last hoorah, however. College shops and boards fell by the wayside in the early 1970s, a victim of the trend toward do-it-yourself fashion that began in the late 1960s.

"Mademoiselle": ## The Arbiter of Campus Taste

College shops weren't the only place for girls to get retail's sanctioned collegiate look. Every August from 1939 until 1979, *Mademoiselle* magazine came out with an inch-or-more thick issue jam-packed with ads for dresses, suits, shoes, sweaters, skirts, and accessories, all guaranteed to be what the well-dressed college girl would wear that fall. Other magazines, such as *Glamour* and even *Vogue*, had college issues, but *Mademoiselle* focused on the college girl the whole year round, not just for back-to-campus ad sales. And only *Mademoiselle*—borrowing the idea from the department stores—had a group of young women, plucked from their readership, known as their College Board. The girls who joined the *Mademoiselle* College Board were arbiters of campus taste in matters of culture as well as clothing, contributing reports on fads and hijinks as well as more serious ruminations on sex, race, and the future. In 1948 (to choose a representative year), girls attending accredited institutions who wanted to join the College Board submitted a trial report on any phase of campus life in two double-spaced typewritten pages, along with their photo and other personal information (major and minor, interests and activities, paid or volunteer work history).

Most importantly, by completing three written assignments during the school year, College Board members had the opportunity to become one of twenty guest editors annually chosen to spend the month of June in New York City, editing August's special college issue. "You're not only paid for your work, you're feted in a round of extracurricular activities which make your guest editorship an exciting whirl at the same time it's a job. And you get top-notch experience, which will impress future employers," noted the magazine in an ad beckoning would-be board members to "jump on our magic carpet."[65]

For at least one guest editor, the magic carpet quickly descended into hell. *The Bell Jar* (1963) was a thinly fictionalized memoir of Sylvia Plath's month in New York working as the managing editor on *Mademoiselle*'s August 1953 college issue. She clearly tried hard to be the perfect guest editor. A chipper smile hiding her mental anguish, Plath was snapped on the St. Regis Roof in a "before-dinner confab" with another GE and their dates, at the apex of a five-pointed star of Guest Editors and, most famously, in a sleeveless striped dress with a crisp white collar—a picture that eventually graced the cover of *The Bell Jar*.[66] She reported on her meeting with writer Elizabeth Bowen, interviewed five male poetry teachers for an article on "Poets on Campus," and delivered some appropriately banal fashion editorial text. "We're stargazers this season," she wrote in a paragraph on the "last word" in 1953 college fashions, "bewitched by an atmosphere of evening blue."[67] But Plath's suicidal desperation permeated her "Mad Girl's Love Song," a poem whose urgent imagery instantly rendered completely forgettable the work of a Bryn Mawr student whose pastoral "Almanac" had the misfortune of appearing alongside it on page 358. Plath made her first suicide attempt on August 23, 1953, while the *Mademoiselle* she guest-edited was still on the newsstands.

Sylvia Plath may have been the most famous alumna of the program, but on the whole, *Mademoiselle*'s guest editors were an overachieving lot. A 1942 article following up on previous GEs noted they were "one tidy batch of successful careerists" by anybody's assessment: several worked in fashion, publishing, and advertising, two worked behind the scenes at CBS, and one was an analytical chemist for a pharmaceutical company.[68] Other notables with the right to list "Guest Editor" on their résumés include authors Gael Greene and Joan Didion (both '55), actress and model Ali McGraw ('58), and fashion designer Betsey Johnson ('64).

Like so many college campuses of the era, the Guest Editor program went coed in 1972. It was not a natural fit. As writer Ellen Melinkoff observed, the newly installed male GEs "always looked like they'd been sent to entertain the harem."[69] In a photo spread from the 1973 college issue, the two token boys projected a certain deer-in-the-headlights quality, as if they weren't quite sure how much they should be enjoying having their hair styled alongside the rest of the female GEs.

Exactly how much pull did *Mademoiselle* exert in the college marketplace? In May 1947, the magazine's editorial board sent a telegram to their advertisers noting the "special influence of *Mademoiselle*'s annual August issue" and suggesting that these manufacturers and stores band together with *Mademoiselle* to keep clothing prices down. Keeping featured merchandise affordable to collegians faced with rising tuition rates and housing costs was "of ultimate interest to all." The magazine was

Can You Pass the College Board Fashion Exams?

 The following comes directly from a 1930 advertisement for Stern's College Shop. Not surprisingly, there were no wrong answers—as long as one bought the advertised merchandise. Simplicity was not a key word here. The fashions were both sophisticated and pricey ($1.00 in 1930 equaled roughly $11.50 in 2005).* Fur coats and silk undies never came cheap.

1. *What is called the campus uniform?*
   "Jil" cotton mesh imported French polo shirt, 2.50. Worn with pleated wool crepe skirt, 7.50.

2. *What other clothes are right for campus?*
   The three piece tweed knitted suit, 19.50. . . . The two piece knitted dress with matching beret, 16.50. . . .

3. *What is the pet campus headwear?*
   Flannel beret, 1.25. Silk triangle, 1.95.

4. *What shoes are best for campus?*
   Calfskin "clodhopper" shoes with fringed tongue, 8.50. (High heel shoes are worn only in the evening and over the weekends. A favorite is the open shank white crepe evening sandal, 16.50.)

5. *What would you wear to a "midnight feed"?*
   Three piece silk lounging pajamas, 12.75. . . .

* American Institute for Economic Research Cost-of-Living Calculator (http://www .aier.org/colcalc.html [accessed June 20, 2005]).

6. *In what should you arrive at college?*
   The featherweight wool frock, 19.50. The flecked tweed coat and beret and silk frock ensemble, 39.50. . . .

7. *Name the coats essential for the fall and winter term.*
   The black town coat with Persian lamb, 89.50. The classic belted polo coat, 29.50. The muskrat coat, 100.00.

8. *What kind of dresses do you wear to the Saturday night dances?*
   Transparent velvet "double date" frocks, 29.50. The jewel studded canton crepe frock, 39.50. The chiffon frock with new flowing sleeves, 29.50.

9. *What is smart for a football game with a tea dance afterwards?*
   . . . The lapin fur jacket suit with wool crepe frock, 125.00.

10. *What will assure your success at the proms?*
    The black net and paillette dance frock, 39.50. The bolero back transparent velvet evening wrap, 39.50. The "moonlight white" satin gown, 39.50.

11. *What underthings are favored?*
    Glove silk for everyday, crepe de chine for best.

12. *What accessories are smart with weekend and evening clothes?*
    The new fashions in jewelry, gloves, hosiery, hats, shoes, neckwear, handkerchiefs—featured in Stern's College Shop.

"deluged by enthusiastic replies," it reported in a self-congratulatory ad, which noted that any time a reader decided "to plunk out a wad of dough for any fashion pictured in this issue, you'll be getting value." It's impossible to know exactly what pricing decisions the advertisers made and why, but the fact that *Mademoiselle* had the chutzpah to suggest such a cartel in the first place indicates it did indeed carry a big stick in the marketplace.[70]

These days the college shop is a thing of the past, and even the venerable *Mademoiselle* has thrown in the towel after sixty-six years of publication. But when it comes to sales figures, clothing companies still know the value of peer pressure. Just before the end of summer vacation in 2004, lingerie giant Victoria's Secret announced "Pink," a new line of "cute, but comfortable" cotton loungewear aimed squarely at the eighteen- to twenty-two-year-old market. In a twenty-first-century twist on the Cinderella story, the company conducted a nationwide search for young women to act as their "ambassadors" on nineteen college campuses. Among the chosen were majors in marketing and fashion merchandising, and at least one young woman who hoped for a career in politics—though just how her future constituency will view her arrival, along with other members of "Team Pink," at Victoria's Secret's Manhattan flagship store, dressed in short-shorts and tank top and riding in a pink and white Hummer limo, remains to be seen.[71]

Back at her home campus, an ambassador's first promotional duty was to hide a thousand pink and white polka-dot toy dogs, which could be exchanged for merchandise and a chance to win a similarly painted Vespa scooter. Not everyone appreciated what the *Arizona Daily Wildcat* termed a "display of shameless marketing and stuffed animals." One wiseacre student columnist succinctly summed it up: "Be grateful these dogs don't poo."[72]

Returning home after curfew, a student at Oxford University sneaks into her dormitory (ca. 1950s).

In Loco Parentis and Other Campus Rules

A young man at college may be led into temptation; yet he may return, wipe off the filth, and his indiscretion be forgotten. But stains cannot be wiped off from the character of girls.

REV. SAMUEL HARRIS,
"THE COMPLETE ACADEMIC EDUCATION OF FEMALES,"
NEW ENGLANDER AND YALE REVIEW (MAY 1853)

Like Adam and Eve, you know a thing or two, you are free to do well or to do badly. It's a risky business. . . . and the exciting thing is that you are on your own and can do as you please," read a line in a 1940 guidebook.[1] It was exactly this freedom that struck fear into parents and school administrators. If, as advice writers were wont to point out, a freshman walking across campus for the first time had the opportunity to remake herself, in loco parentis and other rules were there to make sure she didn't stray too far from accepted standards of feminine behavior. "[A] girl entering college needs guidance," wrote the authors of *She's Going to College*, by profession a college physician and YMCA administrator: "For her whole environment changes and for the first time she is independent—free from parental supervision. . . . [S]he can make the friends she chooses—the wild crowd, the sports crowd, the dressy crowd, the studious crowd . . ."[2]

While parents of young women have always worried about worldly dangers such as sexual predation and rape, they also worried about their daughters' behavior. "Lack of supervision" and "the wild crowd" was a combination to strike fear into a parent's heart.

This was especially so where the first generations of college girls were concerned. Male collegians had not blazed a particularly reassuring precedent from a parental viewpoint. Instead, college men had a history of being unresponsive to and even outright rebellious toward campus authority figures. From the late eighteenth into the early nineteenth centuries, power struggles between undergraduates and administrators led to a regular course of student riots and revolts at campuses throughout the United States. Windows were smashed, tutors beaten, professors stoned, pistols fired, and students expelled in a wave of violence that made the student uprisings of the 1960s seem tame by comparison. Some of the clashes seemed almost cartoonish: in 1833, two students at South Carolina College reached for a plate of trout at the same time, and one died in the ensuing duel. Later generations of nineteenth-century college men maintained the spirit of revolt in their ongoing contempt for administrative authority. This was largely expressed by rampant cheating, not for personal gain but to save weaker classmates from being flunked, an administrative action considered to be "an intolerable attack on the student community." Rules against drinking, card playing, and profanity were rarely enforced.[3] Freshman and sophomores fought pitched hazing battles: tugs-of-war, cane fights, and regular bouts of unorganized pushing and shoving. These often led to black eyes and bloody noses, sometimes to broken bones and worse. A student died at MIT in 1900 after his neck was broken in a "cane rush," an aggressive tussle during which frosh and sophs battled to get the most hands on a four-foot-high cane. Two other participants were knocked out cold during the same event.[4]

Clearly, the dangers of independent living were there for sons as well as daughters, but prevailing sentiment held that the latter were more likely to suffer lasting harm from youthful indiscretions. Bones broken in a cane rush between male students would mend, but a girl's reputation was altogether less likely to heal from even the least appearance of inappropriate behavior. "Many a boy is wrecked in his [college] course, many a one stumbles and recovers himself," wrote Vassar's geology and natural history professor James Orton in 1870, "but a girl cannot retrace a false step as her brother can. For her once to fall is ruinous."[5]

Girls away from their parents' watchful eyes needed "protection from improper society and connections of love," wrote the Reverend Samuel Harris in 1853. It was the duty of the school to provide such protection: "Parents imperatively demand this; the very first requisite, in intrusting a daughter to a school, is the assurance of her safety; the assurance of a protection vigilant and affectionate like that of a parent."[6]

The detailed rules of in loco parentis helped colleges erect a line of protective fence around their charges, both male and female. A Latin phrase meaning "in the place of a parent," in practice "in loco parentis" meant that colleges had the right—even responsibility—to restrict and discipline their students. The Catholic girls' academy that later became St. Joseph's College for women in Emmitsburg, Maryland, described the ideal in their "Prospectus and Catalogue" of 1875–1876:

> The Sisters who conduct the establishment consider themselves conscientiously bound to respond to the confidence which parents and guardians place in them, by . . . strictly attending to their [students'] intellectual development, cultivating that refinement of manners which will fit them for society and giving them that physical care which they would receive under the parental roof.[7]

This type of institutional parenting was a byword in secular colleges as well. In 1862, Vassar booster Moses Tyler tried to answer parents' questions about the planned college in a laudatory article in the *New Englander and Yale Review*: "How would judicious papa and mama, away in Minnesota, enjoy the thought of sending pretty Susy (Æt. 16 summers) to recite lessons and hear lectures . . . for three or four years, eating and sleeping meanwhile at some boarding house in town, selected 'according to her own preference'? "[8]

It went without saying that little Susy's preference mattered not a whit. The boardinghouse, authorities agreed, was not an appropriate place for college girls to live. In 1858, educator and Antioch College president Horace Mann warned the regents at the University of Michigan, then considering the bold step of coeducation (Antioch had been coed since its opening in 1853), against letting girls live off campus—the effects of which were potentially so dire that Mann preferred young women to remain unschooled lest they be sullied: "If, for instance, they must be permitted in a city like yours [Ann Arbor] to board promiscuously among the inhabitants, I should prefer that the young women of that age should lose the advantages of an education, rather than incur the moral danger of obtaining it in that way."[9]

The problem with the boardinghouse was that even if a girl roomed with "one of the best families in town," there was no guarantee that they would properly restrict her behavior. "It has been shown beyond a shadow of a doubt," wrote a concerned professor in 1910, "that these 'best families' usually hesitate to exercise any moral supervision over the girl roomer so long as her conduct does not reflect much public discredit upon their house."[10] What a boardinghouse lacked, a dormitory run under the strictures of in loco parentis provided—supervision and lots of it.

A Room of One's Own—Sort Of

The home life is an essential element in woman's education," noted Sarah Josepha Hale in 1864, approving the decision to house all of Vassar's students under one roof.[11] Indeed, early college catalogs often stressed the homelike atmosphere of their dormitories. This was certainly intended as balm to homesick girls, but it also indicated that a certain level of pseudoparental control was to be provided to resident students. In 1905, Slater Memorial Homestead, the lone dormitory

Students relax in this smoking room at Grace Dodge Hall, Teachers College, Columbia University, 1934.

building for women at Brown University, was said to possess "not a little of the old-time charm to be noted in many of the best Rhode Island mansions" and was liberally supplied with "such pictures, books, and tasteful rugs as conduce to that refined atmosphere that is so important for college girls." The Florida State University for Women considered its dormitory to be the "exemplification of a cultured home" in which to "brighten, strengthen, and sweeten the womanhood of our country." Slightly more than a decade later, in 1920, the University of Oregon described its women's dorms as "thoroughly home-like," the better to provide coeds a wholesome, studious, and most importantly, "well-regulated" experience.[12]

And who better to regulate the home than Mother dear—or at least a maternal figure? This, too, the well-equipped college could provide. Writing in the *New York Times* in 1910, a male professor at the Kansas State Agricultural College expressed the opinion that "every young girl living away from home" was "in the need of a foster mother":

It is hoped that the day is not far distant when college authorities will see fit to select officially a "Mother" in the spirit of some well-trained, sweet-spirited woman to whom girls may go with their problems and perplexities and receive parental advice and encouragement that any case may require.[13]

Ideally, he felt, this woman should be an ex-teacher with children of her own. In fact, most college girls were well acquainted with, if not loving maternal figures, then forceful females in command: dormitory matrons, sorority housemothers, deans of women, and at some schools, female presidents. An Amherst student in the 1840s on his way to a blind date at Mount Holyoke confided to his diary that he feared running into Mary Lyon and her "assistant dragoness."[14] Vassar's first "lady principal," Hannah Lyman, ruled with the proverbial iron fist in a velvet glove, though given her edicts on simplicity in dress, she probably would have preferred a cotton one: among other details, she was known to personally measure hem lengths.[15] M. Carey Thomas at Bryn Mawr, Aurelia Henry Reinhardt at Mills, and Lucy Hale Tapley and Florence Matilda Read at Spelman were just a few of the strong personalities in charge of the women's colleges who inspired varying degrees of affection and awe in their students. Sometimes they even seemed omnipresent. A Mills student in the late 1930s remembered working all night typing papers for classmates at ten cents a page, and then, when the dormitory doors were unlocked at 5:00 A.M., heading off campus for a hearty breakfast at the local greasy spoon. She was amazed when President Reinhardt publicly announced at a later occasion that she would "not have Mills women eating at the White Tower Coffee Shop at five in the morning."[16] The student wasn't punished for her transgression, but she never discovered just how Reinhardt found out about it. At Spelman, President Read never hesitated to fire off a letter to a student's parents if she spotted inappropriate behavior.[17]

In short, the "home life" at college meant the institution controlled students' comings and goings in a way that seems almost unthinkable now. The author of *The College Girl of America*, a 1905 review of both women's and coed campuses, noted that one of the first questions asked about student life at any institution was "How are the young women governed? How much liberty do they have?" She answered with specific regard to Wellesley, but her words might have applied to most other turn-of-the-twentieth-century college campuses: the girls were "subjected only to such rules as would naturally govern the action of any well-bred girl." In other words, the young women on college campuses were subject to a plethora of rules, regulations, and chaperonage. Lights-out, curfews, and room inspections were facts of daily living in the dormitories, as were the restrictions concerning the hours and locations in which residents could receive both male and female guests. Smoking and drinking were forbidden. Off-campus behavior was also policed: rules governed visits to nearby towns, what shops and amusements students could patronize while there, and with whom they rode in automobiles. At turn-of-the-twentieth-century Wellesley, for example, students did not go to town in the evening or "go anywhere else where a chaperon would be required, without having some older person with her."[18]

The rules and regulations concerning when and under what circumstances women students could leave their dormitories in the evening and on weekends were specifically known as "parietal rules." They varied from college to college, but basically required women to sign out of their dormitories, noting where and with whom they were going, for weekend and/or night activities and then to return before a certain hour when the doors were locked against latecomers, who could accrue penalties for breaking the rules. Curfews and sign-out procedures helped colleges acting in loco parentis to keep track of their female students' whereabouts and protect their "reputations." Ostensibly these procedures ensured the safety of women students—but they also helped colleges control illicit S-E-X on campus. Girls were not allowed to have male visitors in their dorm rooms, and vice versa (these restrictions were eventually relaxed, to allow men to visit at certain hours or days or under certain circumstances—as long as the door was open or only in reception rooms on the first floor, for example).

Ella Yates attended Spelman in the late 1940s. She remembered that President Read "ran the college like a small boarding school, and that's what put parents at ease." Many of the rules mirrored those at white women's colleges (permission was needed to leave campus, lights-out was at 10:00 P.M., daily chapel attendance was mandatory), but some were more restrictive. In addition to a dress code that banned slacks, the students' hair, makeup, and jewelry were monitored, lest they appear anything other than demure. "To avoid awkward situations with the opposite sex," girls went shopping off campus in groups of two or more.[19]

Reflecting a double standard, the rules were of course stricter for women than for men: a student at Middlebury College in the mid-1960s recalled how "women students had to be in their dorms by ten or eleven every weekday night; women students could not wear pants to classes or the library; and while men students could drink alcohol openly outside their dorms, women students could be suspended if caught drinking."[20]

The strictest curfew and/or lights-out regulations might be relaxed when students became seniors. In 1941, forty-eight seniors at the Florida State College for Women were allowed to partake in a less-regulated living situation in a special Senior Hall at one of the dormitories. These girls were specially chosen by a committee consisting of other seniors, including previous residents of the hall, and a faculty member. They had to have a C average and a "clear comprehension and acceptance" of college policies, as well as an ability to weld "good influence through example." Based on their good moral character and having passed the scrutiny of the committee, the worthy residents of Senior Hall were allowed to keep their lights on as long as they wanted, were not required to sign out (except for weekend trips), and could stay out until midnight.[21]

During the administration of President Read, there were no special privileges for Spelman seniors. Indeed, the rules only got tougher, according to a 1940s alumna:

> When I was in my last year, Miss Read told us that seniors would not be allowed to visit their parents more often than once every six weeks. She felt this was the best way to teach us independence. She didn't want to

see a class full of spoiled young women who would not know how to live their lives once they graduated.[22]

Read didn't coddle her seniors, perhaps knowing that independence and the inner resilience it fostered would help young black women face a world where segregation and Jim Crow still ruled the day.

At some schools, a practice known as "self-reporting" helped students internalize institutional rules. The practice originated at the Ipswich Female Seminary in the 1830s. Mary Lyon and Zilpah Grant did their best to create a homelike atmosphere at the school, where girls lived and studied under the watchful eyes of their teachers. After students were caught whispering in class one day, they were asked to stop doing so, and to report on their success or failure at the end of a week's time. This proved so successful that a regular course of public confession of student efforts to abide by school rules was instituted. When Mary Lyon moved on to establish Mount Holyoke, public "self-reporting" went with her; it eventually became a feature at many women's colleges—though usually on the honor system. Self-reporting established "the real authority of the Principal in the hearts of the pupils," according to Grant, seating the administration's power "rather *in* them than *over* them."[23] It also required self-discipline. One marvels at the forty-four women at Bucknell University in Lewisburg, Pennsylvania, who confessed in 1930 to smoking in their rooms in defiance of a college rule, and meekly accepted a six-month dating ban as their punishment from the Women's Student Senate. So many women called to cancel dates that an honorary fraternity had to call off a scheduled dance.[24]

Dormitory Dangers

The numerous bad examples set by students at the men's colleges weren't the only thing to worry parents of the earliest college girls. While many looked to Vassar's all-under-one-roof housing policy as an innovation, *Scribners* magazine editor J. G. Holland warned in 1869 that shutting a young woman "away from all family life for a period of four years" into a large dormitory like Vassar's was "unnatural, and not one young woman in ten can be subjected to it without injury. It is not necessary to go into particulars, but every observing physician or physiologist knows what we mean when we say that such a system is fearfully unsafe."[25]

Holland avoided details, but the anonymous physician author of *Satan in Society* (1880), an exposé that revealed the various ways in which modern society was going to hell in a handbasket, was more than willing to spill all. His subject was girls' boarding schools—he called them "hot-beds of iniquity at the best"—but Holland might well have applied the anonymous physician's words to the women's college dormitories:

> A single "bad girl" in a boarding school will corrupt, or at least taint, the entire number. It is well nigh impossible for a pure-minded and innocent young girl to avoid listening to or beholding, if she do [*sic*] not finally participate in, the debasing conversations and practices of her co-pupils, and we know there are some things which no young lady can listen to or behold without pollution.[26]

The debasing practice of which he spoke was female self-abuse ("Alas, that such a term is possible!"), another name for masturbation, then considered the cause of all sorts of horrible physical and mental consequences for practitioners of both sexes. Broken health, general debility, and "remarkable derangements of the gastric and uterine function" were just some of the disorders to which the female self-abuser was susceptible.

Shocking innuendo may have grabbed the attention of school administrators, but historian Helen Lefkowitz Horowitz suggests that Holland and other critics of the large dormitory feared the "autonomous life" students developed at college "with its independence and intense female friendships" as much as the vice and disease they hinted at. Holland, in particular, was well placed to influence dormitory design: his cousin by marriage was none other than Smith College's first president, L. Clark Seelye. When Smith opened in 1875, its students were kept "symbolically at home" in small, homelike cottages that accommodated roughly thirty to fifty girls under the watchful eyes of a "lady-in-charge" as well as a female faculty member. Instead of living and attending classes in one main structure, the cottages offered more student supervision in a familial setting. The students then went to classes in a variety of buildings. As originally implemented, it was hoped that this arrangement would nip in the bud some of the more "disturbing" aspects of an all-women student culture, such as crushes and strong-mindedness. Other colleges looked to the Smith model: when the main building at Mount Holyoke burned to the ground (with no injuries) in 1896, administrators took the opportunity to rebuild along the lines of the cottage plan.[27]

In 1878, Notre Dame of Maryland (a girls' school at the time, still close to twenty years away from receiving collegiate status), reassured parents of the technological and safety advances in their dormitory.

[The building is] constructed and furnished with every accessory and appointment for comfort, convenience and safety. It is thoroughly ventilated, well heated by hot water, lighted by gas, and each story is provided with excellent spring water, speaking tubes, electric bells and clocks. As security against fire, there are two fire plugs in each story with hose attached; to call assistance at any moment of danger, an electric alarm has been placed in the tower.[28]

In an era when buildings were largely of all-wood construction, fire was always a threat. On March 17, 1914, a major blaze gutted Wellesley's College Hall and left more than two hundred students, fifty teachers, and fifty maids (!) without a campus home or, in some cases, their personal belongings. Thanks to the cool thinking of residents well trained by fire drills, as well the actions of the student fire brigade, no one was injured. Damage was estimated at $900,000 (over $17 million in 2005 dollars), with only a scant quarter of that amount covered by insurance.

It was a major blow to the life of the college as a whole, but thanks to the leadership of President Ellen Fitz Pendleton, classes resumed and fund-raising efforts began within three weeks of the disaster.

Compulsory Chapel Services

Prior to the 1920s, one of the most frequently broken rules was the one mandating weekly chapel attendance. This was a holdover from the men's colleges (which, after all, had originally meant to train clergy), but it also reflected the idealized Christian gentlewomen that the women's colleges had at their start hoped to make of their students. Once again, students at the men's colleges did not set a good example. At Harvard in the 1780s, a professor noted in his diary that there were "disorders coming out of chapel," and a week later recorded that he found "Bible, cloth, candles" needed for the service had been "laid in confusion upon the seat of the desk" by a prankster. A decade later, a student noted in his diary that a stink bomb had been set off in the chapel.[29]

Even when their behavior was more decorous, many students simply refused to listen. Colleges could mandate student attendance at chapel services, but not their attention once the pews were filled. This appeared to be a universal problem across the centuries. A Harvard student in 1831 once sat through four Sunday sermons because, as he noted in his diary, "There were two very pretty girls in the pew just in front of me, and I'm afraid I attended more to them than to the sermon."[30] Even at the religiously affiliated Oberlin, a coed in 1860 recorded going to a sermon where "my own thoughts did me good. I listened little to the former but much to the latter," while another recalled laughing and passing notes at a Thursday service.[31] A 1927 editorial in the Hood College newspaper castigated girls who persisted in "passing mail, whispering to their next door neighbors, and turning and twisting in their places" before services began. These were the same students, the editorial continued, who sat in the back of the chapel and paid little or no attention to the speaker. The

Fisk students at morning prayers, 1900. Two decades later, students would strike against compulsory chapel, among other things.

problem was an ongoing one. "If you are tired and disgusted with hearing about the subject discussed—just remember that the discussion will persist as long as the noise and inattention," promised the editor.[32] A student at Amherst in the 1840s summed up not only his own feelings but those of generations of college students who came before and after him: "I really think these public prayers do more harm than good to the religious feeling of a majority of the students; they are regarded as an idle bore."[33]

It was the mandatory, daily nature of chapel that upset students. For example, at the turn of the twentieth century students at the nonsectarian Florida State College for Women were "required to attend devotional exercises, consisting of the reading of a selection from the Bible, singing and prayer, held in the College Chapel every morning of the school

week." Dormitory residents were further required to attend Sunday services at the church of their choice on a regular basis.[34] That made for
mandatory religious observances five or six days of the week—at a public
school no less. Long after most schools had ended their compulsory
chapel requirements, a student who attended Mount Holyoke in the
1940s recalled that all students "Christians, Jews, whatever" were "net-
ted into compulsory chapel service three times every two weeks and two
Sundays out of four."[35]

It could all get on a girl's nerves. Many schools had a system of
excused absences which a student could use to get out of chapel a few
times a year, but sometimes these weren't enough. In Jean Webster's
1903 novel *When Patty Went to College*, the high-spirited Patty Webster decides to skip Sunday chapel for what may be the fourth time
("I've rather lost count," she later confesses). All the girls are allowed
three cuts a month (evening chapel counts for one, Sunday service for
two), but Patty is reckless with her overcutting. If caught without a
good excuse, she will be deprived of her privileges for a month, "and
you can't be on committees or in plays or get leave of absence to go out
of town." But it is a beautiful spring morning, the perfect sort of day for
a nature walk. "I'm sure it would be a lot better for my spiritual welfare," she tells her disgusted roommate. When she runs into a visiting
bishop on the trail above campus, Patty confesses: "It was just—the
obligatoriness" of chapel attendance that has caused her to rebel, along
with the fact that on a campus where "you have to have a reputation for
something . . . or you get overlooked." Patty has chosen badness—"I
have quite the gift for it." She is nonetheless chastened by her
encounter with the bishop. Patty confesses her overcutting to the Self-
Government Committee and bravely takes her punishment: she is no
longer chairman of the senior prom. Her friends are amazed by her new
outlook: "What's the matter, Patty? . . . Don't you feel well?" laughs her
play-by-the-rules roommate.[36]

Author Jean Webster graduated from Vassar in 1901. She certainly
remembered the yoke of compulsory chapel and wrote the freewheeling
Patty's character as true to form as she remembered her own college life

to be. She had, after all, only graduated two years prior to the publication of *When Patty Went to College.*

By the 1920s, college women and men began to revolt against compulsory chapel services. In November 1926, after two years of discussions, Vassar dropped required chapel attendance and replaced it with a voluntary system. In addition to regular Sunday worship, a fifteen-minute service consisting of a prayer, singing, a Scripture reading, and "perhaps a short address" would be held Tuesday through Friday evenings, while Monday would be reserved for meetings of the entire school, if and when needed.[37] A questionnaire taken at Vassar a year after the voluntary system was instituted showed that most students never attended chapel and went to church only about five times between November and May. Despite these statistics, the *New York Times* reported that after compulsory chapel was dropped, enrollment in Vassar's religion department doubled. It was, the reporter concluded, the result of a growing interest in the individual:

> The new girl is interested in conduct, not in faith. She has a code of ethics based on reason, its first rule being truth to one's self.
>
> "There's a new creed," she [the new girl] says, "a creed far stricter than the old one, and that's You. . . . You are your own god. You've got to live up to your own faith."[38]

This seemingly wholehearted rejection of traditional worship was surely enough to cause more than one parent raised on that old-time religion to there and then void out the next installment on Susy's tuition.

First there were the sinfully syncopated rhythms of jazz, then hip flasks, smoking rooms, sexually adventurous flappers, and now, on some campuses, the end of compulsory chapel. It appeared that the younger generation had started down a slippery slope to godlessness. Anna Eloise Pierce, dean of women at the New York State College for Teachers in Albany, fought against the tide. In 1928, she penned the manual *Deans and Advisors of Women and Girls,* which included an entire chapter on the "Right Student Spirit" as well as a list of "Suggestions for Developing

Sincere Religious Life in Girls." These included personal conferences, group talks, and the employment of residence-hall personnel who had "the necessary spirituality and who can acceptably insure it in others." The list went on from there, but the general idea seemed to be to surround girls with "the religious influence which emanates from instructors and other persons" on campus.

The author also compiled a "list of vices and virtues" which she suggested be used as the basis of either individual or group discussions. Seven double-columned pages followed, each filled with groups of words that wouldn't be out of place in a thesaurus. Here's an example from the "List of Vices and Near Vices":

12. Carnal:
    (a) Incontinent
    (b) Indecent
    (c) Lascivious
    (d) Lecherous
    (e) Licentious
    (f) Libertine
    (g) Lustful
    (h) Unchaste
    (i) Vulgar
    (j) Wanton[39]

Pierce admitted that some of the vices listed might "seem so excessive and awful" that they shouldn't be discussed with innocent girls. "It must not be forgotten," she defended herself, "that a large percentage of criminal and evil women, guilty of these very vices, trace the beginnings of their downfall back to their girlhood or young womanhood when they adopted the practice of the near vices or the little sins."[40]

Cornering a homesick freshman and asking her to discuss "lecherousness" was therefore really only in her best interests. What is certain is that many college girls continued to practice near vices and little sins, sometimes right under the collective nose of the faculty.

Breaking the Rules and Facing the Consequences: A Tale from the Turn of the Century

In 1871, Vassar's faculty minutes recorded that "five students have smoked cigarettes, three have drank wine, three have corresponded with Bisbee students [a local men's school], two of them with strangers." As a result, the girls were placed on probation and lost both the right to leave campus and to receive gentleman callers. Perhaps most shamefully, the offenders' names and punishments were read aloud in chapel "in the presence of [their fellow] students."[41] Cigarettes and wine seem the quaintest of vices to modern eyes, but six years later, some enterprising students at the Rockford Seminary in Illinois got up to more serious hijinks—all in the name of education of course:

> At one time five of us tried to understand DeQuincey's marvelous "Dreams" more sympathetically, by drugging ourselves with opium. We solemnly consumed small white powders at intervals during an entire long holiday, but no mental reorientation took place, and the suspense and excitement did not even permit us to grow sleepy. About four o'clock on the weird afternoon, the young teacher whom we had been obliged to take into our confidence, grew alarmed over the whole performance, took away our DeQuincey and all the remaining powders, administered an emetic to each . . . and sent us to our separate rooms with a stern command to appear at family worship after supper "whether we were able to or not."[42]

Thus ended, rather ignominiously, an experiment by "five aspirants for sympathetic understanding of all human experience," as recounted by none other than settlement worker, Hull House founder, and Nobel laureate Jane Addams. At the time of the experiment in the late 1870s/early

1880s, opium was not yet an illegal substance and was in fact frequently used as an ingredient in patent medicines.[43]

Nonetheless, Addams and her friends' re-creation of an opium den on the Rockford campus was the sort of worst-case scenario that gave nightmares to parents and other adults responsible for the young. The consequences could have been much worse. Schools had the authority to dismiss students who could not or would not follow the rules. The 1908 edition of the Florida State College for Women's catalog included a section on "Supervision and Discipline" which was representative of that of most colleges at the time:

> All students are required to attend to their duties faithfully and well, as the condition for their continuance at the College. The discipline is strict and firm, but not harsh or severe. Every effort is made to develop womanly traits of character, to foster self-respect, and to stipulate the students to put forth their best efforts to fit themselves for the duties and responsibilities of life; but students who persevere in idle or vicious habits, who are insubordinate or disrespectful will be dismissed from the institution.[44]

This was not an empty threat. Historian Lynne Kleinman told the story of Thelma Richards, a sophomore at Milwaukee-Downer College who, on a Sunday morning in October 1919, signed herself out to go to church. What happened next was the subject of a letter sent to Thelma's parents by Dean Mina Kerr:

> Instead of going there, she spent the morning attending the movies. This was, of course, dishonor and falsehood in that she went one place when she was registered for another place. Moreover, the college stands for keeping the Sunday, and we do not permit our students to go to theatres on Sunday. She has confessed the action.[45]

As a result of her outing, Thelma was fined and suspended from the Student Government Association. She and her parents were warned that

Of course, rule breaking could be fun! Here, in the 1950s.

if she were caught breaking the rules again, she might be asked to leave the college.

Parents and administrators didn't always see eye to eye when it came to punishing daughters who infringed upon the rules. Instead of thanking the dean for reporting his daughter's sneaky, lying, Sabbath-breaking behavior, Thelma's father came out swinging in her defense. Surely, he wrote in reply, Thelma signed out of her dormitory with the full intention of going to church, only to change her mind and head to the movies afterward. Indeed, it was Mr. Richards's opinion that "a good Christian portrayal of character in Sunday movies may produce good spiritual and moral results, even better than a sermon."[46] One can only imagine Dean Kerr's reaction to this inspired suggestion, but eventually both parties agreed that others had led Thelma astray and that she now understood the need to obey rules.

Then another letter from the dean arrived:

Again, I must write to you about your daughter. On Saturday evening, November 8, she left the college soon after eight o'clock and several blocks from the campus met two young men in their machine. Thelma and another student had made a previous appointment with these two men. The four of them drove about the city, went to the Badger Room of the Hotel Wisconsin, returned to college about twelve o'clock, and reentered the hall by a basement passageway.[47]

To make things worse, after they had been reported by the faculty head of their residence hall, Thelma and her friend made a completely false confession to Dean Kerr before finally breaking down and telling the truth. Taking all this into consideration along with the fact that Thelma was still under discipline for her unauthorized movie going, the dean lowered the boom: "Will you come to Milwaukee to take her home? We would like to have her leave here as soon as possible." Thelma, the dean asserted, needed "to be with her family and to have their constant watchfulness and care."[48] Dean Kerr seemed to suggest that in such an extreme situation, in loco parentis couldn't compare with the firm discipline meted out by loving parents.

Mr. Richards did not concur. Once again, he sprang into action. In the exchange of letters with the college president that followed, he questioned whether Thelma was indeed the guilty party or if she had again been led astray by undesirable companions. If she had committed any wrongdoing, he claimed, the college itself was responsible, suffering as it did from what Mr. Richards termed a "delinquency in management." His daughter's behavior, alas, left little doubt as to the identity of the real delinquent. The college president soon reported that Thelma had gone AWOL from campus yet again, this time with the flippant explanation that "she supposed she was no longer under college control." In the end, the silent-to-history but no doubt long-suffering Mrs. Richards came to pick up her rowdy offspring, though President Sabin magnanimously offered to accept Thelma back the following semester.[49]

Campus Crime

Thelma's behavior, as she was no doubt told, hurt no one but herself. Other students' misadventures had more widespread consequences, and unfortunately showed that despite all the chapel attendance, self-reporting, and in loco parentis, student safety could never be guaranteed.

In the dormitories, theft was a problem. A dropout stalked Smith's dormitories in 1901, stealing money and jewelry worth $3,000 before she was arrested. The press attributed her action to "some form of mania" (it also noted that the thief was "brunette, small and slender, and quite attractive"). The administrators at Adelphi College in Brooklyn were decidedly less successful with a sting operation designed to capture a dormitory thief in 1909. When a student was suspected of several small thefts, the faculty planted a purse containing a marked dollar bill in a room where the thief was expected. Then a faculty member decorously knelt by the keyhole and waited. The bait was taken, but the peeping professor managed to look away at the opportune moment and missed seeing the culprit in action. A search of the suspected girl turned up nothing, so the faculty went ahead and searched the rest of those who had been in the room where the trap was laid. No purse was found, but the searches caused an uproar among the girls, their parents, and the student body at large, all of whom, the *New York Times* reported, were "at a white of indignation" over the turn of events. The peeping was not the problem. It was the search—how dare the faculty impugn the students' character by acting as though each were a common criminal?[50]

Sometimes, the unimaginable happened. In April 1909, Smith College was rocked by a tragedy that seems all too familiar today. Twenty-three-year-old Helen Marden was "one of the most popular members of the . . . senior class," a brown-eyed blonde who "was clever but not at all studious" and possessed a lovely soprano singing voice. With her love of music, it was not surprising that she had chosen Porter Smith, a member of the Dartmouth Glee Club, as her beau. Some of her friends thought Smith was Helen's fiancé, though her family "believed no real engagement existed."[51] In any event, Helen had regularly traveled to Dartmouth for "games, dances, fraternity house parties," and finally, Porter Smith's commencement in 1908.

Then something happened. Helen broke the engagement—if there ever was one. After the fact nobody seemed to know just why, though friends later alleged she wanted to pursue a career as an opera singer. The spurned lover showed up on the Smith campus "and so persistently followed Miss Marden . . . that she did not attend chapel services" on the morning of April 20 "because she was afraid of meeting" him. As she crossed the campus around 9:00 A.M., however, Porter Smith caught up with her. According to a newspaper account of what followed, "they walked a few rods without attracting any attention until Smith fired the first shot." Helen screamed and collapsed in front of the Students' Building. Smith fired two more bullets into her back, then shot himself in the head. He died immediately, Helen a few hours later. Porter Smith's family later reported that he had been suffering from "nervous prostration" and melancholy since his graduation.[52]

Fighting Back

Thankfully, most college girls graduated without having encountered anything as shocking as the tragedy at Smith. The rules and regulations in most cases functioned as they were supposed to, and kept girls safe, if occasionally restless. This did not mean that they followed the rules with nary a peep of dissent. "O I shall be so glad to get home where I can speak above a whisper and not have to move by line and plummet," wrote a student at Mount Holyoke in a letter to her mother in 1844.[53] Almost one hundred years later, freshman girls at the University of Oregon complained about the strict rules on their campus to a sociologist studying the "Adjustment Problems of University Girls in Collective Living," who noted that 36.8 percent of 1933's freshman found dormitory rules too strict. "I don't see why the campus has put so many silly rules on us," said one; another reported she couldn't get used "to accounting for every little thing I do" and as a result had "constantly broken the rules this year." Yet a third wondered why her parents told her she'd "be coming to a campus where my own judgment counted for something." Instead,

> Since I have been here I've found that the rules are so thick that one can't breathe! Why I have to get permission from my parents to the Dean before I can even visit my parents! Isn't that absurd for college girls? . . . Rules make me want to rebel all the time! . . . I'm sick of them.[54]

Wanting to rebel was different than rebelling, of course, and complaining about rules (or the food or class assignments) was collegiate tradition at its finest. But students sometimes did more than bellyache. Young women at Antioch in the 1850s refused to cooperate with the matron who presided over the girls' dormitory (described by one girl as a "prune") to such an extent that the woman left, thinking her charges "quite uncontrollable."[55] In 1898, the semisecret "Memoir Club" at the Maryland College for Women pointedly mocked school rules on their page in the yearbook:

  I. All lights must be out at 9.45 P.M. for a few moments at least.

  II. No feasts allowed until twelve M., when the Faculty should be in their beds. . . .

IX. Hook whenever you can without being caught.

X. "Do others, or they'll do you."[56]

To "hook" meant to skip class, or play hooky. This was innocent fun next to the bald-faced cynicism of the last injunction, which assumed that everybody was out to get everybody else, and only by being ruthless first could one get ahead. Flaunting lights-out rules and sharing the risk of being caught out-of-bounds at a midnight feast rounded out a set of antiauthoritarian rules that echoed the endemic disrespect for authority that was a tradition among college men.

At the turn of the twentieth century, *Ladies Home Journal* published articles on "College Girls' Larks and Pranks" (a four-part series in 1900) and "Christmas Pranks of College Girls" (1906).[57] These were presented as factual, albeit anonymous, reporting from the nation's women's and coed college campuses. On the surface, the articles presented college girls as little more than carefree children at heart and, as historian Lynn Gordon suggests, may have "softened the disturbing image of educated women" in the public mind.[58] Viewed from another angle, however, some of the pranks appeared to be a marvelous way to fight back against authority in the guise of strict dormitory curfews and college administrators. "[W]ithout restrictions to overcome," wrote the anonymous "Graduate" who penned the "Larks and Pranks" series of articles, "a prank is apt to dwindle into a kind of romp, or a milk-and-water affair." Many of the pranks she reported were robust and not for the faint of heart. In one, a group of coeds who regularly took the sun perched on a ledge outside their dormitory window pitched a realistic dummy over the edge, then laughed uproariously when a group of male students rushed to its aid. Another prank involved the "suspicious little teacher, who always left her door open at night to make sure there was no visiting" after lights-out. The girls came up with a ghost scare so successful that the teacher ever after bolted her door at night, leaving her charges free to make their midnight rounds.[59]

In fact, college girls were not afraid to act in a manner that set them directly at odds with faculty and administration over perceived injustices. Women students at Antioch in 1853 were particularly irked when president Horace Mann refused to allow the male and female chapters of Alethezetean Society (the school's first student literary group) to permanently hold joint meetings. They viewed the decision as rank hypocrisy: they sat in classes with men, yet the faculty found the idea of a coeducational literary society "too radical" (or so claimed one of the students involved). Four years later, the women's Alethezetean Society was denied permission to hold a public exhibition, even though another women's literary group had already done so, albeit in conjunction with a men's organization. The aggrieved society immediately disbanded, and in a bold public action, several of its members wore mourning clothing to Antioch's first ever commencement ceremony. Newspapers took note of the "dozen or more" women dressed not in the sweet girl graduate's traditional white dress, but in widow's black.[60]

This was not the sort of publicity the college president, respected educator Horace Mann, wanted for his new endeavor in coeducation. The college blamed the situation on what Mrs. Mann later called "women's rights women of an ultra stamp." The women students vehemently denied this charge, and focused instead on the double standard. "Antioch College offers to both sexes 'equal opportunities for education,'" wrote a student mourner in a letter she intended for publication. "I had not heretofore learned that the opportunities were to be limited to the classroom, but thought that what pertains to the development of mind was to be shared equally by both sexes, hence my mistake." In the aftermath of the commencement demonstration, one of the women left the college. Of those who remained, at least some seemed to have been radicalized by the events. According to academics John Rury and Glenn Harper, the "controversy marked only the beginning of women's rights agitation at Antioch."[61]

At the historically black colleges, students fought against rules and regulations put in place by usually well-meaning but oftentimes paternalistic white faculties and administrators. In the words of historian Maxine D. Jones, "college officials sought not only to provide a thorough education for former slaves, but also to develop their moral character and to prove to skeptical whites that their stereotypes of blacks were wrong. Thus discipline was strict and punishment severe."[62] As the nineteenth century passed into the twentieth, this led to increasing friction on black campuses, as students agitated for greater autonomy and an end to white paternalism.

In 1887, twenty-five "girl boarders" (as a news account referred to them) at Talladega College in Talladega, Alabama, protested the school's new money-saving plan that saw teachers eating a better quality of food than students in a separate dining room. After they were scolded for singing protest songs, the boarders appeared at the breakfast table with red ribbons pinned to their blouses as a silent demonstration. A local newspaper reported that the student ringleader was dismissed as a consequence (the school said she left campus before the disturbance occurred), but the upshot was that the eating plan was modified in the students' favor.[63]

Eight years later, Talladega women banded together in support of Irene Waller, a student who had been locked in her room as punishment. Worried that Waller wasn't receiving enough to eat, the girls threatened to boycott classes and work assignments until assured she was being adequately fed. The most a few girls did was come to class late, but that was enough for the school to restrict the protest leaders to their dorm rooms and forbid them visitors, except for faculty members who counseled the girls in the hope they would repent of their wrongful conduct. This proved less than successful. "I do not remember ever to have met such defiant insolence either in my experience as a country-school teacher, or in my connection with two college faculties in the north, or in my more than fifteen years here as I then observed and received," sputtered college president Henry S. DeForest in the wake of his interview with Georgia Patterson, who had declared that the faculty "walked over the students" because of their race.[64] For her impudence, Miss Patterson was suspended. She left Talladega College on March 4, 1895, accompanied by six male student sympathizers, none of whom sought the required permission to leave campus, a decision for which they were later "reproved and admonished" by the faculty Nineteen other young women who had taken part in the original protest were reprimanded, and five placed on special probation with the understanding that any further disobedience would result in their suspension.[65]

In the 1920s, the sparks flew at some of the historically black colleges when students began to agitate for more autonomy as to wardrobe and behavior, as well as greater representation in administrative decision making. Many of them were World War I veterans, who after facing racism as they helped "make the world safe for democracy" then turned their attention to conditions at home. Along with the Harlem Renaissance of art and literature and Marcus Garvey's black nationalist movement, the student strike at Fisk University (as well as those at Hampton Institute and Howard University) was part of what historian Raymond Wolters referred to as a "rising tide of Negro protest," also known as the New Negro movement.[66]

In the mid-1920s, student life at Fisk was governed by a strict Code of Discipline and an autocratic white president, Fayette Avery McKenzie. Hours were set for eating (6:30 A.M. breakfast was compulsory), sleeping (lights-out at 10:00 P.M.), and studying. Chapel attendance was mandatory and smoking was prohibited, to mention two rules that were being dismantled at other campuses even as Fisk held tight. Students of the opposite sex were forbidden "to meet each other without the presence and permission of the dean of women or of a teacher. A girl and boy could be sent home for walking together in broad daylight," reported the Fisk *Herald*.[67]

Coeds were required to wear high-necked, long-sleeved dresses (silk and satin were forbidden) with black hats and cotton stockings, at a time when white students at the nearby Peabody College were allowed to wear flapper fashions, including sheer stockings. Not surprisingly, the dress code was a particularly sore spot with coeds, as a young woman participating in the strike recounted in the *Chicago Defender*:

> The girl part of the student body might have been able to get along with
> the orders forbidding them to talk with the boys on campus or in college

buildings. They might even have been peaceful, but not satisfied, with the order which forbade them dancing with boys, but when they are to keep on wearing cotton stockings and gingham dresses it was too much.[68]

White administrators viewed these conservative regulations as a way to counteract prevailing stereotypes of black adolescents as "particularly sensuous beings who would abandon themselves to indulgence if they were not subjected to firm control," in the words of Raymond Wolters.[69]

After their requests for the establishment of a student council, news-paper, honor system, and Greek-letter societies, and the reorganization of sports teams, were ignored, Fisk students went on strike. Beginning on February 4, 1925, when a hundred male students ignored the 10:00 P.M. curfew and instead marched on campus singing, chanting, and breaking windows, students boycotted classes for ten solid weeks. By faculty esti-mate, half the college's population of three hundred students were still avoiding classes five weeks into the strike. On April 16, president McKenzie resigned. Although students would have preferred a black man, McKenzie's white successor, Herbert A. Miller, proved to be flexi-ble and sympathetic to their demands for greater autonomy. Student leaders who had been suspended during the course of the strike were readmitted. A student council was established, the Fisk Code of Disci-pline revised and an honor system installed, fraternities and sororities organized, and a new football coach hired.[70]

Good-bye, In Loco Parentis

Without question, the parietal rules chafed at students. At Hanover Col-lege in Hanover, Indiana, a "recently revived" coed curfew of 6:00 P.M. led to a campuswide student walkout in 1926. The strikers returned to class two days later, after a faculty member explained there had been a "gross misunderstanding" and the curfew rescinded. Fraternities and sororities at St. Lawrence University in Canton, New York, in 1931 threatened to "strike against all extra-curricular activities" unless their demands extending sorority curfew to 3:00 A.M. and abolishing a "recent ruling forbidding the parking of girls on fraternity porches during the daytime" were met.[71]

By the early to mid-1960s, changing attitude toward premarital sex were making mockeries of both honor systems and the increasingly complex parietal rules at many colleges, at least in the eyes of students. By 1962, Vassar's long-standing, unwritten "open-door" policy by which students could have men in their rooms at certain hours was frequently ignored in favor of the privacy afforded by locked doors. Given the change, a student committee asked for Vassar's definition of the "highest standards" the college expected "every girl to uphold." President Sarah Gibson Blanding (the first woman to hold that position at Vassar) called a compulsory convocation in response, and told students that premarital sex or excessive drinking were grounds for expulsion. What once would have been accepted without question was now subject to debate: did Vassar have the right to dictate student morals? A poll taken by the student newspaper showed that by a thin majority of 52 to 40 percent, most students agreed with Blanding. The opposition was vocal, however, and one especially tart response made it into both the *New York Times* and *Newsweek*: "If Vassar is to become the Poughkeepsie Victorian Seminary for Young Virgins, then the change of policy had better be made explicit in admissions catalogues." "I don't think," another Vassarion noted, "that any girl is going to tell her boy friend: 'I can't go to bed with you because Miss Blanding said I shouldn't.' "[72]

Indeed, students always found ways to work around parietal rules. At Columbia (men only until 1983), for example, girls were allowed in men's dorm rooms from 2:00 to 5:00 P.M. on alternate Sundays, as long as the door was left open the "width of the book," which at least one student interpreted as the width of a matchbook. At Brown (men only until 1971), the lights were to be left on and the door open six inches when a girl was visiting, but couples got around those requirements by leaving the "lights on in the bathroom and the *closet* door open" reported a girl with firsthand knowledge. Other restrictions seemed increasingly quaint:

at Oberlin, pairs of students using the lounges were required to keep four feet on the ground; at the University of Rochester, it was three feet. Student newspapers decried the "lockout scene" at the women's dormitories—a mass entanglement of passionate last embraces before the girls had to be inside. At Bennington, a Vermont women's college long considered a bastion of nonconformity (*Datebook* magazine dubbed it "Kookie U." in 1962), a curfew of 6:30 A.M. begged the question of why have one at all.[73]

Cornell began revising its social code in 1966. One result was that junior and senior girls had "virtually no curfew," reported the *New York Times*. "We don't ask what they do and don't want to know," said the assistant dean for residence halls. She ruefully admitted that even though the girls were "presumed to be responsible," not all of them were. The same year, some three hundred coeds at Clark University in Worcester, Massachusetts, "overwhelmingly" voted to ban curfew for upperclasswomen who resided in the dorms.[74]

Students on less enlightened campuses took a tip from the social protest movements and turned to civil disobedience to show their displeasure. At the University of Georgia in 1968, 150 male and female students participated in an overnight sit-in at the school's administration building, demanding more liberal rules for women students, including the right to drink on campus if they were over twenty-one and, of course, later curfew hours. A similar tactic was used at Gettysburg College in Pennsylvania, where students held a "sleep-in" for extended women's curfew hours. In the fall of 1968, residents of Barnard's new Plimpton Hall women's dormitory willfully violated university regulations regarding male visitors, after voting to abolish Plimpton Hall's curfew in favor of being allowed to have men in their rooms at any hour. Ninety-one girls lined up to add men's names to the guest register—even though many didn't actually have male guests that night. When the doors were locked at the normal hour of 1:30 A.M., twenty-five men were still in the building.[75] By the following year, one of the few remaining housemothers at Barnard (or elsewhere, for that matter, as they were disappearing as fast as in loco parentis) as much as admitted defeat to the *New York Times*: "[N]ow it's pretty much down to checking whether a girl is dead or alive. Families have given up thinking we can do much about their daughters."[76]

The death of the parietals was hastened along when the traditionally single-sex Ivy League and Seven Sisters colleges began admitting the opposite sex to their dormitories as well as their classes in the late 1960s. Who could have imagined at any time prior to the decade when it actually occurred, that after one hundred years of women-only education, Vassar would admit male students in 1969? Or that over the next several years, Yale, Harvard, and Princeton would admit women? In the late 1960s, coeducation was a sign of the times, both philosophically and demographically. Male and female students saw coeducation as the next step away from the reviled parietal rules and toward self-determination of their private lives. Feminist students saw it as a sign of equality concomitant with the women's liberation movement just getting underway. Trustees and administrations saw it as a way to fill coffers in the face of shrinking applicant pools.

What gave parents pause, however, was the thought of coed dormitories. There had been earlier experiments in coed living—at the University of Kansas in 1959, for example—but when women breached the traditionally men's campuses, the press had a field day, predicting that sex in the streets would surely follow the advent of coed toilets.

In practice, however, proximity to the opposite sex was often anything but romantic. Harvard's dormitories went coed in 1970. The following year, sophomore Fran Schumer moved into Adams House, "the oldest and most luxurious" student residence on campus. Adams had its own swimming pool, "a decadent Grecian tub of marble and tile with its own Gorgon's head," where male students skinny-dipped prior to coeducation. In a show of savoir faire (and considerably more), the women students decided they would too. "It was remarkable what a depressing effect all this had on sex," Schumer remembered. The sight of "breasts and other freewheeling parts flapping about" during Sunday night water polo drove her back to women's only swims. It all hit the fan when the *Daily News* ran a story about Harvard's "Nudie Co-ed Pool."[77]

When a similar flap hit Wellesley in 1976, in loco parentis was already a thing of the past, and the incident passed in what became a collective yawn of disinterest. In the spring of that year, the overanxious father of a Wellesley senior sent a letter to the parents of the entire two-thousand-member student body, claiming that "sexual immorality" was being taught "24 hours a day, seven days a week" thanks to the school's unlimited dormitory visiting hours. Wellesley's dormitories were not coed (indeed there were no male students), and no unescorted guests were allowed anywhere in the building. Nonetheless, the father claimed that "unknown men of unknown ethics" prowled the hallways, where peer pressure forced residents "into promiscuous, unhealthy or unnatural sex habits," and demanded that the faculty and trustees fulfill their in loco parentis "obligation to provide a moral environment." He enclosed a petition to be brought before the trustees deploring the "sexual freedom permitted in the dormitories" and asking for the establishment of a separate, cloistered residence where men would not be allowed.

But Wellesley's dormitory policy had already been in effect six years when the father wrote his letter. Students denied that their residences were the sites of orgiastic gatherings, and members of the board of trustees expressed "great confidence" in the school's administrators and in the maturity of the student body, as did many parents.[78] By the time the father sent a second outraged letter (in response to the trustees' failure to take action), opinion among the vast majority of Wellesley's students, parents, and administrators had solidified: the man was little more than a crackpot. In loco parentis was dead—at least for the time being.

*A sewing class diligently stitches at Howard University,
Washington, D.C., ca. 1900.*

Book Smart or House Wise?
What to Study

Proud Daughter: "I have made 100 in algebra, 96 in Latin, 90 in Greek, 88-1/2 in mental philosophy and 95 in history; are you not satisfied with my record?"

Father: "Yes, indeed, and if your husband happens to know anything about housekeeping, sewing and cooking, I am sure your married life will be very happy."

APOCRYPHAL STORY, CIRCA 1900[1]

Perhaps you were one of those annoying people who devoted their high-school years to following your dream of getting into a good college, maybe even one of your parents' alma maters. You studied hard, played junior varsity field hockey (not particularly well but with great conviction), and tutored astronomy to at-risk youth in your spare time. Getting into the right college was oh-so-important because you knew you wanted to be an engineer at NASA ever since the first time your mother read *Goodnight Moon* to you at bedtime.

Well, bully for you, I say! None of the usual hemming, hawing teenage uncertainty at your house, no sweating indecision about picking a major or a school. That was for the rest of us, a batch of confused puppies who never looked at life beyond high-school graduation unless it was to contemplate how cool it would be to eat all the cookies in the bag with no one there to tell us we shouldn't. "Vocation" and "avocation" were but tricky words you might run into on the SAT. The world was our oyster, and never mind about tomorrow, etc., and so forth.

Sadly, I have always been highly allergic to oysters and other shellfish. Part of my problem regarding college was the overwhelming array of choices with which I was faced. English literature? Too predictable. Journalism? This was my mother's suggestion, ergo instantly rejected. Fine art? A suitably hip choice, but I was stymied by a distinct lack of talent. Business? Are you kidding? Teaching? That was for squares, albeit ones with a great vacation package. Mathematics? Economics? Theater? I was a rabbit in the headlights of a swiftly approaching disaster. Library science? Home economics? Engineering? Too late I realized I was paralyzed by indecision.

Which is how I wound up an art history major.

The earliest college girls simply didn't have the problem of too many choices. The girls who enrolled at Oberlin in the nineteenth century, for example, took either the Ladies Course (described in the 1867 catalog as "designed to give Young Ladies facilities for thorough mental discipline, and the special training which will qualify them for teaching and the other duties of their sphere") or the Classical Course (which consisted of the usual Greek, Latin, and higher mathematics).[2] Other schools offered a literary course and perhaps a scientific course in addition to the classical. Easy!

Or maybe not. In 1867, a young woman at Oberlin who elected to take the Classical Course faced a freshman semester devoted to reading Greek authors Xenophon and Cicero in the untranslated originals, a class in algebra, plus lectures on rhetoric and composition.[3] In the 1870s, freshmen at Vassar concentrated on Latin, Greek (French or German could be substituted), rhetoric, and mathematics.[4] My first semester appears positively brainless in contrast. I took classes in art history, English, drawing, and algebra. It's even worse once you know that I didn't bother to attend the drawing class at all, and I may have dropped algebra too.

I wouldn't have been alone in being overwhelmed by a nineteenth-century curriculum. When Vassar opened in 1865, its administrators quickly discovered that many of the students were not fully up to the rigors of the collegiate course of study. President John Howard Raymond classified two-thirds of the first class as "irregular" students and initiated a preparatory department where girls could complete the needed course work.[5] The preparatory department became a common feature at women's colleges that followed in Vassar's wake, and allowed girls who hadn't had the opportunity to study the classics, higher math, or other collegiate subjects at their local schools to better prepare themselves for the required entrance examinations. As the idea of women going to college became less of a novelty and high-school education became more standardized, the preparatory departments were phased out. Vassar closed its preparatory department in 1914.[6]

Looking at these early curricula doesn't indicate the controversy that lay beneath the surface. In 1829, when a collegiate education for women was a faint gleam in the eye of the most advanced thinkers, a letter to the editor of the *Salem Gazette* in Massachusetts explained why women's educational needs were different from men's:

> A woman is not expected to understand the mysteries of politics because she is not called to govern; she is not required to know anatomy, because she is not to perform surgical operations; she need not embarrass herself with theological discussions because she will neither be called upon to make nor to explain creeds.[7]

It was a simple matter of practicality. Men had many professions: politics, medicine, and the pulpit among them. Women had one duty: "It is, to be a wife, a mother, a mistress of a family. The knowledge belonging to these duties is your professional knowledge, the want of which nothing will excuse."[8]

This was a long-lived argument: seventy years after the letter to the *Salem Gazette* was published, an anonymous "American Mother" writing in the *Ladies Home Journal* wondered whether a "college education was best for our girls":

> Not once in a woman's life, perhaps, will she be called upon to quote from an Assyrian-Babylonic epic, or to dissect a cat. But three times every day a meal must be cooked under her supervision. At any minute . . . she may be called upon to make a poultice for a sick child, to change the sheets under him, to know why the bread is sodden and the meat uneatable, to give medicine intelligently to the baby in her arms.[9]

The American Mother argued that the four years college girls spent in irrelevant studies of "every branch of knowledge from the language spoken by the Ninevites to the measurements of a gnat's foot" were four years that would otherwise be devoted to learning at home, as their mothers did, "half-unconsciously, how to cook, to sew, to bring up children, to control servants, to take care of the sick," if not actually practicing these homemaking skills at her family's home or in a new one of her own.

Not everyone thought that womanly duties and intellectual pursuits were mutually exclusive. Sue W. Hetherington pointed out in an 1873 article that even though Harriet Beecher Stowe wrote *Uncle Tom's Cabin* "in the intervals of culinary duties . . . the book was a success, and we have no evidence that the dinner was a failure."[10] Still, the organization and opening of Vassar spurred public discussion not only over this question but about female intellectual capacities in general. In 1897 an essayist named G. G. Buckler reduced the argument to four questions:

(1.) Is woman mentally and bodily fitted to engage in the higher branches of literature, science, and art?

(2.) Is it for the good of the community that she should engage in these higher branches?

(3.) Has she ever produced, or is she likely to produce, anything first-rate in these higher branches?—a question leading to the fourth and final one,

(4.) What is woman's proper sphere?[11]

Buckler's penultimate question regarding the likelihood of a woman producing "first-rate" works of literature, art, or science touched on what seemed in the mid to late nineteenth century to be certain evidence of women's lesser mental abilities.

The Women of Genius Are Men, or Could Women Think at All?

Just as American women were beginning to enter the halls of higher education, not to mention beginning in earnest the drive for woman suffrage (the Seneca Falls Convention was held in 1848), American men of science turned to the question of physical and psychological differences between the sexes. As historian Cynthia Eagle Russett has pointed out, the result of these inquiries provided "scientific" support for separate spheres ideology.[12] In other words, that women were best suited to home and hearth and men the outside world of work and business was the result of a biological determinism that suggested such gender differences were innate, not the result of environmental factors.

To give but one example of mid-nineteenth-century research into the differences between men and women, anthropologists and "craniologists" (who specialized in the study of skull and brain) believed there was a correlation between brain size and intelligence. The larger the brain, they argued, the greater the intelligence of its owner. Women's brains, they agreed, were about 10 percent smaller and lighter than men's. There could be no mistaking the import of "the missing five ounces of female brain," as it became known from a widely read and reprinted article titled "The Mental Differences between Men and Women" (1887). As a French writer described it, "even in the most intelligent populations . . . the skulls of a notable proportion of women more nearly approach the

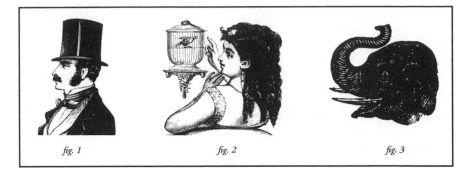

fig. 1   *fig. 2*   *fig. 3*

Man, woman, elephant: compare and contrast.

volume of the skulls of certain gorillas than that of better developed skulls of the male sex."[13] Women, it seemed, had more in common—intellectually speaking—with apes than with human males.

While theories of brain weight and its relation to intellect continued to be popular until after the turn of the twentieth century, some early observers pointed to an obvious flaw with the argument. If brain size and weight were indeed related to intellect, then, as one nineteenth-century feminist dryly observed, "Almost any elephant is several Cuviers in disguise, or perhaps an entire medical faculty."[14] Even though the gray matter of the brilliant French paleontologist and comparative anatomist Georges Cuvier (1769–1832) appeared on a list of the heaviest brain weights recorded to date, it kept some rather mixed company. As noted by a skeptical Havelock Ellis, a British physician, writer, and sex researcher, among the other brains on the list were those of "a totally undistinguished individual, an imbecile, the Russian novelist Turgenev, an ordinary workman, [and] a bricklayer."[15] Such observations suggested that brain weight and size had little to do with actual intelligence.

Undaunted by these naysayers, leading craniologist/neurologist Paul Broca speculated that women's smaller brains were due to the fact that they were "on the average, a little less intelligent than men . . . We are therefore permitted to suppose that the relatively small size of the female brain depends in part on her physical inferiority and in part upon her intellectual inferiority."[16] It was a dizzying turn of circular logic: not only were women less intelligent because their brains were smaller than men's, but their brains were smaller because they were less intelligent.

The argument that the female brain was less developed than that of the male reflected a belief that women were, as a whole, more infantile than men. Anthropologists suggested that, skeletally at least, women were a sort of missing link between adult males and children: "The outlines of the adult female cranium are intermediate between those of the child and the adult man; they are softer, more graceful and delicate." Psychologically, too, women were more childlike than men, "characterized by a greater impressionability . . . warmth of emotion, submission to its influence rather than that of logic; timidity and irregularity of action in the outer world."[17]

It wasn't until the development of the Stanford-Binet IQ tests around the time of World War I that the arguments over gender, brain size, and intelligence were fully put to rest. In the interim, a theory based on an ultimately discarded hypothesis of Darwinism—that of "male variabil-ity"—was developed into a supporting argument for questions about women's intellectual capacities. Where, asked the critics of higher edu-cation for women, were the female geniuses?

Men, the argument went, exhibited greater "variability" of intelli-gence, with some individuals spiking into the heights of genius while oth-ers plunged into the troughs of imbecility. Women, meanwhile, clustered like frightened sheep around the central rankings, and displayed a numb-ingly average intellect. Intelligence of the highest order was simply beyond their reach. Women of genius were "rare exceptions in the world" and those who existed displayed a suspicious "something virile about them," according to nineteenth-century criminologist Cesare Lombroso, most famous for his now-discarded system of typing criminals according to physical characteristics. Or, in a blunt aphorism from the French liter-ary brothers Edouard and Jules de Goncourt, "[T]here are no women of genius, the women of genius are men."[18]

From our twenty-first-century vantage point, these and other exer-cises in "scientific" inquiry (which continued unabated throughout the latter half of the nineteenth century) are equal parts hilarious and stupe-

fying. At the time, however, they had a real impact on arguments for and
against the higher education of women, not to mention their entrance
into the professions and the political arena, both as voters and as politicians. Woman's brain "was not capable of originating, though it copies
very well," wrote Dr. William Hammond, a retired surgeon general of the
United States Army, in a cantankerous 1883 essay devoted to the reasons
why the right to vote should not be extended to women:

> [V]ery few women are capable of an intense degree of abstract thought, no
> matter how much education they have received. . . . No great idea, no great
> invention, no great discovery in science or art, no great political, dramatic
> or musical composition has ever yet emanated from a woman's brain.[19]

Why, then, if women lacked the capacity for abstract thought, let
alone genius, should they pursue the highest reaches of academia?
Drawing on the assumption that the quality of woman's intellect was, at
best, fair to middling, psychologist Edward Thorndike argued in 1906
that graduate education was wasted on women:

> The education of women for such professions as administration, states-
> manship, philosophy or scientific research, where a few very gifted indi-
> viduals are what society requires, is far less needed than education for
> such professions as nursing, teaching, medicine or architecture, where
> the average level is the essential. . . . On the other hand post-graduate
> instruction, to which women are flocking in great numbers, is, at least in
> its higher reaches, a far more remunerative social investment in the case
> of men.[20]

Women who sought postgraduate degrees were simply barking up the
wrong tree, as the female brain was built for something other than sustained analytical thought. Higher academics may have been a bad invest-
ment where woman was concerned, but her greatest assets—the twin
realms of emotion and intuition—had their own value:

Who, however, will venture to say that the brain which evolves a mother's love, a wife's fidelity and self-abnegation, a sister's devotion, a woman's gentleness, forbearance, constancy, is not a better brain than the one that prompts to the making, executing, and interpreting of the laws, to arctic voyages, to the discovery of electric telegraphs, or to the building of wonderful suspension bridges?[21]

Let's see, which would I choose: self-abnegation or wonderful suspension bridges? Whittled down to those two choices, it's no wonder so many women and girls fought public opprobrium to go to college.

While most of the arguments about gender differences and intellect were eventually discredited shortly after the turn of the century, the belief that women's brains were more suited to intuition rather than intellect persisted well into the twentieth century. Indeed, according to psychologist Helene Deutsch, M.D., in 1944, intuition *was* "woman's source of genius." Deutsch warned students not to sacrifice the "treasure" of intuition and other "valuable feminine qualities" to intellectualism. "All observations point to the fact that the intellectual woman is masculinized; in her, warm intuitive knowledge has yielded to cold, unproductive thinking."[22] It was a rare college girl indeed who could retain her femininity while exercising her intellect:

> Only exceptionally talented girls can carry a surplus of intellect without injuring their affective lives, for woman's intellect, her capacity for objectively understanding life, thrives at the expense of her subjective, emotional qualities. Modern education unfortunately neglects this truth, and girls are very often intellectually overburdened.[23]

Deutsch's two-volume study of female psychology was aimed at other members of the profession, as well as teachers and parents. Similar ideas were presented directly to students (presumably including intellectually overburdened female ones) in *Marriage Guidance* (1948), a college-level family-living textbook. The very first chapter ("Preparing for Marriage") explained the differences between male and female thought processes and how they affected relations between husbands and wives. Women arrived at decisions by intuition, whereas men had a "taste for abstract subjects: for science, philosophy, theories, and ideas." Untrammeled as they were by "rigid channels of logic," women frustrated men in conversation by jumping "intuitively to conclusions." Luckily for the sanctity of marriage, "it is not rare to find women who by careful training have accustomed themselves to think things out in logical sequence. Some women, too, have schooled themselves to take a comprehensive view of important questions in which they are intimately concerned."[24]

Sitting in a classroom with female students, did a professor teaching a course with *Marriage Guidance* really have the guts to assign the following without first barricading himself behind his desk? "Topics for Discussion. 1. One must admit that men are both physically and intellectually superior to women."[25]

"A Just Appreciation of Woman's Home Sphere"

Mindful of the arguments that four years of college education somehow left women unfit for their duties as wives and mothers, many early colleges made sure to emphasize how an education gained at their institution benefited the femininity of their students. In an 1857 letter to the editor, an Oberlin professor reassured the public that "the ladies are educated to be *women* not *men*" at that particular institute.[26] Similarly, the 1865 "Prospectus of the Vassar Female College" promised that in addition to the groundbreaking curriculum of Greek and higher mathematics, the college would do its best to instill in its students "a just appreciation of woman's home sphere; [and] to foster a womanly interest in its affairs." The Prospectus went on:

In society also woman has a special place and mission, which should not be lost sight of in the composition or conduct of her educational course. It is hers to refine, illuminate, purify, adorn—not under any ordinary circumstances, to govern or contend. She should be as intelligent as a man, as broad in the range of her information, as alert and facile (if less robust) in the use of her faculties, more delicate and pure in her tastes; her moral aims should be equally definite, her moral tone equally high; but her *methods* should be all her own, always and only *womanly.*[27]

According to James Monroe Taylor, Vassar's president at the turn of the twentieth century, "this ultra-feminine tone of the College disappeared quickly with the 'female' from the name." On campus, an unanticipated but fervent student culture refused to be pigeonholed, while faculty members like the protofeminist astronomy professor Maria Mitchell worried less about womanly propriety than creating what she called "the best educated women in the world."[28] Meanwhile, scores of well-adjusted graduates meant the college no longer had to bend over backward to reassure both prospective students and their parents of the "womanly" nature of a Vassar education.

Without denigrating woman's ability to think or her right to higher education, some institutions decided that college girls indeed required an education that placed an emphasis on particularly womanly needs. The Woman's College of Baltimore was founded in 1885, and its first president, Dr. John F. Goucher, believed that the "ordinary girls college" graduated "an occasional scholar, some pedants, many teachers and a few—a very few—all around girls." The Woman's College of Baltimore (renamed Goucher College in 1910) sought to increase the number of the last by developing "womanliness" in its students. A woman needed a combination of "alertness and poise, judgment and skill, taste and tact, a nature enriched with varied and exact knowledge, beautified by culture, chaste and strong through discipline, lofty in ideals, and possessing the incomparable grace of unselfish ministry" to successfully fulfill her "special work" as wife and mother.[29]

That a college education somehow unfit women for household duties was perhaps the most resonant criticism of college for women, only being quieted by the women's liberation movement of the 1970s. In 1896, Dr. S.

Weir Mitchell, the developer of the so-called rest treatment for hysterical women, spoke to the students at Radcliffe. (One of the reasons Charlotte Perkins Gilman wrote the feminist classic "The Yellow Wallpaper" was to rebut Mitchell's method, which despite its name was less blissful spa than solitary confinement.)[30] The *Ladies Home Journal* published his remarks as an article, "When the College Is Hurtful to a Girl," in 1900. Mitchell told his audience a cautionary tale of three unhappy husbands:

> All married sweet girl graduates. . . . All three were uncomfortable because their wives had no more idea of household management than they. One declared, in fact, that he had to run the household himself. His wife did know the romance literature and was a fair Grecian. The wife of another found no interest in the care of economical house, and said: "Where was now the good of her mathematics; she had not time for them."[31]

Mitchell suggested that girls gain "a sensible competency in common household knowledge" prior to college; he felt that sewing, cooking, "the art of washing and ironing" could be taught in grammar and high schools alongside the regular curriculum. Mitchell was just getting warmed up: later in his remarks, he looked out over the crowd of hopeful young women and told them: "You are here in competition with men. I do not like that. The professor expects of you virile standards of work and results; you are, therefore, as I think, in an atmosphere of peril, and . . . for some of you life here will leave you certain regrets"—just the sort of cheering talk guaranteed to appeal to hard-working and ambitious college girls.[32]

Horror stories of college girls who spoke fluent Greek but couldn't cook an egg appeared frequently in the turn-of-the-twentieth-century popular press. "Oh, yes, they sent Harry to college to learn engineering . . . ," the *Ladies Home Journal* quoted a disgruntled graduate in 1910. "They sent me to learn housekeeping off of the same courses—with a little supplementary French instead of stoking!—and you see how I've learned it! Can't even bake a loaf of bread!"[33]

She was unable to bake a loaf of bread for "a whole year" after graduating, she told her friend the magazine writer, because she "had so much

Speakers

Over the years, college girls were subjected quite regularly to a curious selection of speakers. In 1883, Wellesley student Charlotte Conant reported in a letter to her parents that she and her fellow students were subjected to "Lenten sermons by Dr. Morgan Dix of New York. He attacks 'higher education' with much vehemence, grouping it with co-education, women's suffrage, and 'trouserloons' all together as if they were all of one and the same piece. . . . He contradicts himself, to say nothing of making statements unsupported by a bit of proof."* At Smith College's commencement in 1955, politician Adlai E. Stevenson urged the graduates to fight against conformity—by becoming wives and mothers. "When the time comes, you'll love it," he told the assembled masses.† And in 1984, comedian/talk-show host Dick Cavett told Yale's coed graduating class a joke about how, when he was an undergraduate at what was then an all-male campus, stolen nude posture photos from Vassar "found no buyers." One of the girls in the audience that day was feminist Naomi Wolf who years later took Cavett soundly to task for his remarks in a *New York Times* op-ed column.‡

* Quoted in Martha Pike Conant, *A Girl of the Eighties: At Home and at College* (Boston: Houghton Mifflin, 1931), 149.

† Edith Evans Asbury, "End Conformity, Stevenson Urges," *New York Times*, June 7, 1955, 36.

‡ Naomi Wolf, "A Woman's Place," *New York Times*, May 31, 1992, 19.

to get over." The need to "unlearn" what college taught was a frequently mentioned criticism of the liberal arts curricula (perhaps the missing five ounces of brain contributed to this inability to hold two or more thoughts in one's head at the same time). The unhappy graduate continued: "Who in Peoria cares if Hamlet was or wasn't mad? People here want to know if you can make good hats and get up a dinner. . . . I tell you, Anne, college doesn't prepare, that's the trouble with it."[34]

Popular though the idea was that college kept women from learning housekeeping skills by filling their heads with unnecessary things like dead languages, opposing arguments could be found—sometimes in unusual places. *Winsome Womanhood* (1900) was a guidebook of "talks on life and conduct" with distinctly religious overtones. Its author, Margaret E. Sangster, was a deeply devout woman as well as a prolific writer and editor—most famously of *Harper's Bazaar* from 1889 to 1899. Sangster was of the opinion that the "whole education of a girl from her infancy onward should be a preparation for motherhood," but she had a rather higher opinion of the expansive nature of women's intellect than the *Ladies Home Journal*. A college education was simply no excuse for not knowing how to cook:

> Ill-prepared and wretchedly served meals are a disgrace to an intelligent woman, the deeper disgrace if she be college-bred . . . a young woman to whom the curriculum of the schools presents no insuperable difficulty must not stumble over the making of a loaf, or the cooking of a roast. We hear a great deal of nonsense about the effect of higher education on a young woman, as if there were in it any essential handicap to unfit one for domestic life. Absolutely there is nothing in ordinary housekeeping which need daunt any fairly intelligent girl, who can pay attention, take pains, and observe directions.[35]

There you had it: a girl who was smart enough to go to college was smart enough to learn to cook. Whether she *wanted* to cook was another matter, not given nearly enough attention by the experts.

"As to my career, that of housewife and mother," said one unsatisfied graduate in 1952, "college trained me very ill . . . Because of my liberal education, I would much rather read a book than cook a meal, and I would much prefer to play a Bach fugue than can peaches or scrub the kitchen floor. I have needed all my philosophy to reconcile myself to accepting the monotony of household chores."[36]

But really now, who wouldn't prefer to do just about anything other than scrubbing the kitchen floor? Housework was no less monotonous to the high-school graduate than to the Ph.D., and to suggest otherwise smacks of classism similar to that in arguments against middle-class women working outside the home which ignored the fact that lower-class and poor women had been doing so for centuries with no uproar about their femininity.

Studying for Housewifery: Practical Education

Beginning in the late nineteenth century, a new discipline suggested that perhaps cooking skills and college study weren't mutually exclusive— that a woman might be both "book smart" and "house wise." Ellen Swallow Richards (1842–1911) studied chemistry at Vassar and graduated in 1870. When the chemical firms she approached for employment refused to hire a woman, she applied to the Massachusetts Institute of Technology, where she was accepted as a special student. Admitting Richards as a regular student would have meant setting a precedent for other women to follow in her footsteps—and MIT was not ready for coeducation. It was barely ready for its new special student. Segregated into her own corner of the chemistry lab, Richards later said she was treated "very much as a dangerous animal might have been." In the words of historian Sarah Stage, Richards used "the camouflage of domesticity" to offset negative comment from her fellow classmates: she sewed on their buttons and swept out the laboratory.[37]

In 1873, Ellen Richards became the first woman to be awarded an undergraduate degree from MIT. But the school discouraged her from continuing with her doctoral studies—it did not want to grant its first Ph.D. in chemistry to a woman. Nevertheless, in 1883 she became MIT's first female faculty member. Her experiments in "sanitary chemistry" led to books like *The Chemistry of Cooking and Cleaning* (1880) and *Food Materials and their Adulterations* (1885). Then, in 1890, she opened the New England Kitchen, a Boston "food depot" that provided cooked meals to the poor, along with a dose of her theories on nutrition. Seven years later, Richards transformed the Boston School of Housekeeping from an unsuccessful servant-training program into what she termed "a professional school for home and social economics."[38]

Richards believed that domestic science could provide a valid career path for college-educated women. Others, notably the Seven Sisters colleges, considered it little more than nonacademic course work in household skills. "There are not enough elements of intellectual growth in cooking or housekeeping to furnish a very serious or profound course of training for really intelligent women," was Bryn Mawr's rebuke.[39] Richards regrouped, and formed what became the American Home Economics Association in 1909, hoping that by organizing and professionalizing the discipline it would receive the academic notice she felt it deserved.

What made the collegiate study of domestic science possible at all were changes in the curriculum during the mid-nineteenth and early twentieth centuries. Simply put, instead of the strict classical curriculum, elective course work allowed male students (who had been arguing for this for years) to prepare for vocations beyond the law or the pulpit. Since the original women's colleges followed Vassar's lead in teaching the classics, they mostly approached these changes with caution. Bryn Mawr was an exception. From its opening in 1884, it followed something called the "Johns Hopkins Group Plan." This sounds surprisingly modern: there was "a core of required courses, a choice of sequences comprising a major area of study, a limited choice of electives for a distribution requirement, and finally a few completely free electives." Almost all the women's and coed colleges eventually experimented with adding different levels of electives, whether it was on a group plan similar to that at Bryn Mawr or by other design.[40] Out west, the land-grant colleges were specifically created (with men in mind, though the schools themselves were largely coeducational) to provide programs in agricultural science and practical mechanics—not Greek and Latin, though these subjects also might be included in the curriculum. This type of vocational training for men also came in for its share of criticism. During debate prior to the passage of the first Morrill Act, a senator from Minnesota huffed "we want no fancy farmers; we want no fancy mechanics."[41]

But the die was cast. A 1920 pamphlet advertising women's programs at the University of Oregon described the differences in these "two broad educational tendencies": "one, education for culture, for self-development, for the fullest realization of all the powers and capacities of the individual; the other, education as a preparation for some vocation or calling."[42]

The educators at Oregon spoke in concrete terms, dividing liberal arts courses (the "cultural" ones) from those in the professional schools (the "vocational" ones). For women, vocational education meant domestic science/home economics—at Oregon, in its Department of Household Arts.

While the Seven Sisters remained lukewarm for the time being, other schools were more amenable. At the turn of the twentieth century, students of the domestic economy course at the Catholic women's College of New Rochelle could take a class in laundry work. This was described as a "good, practical course in the washing and ironing of plain and starched pieces; the doing of fine laces; the removal of stains."[43] It sounds funny now, but it was practical knowledge for the young woman whose future probably consisted of running a middle-class household.

Laundry work had other implications at other schools, however. Around the same time, the Industrial Department at Spelman Seminary also offered a course in laundering, as well as chamber work, table work, dishwashing, cooking, ironing, and plain sewing. Certainly a course in washing at all-black Spelman meant something different than it did at the mostly white College of New Rochelle. According to Spelman's 1887–1888 catalog, vocational training was "essential" in making its students "self-reliant and self-supporting." In a 1902 speech on "What Spelman Seminary Stands For," General Thomas Jefferson Morgan of the American Baptist Home Mission Society elaborated on how the "knowledge of ordinary household duties" learned by the young women at Spelman would "enable them to earn by their own labor their bread and butter" whether "in their father's house, in their own homes, or in work for others."[44] Separate spheres ideology that made white women angels of the hearth did not hold for black women, who in slavery days labored alongside men in the fields (and then performed domestic duties back at their quarters). In the post-emancipation era, black women were expected to be wage earners as well as homemakers. Preparation for what Spelman president/biographer Florence Read later referred to as "the practical duties of life" also reflected Booker T. Washington's theory that vocational training was the best way for African Americans to get ahead in a segregated society.[45]

It was also a matter of money. The white missionaries who founded Spelman did so with the goal of training teachers and community leaders. But by the turn of the twentieth century, the Freedman's Bureau had closed and many other sources of funding for black education efforts in the South had dried up. Northern philanthropists stepped into the breach—largely white businessmen who perhaps felt more comfortable with the idea of young black women trained in dressmaking and cooking than as leaders in the attempt to uplift the race as a whole. In 1907, Spelman received 16 percent of its budget from The John F. Slater Fund for industrial training. Nevertheless, according to educator Johnetta Cross Brazzell, "there was a conscious effort on the part of the Spelman administration" to keep students from concentrating on entirely industrial courses by requiring them to enter literary classes as well. This kept "the curriculum on a steady course that was firmly grounded in the classical/literary education arena" but allowed the school to receive sorely needed funds.[46]

At Teachers College, Columbia University, courses in the school's "laundry laboratory" helped train women for wage-earning professional work outside the home. Shortly before a new Department of Household Arts building opened in 1909, the *Teachers College Record* explained that while

Students rinse and wring in the laundry laboratory at Teachers College, Columbia University, 1910.

the primary goal of the department was to train teachers of "the household arts and sciences . . . for public, technical and collegiate education," it also sought "to equip professional workers," who would go on to manage "institutional households" such as hospitals and dormitories, or find jobs as dietitians, social workers, lunchroom superintendents, or managers of institutional laundries. "As the engineering college has opened new professions for men," the *Record* proudly stated, "so it is believed this School will aid in establishing similar opportunities for women in the domain of the household, both domestic and institutional."[47] This was exactly the sort of social or municipal housekeeping championed by Progressive Era reformers and politicians, who envisioned properly trained women improving living conditions in communities and institutions as well as their homes.

But lofty ideals were not what the *New York Times* focused on five years later. "The terrors of Greek, the intricacies of mathematics, the mysteries of psychology—all pale before the laborious toils of the laundry course, which requires good, stout muscle and a cheery heart rather than quick wits and a vocabulary," reported the *Times*. As portrayed in the article, the young women in the Department of Household Arts were a giddy bunch of intellectual lightweights, who "whooped with fiendish glee" at the sight of a new and difficult stain, and disdained classical education. "I hate your old Latin and Greek; what good does it ever do?" said one. Another described how a young man "died laughing" when she turned down his invitation to lunch because she had to wash woodwork. "And he had the audacity to ask me if I wore my suffrage button to that class."[48]

The point of the article was simple: "Nothing feminist about Teachers College, but good old-fashioned ideas and ideals." There was no nonsense about suffrage or getting a man's education for these girls. Instead, students couldn't "imagine anything more fun than keeping house" and looked forward to pleasing a mother who "thinks the modern girl is an abomination." The irony, of course, was that the reporter skipped mentioning Teachers College's progressive ideas about the worth of women's work.[49]

Vassar and the white women's colleges that followed in its wake were founded on the notion that women deserved and were capable of an education on a par with that offered in the best men's colleges, a curriculum based on the classics and higher mathematics. Domestic science, even with its Progressive Era emphasis on municipal housekeeping, was antithetical to these ideals. Nevertheless, in the face of numerous articles about college girls who lost all ability to cook or clean when they studied Greek, the women's colleges went on the defense. Articles appeared in magazines and newspapers in which their presidents defended liberal arts education as excellent training for the future housewife. "A good mathematician is not necessarily a poor cook; on the contrary, the habit of concentration is as necessary to success in the latter profession as the former," wrote Mount Holyoke president Mary E. Woolley in the pages of the *Ladies Home Journal* in 1910. Several years later she reiterated her stance to the *New York Times*, this time defending Mount Holyoke's decision to drop its domestic work requirement (which, she reminded readers, "was never a form of domestic teaching"). "The best home-maker is the well-balanced, well-rounded woman . . . whose mind is trained . . . to meet and master things, whether or not she has had practical training in household detail."[50] Barnard's first alumna president, Virginia Gildersleeve, struck a by now familiar note in 1911: "Even if Greek and geology do not help a woman to cook a better meal—and I am not sure that they do not—this is no reason to condemn a college education. The ability to think straight, to weigh facts quickly and soundly" were just as "practically valuable to the woman who runs the household" and watched over children as to the man who passed "his days as a stock broker or lawyer."[51]

Imagine, then, the surprise when in 1924 Vassar opened its Department of Euthenics. No, it wasn't Greek for housekeeping, though it did come from that language's verb "to flourish." At the turn of the twentieth century, Ellen Richards defined euthenics as "the science of the controllable environment" a term she preferred to "home economics." Neither it nor another of her alternate suggestions, "oekology," caught on, the latter because it had already been claimed by the biological sciences as "ecology." Vassar's new president, Henry Noble MacCracken, viewed euthenics as a way to both placate conservative trustees and modernize the curriculum by linking "science and humanities, theory and practice, learning and life."[52] Women needed additional training to stay in step with industrial progress, MacCracken told the *New York Times.* "A woman who goes in for building a home can no longer do it with nothing but her four years of academic education. She must be trained for her job."[53] There was also a $550,000 gift from trustee Minnie Blodgett (class of 1884) and her husband (lumberman and philanthropist John Wood Blodgett) earmarked for a grand new Hall of Euthenics, completed in 1928. Not everyone at Vassar was pleased with the decision. "You are driving women back into the home, from the slavery of which education has helped us to escape," said psychology professor Margaret Washburn.[54] It nevertheless appeared to be the wave of the future.

The Woman-Oriented Curriculum

In a 1948 ad for Borden, Elsie the Cow and her husband, Elmer, got into a bit of a tiff. As she draped an oversize graduation gown on a lovely young heifer who gazed dreamily into the mirror, Elsie asked rhetorically, "Do college girls make better wives?" Given her husband's scowling face and the mortarboard-wearing baby bull on his lap, Elsie should have known the answer wasn't going to be in the affirmative:

> "No daughter of mine is going to any college—if that's what you're getting at!" snapped Elmer, the bull. . . ."*College is Okay for boys, . . . Beauregard is sure going to be a college man! But college for girls is a waste of money.* Gives 'em too many high-toned ideas. I say woman's place is in the home."
>
> "Oh, *that* old saw again!" sniffed Elsie. "Seriously, dear, don't studies like economics help a girl run her home better?"[55]

In the space of time it took to sell a gallon of milk, the two cartoon cows related the argument that women who were going to be homemakers didn't need the high-toned ideas a liberal education would give them, and conversely, that aspects of that same education benefited girls by making them more efficient housewives and better-informed mothers. Elsie went on to point out two more proeducation arguments: that the "specialized training" college provided might help a woman support her family in the unanticipated absence or unemployment of the traditional head of household, and that it helped a wife "keep *her husband* interested in *her*."

Elsie and Elmer's argument resolved only to the extent of agreeing that the way to a man's heart was through his stomach and lots of Borden dairy products, but throughout the mid-twentieth century the question of specialized training for women was highly discussed. "What shall we teach women?" asked Vassar anthropology professor Dorothy D. Lee in 1947. "Should we fill our colleges with courses on baby tending and dressmaking?" Lee advocated teaching women the liberal arts "with a difference." In

"Do college girls make better wives?"

ASKED ELSIE, THE BORDEN COW

"NO DAUGHTER of *mine* is going to any college — if that's what you're getting at!" snapped Elmer, the bull.

"For goodness' sake!" gasped Elsie, the Borden Cow. "What's wrong with college?"

"College is Okay for boys," answered Elmer. "Beauregard is sure going to be a college man! But college for girls is a waste of money. Gives 'em too many high-toned ideas. I say woman's place is in the home."

"Oh, *that* old saw again!" sniffed Elsie. "Seriously, dear, don't studies like economics help a girl run her home better?"

"You mean run her *husband* better!" corrected Elmer. "A girl can learn plenty of money economics shopping for her family — and all the cooking economics she needs to know from Borden's cook books!"

"How nice of you to remind me of Borden's!" beamed Elsie. "I wanted to tell everybody about the tasty and nutritious dishes they can make with *Borden's* Chateau.* It has a glorious, mellow-mild flavor that's grand in cheese sauces, soufflés, cheese omelets and Welsh rabbits."

"That's what comes of giving a woman a college education," groaned Elmer. "They get to know too much."

"But there's so much to know about Chateau!" protested Elsie. "It slices, it spreads, it melts! Children really love it, can't seem to get enough of it." ·

"Well I've had enough — and more—of this sales talk," frowned Elmer. "Let's get back to wives!"

"*All* wives," said Elsie, "love the speed and convenience of *Borden's Instant Coffee.* No pot, no mess. Just measure Borden's Instant Coffee into a cup, add boiling water, and you have the grandest coffee ever

got a husband on his feet of a morning."

"*Got a husband on his feet!*" mimicked Elmer. "I'll bet some college dame thought up that one."

"Then, you bet wrong!" laughed Elsie. "Seriously, dear, Borden's Instant Coffee is truly superb coffee, rich and full-bodied. It's 100% *pure* coffee, you know."

"Sometimes you get me so addled," moaned Elmer. "I don't know what I know."

 "But surely you know," teased Elsie, "that it's a wise thing for every girl to get some specialized training. It helps her earn a living — if she has to. And it helps her keep her husband interested in *her.*"

"NOW it comes out!" pounced Elmer. "A girl goes to college to learn how to hold her man!"

"No," said Elsie, "a girl goes to the *kitchen* and makes really *good* food with Borden products. There's no better way to hold a man!"

*T. M. Reg. U. S. Pat. Off.

— if it's *Borden's* it's g<u>ot</u> to be good!

MELTS LIKE A DREAM! Just try grilling Chateau topped with bacon strips on English muffin halves or toast. That mellow-mild Cheddar flavor is *irresistible!*

100% PURE COFFEE — nothing added! Borden's Instant Coffee is rich, full-bodied. It'll thrill your coffee-loving soul! Made in the time it takes to pour boiling water!

FIT FOR A GOLDEN SPOON! It's Lady Borden Ice Cream, and there's never, until now, been ice cream like it. Such richness, such creaminess, such flavor! *Taste it*, and see!

©The Borden Company

Elsie and Elmer debate the question. Borden, 1948.

addition to facts and theories pertinent to whatever discipline was being studied, courses would include content specific to women's role. Psychology, for example, should introduce female students "to the human situations with which women deal." Forget rats, mazes, or even putting a hapless freshman through her paces in double-blind studies. Instead, Ms. Lee argued, "we should also give her [the student] some idea of how a man will act in the confusion of living: celebrating in a night club, or when his car stalls in traffic, or when he loses his job, or when his son wins a prize."[56]

Like their antecedents at the turn of the century, proponents of the specifically "woman's curriculum" in the 1940s suggested that alumna of traditional liberal arts programs had to "unlearn" their college education in order to "find value in homemaking or selling or working in an office."[57] It wasn't so much that the liberal arts "failed" women, as was suggested, but that women needed a specialized program, one that would not merely deal in the generalities of child psychology, for example, but should "prepare the mother to cope with a tired four-year-old, and, in addition, to get meaning out of this" and further to "come out of this situation refreshed not cross and wilted."[58] It was the liberal arts focused through the prism of *kuche* and *kinder*, with an underlying assumption that housewife was the career that most women, if not aspired to, nonetheless found themselves in.

Arguments for and against a "functional" education for women made headlines in the 1940s and 1950s. The head of Mills College in Oakland, California, a man named Lynn White, Jr., called for a curriculum that would help a college graduate "foster the intellectual and emotional life of her family and community" by training her in interior design, child care, and "the theory and preparation of a Basque paella, a well-marinated shish kabob [and] lamb kidneys sautéed in sherry."[59]

Agree with him or not, but White was a bold thinker. He seriously suggested that a college class in flower arrangement might well represent a new height in Western civilization:

> Although many may jeer at the notion, when at last flower arrangement
> is admitted to our college curricula without reluctance we many know

In the early 1950s, home-economics students at Cornell learned how to properly use and maintain an iron.

that our higher education is beginning to overcome its ancient disregard for the values which confirm the home and to transcend its traditional male-mindedness.[60]

Color me jeering. Mills never switched to an entirely vocational curriculum. One school that wholeheartedly embraced the idea of the woman-oriented curriculum was Stephens College in Columbia, Missouri, which announced its new division of home and family living in 1942. Homemaking and motherhood were, for most women, "the equivalent of professional pursuits" said Stephens president James Madison Wood, and the home and family living division gave "new emphasis and prestige" to these studies. In addition to courses on marriage and the family, there were a bevy of classes related to child rearing: kindergarten and nursery school methods, children's literature, child psychology, fine and industrial art for young children, child health, child nutrition. There was also a class on household equipment.[61]

Eight years later, *Senior Prom* magazine got down to brass tacks about Stephens College. "What should a girl learn in college?" asked a pair of articles focusing on the school in September 1950. "The same things as a boy? Stephens said no." So, while "Susies" (as Stephens students were nicknamed) might take a course in commercial aviation ("yes in a *girls'* school!" squealed *Senior Prom*), the goal of all campus activities was "to develop the whole personality of the student."[62] Hence, its Personal Appearance Clinic ("Instruction is available in how to select and apply make-up, what to expect of a manicure, how to brush hair, etc.") and the marriage course: "Vague dreams about marriage sharpen into facts and reality as students discuss with the instructors such vital matters as choosing your husband, courtship and engagement, the wedding and honeymoon."[63]

Marriage was the "major occupation of women," *Senior Prom* noted, thus it should be studied as "objectively as television, journalism, or fashion design."[64] The course was a popular one, attended by almost 60 percent of second-year students.

At the time, Stephens was a two-year junior college that verged on a finishing school (students, for example, could bring their horses), whereas Barnard College in New York had a sterling academic pedigree as Columbia University's "coordinate" college for women.[65] But Barnard, too, felt the midcentury pressure to feminize its curriculum. "Modern Living" was a course for freshman girls in which they studied nutrition and family life. Seniors had the option of taking "The Family," a class on courtship, marriage, and careers. Barnard president Millicent McIntosh straddled the line between visions of the college-educated woman as "kitchen mechanic" or overeducated bookworm. Girls didn't need courses in "baby-tending" to prepare them for moth-

"They want cake, but can they bake it?" Quick, 1952.

erhood, McIntosh noted, and she stressed a need for an educational philosophy that didn't "belittle the home as a place unworthy of [a woman's] best, and does not glorify the 'job' as important beyond everything else"—words that will resonate with almost every twenty-first-century woman who tries to balance career and motherhood.[66]

McIntosh was quoted in the poignantly titled "College Girls: If They Could Only Cook," an article that appeared in a 1952 newsweekly. "What," the article asked, "are American college girls—three-fourths of them slated for marriage—learning about the switch from campus to kitchen?" Once again, it seemed that the textbook had trumped the cookbook. "Modern" theories which held that "girls should study what boys study; that a college's main aim was to turn out 'thinking citizens'; and that the road for both sexes leads through classic poetry, medieval history and advanced botany" turned out too many women who didn't "want to cook, or sew, or care for their children, if they can help it." Girls

College Girl Bookshelf:
"Waverly" (1963), by
Amelia Elizabeth Walden

 Jane Townsend is a teenage tomboy from the Midwest. She fixes cars, rides horses, and dates boy next-door Bobby Phillips, with whom she has a long-standing pact to study law at State University before going into practice together. Her father has other plans, however; he thinks motherless Jane needs the "softening influence of a woman's school." And so he sends her off to Waverly, a famous women's college in the east, where Jane fears the curriculum consists of "how to pour tea and speak a little French or Spanish . . . and wear fussy clothes and go to dances where you flirted with boys you didn't care anything about." *

Her first view of her dormitory room isn't encouraging. From curtains to bedspreads and desk blotters, it's done entirely in pink—a color Jane detests (of course). Indeed, her acceptance of the color is a metaphor for becoming a woman, but it's not an easy evolution. Consider her forced makeover at the hands of her dorm mates:

> She pulled at Jane's sweater, trying to get it over her head. Jane struggled but Kathie came to Ann's assistance. Together they yanked it off. A tug on the zipper and Jane's skirt was on the floor.
> "Let go of me!" she shouted. But Kathie held her arms over her

---

* Amelia Elizabeth Walden, *Waverly* (1947; reprint, New York: Berkley Highland Books, 1963), 7.

head while Ann slipped the dress over it. For moment they were all arms and pink velvet. Then the dress was over her head and billowing to the floor.†

When Kathie accuses Jane of being "afraid to look and act and feel like a woman," there's almost no reason to finish reading the book.‡ We know spirited Jane will prove her wrong, and that for a moment nobody will recognize the tomboy turned lady when she gets home for summer vacation.

† Ibid., 104.

‡ Ibid., 127.

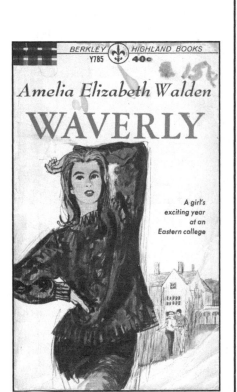

BERKLEY HIGHLAND BOOKS
Y785 40¢

Amelia Elizabeth Walden

WAVERLY

A girl's exciting year at an Eastern college

Tomboys learned how to be ladies at Waverly (1963).

who studied the liberal arts might make brilliant career women, but they averaged "less than two children. Statistically, a high proportion seem likely to have broken marriages and nervous breakdowns."[67]

Bancroft Beatley was the head of Simmons College, a Boston-based institute of higher learning which at midcentury prided itself on its dedication to women's vocational education. He, too, sketched a dark future for the traditional liberal arts student. Female graduates of such programs might be interesting, well-read people with discriminating tastes in art and music, he acknowledged, but "unless these women also have made satisfactory adjustments to home and family life . . . unless they are making their lives count in some way for the common good, they will not be happy people."[68]

Few commented on the lack of opportunity for women in the professions, inequities in compensation and promotion, the lack of affordable child care, or the necessity of a husband who pitched in with household chores. More common was the belief that it was "unrealistic to expect most men, fully engaged in other occupations, to carry the main burden of work and child rearing in the home," as a pro-women's curriculum educator noted in 1955.[69]

"The one lesson a girl could hardly avoid learning, if she went to college between 1945 and 1960, was *not* to get interested . . . in anything besides getting married and having children, if she wanted to be normal, happy, adjusted, feminine, have a successful husband, successful children, and a normal, feminine, adjusted successful sex life," wrote Betty Friedan (Smith '42) in *The Feminine Mystique* (1963).[70] Friedan castigated the "sex-directed curriculum" of colleges more concerned with training students for married life than for the life of the mind. Friedan did research at her alma mater and other women's colleges in the 1950s and was shocked by what she saw as the complacency of students who knitted their way through classes, their handiwork symbolic of the domestic futures Friedan believed they'd already mapped out. (This had already been noticed by French writer Simone de Beauvoir. In *America Day by Day* [1953], she described women's college students "dressed like boys, painted like street-walkers" knitting through classes in what she attributed to "an anticipation of marriage and maternity.")[71]

Friedan thought the "feminine mystique" was promulgated by students who compared engagement rings and sweater patterns more frequently than class notes and career plans, and by professors who didn't challenge the assumption that the curriculum needed to be feminized. Long before girls reached campus, they encountered the mystique in magazines and prescriptive literature aimed at teenage girls and adult women, in articles and stories that told readers to value social relationships over study, and to hide their intelligence lest boys find them competitive, bossy, and unattractive.

Nobody Likes a Grind

The teen magazines urged readers to act like regular girls, not intellectual harpies. In 1958, a girl named Dinah wrote to a teen advice columnist with what was then the non-titter-provoking name of Gay Head. Dinah's problem? She was a conscientious student whose friends resented it "when I want to study instead of being with them." Dinah considered studying important; how could she explain this to them? "Studying *is* a big job and you want to be sure that it's a job well done," replied Miss Head. "But if you really do the job right, you won't let it become a full-time occupation. Take out enough time to bone up on an extracurricular assignment—learning how to keep friends."[72]

Keeping friends was important, especially for girls, because it implied popularity and the concomitant eager-to-please disposition that was associated with femininity. Loners who studied too hard found themselves the subject of epithets like brain box, book bug, or book beater, to name a choice few from the mid-twentieth century.[73]

Perhaps the most familiar of the many less-than-complimentary names for students who ignored social activities in favor of their studies is also one of the oldest: "grind." *A Collection of College Words and Customs*, published in 1856, noted that "students speak of a very long lesson which they are required to learn . . . as a *grind*."[74] It followed that "grinding" was hard study, and eventually "grind" became a derisive term for students who spent too much time with their books.

According to one of the coeds interviewed in Sex and the College Girl (1964), "you could judge how good a girl's sex life was by how much knitting she got done each semester. 'It took me two years to finish this sweater,'" she proudly told author Gael Green. College Knits pattern book, 1958.

For the most part, grinds were not well regarded by their fellow students. A 1905 survey of "the American College Girl" explained the type to readers: "The 'grind' is not popular among the girls of any college set, and since like seeks like, her friends are ordinarily "grinds" like herself,—creatures apart from any set. . . . A 'grind' is not very interesting socially, and she generally is let alone."[75]

The poor grind! Students didn't like her, and sometimes neither did the faculty. At the turn of the century, the founder of the Woman's College of Baltimore believed that "the truest womanliness is not attained by the 'grind.' " To avoid this fate, he vowed to train his students "as much . . . in social ease and grace as in profounder things."[76]

Grinds didn't get more popular over time. According to the authors of a 1952 study of college graduates, the very word called up "an immediate mental picture" of:

> a girl with flat shoes, horn-rimmed glasses, and a shiny nose which she keeps buried in Shakespeare, Schopenhauer, and Shelley; a girl who is not interested in dancing, sports, or small talk; a girl who has the musty air of the library instead of a drop of perfume behind her ears. To date her or court her would be just like having to stay after school, and therefore unthinkable. Obviously, while her former classmates traipse off one by one to be fitted for their wedding gowns, she will be sitting at home reading a good book.[77]

No book, they seemed to say, could possibly be *that* good. The key, then, was to balance schoolwork and social life lest all work and no play make Jane a spinster. A 1948 article describing various ways by which girls could put themselves through college told of Vera, a Vassar senior who majored in astronomy. A top-notch student, she earned scholarships and cash working in Vassar's astronomy lab and doing astronomical research at a navy lab. "Is Vera a 'greasy grind' with no interest but science?" asked the author rhetorically.[78] The answer was an emphatic no. Vera understood the ins and outs of popularity and the necessity of balancing her intellectually rigorous (and potentially man-threatening) work with down-to-earth extracurricular activities such as singing in the choir, reporting on the school newspaper, and taking classes in music and philosophy. Vera's diligence paid off: she not only worked her way through her college but, the article stressed, met her husband-to-be along the way.

With a little attention to detail, a girl could divest herself from the "greasy grind" stigma. In 1960, *Teen World* magazine gave the example of Patricia, a very bright high-schooler who hated her role as a brain. Luckily for her, she was not only gifted academically but socially as well. Thus, when a fellow member of her science class asked her the words to a popular song, Pat was "only too happy to oblige" with an open display of popular culture knowledge:

> She began singing to her friend in a low voice, and suddenly realized that the teacher and class were all turned her way, listening.
>
> "Now, Miss R., if you've finished," the instructor said, amused, "we'll go on with the experiment."[79]

While the embarrassment may have stung a bit, Patricia's social experiment was a grand success: both class and teacher realized that at heart she was a regular Jill, her brain big enough for both algorithms and rhythm 'n' blues. Readers learned that it was possible to be both smart and popular—though the emphasis always tipped toward popularity.

Lesson 1: Never Flaunt Your Learning

"Brains Are for the Birds!" (1957) was the eye-grabbing title of a story that appeared in *Redbook* magazine. Twenty-one-year-old Kathy Adams is a stenographer at an advertising agency who yearns for intellectual integrity. "I'm tired of being known as a—a fluff ball with legs!" she declares. Unfortunately, she is more bombshell than egghead—in the illustration accompanying the story, she resembles Marilyn Monroe. In a misguided attempt at self-improvement, she dumps her current office beau (the broad-shouldered, blue-eyed Johnny Egan) for the Jason

Agency's resident horn-rimmed-glasses-wearing intellectual, David Keller, by faking an interest in his work. She is disappointed, however, when, instead of discussing advertising techniques, he asks her to be the model for *Servisheer* hose—one of his accounts. "I could make Mister David Keller notice my legs without even intending to, because I was using natural ammunition. But when it came to making him notice me for an intelligent female, I was just shooting at him with an empty gun!" she despairs in an interesting choice of phallic metaphor. But when Keller calls her "a little bird-brain," Kathy realizes her fling with intellectualism is over. "I'm just a d-dumb bunny, and I was trying to be intelligent!" she sobs to Johnny Egan, who is conveniently available to pick up the pieces. He holds her tight and says "Don't worry, . . . when we're married, you can go to night school. Every night. I'll be the teacher."[80]

At the end of the story, Kathy's happily married to Johnny and "majoring in biology"—wink, wink. The moral of the story? Women shouldn't try to rise above their station, and men don't want their wives to be intellectuals.

"Brains Are for the Birds!" may have been a fluffy little story not meant to be taken seriously, but it was another reflection of cultural ideals surrounding female intelligence (not to mention working women). Teen girls and adult women were constantly reminded that men wouldn't date or marry women who appeared to be smarter than they were. Four years before the story appeared, *Redbook* pointed to a series of "leading soci-

Don't bore your boyfriend with books! Dura-Gloss Nail-Polish, circa 1940s.

ological studies" which showed that most men wanted a woman who was "appreciably less intelligent than *they* were":

> [O]n the whole, men are attracted to women to whom they can feel intellectually superior. They tend to marry girls whose I.Q. and educational attainments are less than their own. Indeed, investigations show that the average male has a very marked tendency to shy away from girls whom he suspects of having as many or more brains than he has.[81]

The article went on to state that college men were less frightened of brainy women than their working-class brethren, though it appeared they were pickier in other respects. According to a poll of male students at "two leading Eastern universities . . . the ideal wife is 5 feet 5 inches, weighs about 120 pounds, does not wear glasses, possesses sex appeal and a good figure," and was herself a college graduate. More telling, perhaps, was another desirable wifely characteristic mentioned by the college men: they agreed that the woman they married "must not have too dominating a personality."[82]

The assumption that dominating, intellectual women didn't make good wives hadn't changed much, if at all, from the previous century. "How many conquests does the blue-stocking make through her extensive knowledge of history? What man ever fell in love with a woman because she understood Italian?" demanded social theorist Herbert Spencer in the nineteenth century.[83] Spencer probably didn't trifle with popular fiction, but a similar message underlay an 1865 story in *The Living Age*. Handsome Roger Hamley is invited to dinner at the Gibsons, where his host expounds upon "a paper on comparative osteology in some foreign journal of science." Bored by this mealtime lecture, young Cynthia Gibson looks up from rolling bread pellets to meet Roger's admiring gaze. She admits she isn't paying attention: "[Y]ou see, I don't know even the A B C of science. But, please don't look so severely at me, even if I am a dunce!" she tells him coquettishly. When her mother berates Cynthia for hiding her education under a bushel by talking "such nonsense," her bookish sister Molly woefully acknowledges that she, too, would "rather be a dunce than a blue-stocking."[84]

While it mortifies her mother, Cynthia's behavior is just what twentieth-century advice writers and others advised young women near or at college age: that catching a man meant hiding one's intellect— at least to the extent of not upstaging their dates. Alice-Leone Moats didn't mention college as an option in her etiquette guide for would-be debutantes, *No Nice Girl Swears* (1933). After all, the debut tradition- ally marked a young woman's entrance into the marriage market, where a college education was a hindrance, not a help. Therefore, Moats's suggested method of making conversation at cotillion dinners centered on looking "vastly interested and amused at everything" said by one's male neighbors at the table. "She needn't make an effort to appear bril- liant—brains are a handicap to a debutante." Those "erudites" who insisted on discussing "Hindu philosophy or Greek sculpture" at dinner would find themselves ignored on the dance floor in favor of "a belle who, if she has ever heard of Phidias, has the sense to keep it in the dark."[85] (For belles in the dark, Phidias, circa 430–460 BC, was a Greek sculptor and architect, one of the artists responsible for the Parthenon.)

Nor was Moats the only advice writer who counseled hiding one's intellectual light under a bushel. In *Love at the Threshold* (1952), a guidebook aimed at young adults, author Frances Strain railed against what she termed the "highbrow" girl: "The *highbrow* girl has brains. She knows all the answers and knows them first. She can take a job, any job, and keep it. She can earn more money than her boyfriend. In a contest she always wins. But her friends sometimes say of her, 'She's so smart, I hate her!' " Outperforming boyfriends at both work and play defied accepted standards of feminine complacency and noncompetitiveness, and threatened both friends and would-be suitors.

Instead of pride in their academic accomplishments, young women were urged to hide them away—literally. A Phi Beta Kappa key, that sym- bol of high academic standing, branded a woman as an intellectual as quickly and even more precisely than a pair of horn-rimmed glasses. Gals on the prowl were advised to ditch the offending bibelot in the nearest trinket box. "It takes discipline to hide a Phi Beta Kappa key and wear instead a piece of swank costume jewelry," sympathized Frances Strain, "but it pays if a girl is matrimony bound."[86] Literary critic Diana Trilling argued against the "woman-oriented" curriculum a year later, but she noted "that obsessive problem of educated women: how to behave intellectually. Shall they be passive or aggressive? Shall they flaunt their Phi Beta Kappa keys or make them into slave bracelets?"[87] The cartoon drawing that accompanied Trilling's essay in a 1953 anthology titled *Women Today: Their Conflicts, Their Frustrations, and Their Fulfillments* showed a mortarboarded mom bent over a changing table, while her baby happily gummed her PBK key.

According to Strain, the solution to this social contretemps was as easy as masking one's outsized brain with a clever little hat: "If girls are highbrow, they must keep it pretty dark. It's a potential sin, and if it is acute, to expose it is sure to make men take to their heels. The highbrow girl must cultivate the simple life, fun, sports, dress, new hats, love-making, to give her balance and make her an all-around woman."[88]

A practical use for a Phi Beta Kappa key, 1953.

The "all-around woman" was not so bright as to outshine her mate, nor was she so dull as to bore him at home or embarrass him in public. Finding the balance, however, was a tricky proposition at best. The girls who made up the core audience for *Teens Today* magazine learned, if not how to walk this tightrope, then at least of its existence from a pair of articles in the September 1959 issue. In "College Boys Agree: We Date to Love and Learn," real life university students (or so the editors said) gave their opinions on perfect dates. Pete explained the difference between smart and too smart:

> "I didn't think boys really liked girls with big brains," the interviewer said quietly.

Pete considered then shook his head. "That's not so; what you mean is that guys don't go for girls who sound like walking Britannicas. See, what I'm saying is we want a girl who's able to think; a doll who's curious about all kinds of things . . . politics, the theory of economics, Freud; everything and anything, that's my whole point. A guy starts thinking about all kinds of new things when he's in college and he wants to talk about them."[89]

Did he really? The evocatively titled "I'm Sick of Acting Like a Moron!," which appeared in the same issue, suggested otherwise. After a series of frustrating dates with her domineering boyfriend Cal, Marilyn discovers that "smart enough" was all men wanted in a woman:

Well, so finally I learned: Pretend that all I knew about were the "approved" things. That included sewing, knitting, tatting, crocheting . . . English grammar and English lit., history, sociology, school gossip, dancing and the weather. Not approved were, all sports except badminton, politics (local, national and international), automobiles, airplanes, atomic energy . . . economics (the theory of), Wall Street, labor unions, management, strikes, depressions, recessions, inflation—and anything that gave the impression I might be *thinking*. Heavy thinking, you know?[90]

Acceptable or not, Marilyn then does some heavy thinking of her own and concludes "it's a lie" when boys say they want a girl with "sense" (a synonym for nonthreatening levels of intelligence). It isn't "just the Big Brain they hate; it's also the Equal Brain!"[91]

In one last display of her big brain, however, Marilyn helps Cal with an unfamiliar word:

"Say, what are you, one of those—femi—femi—"
"Feminists," I filled him in icily.[92]

Marilyn declines to define herself as such, but one can always hope that readers rushed off to the dictionary for a look-see; the word "feminist" did not appear with any sort of frequency in teen-girl magazines in 1959.

Women's Rights to Women's Studies

It had not been a popular subject a hundred years earlier either. There were worries almost from the start that college would be an incubator for "women's rights women," i.e., followers of the woman suffrage movement that simmered throughout the second half of the nineteenth century and came to a full, rolling boil in the early years of the twentieth. The supporters of women's education and founders of women's colleges were not by and large supporters of women's political rights. Neither were the great majority of nineteenth-century college girls. Indeed, the women's rights woman was the antithesis of the Christian gentlewoman the colleges hoped to mold.

However, a link between women's rights and higher education was forged at the Seneca Falls Convention in 1848, when Elizabeth Cady Stanton and Lucretia Mott included the lack of access to higher education as one of Woman's grievances against Man in the Declaration of Sentiments: "He has denied her the facilities for obtaining a thorough education, all colleges being closed against her."[93]

College itself could be a radicalizing experience. For example, it was only after Antioch officially put the blame on women's rights agitators for the mourners' demonstration at its first commencement that campus suffrage activity began in earnest, according to academics John Rury and Glenn Harper. In the 1860s, a woman student was prevented from speaking at commencement because she wore a Bloomer suit and refused to change into a dress. During the following decade, one of the literary societies invited speakers advocating women's rights to the campus.[94] The fictional heroine of *An American Girl and Her Four Years in a Boys' College* (1878) also discovers women's rights at college. Will becomes "one of the earliest converts" to woman suffrage when movement leaders make her university

The Anti-Suffrage Argument

From our privileged place in history, one has to wonder—what was the rationale against giving women the right to vote? In 1898, suffragist Frances M. Abbott (Vassar 1881) summed up the opposition's arguments: "[T]hat it would be useless, expensive, detrimental to the best interests of women, inimical to marriage and otherwise destructive to the home; that women do not want it, that they are not mentally fitted for it, that it would impose upon them greater physical burdens than they could endure, that the polls are not fit places for women, that the female sex cannot perform military duty, that women are sufficiently represented as it is, that the ballot would brush the bloom of delicacy from the female temperament, that it would be subversive of the best interests of the Republic, that it is against nature. . . . that many of the foremost advocates of the cause are not beautiful, that they are careless in dress, that they are old maids, that they are not church members, that they do not eat ice-cream with forks, that they are cranks, and, generally speaking, poor, unfashionable and unpopular."*

* Frances M. Abbott, "A Comparative View of the Women Suffrage Movement," *North American Review*, February 1898, 142–3.

town a basis of operations. For a required sophomore debate, she chooses the question "Shall the ballot be given to women?" "Plenty of boys were willing to take the negative," but Will has a hard time finding someone to assist her with the affirmative, many of the coeds being "bitterly opposed" to the idea. She finally finds a sporting male to take the affirmative with her, but of course it is Will's earnest eloquence that carries the day.[95]

Maud Wood Park was one of two students (out of almost seventy) who wrote in favor of woman suffrage for a class assignment at Radcliffe in 1895. After a disappointing visit to a national suffrage convention in Washington, D.C., dominated by middle-aged and older women (one of whom presented her state's report in rhyme), Park founded the College Equal Suffrage League in 1900 for the express purpose of attracting younger educated women to the cause.[96] In 1908, it became the National College Equal Suffrage League with Bryn Mawr president M. Carey Thomas at its head and Park as vice president. Between 1908 and 1917, when it disbanded, the league brought the debate to college campuses, via chapters comprising students, faculty, and governing boards. Its members marched in parades wearing banners emblazoned with the names of their colleges, and took part in other demonstrations.[97]

Not all observers welcomed these developments. When Vassar's President Taylor forbade a suffragist from speaking on campus in 1908, a charismatic junior named Inez Milholland persuaded forty students to attend the rescheduled meeting outside college grounds (legend has it at a cemetery).[98] Barnard founder Annie Nathan Meyer assured the *New York Times* in 1910 that rumors of suffragism on campus were greatly exaggerated and that the graduating seniors had in fact "formally voted against woman suffrage on class day."[99] The *Times* flatly blamed outside agitators for "trying to butt in . . . with their disturbing suffrage propaganda" in an editorial a week after Meyer's letter: "The organization of suffrage clubs in the women's colleges is not spontaneous, the idea of it is hardly tolerated by the majority in the undergraduate bodies."[100] Also in 1910, the Massachusetts Association Opposed to the Further Extension of Suffrage to Women sponsored a college essay contest with the subject "The Case Against Woman Suffrage."[101]

College *was* a hotbed of suffrage activism, asserted "E. K. R." in a 1911 letter to the *New York Times*. A daughter just returned from "one of the prominent colleges" told him "without doubt most girls come out of college suffragettes." He vowed that none of his three remaining daughters would follow in her footsteps:

In early 1917, suffragists picketed Woodrow Wilson's White House. February 1 was college day in the picket line.

It seems to me too bad that our girls should have their poor little heads filled up with this nonsense, thereby constantly increasing the already large army of spinster ladies in the United States of America; for what young man, except one of those long-haired poltroons [i.e., effeminate cowards], would marry a girl who is both a college graduate and a suffragette?[102]

A girl may have discovered the cause of suffrage while at college, but it wasn't anything she was being taught in class. While the fight for suffrage was taking place, and until long after women were granted the vote in 1920, college girls studied the canon of what a later generation would call the "dead white males" of literature and other disciplines (though at that time, of course, some of them were still alive). The study of women's history or feminist psychology was a completely alien idea. The lens of gender as we think of it in the twenty-first century simply did not yet exist.

Even so, as Barbara Miller Solomon points out, courses in home economics or the social sciences "in the hands of imaginative professors" foreshadowed the field of women's studies. At the University of Kansas, a male professor taught a sociology class on "The Status of Women" to female graduate students in 1892. In the first decades of the twentieth century, women taught classes on "The Legal and Economic Position of Women" (University of Chicago) and "Women in Business and Industry" and "Vocational Opportunities for Women in the Pacific Northwest" (University of Washington). At Wellesley, a class on consumerism used Charlotte Perkins Gilman's feminist *Women and Economics*, while Goucher had a course on the history of the women's rights movement.[103]

Other than these rare classes (and rare teachers), there was no organized study of women's ideas or problems. What's more, once the vote had been attained, it seemed most American women slid into apathy when it came to feminist causes. Nevertheless, a brave few soldiered on. In the mid-1930s, historian and textbook writer Mary Ritter Beard established the World Center for Women's Archives and worked to "put women in the record" of history. Several months after the center was incorporated in February 1936, she explained to the graduating class of the New Jersey College for Women why it was important to reclaim women's place:

> What is called equal education is in fact but co-education in men's minds and manners, and in men's politics, men's wars, men's business adventures, men's books, men's theories and practices. The assumption is that women have no history of their own worth much recognition, if any; that women have no ideas pertaining to their social role; that they have no interpretations of history to offer, and that they derive their notions of the proprieties from men.[104]

Sponsored by First Lady Eleanor Roosevelt and suffrage leader Carrie Chapman Catt, among others, the World Center for Women's Archives sought to right these assumptions by preserving documents of women's history and making them available for use by scholars and the public. The collection was richly varied, including maps, charts, and records belonging to Amelia Earhart, forty-four bound volumes of *The Woman's Journal* (an early suffrage publication), and the papers of organizations such as the National Council of Jewish Women and the National Association of Women's Lawyers. But lack of funds and gathering war clouds caused the archives to disband at the end of 1940, its materials sent to other repositories.[105]

The woman-oriented curriculum grabbed headlines in the 1940s and 1950s and made feminism seem quaint and outmoded. "Today there is no time for feminism," claimed Mrs. Chase Going Woodhouse, the director of the Institute for Women's Professional Relations, in a 1940 speech at a home-economics convention. Women had "passed that stage," though she also noted that women in the professions had lost ground during the past decade. Eight years later, in a speech to business and professional women, the dean of women at Syracuse University proclaimed feminism "outdated." Her argument that women had "developed a martyr complex for ourselves that . . . not only perpetuates discriminations, but makes for the creating of new ones" would find support among today's antifeminists.[106]

When professor Gerda Lerner offered to teach a course in women's history at New York City's New School in 1963, it didn't attract the minimum number of students—ten—required for the course to be given. Yet only seven years later, *Newsweek* pronounced women's studies "one of the hottest new wrinkles in higher education."[107]

Obviously, a lot happened in the interim. Feminism was once again in the public mind thanks to the publication of *The Feminine Mystique* in 1963 and the foundation of the National Organization of Women (NOW) in 1966. By the end of the decade, America's campuses were in a state of ferment. White and black students who spent the early '60s taking part in voter-registration drives and freedom rides organized by the Student Non-Violent Coordinating Committee (SNCC) and other civil rights groups brought ideals of racial equality and civil disobedience back to campus with them. Some joined up with radical "New Left" student groups like the Students for a Democratic Society (SDS). Many people took part in the frequent and sometimes violent campus demonstrations against the war in Vietnam. From their experiences in both the Civil Rights and student movements, women learned how to work collectively for social change. But they also encountered sexism, most famously exemplified by Stokely Carmichael's pronouncement in 1964 that "the only position for women in SNCC is prone."[108] A statement on women's liberation met with derision and catcalls from male members when it was read from the podium at the SDS convention in 1967.

As part of the protest movement, students held teach-ins and "free university" classes on racism and black history in addition to those on pacifism and conscientious objection, and at the Free University of Seattle in 1966, a course on women's history.[109] From these roots grew the demand for including in the traditional curriculum such interdisciplinary courses as, first, black studies (at Vassar in 1969, thirty-five African-American students demanding a degree-granting program in black studies held a sit-in that blocked the administration building for several days), and, finally, women's studies.

Also in the 1969–1970 time frame, the Modern Language Association set up a Commission on the Status of Women. A survey was undertaken by commission chair Florence Howe, who with the help of two graduate students asked five thousand English and modern language departments about their employment opportunities for women. The results, Howe later recalled, were "gloomy": while 55 percent of graduate students in 1970 were female, only one out of nine or ten of their teachers were; fewer women than men taught at prestigious institutions; women earned lower salaries, were less frequently tenured, and were more likely to teach lower-level courses. "In short," Howe summarized, "women are at the bottom of our profession in rank, salary, prestige, or all three." Among other things, Howe called on the membership of the MLA to "work to change the study of literature so that it does not continue the sex-role stereotyping of its tradition" and to stop ignoring women writers in favor of "a male-dominated curriculum and a male-centered criticism."[110] A gauntlet had been thrown down to academics.

San Diego State College (now University) offered the first woman's studies program in 1970. A statement of purpose declared it "an attempt to repair the damage done to women by the omissions and distortions of traditional education and to illustrate at least one way of releasing the power and potential of more than half the population of this country." But the new discipline had its detractors. "The idea is slightly absurd.

Why don't you stop these attempts at fragmentizing higher education and devote yourself to real scholarship?" was the reply from an engineering professor at Cornell University in response to a questionnaire about the school's new program in women's studies, which opened shortly after the one in San Diego. Another answer to the questionnaire proclaimed that "Black studies is divisive enough. Female studies would inevitably be aimed towards political goals, which I am far from sharing."[111] Even today, women's studies is attacked by academics for its "unfocused" interdisciplinary nature, and mocked by antifeminists for the touchy-feely nature of "consciousness raising" and for what they consider its fractious identity politics. (The discipline could be confrontational, as when women of color challenged white feminists to stop assuming they spoke for all women and to start thinking in terms of "feminisms.")

Although it remains a favorite whipping post for antifeminists (a 2002 report issued by the conservative Independent Women's Forum excoriated the entire discipline for not only the purported "errors of interpretation" and "sins of omission" found in five textbooks, but for "serious errors of taste" regarding their choice of illustrations), women's studies remains a popular choice on college campuses. Perhaps its introductory courses in particular help young women find a sense of identity and self-esteem at a time in life when they need it the most. Historian Marilyn Boxer traced an exponential growth in women's studies: "The 150 programs counted in 1975 had doubled by 1980, reached 450 at mid-decade, and exceeded 600 by the early 1990s."[112]

As evidenced by the controversy women's studies engenders all these years later, the question of how to educate women has not yet been definitively answered. In the early 1990s, Ursuline College, a small, Catholic, mostly women's school in Ohio, announced a newly revamped curriculum tailored to "the different way women learn." The college based its new teaching style on research by psychologist Carol Gilligan and others that suggested women learned better in small, cooperative, nonconfrontational groups, linking academic course work with personal experience. Students testified to the efficacy of Ursuline's core program in making them feel empowered: "Coming here has enabled me to be my own person—able to say what I felt instead of what everyone else wants me to say," recounted a first-year student.[113]

But academics and others questioned whether this was "feminism doing the work of sexism," in the words of Judith Shapiro, then provost at Bryn Mawr. Was suggesting that women thought differently from men merely reinforcing existing stereotypes of female behavior? Feminist journalist Susan Faludi called it "a self-fulfilling prophecy": "Saying that we're more maternal and caring and cooperative and contextual just reinforces that behavior." But when asked by a journalist what Ursuline College graduates gained from the program, Sister Rosemarie Carfagna simply replied, "Moxie."[114]

Two members of the New York University Women's
Fencing Team practice for the Intercollegiate Women's
Fencing Championships in 1933.

Fit in Mind and Body

And so Miss G—— died, not because she had mastered the wasps of Aristophanes . . . not because she made the acquaintance of Kant . . . , and ventured to explore the anatomy of flowers and the secrets of chemistry, but because, while pursuing these studies, while doing all this work, she steadily ignored her woman's make. Believing that woman can do what man can, for she held that faith, she strove with noble but ignorant bravery to compass man's intellectual attainment in a man's way, and died in the effort.

EDWARD H. CLARKE, M.D.,
SEX IN EDUCATION, OR, A FAIR CHANCE FOR THE GIRLS (1873)

One long-standing argument against the education of women had to do with the supposed "delicacy" of their constitutions. Unlike her brother, the girl child required special treatment, without which she was subject to dire physical consequences. In the mid-nineteenth century, a properly raised daughter was

guarded from over fatigue, subject to restrictions with regard to cold, and heat, and hours of study, seldom trusted away from home, allowed only a small share of responsibility;—not willingly, with any wish to thwart her inclinations—but simply because, if she is not thus guarded, if she is allowed to run the risks, which, to the boy, are a matter of indifference,

she will probably develop some disease, which, if not fatal, will, at any
rate, be an injury to her for life . . .[1]

A girl was particularly susceptible to such life- or fertility-threatening
injuries because of the nature of her reproductive system in particular
and the way in which nineteenth-century medicine viewed the human
body in general. According to contemporary wisdom, menstruation was
particularly stressful on the female body. Mental stimulation—studying,
for example—during the menstrual period drew a woman's bodily energies away from her uterus with what many medical writers assured readers were dreadful and long-lasting consequences. The danger was
especially great during puberty, when a girl's system hadn't yet grown
accustomed to the monthly flow. The weeks and months prior to menarche, and thereafter until regular menstruation was established, were of
particular importance. Unless the development of the female reproductive system was accomplished during puberty, it was "never perfectly
accomplished afterwards."[2] Healthful menstruation was important to a
girl's future "happiness in marriage, easy child-beds, and the constitution
of children." Neglecting menstrual health therefore violated "a duty owed
to others as well as herself." Not coincidentally, this crucial developmen-
tal phase (roughly from age twelve though twenty, according to
nineteenth-century medical men) overlapped the time young women
were most likely to enter college.[3]

Education also caused health problems in younger girls, even those
who never went on to college. George Napheys, M.D. (1842–1876), a
popular medical writer whose The Physical Life of Woman went into
many editions after its 1869 debut, marked boarding-school life as one
of the "fertile sources" of menstrual disturbances in adolescent girls.
No one rated the education of the mind higher than himself, he told
readers, but he did not "hesitate a moment to urge that if perturba-
tions of the [menstrual] functions become at all marked in a girl at
school, she should be taken away." It was better for her to live in idle-
ness for a year than to "become a dead-weight, through constant ill-
health, on her husband in after life."[4] "Overwork at school" was also a

cause of chlorosis, popularly known as "green sickness," a generalized anemic condition involving lethargy, lack of appetite, vague pains, bad temper, and "depraved tastes—such as a desire to eat slate-pencil dust, chalk or clay," as well as its titular symptom, a greenish tinge to the complexion.[5]

The "Sex in Education" Controversy

The link between education and female ill health was widespread in popular medical literature, but the book that brought the argument to the forefront of American discourse was Dr. Edward H. Clarke's *Sex in Education, or, A Fair Chance for the Girls* (1873). Clarke was a retired Harvard medical professor who, he emphasized, was not against the education of girls, merely against educating them in the same manner as boys, whether at coeducational campuses or at woman's colleges.

A "fair chance" in education for girls meant observing the laws of "periodicity": every four weeks, between the ages of fourteen and eighteen (perhaps even until the age of twenty-five), girls needed to take a break, in part or in whole, from both study and exercise, thus giving "Nature an opportunity to accomplish her special periodical task." This monthly diminution or cessation of study was a "physiological necessity for all, however robust" their appearance.[6] Girls who ignored their reproductive organs in favor of study "graduated from school or college excellent scholars, but with undeveloped ovaries. Later they married, and were sterile" or suffered from a variety of ailments, including "neuralgia, uterine disease, hysteria and other derangements of the nervous system."[7]

Of all the arguments Clarke made in *Sex in Education*, perhaps the most damaging by virtue of its sheer staying power was that study made women masculine. The "arrested development" of the reproductive system that resulted from study during the menses led to a corresponding change in intellect and psyche, "a dropping out of maternal instincts, and an appearance of Amazonian coarseness." Clarke's assessment of these masculinized women was as brutal as it was blunt: they were "analogous to the sexless class of termites" or "the eunuchs of Oriental civilization."[8]

Clarke devoted an entire chapter to horror stories of top students whose health collapsed from the combination of overstudy and uterine neglect. Miss D—— attended Vassar from the age of fourteen, and "studied, recited, stood at the blackboard, walked, and went through her gymnastic exercises, from the beginning to the end of the term, just as boys do." One day, she fainted while exercising. This happened again and again, until she was compelled to "renounce" physical education altogether. During her junior year, she began to suffer monthly pain and a lessening "excretion" of menstrual blood. Friends and faculty suspected nothing from her apparently healthy appearance. She graduated "with fair honors and a poor physique," and began an inexorable slide into "steadily-advancing invalidism." Clarke diagnosed "an arrest of the development of the reproductive apparatus," confirmed by his examination of Miss D——'s bosom, "where the milliner had supplied the organs Nature should have grown."[9] (Imagine how this particular slander would have played a century or so later, when America's bosom fixation was firmly in place. Tying collegiate education to A-cup status would have drained the campuses of all but the most resigned academic martyrs.)

Miss E—— was the daughter of a well-known scholar and "one of our most accomplished American women." She, too, "studied, recited, walked, worked, stood . . . in the steady and sustained way" of male students. She seemed healthy until, "without any apparent cause," she ceased menstruating. An "inveterate acne" appeared, followed by "vagaries and forebodings and despondent feelings," insomnia, and loss of appetite. "Appropriate treatment faithfully persevered in was unsuccessful in recovering the lost function," and Clarke was "finally obliged to consign her to an asylum."[10]

Perhaps most disturbing was the example of Miss G——, who graduated at the head of her class at an unnamed coeducational western college. Although she was robust throughout her collegiate career, the damage was nonetheless done. After graduation, her health failed, eventually leading to her death some years later. A postmortem revealed degeneration of the brain. It was "an instance of death from over-work" combined with carelessness where her femininity was concerned.

Tragic though Miss G——'s untimely demise was, it may have been preferable to the ends met by other broken-down scholars, as dutifully reported by Clarke. Miss A——, for example, became hopelessly and violently insane after her marriage, whereas Miss C—— was hospitalized with hysteria and depression. Miss F——, long the victim of hypochondria and insomnia, was just returning to health under Clarke's "careful and systematic regimen" when she was killed by a sudden accident.[11]

Packed with such sensational tidbits, it's not surprising that *Sex in Education* was an immediate best-seller. In a preface to the second edition, the author himself modestly pointed out that the new printing followed "little more than a week after the publication of the first."[12] A bookseller in Ann Arbor, Michigan, reported selling two hundred copies in a single day.[13] A flood of journal articles and at least four books replying to Dr. Clarke followed—most impressive when one remembers there were no morning talk shows, no Internet discussion groups, no electronic media whatsoever to whip the waves of controversy. The answering volumes were mostly penned by women, and as a contemporary reviewer wryly observed, "the ladies, it is needless to say are 'down' on the Doctor with more or less temper, according to knowledge and position."[14]

Eliza Bisbee Duffey's "temper," as recorded in her *No Sex in Education; or, An Equal Chance for Both Girls and Boys* (1874), still echoes tartly down the years:

> If there is really a radical mental difference in men and women founded upon sex, you *cannot* educate them alike, however much you try. If women *cannot* study unremittingly, why then they *will* not, and you *cannot make them*. But because they do, because they choose to do so, because they will do so in spite of you, should be accepted as evidence that they can, and, all other things being equal, can with impunity.[15]

Instead of Clarke's stunted, small-bosomed victims of physical collapse, argued Duffey, education created "women with broad chests, large

In 1943, a group of Oklahoma State coeds showed health, vitality, and just how wrong Clarke's Sex in Education *turned out to be.*

limbs and full veins, perfect muscular and digestive systems and harmonious sexual organs," who could keep pace with men either in a foot race or intellect to intellect.[16]

Mrs. Julia Ward Howe scoffed at Clarke's contention that "you cannot feed a woman's brain without starving her body."[17] The venerable poet, novelist, women's rights advocate, and clubwoman gathered essays refuting Clarke in *Sex and Education: A Reply to Dr. E. H. Clarke's "Sex in Education"* (1874). Howe and others questioned the quality of Clarke's research—particularly the statistically small number of supporting cases he presented—while reports from far-flung coed campuses such as Antioch, Oberlin, and the University of Michigan confirmed the health and vitality of both female students and alumnae.

The argument even wound its way into *An American Girl and Her Four Years in a Boys' College* (1878). Will Elliott and her sister coeds at Ortonville react to Clarke's work with "disgust and amusement."[18] Caught up in the hubbub surrounding the book, Will wonders "what the dear old humbug has to say against girls." After reading *Sex in Education*, she astutely notes the recent origin of the "precious" doctor's concern:

> Women have washed and baked, scrubbed, cried and prayed themselves into their graves for thousands of years, and no person has written a book advising them not to work too hard; but just as soon as women are beginning to have a show in education, up starts your erudite doctor with his learned nonsense, embellished with scarecrow stories, trying to prove that woman's complicated physical mechanism can't stand any mental strain.[19]

Will was on to something here, not only that lower-class women had worked for centuries without alarm being raised as to their physical health, but also the question of Clarke's own motives. In *Sex in Education*, Clarke declared that his alma mater and former employer, Harvard, was a "red flag" target that "the bulls of female reform" were "just now pitching into." Answering those who would open up his beloved Harvard to coeducation, Clarke argued that, even despite its "supposed" riches, the expense to fit Harvard to meet the "special and appropriate" needs of women students was one the school "could not undertake" without an additional million or two dollars.[20] Or so he said.

Clarke's arguments disturbed faculties as well as students. In an 1877 report to the board of regents, a visiting committee to the University of Wisconsin worried about "the fearful expense of ruined health" and decided that it was "better that the future mothers of the state should be robust, hearty, healthy women, than that, by over study, they entail upon their descendents the germs of disease." No doubt considering the university's twenty-odd years of healthy female students, President Bascom replied that study was, in fact, "congenial to the habits of young women" and politely noted that "the visiting committee is certainly mistaken."[21]

As women entered college in greater and greater numbers, and their prophesized collapse did not occur, arguments linking women's health and education eventually disappeared. The decline was gradual, however; the 1894 edition of *The Physical Life of Woman* still made the link between women's education and ill health, while magazine articles just before the turn of the twentieth century sought to reassure readers—especially parents of daughters—that college girls were as robust and happy as those who stayed at home. Concerns about higher education and ill health lingered well into the twentieth century. Writing in 1911, Dr. William Lee Howard was mostly concerned with the deleterious effects of basketball and other strenuous forms of exercise on youthful reproductive systems, but he also advocated girls staying home from school during the menstrual period. He took his appeal straight to parents:

> Which had you rather YOUR daughter should have, a certificate of perfect health, with the knowledge that when she marries she can become a mother without danger to herself and child, that she can remain happy in the nursery instead of miserable in the hospital, or a diploma stating that she can read French poetry and write an essay upon "Woman's Career"?[22]

The nervous strain and "ceaseless activity" of college life itself were other threats to health. One writer blamed the resultant "worn nerves and impaired digestion" on the combination of poor eating (all those hard-to-digest pies and doughnuts at midnight spreads), and colleges that didn't enforce the "ten o'clock" rule but rather allowed girls to sit up all night studying. She also blamed extracurricular activities, whether they were athletic, literary, or benevolent in nature. Few escaped her inclusive list:

> basket ball, hockey tennis; the glee club, the mandolin club, the French and German clubs; the literary societies; the fraternities; the work on literary magazines; the little plays so frequently given by societies; the meetings in connection with social settlements and other benevolent or

religious associations; the teas and suppers; and, worst of all because the most taxing, the senior dramatics which cap the climax of fatigue.[23]

Alas, she didn't explain just what made the senior dramatics so taxing. She did, however, describe how a girl who for two weeks participated in extracurricular activities every night until midnight and then studied until 2:00 A.M. came down with, not the mononucleosis that nearly every modern college student seems to have a brush with, but appendicitis.

Calisthenics for Ladies

Emma Willard, Catharine Beecher, and Mary Lyon all recognized the healthful benefits physical activity conferred on young women and incorporated various exercises into their successful educational programs. Beecher and Lyon in particular used the exercise system known as calisthenics. In 1834, Amherst professor and physical-education advocate Edward Hitchcock defined the term as "the classical name for female gymnastics"; another practitioner noted it derived from "two Greek words signifying beauty and strength."[24] This did not mean the sort of acrobatic tumbling and gravity-defying apparatus work we associate with today's Olympic-level female gymnasts. As practiced beginning in the early part of the nineteenth century, calisthenics were a synchronized series of movements usually done while rooted to one spot on the floor, either with or without music. Some practitioners advocated the use of the bowling-pin-shaped Indian clubs (so named after British soldiers stationed in colonial India adapted native exercises employing similar devices), beanbags, or other weights for added benefit.[25] Most importantly, calisthenics were always "carefully accommodated to the delicate organization of the female sex," as noted in an 1856 guide.[26] Engravings in the same book showed gymnastic exercises for men which involved rope climbing, pole vaulting, and the parallel bars, while women stood in place and gently waved their arms or small wooden dumbbells. Which isn't to say that calisthenics weren't rigorous in their own way. Catharine Beecher outlined her suggested routine of fifty exercises in *Physiology and Calisthenics for Schools and Families* (1856). Students began by beating their chests (to "enlarge the chest and lungs"), then came arm extensions and stretches, followed by deep knee bends, leg raises, and high stepping, among other movements.[27] But Beecher also stressed the "simple *gracefulness* of movement and person" that resulted in girls who practiced calisthenics. When another popular health reformer, Dio Lewis, updated some of Beecher's exercises, Beecher found the modifications "objectionable"; Lewis's adaptations were "so vigorous and *ungraceful* as to be more suitable for boys than for young ladies."[28]

William Hammond was a snarky Amherst undergrad when he visited Mount Holyoke in the 1840s. As he recorded in his diary, the sight of students engaged in calisthenics failed to impress him:

> Saw some of the young ladies exercise in calisthenics, a species of orthodox *dancing* in which they perambulate a smooth floor in various figures, with a sort of sliding stage step. . . . The whole movement is accompanied by singing in which noise rather than tune or harmony seems to be the main object. By a species of delusion peculiar to the seminary they imagine that all this [is] very conducive to health, strength, gracefulness, etc.[29]

Delusional or not, calisthenics were part of a larger mid-nineteenth-century movement toward health reform which appeared just as the American population began to relocate away from the agricultural countryside with its numerous opportunities for healthy outdoor exercise and the consumption of fresh produce and meat, to the industrial city where adulterated foods were the norm and the majority of workers and students were engaged in what was considered dangerously sedentary "brain work." Combined with questions about the ability of females to remain reproductively sound while engaged in heavy study, it's not surprising that Matthew Vassar and his associates included a "Calisthenium" in the plan for his women's college.[30]

The author of *Ladies Home Calisthenics* (1890) described woman's combined obligations of physical fitness and maternity:

> The health of coming generations and the future of a nation depend in great part upon the girls. They are to be the coming mothers; and, as such, obligations for the formation of a new race are incumbent upon them. These obligations they can by no means fulfill unless they are sound in mind and body.[31]

In this regard, the practice of calisthenics was nothing less than patriotic. The exercises helped women build strength for their most important job—reproducing the race, specifically, the white middle and upper classes in the face of increasing non-western-European immigration at the turn of century. And the exercises themselves were deemed "ladylike"—unlike the strenuous, sweaty game of basketball.

Basketball

The game was invented in 1891 by Dr. James Naismith of the YMCA. A year later, it was adopted into the physical educational program at nearby Smith College and quickly became a popular staple of women's physical education in both women's and coed colleges. And why not? Basketball was fun. It was fun when we played it, boys and girls together, in our fifth-grade gym period and I made a completely accidental midcourt hook shot that secured both the notice of and later a valentine from Mark Elbach. Imagine for a moment how much fun it must have been for a group of girls in the 1890s. Raised with restrictions of both clothing and behavior, they got the chance to shed both corsets and decorum in an unfettered physical competition that the more sedate practice of calisthenics didn't offer. Watching girls play basketball "in bloomers and sweaters" in 1898, an observer marveled a bit wistfully at their freedom in dress and movement. "The alumnae of only ten years' standing were

Title IX

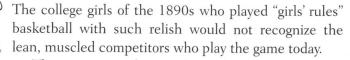

The college girls of the 1890s who played "girls' rules" basketball with such relish would not recognize the lean, muscled competitors who play the game today.

The exponential growth and development of women's college basketball and other sports were due to Title IX of the Educational Amendments Act, passed in 1972. Title IX prohibits sex discrimination at any educational institution that receives federal funds. Under its authority, schools are required to provide equal opportunities and funding to men's and women's athletic programs proportionate to the number of men and women in the student body.

At least, that's how it's supposed to work. Detractors decry Title IX as a government-mandated "quota system" that in practice has forced colleges to cut men's programs in sports such as gymnastics and wrestling rather than add them for women. In mid-2005, advocates of the law worried about its future, given the retirement of Supreme Court Justice Sandra Day O'Connor, who was often the swing vote in cases expanding Title IX, and new Bush administration rules for compliance, requiring that colleges merely conduct an online survey to assess female student interest in sports programs. A lack of response would indicate lack of student interest, and excuse the college from providing any further opportunities for women to play that sport.[*]

[*] Karen Blumenthal, "Title IX's Next Hurdle; Three Decades After Its Passage, Rule That Leveled Field for Girls Faces Test from Administration," *Wall Street Journal* (eastern edition), July 6, 2005, B1.

mourning because the college in their day supplied nothing better than boarding-school calisthenics."[32] No wonder the early college girls loved playing basketball so much—it must have been liberating beyond their wildest dreams to run, jump, yell and actually *compete*. "We played as hard as we could. And loved every moment of it," recalled one woman of her days on the court in the years leading up to World War I.[33]

Of course, one couldn't properly play basketball (or practice calisthenics) if one's waist was whittled down to a fashionable twenty inches or so by a tightly laced whalebone corset. The rise of women's athletics contributed to the downfall of the corset and similarly restrictive clothing for daily wear. Catharine Beecher, Dio Lewis, and other advocates of female calisthenics were also devotees of the dress reform movement, and sought to get women out of organ-crushing, health-impairing corsets and into looser, less restrictive inner and outer garments. Just what those new garments should look like was a matter of debate—Amelia Bloomer's ill-fated reform outfit of shortened skirt and baggy pants is still remembered for the ridicule hurled at both it and its inventor in the early 1850s. Nevertheless, early college girls adopted gym uniforms that were essentially divided skirts gathered at the knee into the traditional "bloomer" shape worn with sailor-style middy blouses. Wearing this modified bloomer costume was acceptable in the gym and even in the classroom on some campuses, but only because its wearer was shielded from public display. For example, in 1895 the playing field at Smith College was noted to be "retired enough for the girls to play without embarrassment in gymnasium suits." If gym-suited girls might be visible to passersby, they wore long skirts over the bloomers.[34] Dressed for their team photograph in the 1898 *Oriole* yearbook, the members of the junior and sophomore "basket ball" teams at the all-girl Maryland College for Women in Lutherville, Maryland, ignored their gym uniforms altogether and appeared in ankle-length skirts, fashionable leg-o'-mutton sleeves, and dress reform be damned, corsets tight laced within in an inch of their young lives. These outfits were more fashionable than the baggy, natural-waisted middy blouses and shorter skirts (not bloomers) worn on the outside playing field, and which the freshmen class of 1900 wore for

The fashionably tight-laced sophomore basketball team at the Maryland College for Women, 1898.

their team picture, although one member flaunted convention and short-ened her skirt almost to her knees.

In the nineteenth century, as in our own, the prophets of doom appeared whenever girls had too much fun. There were concerns about girls playing a men's game according to the men's rules, questions regard-ing how vigorous play affected women's health, or whether competition compromised players' femininity. In *Confidential Chats with Girls* (1911), Dr. William Lee Howard warned girls about these and other dan-gers of athletics. Crashing down court in a jostling group of fellow play-ers, leaping high to toss ball into basket or block another's shot, few girls worried about their reproductive organs—but Dr. Howard did. He focused his readers' attention by placing key words and phrases in capital letters:

> Many a foolish or uninstructed girl has made herself a girl of muscles, but ruined her WOMANLY POWERS in so doing. Save all your strength for what Nature intended a woman to DO; don't throw it away in doing gymnasium stunts. . . . Such a girl may have strong arms in which to

The freshman basketball team displays its uniforms. Maryland College for Women, 1898.

carry a baby, but the chances are that some other woman will have to give her the baby to carry.[35]

A girl's muscular arms, it seemed, wouldn't help keep her uterus anchored in the proper place. As described by Howard, the female organs were suspended—barely—by delicate cords ("Never mind the names the doctors call these cords or other ligaments," he snapped at curious readers) which could be jarred loose at almost any second, especially while a girl was still growing. "[I]t takes but little to put [the womb] out of place and have it stay there. The ovaries may be so twisted and put out of order that nothing can be done for them in later life but to cut them out with a knife; then you are ruined as far as womanhood is concerned."[36]

It was a frightening vision of the uterus broken loose from its strings like an out-of-control Macy's Parade balloon tangled in telephone wires on a windy day. Howard later took what promised to be a more sensible tack before he stumbled into a syntactical abyss: "Of course, every girl must exercise, but it must be such exercises as is governed with her sexual organs ever in view."[37] Mental images of naked Twister contests twirl in the modern reader's head, but all he meant was that girls needed to be ever vigilant of their delicate reproductive systems: walking, dancing, even swimming (of course never during the menstrual period) were all acceptably gentle forms of exercise.

As for the types of sports that had taken the women's colleges and female departments of coed campuses by storm, the dangers were far beyond mere physical strain:

> You can over-exercise, become too much excited over contests in the gymnasium . . . No girl of a nervous temperament should go into any athletic contest, team or personal. Such a girl should not play basketball, attempt any stunts on horizontal bars or flying rings . . . Hundreds of girls who are playing contests of basketball, to see which team is going to be the champion of the state or the town, are going to suffer from this excitement.[38]

Like the author of *Sex in Education* a generation or so before him, Howard understood that a young woman's reproductive system was at its most vulnerable in the first years after menarche. Athletic excitement of the sort engendered by gymnastics or basketball at this crucial time caused "growing womanly functions [to] become weakened and sometimes dried up." Rather than training for athletic competition, a girl between the ages of fourteen and twenty was better served by preparation "for her future work—motherhood."[39]

Even proponents of women's athletics worried about their masculinizing effects. Dr. Dudley A. Sargent was the director of Harvard's Hemenway Gymnasium from 1879 until 1919. He oversaw the gymnasium work of Radcliffe students, and developed a system of exercises performed on special machines that was incorporated into Wellesley's gymnasium in the early 1880s.[40] He also wielded a prolific pen. In 1912, he presented an up-to-date summation on women and sports when he tackled the question "Are Athletics Making Girls Masculine?"

Sargent's response was a decided "it depends." He believed that women could take part in almost all athletic endeavors without fear of injury and "with great prospects of success," even though gym work and sports modified the conventional female figure with its "narrow waist, broad and massive hips and large thighs" into something more masculine, with a stronger back and more expansive chest. Women developed beneficial mental qualities in the gym or on the playing field: concentration, will, perseverance, reason, judgment, courage, strength, and endurance were just a few in an exhaustive list. Only a few sports made women "masculine in an objectionable sense," but among them were campus favorites baseball and basketball. These were men's games, and when played by men's rules they were rough, strenuous, and afforded the opportunity for "violent personal encounter," which most women found "distasteful." Combined with the "peculiar constitution of [the female] nervous system and the great emotional disturbances" to which girls and women were subject both on and off the playing field, these games held the potential for disaster:[41]

> I am often asked: "Are girls overdoing athletics at school and college?" I have no hesitation in saying that in many of the schools where basketball is being played according to the rules for boys many girls are injuring themselves in playing this game. The numerous reports of these girls breaking down with heart trouble or a nervous collapse are mostly too well founded.[42]

In addition to physical breakdown, Sargent ominously noted there was "some danger" that women who played these unreconstituted men's sports might "take on more marked masculine characteristics" than simply stronger backs and broader waists. "Many people," he reported, believed that athletics made girls "bold," "overassertive," and robbed them of "that charm and elusiveness that has so long characterized the female sex."[43]

Girls had been playing basketball for almost twenty years on some college campuses and they clearly enjoyed it. How then did they keep from "breaking down" physically and/or otherwise compromising their femininity while at the same time reaping the healthful benefits of playing basketball? In 1899, Senda Berenson, Smith College's athletic director and the "mother of women's basketball," organized a committee comprising women educators to investigate the matter. Their solution was to modify the rules to remove "undue physical exertion" from the game.[44] Among other changes, the modified rules restricted players' movement on the court to one of three assigned zones, prohibited girls from snatching the ball from one another (which was seen to encourage rough play), and forbade any one of them from making more than three dribbles of the ball (a 1928 guide to women's basketball cryptically stated, without further explanation, that many of the committee felt there was a "possible danger in the dribble").[45] In addition to limiting the physical exertion needed to play the game, the rule modifications made the game more psychologically "feminine" by eliminating what the basketball committee referred to as "star playing" while encouraging "equalization of team-work."[46] This meant that players submerged their individual egos for the good of the team, just as women were reminded to practice self-denial for the good of their families. In the words of historian Barbara A. Schreier, "the result was transformation of a man's sport into a women's game."[47]

The first women's basketball rule book was issued in 1901, though it's apparent from Sargent's article that almost fifteen years later not all colleges employed it. Even before the "girls' rules" went into effect, though, boosters described how athletic contests on their campuses emphasized feminine cooperation instead of masculine competition. As the wife of Smith's president, essayist Harriet C. Seelye was no doubt trying to counter negative images of hoydenish girls who lost self-control on the court and became "rough, loud-voiced and bold."[48] In an 1895 article, she described how the "feminine character of the college [was] clearly revealed in the manner" in which formerly male collegiate sports like basketball and baseball were played by the girls. "No charge of masculinity" could be made against girls playing baseball after dinner in long dresses (on at least one occasion it was observed that "the pitcher wore a ruffled white muslin with a train for good measure").[49]

Miss Tomboy and Miss Demure both wear the Paul Jones Two-In-One

$2.00 upwards

MISS TOMBOY wears a middy blouse that's long and comfortable—just the thing for gym and sports. Miss Demure is trim and smart from head to toe. Her middy is evenly cuffed, fits snugly, is just blousy enough to be neat and dainty.

Each wears the new Paul Jones Two-In-One. Two turns of the bottom, a swift unsnapping of hidden tabs, an instant to button them in the back, and this comfortable sports middy becomes a charming garment for street or classroom.

Ask your dealer to show you the exclusive Paul Jones Two-In-One. It is made in a variety of styles and materials and priced at $2.00 upwards. Or write us to send attractive style book and name of nearest dealer.

Paul Jones garments are guaranteed without reserve.

MORRIS & COMPANY
412 No. Eutaw St., Baltimore, Md.

PAUL JONES MIDDIES

Middy blouses were the height of casual comfort in 1922.

While the strenuous nature of basketball required gym suits instead of formal wear, Seelye wrote, the girls who played the game at Smith developed "grace, self-control, and politeness": "In a Harvard-Yale football contest one does not hear opponents saying at an exciting crisis, 'Pardon me, but I think that's our ball,' or 'Excuse me, did I hurt you?' "[50]

Such idealized teamwork and cooperation were the bywords in women's collegiate athletics for years to come. In 1940, the authors of *She's Off to College* described the important life lessons a girl learned when she sublimated her individual will to the greater good of the team:

> A girl learns not to make a grandstand play, not to show off her own skill, but to subordinate her playing to the success of her team. She doesn't cheat. She doesn't call a ball in that's out. She doesn't slouch in the ranks. She plays with all her ability, skill, and good will. These qualities become a part of her and are carried over into other departments of her life, making her a good all-round sport in whatever she undertakes, at college or later.[51]

In this sense, the girl who became a "good all-round sport" was analogous to the girl who was "smart enough": both appellations indicated levels of achievement that didn't threaten male superiority. Good all-round sports learned (or so educators hoped) patience, obedience, self-control, self-denial, and submergence of self—qualities that conformed to traditional views of nonassertive femininity, in the classroom, the home, or the office—and certainly not the "will" Sargent placed near the top of his list of qualities women might obtain on the basketball court. It was a short hop from becoming a good all-round sport on the playing field to "being a good sport" wholly divorced from any athletic connotation in real life. Being a good sport was an attribute that often showed up in midcentury dating manuals' lists of qualities boys liked in girls. In its most frequently used context, being a good sport meant being a member of the get-along gang, and not bothering one's date by complaining or being bossy. According to *CO-EDiquette*, being a good sport at a football game meant wearing clothing that could stand the rough-and-tumble of outdoor stadium seating, because "if you can't sit down because the step is dirty and if you melt in a drizzle, you will be as welcome as white satin at a picnic."[52]

It wasn't until the 1950s that women physical-education teachers sought to eliminate the distinctions between men and women's basketball.[53]

The Unladylike Nature of Competition

Competition itself was a vexing issue for the administrators of women's athletic programs. On the one hand, they acknowledged competition was increasingly important to the American way of life—"why not prepare for it in the gymnasium," asked Bryn Mawr's director of physical culture in 1904.[54] At precisely the same time, administrators at Smith felt that intercollegiate athletic contests were not in "good taste" where its students were concerned—hence those oh-so-polite basketball players. "Valuable as such contests may be for men," deemed President Seelye, "they do not seem suitable for women, and no benefit is likely to come from them which would justify the risks."[55]

Competition was at the root of a problem that factionalized the coeducational campus of Morningside College in Sioux City, Iowa, at the turn of the century. The matter at issue was whether a young woman who could sprint "faster than any man in the school" at fifty and one-hundred yards should be allowed to attend the state intercollegiate track meet. Not surprisingly, the coeds demanded to know why their colleague was denied the opportunity to compete—and quite possibly win—against men. The author of *The College Girl of America* (1905) deemed the imbroglio as evidence of the "unwomanly direction" competition might take.

A quarter of a century later, with woman suffrage secured and a place on the wider stage of public life seemingly assured, Alice Frymir, the author of *Basket Ball for Women* (1928), acknowledged the individual's need to "engage with others in some form or other of competition when he enters his life work. Modern woman has taken her place in the world: in business,

In 1925, Upsala College in East Orange, New Jersey, had a women's football team led by Gladys Scherer, "the Red Grange of woman football." News accounts noted that her team "tackled football with the same enthusiasm that they formerly tackled dancing."

in profession, in politics. She, too, must meet the situations as they exist."[56] It was the fervent hope of the Women's Division of the National Amateur Athletic Federation that she would meet those situations in a ladylike fashion. Founded in 1923, the Women's Division adopted a platform for girls' and women's athletics that emphasized the ideals of team play and recreation over personal glory gained in the heat of competition:

> 4. *Resolved,* In order to develop those qualities which shall fit girls and women to perform their function as citizens, . . .
>   (b) That schools and other organizations shall stress enjoyment of the sport and development of sportsmanship, and minimize

the emphasis which is at present laid upon individual accomplishment and the winning of championships.[57]

Coaches and educators needed to keep "the *educational value* of the game in mind rather than *winning*." Under these conditions, intramural and even interschool play was permissible (unless a girl was in the first three days of her menstrual period, in which case she needed to sideline herself both during practice and on game day).[58]

To further curb the disruptive effects of overstimulation on delicate female constitutions, most colleges spurned women's interschool competition in favor of intramurals—games played between classes or other arbitrary divisions. In the event two schools met, teams were sometimes mixed and divided on the spot, thus cutting out the element of rivalry that led to rough and combative play.[59] "Play days" and "sports days" in which girls from different colleges took part in noncompetitive games further reinforced the ideals of team play and sportsmanship. Just prior to Hood College's first play day in February 1931, an editorial in the student newspaper explained that "the spirit which we aim to foster . . . is not one of inter-collegiate rivalry, but one of team co-operation which definitely contributes to the fostering of sport for sports sake."[60]

At Hood's play day, freshman, sophomore, junior, and senior basketball teams met corresponding class teams from two visiting colleges. Winning was so unimportant that neither the editorial nor another descriptive article in the same issue of the student paper bothered to explain how—or even if—an overall victor would be chosen.

Some schools further eroded the possibility for competitive interschool rivalries by conducting their sports or play days via post or wire. On the appointed day, a college's class teams played one another and mailed the resulting scores to another participating college, where, on the same day, that school's class teams played one another. The scores were compared, and a winning school determined. Given the inevitable lag time, who cared who won? Certainly some did—but enthusiasm is hard to maintain over days or weeks waiting for the mail. Telegraphing the results sped up the process, but physical isolation during the actual games prevented anything so disgraceful as partisan rooting. As late as 1950, a glossy magazine photo of underclassmen playing field hockey at Smith was accompanied by a caption which noted that competition was "between houses and classes, never with other colleges."[61]

The fear of competition trickled down into other gendered arenas of life—specifically dating. Mid-twentieth century dating manuals often recommended sports as ideal date activities: they were fun, you didn't have to talk all the time, and there was an underlying suggestion that they provided a safe outlet for pent-up teenage sexuality. But they also provided a dilemma for girls who were better athletes than their dates: should they play to the best of their abilities and possibly win, or should they throw the game and lose in order to avoid embarrassing their date? Women were constantly reminded that competition with men was strictly verboten. If anything, a beau wanted a helpless little girl by his side, not a competent, muscular Amazon. Being a good sport could mean being a namby-pamby competitor.

Undergraduates were recommended to choose a sport that a future husband would be likely to play—something along the lines of tennis or golf. "Girls nowadays . . . are mainly looking for a chance to improve their skill in individual sports which they can use the rest of their lives," stated a *New York Times* report on the "new freedom" of the college girl. "A girl today who can't swim and play tennis is considered a dub [i.e., "dud"]."[62] This nixed two of the most popular women's college sports for postgraduation fun, because a hypothetical husband wouldn't want "to cross field hockey sticks with you or shoot a basket or two when he comes home from work," as *Mademoiselle* confidently stated in 1940.[63]

Advice writers regularly reinforced this idea to their teen girl (and adult woman) readers. If you insisted on winning, even at golf, you had better be prepared to feign incompetence in other ways according to *Seventeen* in 1959:

Q: I am sixteen and in perfect health. I swim, ride, play tennis and regularly beat my beau at golf. Why then—when I'm out on a date—do I have to pretend to be so helpless I can't open a car door!

A: It's a penalty for beating your beau at golf! Actually, it is a pretense—but a nice one. It gives your escort much the same protective feeling you get taking a child's hand to cross a street. Cater to it.[64]

Good thing the girl who went out for athletics wasn't necessarily doing so because she enjoyed sports. She knew that the quickest way to a man's heart was not necessarily through his stomach. As *Mademoiselle* pointed out in 1940. "There's no better way to make and keep friends, and in particular that top man, a husband, than to play his favorite game—and play it well."[65]

The Freshman Five: Eating and Dieting

Ideally, a rousing game of basketball or spirited round of calisthenics helped a girl balance the calories she took in, which from the amount and range of food provided at meals, must have been formidable. Sarah Tyson Rorer made an investigative tour of several college campuses in 1905 and reported her findings in a *Ladies Home Journal* article titled "What College Girls Eat." Rorer battled against difficult-to-digest foods (including, as we have seen, pies and pastries) and for a "hygienic table" of nutritious viands. She was happy to report that Northwestern employed a trained dietician (a modern innovation at the turn of the century), but overall her impression was a negative one. "To kill the weak and ruin the middling is too great a price to pay for even a college education. The heavy breakfasts with course luncheons and heavy dinners, with teas and 'fudges' between and after, will, I am sure ruin the physique of any woman."[66] The sample menus Rorer provided proved no one went hungry, even on those campuses with modern ideas about digestible foods—

where one might expect to find lighter fare. Breakfasts consisted of fruit, cereal, cream, eggs, biscuits or toast, and coffee. At noon a girl might sit down to a meal of tomato soup, fried veal, mashed potatoes, peas, and stewed celery, topped off with panned apples and cream. Supper was a smaller meal: pressed chicken with mayonnaise dressing, potato chips, olives, canned fruit, and cake.

For the most part, girls thrived on the board they received at college. "Everything is excellent and well and thoroughly cooked," reported Wellesley student Charlotte Conant to her parents in 1880.[67] "We are both growing fatter," wrote Smith student Alice Miller, speaking for herself and her sister, to their parents in 1883.[68] In her study of college women and body image from 1875 to 1930, historian Margaret Lowe has shown how early college girls accepted modest weight gain as a sign of "a healthy adjustment to college life" instead of the alarming development it would become. "It is my ambition to weigh 150 pounds," wrote Charlotte Wilkinson in a February 1892 letter home. By April, her weight was 135½; two months later she proudly informed her mother that it was up to 137.[69]

College girls well knew at any given time how much they weighed because their weight and other vital statistics were carefully monitored. This happened on men's campuses as well, but it took on a special significance at women's schools in response to the medical profession's warnings about the effect of higher education on women's health. Freshmen were subject to a rigorous inspection at the beginning of the school year. Following the nineteenth-century vogue for anthropometry (a pseudoscience that used body measurements to draw anthropological conclusions), girls were asked to strip down, slip on a hospital-gown-like garment, and a detailed set of measurements were made. In addition to height and weight, the circumference of head, neck, thighs, calves, ankles, upper arms, elbows, and wrists might be taken, along with the length of one's head, various measurements from hips to heels, and so on. On some campuses, the exam was repeated at the end of the school year and both sets of results were compared with the average. "Suggestions for special exercises, suitable to the individual needs of the stu-

Anthropometry in Action, or How Do You Measure Up?

 Dudley A. Sargent, M.D., was an early booster of physical education for both men and women (as long as they didn't overdo it). As director of the Harvard gym from 1879 to 1919, he oversaw the anthropometric measuring of several generations of Harvard freshmen. In 1912, he provided the following ideal feminine measurements for what he termed "A Fine Type of Athletic Figure" in the March issue of the *Ladies Home Journal*. Get out your tape measure and see where you fit in! And while you're at it, remember those poor college girls at the turn of the century who were subjected to a similar frenzy of measuring—sometimes twice a year.

	INCHES		INCHES
Weight, 118 pounds			
Height, standing	61¾	Girth of Thigh	21
Height, sitting	33½	Girth of Calf (right)	13½
Girth of Neck	13½	Girth of Calf (left)	13¼
Girth of Chest	31½	Girth of Ankle	8
Girth of Chest Full	33½	Girth of Upper Arm	10¾
Girth of Lower Chest	27½	Girth of Forearm	9½
Girth of Lower Chest, Full	29½	Girth of Wrist	6
Girth of Waist	23¼	Breadth of Waist	8
Girth of Hips	35¼	Breadth of Hips	12½

dent" were based on these examinations.[70] Both students and administrators could easily track a girl's progress toward health.

It is certain that college girls ate with relish. Following Princeton's tradition of eating clubs (a lack of dining facilities in the 1850s led students
to take their meals off campus, and the resulting clubs evolved into social
groups resembling fraternities), Vassar students had supper clubs. Ten
pages of the 1904 *Vassarion* yearbook were devoted to these alliances,
among them the "Nine Nimble Nibblers" and "The Bakers' Dozen."
Members of the latter increased their dining pleasure by adopting special
snacking names such as "G. Inger Snap" and "Grid L. Kakes." Around the
same time, the *New York Times* described the eating clubs at "one of the
Massachusetts colleges":

> one calls itself the "Bow-wows," meeting at intervals to cook "hot dogs"—
> as frankfurter sausages are called—and wearing china puppies attached
> to bits of blue ribbon. Another, "The Eating Six," takes Sunday morning
> breakfasts together. The "Stuffers" have for their motto, "Eat, stuff, and
> be merry, for to-morrow, ye flunk."[71]

The Stuffers made it a point to cook and consume meals in a member's room, and the ingredients could only be purchased using the ten
cents gathered from each girl. One thrifty menu consisted of fruit salad,
omelets, and ice cream. When penury reared its ugly head and not even a
dime was available, the Stuffers shamelessly wrote a story that asked
"What is more agonizing than to see an innocent child enduring the
pangs of hunger?" After a gullible Sunday school paper purchased the
story, the Stuffers rewarded themselves with a high-ticket dinner costing
twenty cents a head.[72]

Today one would be hard-pressed to find a group of college girls who
so proudly admitted their lusty gustatory appetites. Clearly, the Stuffers
and their cohort had a different relationship with food than we currently
do, one seemingly less fraught with anxiety—though concerns about size
and appearance were never entirely absent. Lowe mentions an overweight college girl in the 1880s who begged her mother to keep her

The Freshman Five (or More)

 In 1950, design-heavy *FLAIR* magazine polled an undisclosed number of male and female college freshmen (only college girls were pictured) on their eating habits and weight. On average, each gained eight pounds. Students blamed the extra poundage not on mass-produced cafeteria grub but snacking. And what were the most popular between-meal yummies on college campuses that year? The top responses were:

1. Cola drinks;

2. Coffee;

3. Milkshakes and malteds (a recipe from all-male Haverford College read "2 scoops ice cream; 1 pint milk; 1 squirt vanilla; Syrup; and beat like hell on the mixer");

4. Beer ("or beer, beer, beer as it was written on almost all the answers from men's colleges . . .")

Barring the number two choice, all of these packed a caloric punch, especially in combination with the runners-up: all manner of ice-cream sodas, hamburgers, grilled-cheese sandwiches, cheese crackers, popcorn, potato chips, French fries, peanuts, candy bars, sundaes, and "anything a la mode," as well as a fascinating array of regional goodies, including "spudnuts" (potato-flour doughnuts popular at Southern Methodist University), crème de menthe mixed with beer (a taste treat at Middlebury), and peanut butter/bacon/banana sandwiches (a favorite at the University of Maryland).*

* "Statistics Behind College Figures," *FLAIR*, August 1950, 58.

weight gain a secret from the family physician "or he'd never have any respect for me again."[73] Nevertheless, at the turn of the twentieth century, the standard of physical beauty for women was quite different from the Botox-smoothed, collagen-plumped, extra-attenuated, ultrathin model with implants that rules the media today. In 1912, Miss Elsie Scheel of Brooklyn, New York, was deemed the "most nearly perfect specimen of womanhood" among Cornell's four hundred coeds. Scheel was twenty-four years old, stood five feet seven inches tall, weighed in at a healthy 171 pounds (her favorite food was beefsteak), and possessed a decidedly pear-shaped figure (it measured 35-30-40). Nevertheless, Cornell's medical examiner—the woman who measured all those coeds— judged her "the perfect girl," having "not a single defect" in her physical makeup. (She was also "an ardent suffragette" who "if she were a man . . . would study mechanical engineering" but instead studied horticulture.)[74]

Alas for Elsie Scheel and everyone else built along her solid lines, the flapper popularized the boyish figure after World War I. Mr. J. R. Bolton, a fashion expert consulted by the *New York Times* in 1923, blamed the "athletic tendencies of the modern girl" for the shift to extreme slenderness. The newly ideal girl was five feet seven inches tall and a "perfect 34, with 22-inch waist and 34-inch hips. The ankle should measure 8 inches and the weight not exceed 110 pounds." It was a youthful figure; American women reached their "best proportions at the age of 20," Bolton pronounced. Not surprisingly, "abstinence from candy and pastry" along with "plenty of exercise" were required to maintain this standard of perfection.[75]

By the mid-1920s, reducing diets were the new "national pastime . . . a craze, a national fanaticism, a frenzy," according to one journalist, and college girls were not immune. In 1924, the *Smith College Weekly* published a letter to the editor under the headline "To Diet or Not to Die Yet?" in which a group of girls warned that unless "preventative measures against strenuous dieting" were taken soon, the campus would become "notorious, not for the sylph-like forms but for the haggard faces and dull, listless eyes of her students." A speaker at the American Dietetic Association convention in 1926 warned that "thousands of young girls in schools, colleges and offices were not dieting as they fondly believed, but starving themselves." Modern girls, it seemed, were "so afraid of being overweight" that they were "not willing to be even normal in weight."[76] (Sound familiar, Jane Doe?) The fear of fat had disastrous consequences in 1930, when a nineteen-year-old New York University freshman committed suicide after her weight ballooned from 130 to 235 in the course of a year because of a "glandular disorder." The dean of students believed that embarrassment over her size contributed to her difficulties with studies, though he didn't go so far as to suggest that it also contributed to her death.[77]

Mental Health

Sadly, there was nothing new about college girl suicide in 1930. Worries about test results, grades, and living up to parental expectations were as familiar to nineteenth- and twentieth-century college girls as they are to today's students. The *New York Times* was filled with stories of college girls who found such pressures too great to bear. In September 1884, nineteen-year-old Flora Meyers failed an examination at the unnamed "female college" she attended. Rather than face her parents, she penned a pathetic note in which she described the last five years as nothing but "worry, worry, worry, until I have envied the girls I have seen with scrubbing brushes." She, too, was "fit only for servile labor," she told her parents, whom she could "no longer bear to see . . . slave any longer" for her tuition. And with that, she disappeared. Her distraught father hired a private detective, who searched the morgue and scanned the faces of passing factory and shop girls before Flora was found by a neighbor—working as a servant in a New York City household.[78]

Flora's story had a happy ending (though not for the private detective, who had to sue for payment), but many others didn't. In 1897, Bertha Mellish left her dormitory at Mount Holyoke College. It was presumed that she was headed toward the post office, a three-minute walk away, but Bertha never returned. She was bright, studious, and well liked by

College Girl Bookshelf: "The Bell Jar" (1971), by Sylvia Plath

 The undisputed classic of college-girl alienation, Sylvia Plath's autobiographical novel of adolescent identity crisis and mental illness was originally published under the pseudonym Victoria Lucas in England, Plath's adopted home, a month before her suicide in 1963. It received good reviews from the British press, but American publishers rejected it based on the brutal description in the second half of the novel of Esther's life in a mental institute. It took another eight years for its publication in the United States, where it immediately found a home on the best-seller list and became required reading in many high-school English classes.

That's probably where I read *The Bell Jar* for the first time, though I don't remember exactly when. I do know that it was definitely prior to losing my virginity. I say this because what stuck with me was the protagonist's description of her disappointing first sexual experience and how boyfriend Buddy's equipment reminded her of a "turkey neck and turkey gizzards," a description that left me both terrified and fascinated.

both faculty and classmates. Ominously, she was also reported to have written a story "in which she described vividly the sensations and thoughts of a girl who committed suicide by drowning." Combined with the discovery of "small footprints" leading to a bluff over the Connecticut River and, nine months later, a woman's foot encased in a "black stocking and low shoe" found in a meadow at the river's edge, it was assumed that she had in fact taken her own life.[79]

In the decades to come, Bertha's sad story was repeated over and over

I next read *The Bell Jar* when I was well into my thirties, happily married (no scary Mr. Turkey Neck here!) and satisfied with life in general. This time I was struck by how well Plath's description of the onset of Esther's mental illness fit what I remember of the almost clinically deep depression that descended on my college years: "I was going to cry. I didn't know why I was going to cry, but I knew that if anybody else spoke to me or looked at me too closely the tears would fly out of my eyes and the sobs would fly out of my throat and I'd cry for a week."*

I, too, was subject to overwhelming waves of sorrow, tears that gushed out when I least expected and that were impossible to control. Unlike Plath, therapy helped me find a way to adult happiness, if not her enshrinement as a literary lion (and given Plath's sad end, I'll gladly take the former).

* Sylvia Plath, *The Bell Jar* (1963; New York: Harper & Row, 1971), 112, 75.

again on campuses throughout the United States. Girls waded into college lakes, overdosed on laudanum, took poison, breathed gas, and jumped from dormitory or boardinghouse windows. Indeed, student suicides were a familiar enough spectacle by 1878 that Olive San Louie Anderson included one in *An American Girl and Her Four Years in a Boys' College* (the freshman girl who shoots herself thoughtfully leaves a note absolving coeducation for her rash act, blaming instead a "hereditary mental disease").

Ballyhoo Girl

 Suicide was not the only way college girls dealt with the pressures of life. In August 1935, a month after she disappeared from Antioch College, twenty-one-year-old Anne Sibley was discovered working as a "ballyhoo girl" at a sideshow on Coney Island. "Seen Daily with Freaks" read a *New York Times* headline (an exclamation point was implied). No fancy college degree was required. All she needed to do was "look pleasant and say nothing while the freaks were being paraded on the front platform." Anne also sold tickets and appeared as The Woman with the Disappearing Head. Perhaps most shockingly for the times (when only sailors and criminals inked their skin), she roomed with the show's tattooed lady.*

The story rated mentions in newspapers from Detroit to New York, *Time* magazine, and Westbrook Pegler's controversial column. In the hands of the press, it became a titillating spectacle of a high-toned, upper-class college girl (Anne's father was a Chicago attorney) forced to come down a notch or two. "I learned more at Coney Island in one month than I did in a year at college," she told detectives (who told reporters).† When it was revealed that Anne had flunked out of Antioch before her disappearance, the story's luster dimmed. Who cared that a troubled young woman ran away? An attractive coed turned carnival barker—now that was a story. Only a few local papers bothered to mention that months earlier Anne had been involved in a fatal accident when a motorist swerved to avoid her bicycle, an incident that may well have been behind both her bad grades and flight to Coney Island.

* "Lost College Girl Found Inside Side-Show," *New York Times*, August 4, 1935, 1; "Runaway Girl Student 'Barking' for Coney Island Show," *New York Times*, August 5, 1935, 17.
† "Missing Ohio Coed Found at Coney Island," *Baltimore Sun*, August 4, 1935.

Up through the late 1930s, many of these deaths were attributed to a nebulous condition known as "overstudy." This was different from the loopiness that results from staying up thirty-six hours straight cramming for exams or the performance failure that sometimes results from the same—something with which most current and former students will be well acquainted. It was also different from the breakdowns that college girls were alleged to suffer because of the deadly combination of study and menstruation. According to late-nineteenth-century medical wisdom, the true danger of overstudy was that it led to more severe forms of mental illness. An 1883 textbook on insanity said the condition precipitated "grave delirium," a "rare form of derangement" that caused stricken individuals to pass from delirious excitement to apathy to death in months, if not weeks. The "unbalancing influences of overstudy" were also said to bring on paranoia (a condition one writer in 1892 called "a modern form of insanity").[80] Both men and women were susceptible: an 1875 pharmaceutical dictionary prescribed phosphide of zinc for "impotence of a cerebral origin, i.e., when caused by overstudy." No one, however, suggested that higher education for men was a bad idea because it had a damaging effect on the delicate male reproductive system.[81]

Occasionally, overstudy was posited as the root cause for bad behavior. When a student at New York City's Normal College stole $1,800 worth of jewelry (a small fortune in 1903, when the robbery occurred) from the home of a "schoolgirl chum," her father told the authorities that his daughter's behavior resulted from "nervous prostration brought on through over-study and close application to her scholastic work." This was damage control. The girl had earlier told police that she took the items because "she couldn't bear to be without pretty clothing such as her girl friends wore." Considered alongside the pawn tickets and stolen goods found in her room, her confession suggested full cognizance of her actions. However, a victim of overstudy didn't quite know what she was doing, and deserved pity and treatment rather than jail time. Her father's argument worked: the girl was not charged.[82]

Similarly, overstudy was a convenient excuse when the circumstances behind a student suicide proved embarrassing to parents or inconvenient to academic institutions. When a male student at Wittenberg College in Springfield, Ohio, died at the Columbus State Hospital for the Insane in 1910, his parents blamed hazing for the "severe nervous shock" that led to his death. The school, however, shifted the question of responsibility (and perhaps liability) from itself to the student, declaring that overstudy caused the boy's insanity.[83] The parents of a male student at Bates College who committed suicide in 1927 probably found it less disturbing to publicly (and perhaps privately) blame overstudy than ascribe any other meaning to the "deep friendship" between their son and the male professor to whom he addressed an unfinished last letter beginning "My dear daddy."[84]

Though a benefactor gave Wellesley a dormitory in 1881 to be used specifically as "a home for young ladies who may be fatigued by overstudy" and needed deep rest unobtainable elsewhere on campus, Princeton opened what is officially considered the first student mental health clinic in 1910.[85] It wasn't until the following decade that the idea of student mental health (or in contemporary terms, "mental hygiene") really took off, nudged along, no doubt, by popular interest in Freud and his work. Student psych services were available at a special clinic at Vassar beginning in 1923. Sadly, the *New York Times* reported a stunning twenty-six student suicides during the first three months of 1927, thirteen at colleges or universities, thirteen at what the *Times* called "lower schools."[86]

Reading early to mid-twentieth-century advice books for college students, one wouldn't imagine that the need for student mental health clinics existed. Most books made college sound like a four-year-long party, full of fun and laughter. When depression was mentioned, it was as something over which a student easily had control. *The Freshman Girl* (1925) briefly warned against "neurasthenia"—a soon to be outmoded term for nervous debility brought on by modern living. "Such an abnormal state of mind renders you a prey to a thousand groundless fears, robs you of the enjoyments of life, and makes you more or less of a nuisance to your friends." A "normal, healthy girl" could avoid it by not falling prey to "overanxiety" about her bodily functions.[87]

But what about normal, healthy girls who sometimes worried and felt anxiety about grades, tuition, or relationships? According to the authors of *She's Off to College* (1940), occasional depression could be avoided "by the thrills and delights of your body." It's not as sexy as it sounds. It merely meant the "plunge [into a swimming pool], the skating rink, dancing, a good thing to eat that's very hot—all of them bring you back to reality with satisfaction and delight." Physical activity certainly helps regulate one's emotions as well as lower stress levels, but *She's Off to College* suggested that with a combination of exercise and steady habits of eating, sleeping, and studying a girl could actually "select the dominant moods in which she wants to live."[88] Unpleasant feelings could be simply blinked away without consequence:

> I think there is a split second in which anger hangs in the balance, just as I think there is a split second in which tears hang in the balance. They sting behind the eyelids, but one winks them back and they go away somewhere else. They do not go on forming themselves. They stop. So with anger. It freezes, and the moment of indecision passes.[89]

Passes, that is, until the moment one gets her ulcer diagnosed. Such advice may have made for passive mid-twentieth-century housewives, but it rarely made for happy individuals. Impulse control over sudden flare-ups was one thing, but the authors meant the complete suppression of this powerful, albeit sometimes unsettling, emotion: "the best thing we can do with anger is forget it."[90] Burying one's emotions also benefited friends and colleagues. "Thou Shalt Not Indulge Thy Moods" was one of the ten commandments of life in the collegiate goldfish bowl offered by *You Can Always Tell a Freshman* (1949). "On your bad days have the grace to keep to yourself. . . . Or play ostrich and stick your head in the sand." Bad moods were "as infectious as a nose cold, and just as unpleasant."[91]

Even in the enlightened, post–women's lib 1970s, student guidebooks rarely touched on depression. *Ms. Goes to College* (1975) unblushingly dealt with subjects earlier advice writers glossed over or simply ignored: human sexual anatomy, venereal disease, contraception, and recreational drug use. It even offered a chapter on adolescent identity crises. But consider how it treated "Jennifer," who returned home deeply depressed after a fling with drugs her freshman semester, believing she hadn't lived up to her parents' standards. When asked what she did to end her depression, Jennifer answered: "I didn't . . . I just hung in there and . . . just kind of hibernated." Her mood brightened when she moved to another state, and she eventually returned to school.[92] While stories like this made it clear that there was life after depression, they didn't present much in the way of concrete help to girls currently stuck in its depths.

The "Torches of Freedom"

Prior to World War I, smoking tobacco was a mostly male habit. Smoking by women was "a sad mistake" (though one gaining in popularity), wrote the female author of *Etiquette for Americans* (1898):

> At first—a few years ago—smoking among women was treated as a sort of lark or joke among girls who "didn't mean anything." Statistics of an informal collecting then showed that the habit was settling, and on the increase. . . . At the present rate of progress, women and young girls will be smoking in the streets with men. It is a horror and a crying shame; for the debasing character of the custom will inevitably destroy the delicacy of women.[93]

Despite the writer's sky-is-falling tone, this shocking behavior was at the time mostly relegated to a few iconoclasts while the vast majority of American women avoided tobacco altogether. Most would have supported the position taken by the Board of Temperance, Prohibition, and Morals of the Methodist Episcopal Church which in 1919 deemed the increased use of tobacco among women "appalling" and made an "earnest appeal to women to refrain from the use of tobacco in the name of the country's welfare." Women's smoking, it was feared, would lead to a decrease in "the vigor which has been characteristic of the American people." The Woman's Christian Temperance Union concurred, blamed the war for the increase in smoking among young men and women, and called for further research into the harmful effects of cigarette smoking on the unborn—a stance which at the time was probably seen as further evidence of the WCTU's wet-blanket nature, but seems absolutely prescient now.[94]

To moralists like those in the WCTU, smoking challenged an ideal held over from the era of True Womanhood—that women were morally superior to men. In the words of historian Paula Fass, smoking "implied a promiscuous equality between men and women and was an indication that women could enjoy the same vulgar habits and ultimately also the same vices as men." It didn't help that smoking's early adopters were "disreputable or defiant," hence the habit's association with immorality.[95] The New York City alderman behind a 1922 ordinance barring women from smoking in public (and mandating fines or jail time for scofflaws) colorfully described the moral danger unloosed when a woman lit up:

[Y]oung fellows go into our restaurants to find women folks sucking cigarettes. What happens? The young fellows lose all respect for women and the next thing you know the young fellows, vampired by these smoking women, desert their homes, their wives and children, rob their employers and even commit murder so that they can get money to lavish on these smoking women. It's all wrong and I say it's got to stop.[96]

As the alderman soon found out, it was impossible to stop the wispy gray genie once it left the bottle. Women raised such a ruckus over the smoking ban that the mayor rescinded it the following day.

"Women Cigarette Fiends" were the subject of a 1922 article in the *Ladies Home Journal*, a publication that also excoriated that other new phenomenon, jazz. The most widely stated reason for the rise in women smokers, the *Journal* reported, was the "general emancipation and freedom allotted to . . . [women] in recent years." Popular culture shared the blame: women on stage and screen could be seen "in the midst of luxury puffing away at their cigarettes," thereby seducing audience members hungry for Hollywood sophistication to pick up a pack upon exiting the theater.[97]

And then there was advertising. Convinced in the late 1920s that not yet enough American women were smoking, the tobacco industry consulted pioneer public-relations man Edward L. Bernays, who in turn hired a psychoanalyst. The latter reported that since cigarettes were "equated with men" in the public mind they became "torches of freedom" in the hands of the emancipated woman. Seizing on this phrase, Bernays arranged for ten young women (alleged to be debutantes, not college girls) to march down Fifth Avenue on Easter Sunday 1929, cigarettes proudly in hand, in what was termed "The Torches of Freedom Parade." Although scripted down to the smallest detail (a memo discussed exactly how the women should open their purses, find a cig but no matches, ask another for a light, etc.), the parade was presented as a spontaneous event and the newspapers ate it up. Women were reported to be smoking on the street in numbers greater than ever.[98]

Whether it was the result of brazen manipulation in the name of advertising, the siren song of popular culture, or women's growing desire for social freedoms long claimed by men, the number of cigarettes consumed by women doubled between 1923 and 1929.[99] Most of the new female smokers were young adults.

"Twelve years ago," wrote Elizabeth Eldridge in 1936, "a girl's smoking was regarding as a sin only a degree less scarlet than adding a bar sinister to the family escutcheon."[100] College girls who smoked in the 1920s hid their habit from dormitory matrons by using cracker boxes as ashtrays (when not in use, judiciously sprinkled crumbs concealed their true nature) and burning incense (also a favorite with those who smoked other controlled substances in later eras). Where antismoking regulations existed, getting caught with a cigarette could have serious consequences. Smokers caught with cigarettes in their rooms were among the seventeen coeds asked to leave Michigan State Normal College in 1922. The following year, two coeds at the University of Maryland were suspended for smoking at a dance (and in a very twenty-first-century move, promptly hired an attorney to represent their interests).[101] Smokers risked suspension at Smith and Mount Holyoke, and the Nebraska Wesleyan Teachers College refused to issue teaching certificates to women who smoked. Schools that in the early 1920s didn't have anticigarette rules in place, because smoking had not been a problem on campus before that, now rushed to institute them, among them Northwestern in 1922, Vassar in 1925, and the University of California in 1926.[102]

Administrative arguments against smoking by female students generally mentioned the decline and fall of feminine mores that smoking represented. (Health was not yet an issue; in the 1920s, the medical profession was deeply divided over what, if any, health risks were associated with tobacco use.) In 1922, the University of Wisconsin didn't have a rule against smoking, but the dean of women held that there was "an ethical principle" that made the habit unpopular with coeds. After all, she told the *New York Times*, smokers were "an idle, blasé, disappointed class." An intelligent woman, she declared, couldn't "see herself rocking a baby or making a pie with a cigarette in her mouth, flicking ashes in the baby's face or dropping them in the pie crust." The dean of women at the University of Louisville pronounced smoking a mere fad. "I can't feel that a real, genuine womanly girl would form the habit," she said.[103] Goucher College enacted a smoking ban in 1924, after reports of students smoking in Baltimore tearooms generated bad publicity for the school. "If a student wanted to take her own reputation downtown and smoke it all up, that was her private affair. But to smoke up the fair name of Goucher was something different," noted the *Times*.[104]

Historian Barbara Miller Solomon suggests that the uproar over smoking on women's campuses in the 1920s masked greater anxieties about the flapper generation's sexual mores. Certainly, early advertising played on the link between smoking and sex: a 1926 ad for Chesterfield cigarettes featured a languorous woman who asked her cigarette-smoking boyfriend to "blow some my way."[105] To a nonsmoker, the request sounds revolting—but one can't deny its erotic implications.

Some schools simply accepted the futility of controlling this particular aspect of student behavior and opened special smoking rooms, the better to prevent dormitory fires. Although other schools had done so previously, Bryn Mawr received a great deal of publicity, good and bad, when it opened several smoking rooms in 1925. Given the prevailing attitudes that smoking threatened both morality and long-held values of traditional womanhood, Bryn Mawr's decision was not popular with deans of women. "Nothing has occurred in higher education that has so shocked our sense of social decency as the action at Bryn Mawr," screeched the president of Kansas State Teachers College. When she heard about Bryn Mawr's decision, the dean of women at the University of Minnesota "quickly formulated a policy: 'Smoke and leave school.' " Bryn Mawr's action was directly responsible for the presidents of the eastern women's colleges meeting to discuss smoking rules in 1925.[106]

Bryn Mawr's smoking room was the opening salvo in a battle of wills that took place between the mostly prosmoking student bodies and reactionary administrators on other campuses. Vassar capitulated quickly and opened a smoking room in the student building (it was still forbidden in dormitories, on campus, and in restaurants in Poughkeepsie and neighboring towns).[107] The prosmoking forces at other campuses were less immediately successful. When the student government at Mount Holyoke abolished the school's antismoking rules, the president reinstated them.[108]

In 1927, Hood College's student newspaper printed a roundup of smoking rules from other campuses that showed great differences in how the issue was treated:

> Stanford girls may smoke in the dormitories but not in the eyes of the public. At Smith, no smoking is allowed in the college buildings, but is permitted in the tea rooms. Bryn Mawr provides one room in each of the halls of residence for smoking, while Barnard changes it rules yearly according to the temper of the student body. Wellesley girls just don't smoke.[109]

Actually, the girls at Wellesley did smoke—they just hadn't received the administration's blessing yet. They protested a ban on smoking "within the Township of Wellesley and Natick" by holding what could be described as a "smoke-in" at the town line in 1928. Large numbers of girls sat and smoked on a stone wall in an action that led to the opening of an on-campus smoking room.[110] It wasn't easy: when the head of Wellesley's student government association approached president Ellen Pendleton to ask her permission for a smoking room, Pendleton almost broke down in tears. "You girls are never satisfied," she sighed.[111]

For young women at coed schools, the right to smoke on campus brought with it questions of equality. A letter to the editor of the *Daily Illini* in 1920 asserted that "one has a perfectly good right to ask why men should be permitted to smoke while girls are expelled for doing it." When the coeds at Swarthmore asked for a smoking room a decade later, they pointed to the men who were allowed to smoke on the west side of the campus, while they were forbidden to smoke anywhere. [112]

Not surprisingly, as college women got their smoking rooms, cigarettes ceased to be a symbol of rebellion. "The cigarette has ceased to be a cause," wrote the authors of *Mrs. Grundy Is Dead* (1930), a guidebook based on college students' answers to etiquette questionnaires. "Girls no longer smoke to shock; in fact they protect[ed] older women from the discomfort of being annoyed by them" by not smoking in their presence.[113] By 1933, one observer of the college girl's new freedoms found the cigarette to be "a trifle outdated" in its symbolic capacity. Her description of "the thick blue haze" hanging in the recreation room of "a certain Eastern women's college" on a Saturday night suggested that by now, everybody was doing it.[114]

Smoking had become commonplace, but moralistic arguments against it still cropped up now and then. When in 1944 the *Ladies Home Journal* conducted a survey of attitudes and behaviors of its "sub-deb" readers, it found that 58.3 percent of the sixteen- to eighteen-year-olds who responded were smokers. In noting that only a quarter of twelve- to sixteen-year-olds were nicotine fans, the *Journal* made a judgment that reflected those of previous generations: "Some of us feel it's kind of cheapish for a girl always to be dragging a fag; for a young girl anyway."[115] College rules against smoking in public persisted as well: in 1947, students at Stephens College could smoke in the designated room, but nowhere else on campus "or on the streets of Columbia."[116]

The flapper generation of college girls who fought so hard to install dormitory smoking lounges could not have foreseen that public opinion would turn against cigarettes in the wake of further medical research linking the habit with lung cancer, emphysema, and other deadly or debilitating diseases. "Is Smoking Thing of Past?" asked a 1963 editorial in the Mills College newspaper. It went on to announce that cigarette ads would no longer grace its pages nor those of any other college newspaper, the result of a decision by several major tobacco companies to stop advertising at the college level. In the years before the ban, however, cigarette companies aggressively targeted college students, sponsored contests, handed out free packs, and gave campus leaders "large supplies of free cigarettes in the hope of influencing their admirers to take up smoking," not to mention buying enough ads to become college media's largest single source of advertising revenue. Indeed, it's rather shocking to modern sensibilities to see two or three large cigarette ads in a four-page college weekly from the 1940s or 1950s.[117]

But that was a thing of the past. "Soon," the *Mills Stream* predicted, "if many of those outspoken against cigarettes are successful in their efforts, ads will no longer be shown on television during the hours that children watch programs." The editor at *Mills* was wrong only as to the scope of the ban: all cigarette commercials disappeared from television and radio airwaves in 1971.

Drinking

The cigarette wasn't the only symbol of female rebellion in the 1920s. When it comes to stereotypes of the jazz age, the flask is almost as ubiquitous a symbol as the raccoon coat. But what made alcohol a particularly potent badge of youthful insubordination was that it was outlawed not merely on campus but throughout the United States. The Eighteenth

Amendment was ratified and Prohibition became the law of the land in 1919. For the next fourteen years, the manufacture, sale, and transportation (and, by extension, consumption) of alcohol were illegal acts, punishable by fines or imprisonment.

Yet college students drank heavily during these years. When, in 1930, Congress released poll information taken at campuses throughout the country, the ratio of drinkers to teetotalers was close to two to one.[118] As a further indication of the different attitudes about liquor between the campus generation and their parents, when student newspapers printed editorials or articles denouncing the amount of drinking that occurred on campus, the arguments usually had to do with the law, not with morals or the propriety of drinking itself. "We do not approve of Prohibition in its present form . . . ," wrote the editor of *Daily Princetonian* in 1926, before concluding that "the wide-spread and flagrant disregard for this law by college and university students is a dangerous state of affairs."[119]

Like tobacco, alcohol was perceived as a man's vice, and one that women took an active role in fighting. In the 1880s, the *Christian Herald* noted that a "hostess who simply does not offer wine to any guest under any circumstance is using her [womanly] influence effectively and courageously in the cause of temperance in support of Christian principle."[120] There was more to it than religion, however. The antialcohol reformers listed a raft of booze-related evils, but at least this much is true: in the nineteenth and early twentieth centuries, when a woman was utterly dependent on a husband's income to support herself and their children, a man who drank his wages spelled disaster to his family. Getting one's husband and sons to take a temperance pledge of sobriety protected wives and future wives from the poorhouse. Women organized against alcohol in powerful numbers. Led by Frances Willard (formerly the president of Evanston College for Ladies and Northwestern University's dean of women), the Woman's Christian Temperance Union was the largest women's organization of its time, and along with the Anti-Saloon League, its efforts were integral to ratification of the Eighteenth Amendment. All this helped identify temperance as a "woman's cause" in the eyes of turn-of-the-century Americans, and thus their great shock when Prohibition-era college girls happily took a slug when the gin flask was passed.

Like smoking, alcohol consumption by women was perceived to be tied to sexual immorality. A drink or two relaxed a girl's inhibitions, and if there was a car nearby, trouble was sure to follow. In an address before the National Lutheran Educational Conference in 1924, the president of Roanoke College assailed college girls as "hard-drinking, cigarette-puffing, licentious Amazons":

> What can we do when the daughters of the so-called "best people" come out attired scantily in clothing but abundantly in paint; with a bottle of liquor not on the hip but in the handbag; dance as voluptuously as possible . . . ; call for frequent intermissions to give them the opportunity to quench their thirst from the bottle, and with the man of their choice engage in violent petting parties in the luxurious retreat of a big limousine.[121]

If the college president had any remarks about the behavior of the man who found himself in the backseat of the big limousine with the licentious Amazon of his choice, the *New York Times* did not report them.

In 1926, W. O. Cross was a straitlaced recent graduate of the University of Illinois. He wrote an article for a religious magazine that blamed "college looseness" on coeds, who he said participated in "drinking bouts to an extent astounding." He himself had personal knowledge of "back-door deliveries of huge amounts of gin . . . to a quarantined sorority house." If that wasn't bad enough, he knew "of a trainload of sleeping coaches bound to an inter-university game last Fall in which collegians of both sexes, most quite drunk, staged a pajama dance in the aisles."[122] It was Sodom and Gomorrah on the Sunset Limited. Faculty and administrators at Northwestern University and Indiana University stepped forward to defend their students, most of whom had "higher ideals than will be found in any other group of society." Cross stuck by his guns, though he declined to state just where the wild episodes took place (other than in his imagination).[123]

Even reputable experts could get a little overheated on the subject of college girls and alcohol. *The Freshman Girl* (1925) included an essay on "Good Health" that appealed to a girl's responsibility to future generations:

> Jazz, alcohol, and sexual immorality are sapping the vitality of the race; we are nearing the precipice over which all previous civilizations have plunged, but it is not too late to save ourselves if we can conserve these precious inheritable qualities ["health, sanity and creative energy"] for future generations.[124]

Yet most girls were thinking about fun or fitting in, not eugenics, when they stuck a flask in their garter before a football game or dance. Administrators did their best to stanch the flow of alcohol. In 1927, Hood College in Frederick, Maryland, presented a chapel talk by a member of the local Woman's Christian Temperance Union. She warned her listeners that anyone who violated the Eighteenth Amendment was "a traitor to his country and to his God" and that its repeal would "prove that the democracy for which our forefathers shed their blood has failed . . . , and that atheism and agnosticism will thrive since the side on which God stands has been defeated."[125]

Despite the moral reformers' best efforts, college girls by and large supported repeal of the Eighteenth Amendment. The head of the Women's Organization for National Prohibition Reform announced in 1930 that if a vote were held in the women's colleges, "the result would overwhelmingly be in favor of a change in the present system."[126] The change finally came in 1933, when the Eighteenth Amendment was repealed. Afterward the zing went out of most moral arguments against women drinking. The legal age ranged from eighteen to twenty-one, but depending on how strict the rules were at her college (at Stephens in the 1940s they extended to the period when students were traveling to and from the school) and how gross their violation, a girl could still be expelled or at least in some very hot water with the administration if she were caught with alcohol on campus.

While alcohol didn't turn women into the rapacious nymphomaniacs some fantasized, it did make it more difficult for the average girl to say no or protect herself in any number of situations. "A girl today has to be as adroit as ever in handling a drunken date and in staying sober herself," remarked the author of *CO-EDiquette* in 1936:

> If your date is unsteady on his feet, go home from the party with another couple. And never, under any circumstances, let him drive the automobile. If he gets into a brawl, let him fight it out alone. If he gets sick or unmanageable, turn him over to his fraternity brothers or friends. And if he gets amorous, don't wander alone with him in the moonlight.[127]

All of this is still practical advice today. Otherwise, guidebooks and teen magazines were curiously wishy-washy on the subject of drinking. Most seemed more concerned with appearances than with any of alcohol's adverse effects. Many simply warned coeds who tippled to be sure they could hold their liquor because few men admired a drunken girl or enjoyed "taking care of a sick one."[128]

That boys didn't like to see girls drunk was perhaps the number one reason put forth for college girls to avoid alcohol. *Your Best Foot Forward* was a mid-1950s etiquette guide that offered advice based on questionnaires answered by college students. While it did indeed mention the dangers of drunk driving, it also couched its antidrinking argument in terms of reputation:

> If you are the boy in the case and the girl is the one who hasn't maintained her discretion, take her away from the party and keep her from making a spectacle of herself if you possibly can. It is hard enough for a boy to live down making a fool of himself, but a girl's reputation is even harder to regain.[129]

It was a narrow line to walk: no one wanted to see a girl drunk, but teetotalers made drinkers uncomfortable. "No matter how nicely your date says 'no thanks, she'll have gingerale,' it throws a damper on everybody else. I like a girl who takes the drink, then goes and gets her gingerale later," was the opinion of a male sophomore at the University of Buffalo in 1960. Above all, nondrinkers (and the literature most frequently assumed they were female) were admonished to stick to a simple "no, thank you" and not "get flustered or apologize or deliver any stammered lectures on Temperance" (*CO-EDiquette*, 1936) or "act like her date's a candidate for Alcoholics Anonymous" (*Teens Today*, 1960). In fact, it was "more graceful to accept a cocktail than to appear rude." One could always sip or "coddle it along the rest of the evening," or give it away later.[130]

And they're off! Sadie Hawkins Day Race at
San Francisco State College, 1947.

Sex Ed and Husband Hunting

It is something of a shock to the sweet girl graduate who has spent her youth in digging up the Latin roots, studying the Greek forms and acquiring a working knowledge of French, German and Hebrew, to discover that the only language her lover appreciates is baby talk.

HELEN ROWLAND
REFLECTIONS OF A BACHELOR GIRL (1909)

ne day in 1913, Bryn Mawr president M. Carey Thomas addressed the student body at one of her weekly chapel talks. Generally, these were not religious in nature. Instead, topics ranged from etiquette to women's rights to postgraduation opportunities to, on this particular occasion, sex hygiene. Thomas warned the assembled girls how the kissing games that provided the entertainment at a recent party in New York had disastrous consequences: "One man caught seven girls and kissed them. These seven girls have syphilis. Every effort is being made to suppress it. One of the girls committed suicide."[1]

Today it's hard not to snicker at Thomas's overwrought presentation and downright misinformation, but in its day the talk was pretty much par for the course. At the turn of the century, sex education was still largely a matter of providing what one writer called "just enough anatomical explanation to blunt the curiosity of the young . . . and to warn them away from any sexual thoughts, feelings, or actions."[2] Most colleges required freshman to take a course in hygiene, but these were often less than forthright when it came to describing human sexual mechanics, and often presented that sensitive information in a single, perplexing lecture. Sex educator Mary Calderone remembered how as a student in Vassar's required freshman hygiene course in 1921, she listened as a college physician began the annual sex lecture with the following advice: "Now, girls, keep your affections wrapped in cotton wool until Mr. Right comes along."[3] Almost a decade earlier, the *Ladies Home Journal* had complained that the "slight course in hygiene in the Freshman year—very often stigmatized as a farce" required in the women's colleges left students as ignorant or confused about the facts of life as before. A series of lectures in sex physiology required of seniors did "more harm than good. The girls are so incredibly ignorant that this abrupt enlightenment only shocks and repels them! Some are so overcome that it is not uncommon for one or two to leave the room. . . . When a girl can reach her Senior year in college . . . without the slightest idea in the world where babies come from, what is to be said?"[4] If it left the stalwart *Ladies Home Journal* speechless, the quality of sex instruction in the women's colleges must have been truly abysmal. (It should be noted that the *Journal* made its argument for improved sex education not as an end in itself, but as part of a larger call for women's practical education. In other words, if woman's true career was to be a wife and mother, she'd darn well better know where babies came from.)

The move toward better sex education began in the years following World War I. In 1918 Congress passed the Chamberlain-Kahn Act in response to alarming civilian venereal disease statistics uncovered as a result of the war effort. One immediate result was the distribution of over half a million dollars in 1919 and 1920 to create or shore up social hygiene departments at more than forty college and universities. As historian Jeffrey P. Moran points out, few college students suffered from VD—but they did "form a front line of support for sex education in the future."[5] The 1920s also saw a change in sexual mores among college students. Raised in the belief that all sex was taboo, young men and women at college rediscovered the erotic nature of love. They experimented with "petting," a term that encompassed a range of behaviors from casual kissing to intimate below-the-waist fondling, but always stopped short of intercourse. While True Women revered purity, a young woman on a college campus in the 1920s could indulge without damage to her reputation in sexual behaviors that would have branded her grandmother a strumpet—though marriage remained the ultimate goal.[6]

Just because the younger generation had rediscovered the pleasures of sex didn't mean that their elders approved. Up-to-date flappers surely stifled yawns, giggles, or both at *The Freshman Girl*'s antiquated advice regarding sex on campus, circa 1925:

> By cheap familiarity a girl sins against man's conception of womanhood and makes life more difficult for him than it need be. At her best, the girl who is a friend to a man of her college is kind to his dream. She sells her birthright when she becomes a mere playmate, and forgets that God made her for man's helpmeet.[7]

What mothers considered "cheap familiarity" many daughters simply called petting—and probably made the argument that everybody did it. "There are only two kinds of co-eds," wrote the editor of a college newspaper in 1923, "those who have been kissed and those who are sorry they haven't been kissed." The following year, a study found that 92 percent of all coeds had petted at one time or another.[8]

Given the new attitudes toward sex, it's not surprising that students began to ask for more and better information on both sexuality and marriage than what they received in their hygiene classes. In 1922, Barnard students proposed a biology curriculum that included "the facts of structure, functions, development and hygiene of the sex and reproductive apparatus of the male and female," "the nature and power of the sex impulse" as well as "pathological effects of perverse and unsocial uses of sex," and how to make "a satisfactory adjustment in marriage and homemaking." Around the same time, students at Northwestern University complained that the "faculty was old and fogeyish, and that sex hygiene is not given enough prominence."[9] Finally, at the University of North Carolina in 1925, sociology professor Ernest R. Groves responded to the requests of male students with the first-ever elective college course in marriage. It included information on sexual fulfillment in wedlock, the psychology of family life, and child rearing. It even encroached on a staple of today's self-help industry: how to meet the right girl.[10]

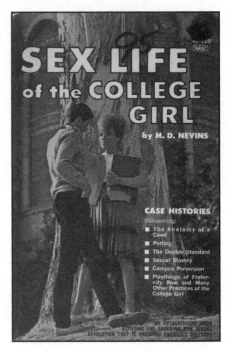

Everybody seemed to be interested in the Sex Life of the College Girl *(1964).*

The so-called marriage courses caught on like wildfire. Where schools wouldn't offer them for credit, students often held their own classes. At Michigan State College in 1938, coeds arranged and attended a series of lectures by doctors and professors about sex and marriage (as did the men, but completely separately). The same year, students at Smith College organized four seminars on the physical and psychological aspects of marriage.[11] When students at Indiana University complained about their required one-hour-long hygiene course (which they attended in sex-segregated sections), the Association of Women Students teamed up with zoology Professor Alfred C. Kinsey who kindly volunteered to teach a new course on marriage and the family. As proposed to the administration, it would be open only to seniors of both sexes (Kinsey asserted that there was no purpose in the practice of segregating men and women) and would cover legal, economic, biological, sociological, and psychological aspects of marriage. Attendees would receive no college credit. To guard against prurient students popping in for only the juiciest bits, those who missed class would be required to read the professor's lecture notes in his office. The administration approved, and on June 23, 1938, ninety-eight students—seventy of whom were women—met for the first lecture. Despite the "seniors only" edict, the majority of people attending the class were postgraduates, with seniors, faculty members and spouses, and even a smattering of underclassmen making up the rest.[12]

Where many of the marriage courses stressed the homemaking aspects of marriage after an initial explanation of sexuality only slightly expanded from the old hygiene days, the course at Indiana University went into explicit detail about sexual anatomy, how to perform intercourse ("The vagina must be spread open as the erect male organ penetrates," read Kinsey's notes for the lecture on "Reproductive Anatomy and Physiology"), and how to prevent pregnancy.[13] Kinsey himself spoke on these topics, while other professors and guests lectured on less racy subjects, such as the economics and psychology of marriage and the sociology of the family. The course was a huge hit. According to Kinsey biographer James H. Jones, "short of free tuition, it is difficult to imagine what could have generated more enthusiasm among students."[14] Kinsey benefited, too; from students in the course, he began to gather the case histories that made up the landmark studies *Sexual Behavior in the Human Male* (1948) and *Sexual Behavior in the Human Female* (1953).

By the 1940s and 1950s, the marriage courses on many campuses put less emphasis on psychology and sexuality and more on personal problems and emotions. These were the sort of "Marriage and the Family" courses that Betty Friedan took to task as part and parcel of the feminine mystique, classes that were so nonacademic that students at the University of Illinois were released from a term paper if they performed six hours of baby-sitting, or at Stephens, could submit a wedding plan as a term paper.[15]

Nevertheless, one might deduce from all this that the college campus of the early twentieth century was a hotbed of sweaty students seething to test the new mores by putting new information to practical use. They may well have been, but administrations had long kept tabs on their female students' comings and goings, and they weren't about to stop now.

Dating Under the Parietal Rules

In order to give girls a place to entertain, special, appropriately chaperoned parlors were set aside for receiving visitors, usually one per dormitory. These were part and parcel of the college experience from the very beginning. Totally lacking in privacy, they caused untold anxiety for generations of both college girls and their suitors. "What one of the Alumni has not at some time made a call at Ladies' Hall?" asked the authors of *Oberliniana*, a slim volume of anecdotes and poetry published in honor of Oberlin's fiftieth anniversary in 1883:

> With what trepidation did he ascend the front steps and give his card to the bell-boy, while groups of girls were passing in and out? Why should so many know of his private affairs? Why couldn't he pay a visit to a young lady without its being advertised? The lady comes. The parlor is entered. No bay-windows or hidden angles. And others are there, too. It seems as if everyone must hear your remarks about the climate. Finally you succeed in becoming oblivious to all externals, when suddenly the ominous Chapel bell peals forth and a moment after all is deserted.[16]

The parlor's awkward, public nature was exactly the point. Men and women weren't supposed to get too comfortable—or too romantic. Protocols were strict, but students always angled to get around them. *Oberliniana* included a story that although probably apocryphal reflected the creativity expended by wily students trying to bend the rules. One of the matrons admonished the coeds to always keep one chair between themselves and any "gentleman caller" who might visit them at the Ladies'

Hall. One evening she was shocked to find a couple "practically occupy-ing the *same* chair" in the reception room. Under questioning, the young man told her they "were only following out your instructions . . . that the ladies and gentlemen should have but one chair between them!"[17] Even the editors of *Oberliniana* had a hard time swallowing that one over a hundred years ago, but you get the point.

At Whittier Hall, a women's residence for students at Barnard and Teachers College at the turn of the twentieth century, there were "spoon-holders" instead of parlors. These were "little nooks and corners con-structed by the sentimental architect in which it is possible for a girl to discuss [Robert] Browning with her 'brother' or 'cousin.' For all male visi-tors must be relatives," explained the *New York Times* in 1906. It was up to "Mother" Daniels, the matron, to see that the spoonholders were empty by 10:30 sharp every night. Mother Daniels was not unsympa-thetic to young love—although she drew the line at ten brothers, she was known to permit as many as a dozen cousins.[18]

Spelman students faced similar restrictions. Before 1920, a man who wished to visit a Spelman student used a designated entrance to the reception room in Rockefeller Hall, where he asked for the girl he wished to see. A messenger was sent to retrieve her, and then the clock started running—literally. At Spelman, visits with the opposite sex were limited to twenty minutes once a month, unless the boy in question was the girl's brother, in which case he might visit once a week. Not surprisingly, Spel-man students frequently discovered brothers they didn't know they had, as did girls on other campuses with similar rules. In 1920, the reception room in Rockefeller Hall was abolished, and students were allowed a two-hour period every Saturday afternoon in which they might receive friends in new dormitory reception rooms, under the watchful eye of a matron, of course.[19]

The parietal rules also wreaked havoc with off-campus dating. Women almost always had earlier and more restrictive curfews than men, and this made for some fancy footwork if they were to get back to their dorms on time. In the 1930s, Stanford coeds were allowed to stay out until 1:30 A.M. Given that the bright lights of San Francisco were an hour away, it took "a gallant Stanford escort to leave a dance as promptly as Cinderella did" in order to have his date back at the dorm in Palo Alto on time. As a result, the 1:30 rule "seriously hamper[ed] a girl's popularity," as Stanford men had no curfew and could stay out as late as they pleased with curfew-free local girls. Similarly, University of California coeds had to be in by 2:00 A.M., a tricky maneuver in the days before the Bay Bridge opened and the last ferry to Berkeley left San Francisco at 1:00 A.M.[20]

College girls frustrated by their school's strictness could find solace in the knowledge that there was almost always a campus where things were worse. In the 1930s, Elizabeth Eldridge declared William and Mary's rules to be the most conservative. The school's rule book included a campus map indicating the brightly lit and well-policed areas "for dates and areas in which women may walk with dates." Eldridge dryly wondered whether proximity to the sights of Colonial Williamsburg resigned "the co-eds to living in this deliciously quaint pattern while on other campuses their gayer sisters go whither they please unquestioned."[21]

Of course, there never was a rule that a cunning college girl couldn't break or at least seriously bend as needed. A sorority member at the University of Nebraska in the 1930s remembered how she and her sisters handled their house's curfew:

> We had to be inside by 10:30 on weekdays and 12:30 on weekends. The rules were very carefully written—inside by 10:30 P.M., doors locked, lights off—but what the rules forgot to mention was that the boys were supposed to be *outside*. And they weren't always, but we followed the rules the way they were written.[22]

Claiming to follow the letter if not the spirit of the law made for a plucky excuse, even if it was unlikely to protect a transgressor from punishment. Another 1930s sorority girl, this one at the University of Wisconsin, recalled that a girl's roommate might "slip down and unlock the door" if she didn't make it back to the dorm before curfew. "But if you got caught, you were in plenty of trouble—heaven help you then!"

In the early 1960s, reporter Gael Greene interviewed 614 students

(538 women and 76 men) from 102 colleges and universities around the country about their sexual attitudes and behavior, and published the result as *Sex and the College Girl* (1964). To a modern-day reader, the book is a paean to frustration. Mid-twentieth-century mores called for young women to be abstinent before marriage, but hormones, love, peer pressure, and personal choice all militated against it. Only the most naïve students or administrators believed that curfews and sign-in times stopped students from having sex. For every girl like the one Greene described in the mid-1960s, who sailed in "two minutes after curfew on a breath of bourbony air with a length of red fabric trailing behind and bubbling: 'What red thing?—Well, what do you know? I got a necktie caught in my panty girdle,'" there were thousands more.[23]

"Where the Girls Are" and Other Guides to Foreign Campuses

Men who prayed to some day lose a tie, a sock, or any piece of clothing under similar circumstances were assisted by guides to the complex and varying rules at local women's schools published by enterprising students at Yale and Princeton. For example, *Going Places: A Guidebook to Eastern Women's Colleges from Virginia to New Hampshire* (1956) included curfew hours, campus maps, and dormitory telephone numbers, as well as names, addresses, and descriptions of local restaurants and nightspots, near and not so near to Yale. A jaunty hitchhiking wolf on the cover made clear the nature of these travels.

In 1965, a group of Princeton men published a similar guide, *Where the Girls Are*. It promised no magic incantations: "You'll have to do most of the work of choosing, locating, and snowing your women yourself. But we can help with some of the duller parts." It sold over eight hundred copies in three weeks.[24] Two years later, it appeared as a fully fledged, commercially published paperback, expanded to more than two hundred pages and covering women's and coed colleges throughout the United States. It's not surprising these guides sold well. Consider the maze of rules in effect at Endicott Junior College in Beverly, Massachusetts:

A handy guide to the parietal rules at the eastern women's colleges for the wolf on the go, 1956.

> **CURFEW** for freshmen for the first six weeks is 7:30 P.M. on weeknights, 1:00 A.M. on Saturday, midnight for a maximum of three Friday nights, and 10:30 P.M. on Sunday. Thereafter, a 9:45 P.M. limit once a week and an 11:00 P.M. once a semester are permitted during the week. Weekend curfews from then until April are midnight on Friday and 1:00 A.M. on Saturday. From then on, weekend curfew is 1:00 A.M. both nights.
>
> Seniors have a 9:45 P.M. curfew on all weeknights (with three 11:00's per semester), 1:00 A.M. on Friday and Saturday, and 10:30 P.M. on Sunday. If a girl is on academic probation or academic restriction, however, she must be in the dorm by 7:30 P.M. for three weekends out of eight. She is allowed to take her proper number of 11:00's.[25]

Not all schools had curfew rules as byzantine as these, but it's clear why the dating man needed a little help getting around. In addition to objective information about curfews, penalties, and overnights, *Where the Girls Are* also presented a lively dose of subjective opinion about the female denizens of the campuses covered. "Nine out of ten California girls are beautiful, and the tenth goes to Stanford" began the entry for that institution. "And what's worse—O infamy—most of them are serious book-weenies." About the Vassar girl: "She goes down well with scotch. She goes down well with gin. She goes down well with bourbon. Even for teetotalers, if such exist, she goes . . . But why go on?"[26]

Needless to say, many college women did not take kindly to the characterizations in *Where the Girls Are*. *Where the Boys Are* (1966) was a tongue-in-cheek response that gave girls the scoop on what they'd find at the Ivies and other men's campuses on the eastern seaboard. Although the cover said it was "compiled by the Editors of the Smith College *Sophian* and the Mount Holoyke *News*," it was in fact written by two men from Princeton (home of *Where the Girls Are*), though allegedly researched by girls at those campuses.[27] They were somewhat hampered by a lack of material: the parietals at the men's schools were nowhere as restrictive as those at girls' schools—one simply didn't need a guidebook to figure out where and when visiting was allowed. But what *Where the Boys Are* lacked in practical advice it made up for in sarcasm—and that was exactly the point. "Be prepared for plenty of pot, plenty of Existentialism, and plenty of Susan Sontag" at Columbia; regarding the Naval Academy at Annapolis, "before you've left . . . you'll know what the post has always known: Uncle Sam does want YOU."[28]

A Dating Handicap?

The more one reads mid-twentieth-century prescriptive literature aimed at teenage girls, the more one wonders that any of them went to college at all. Books and articles suggested that female intelligence should be hidden, lest it frighten men off, and described college as a smorgasbord of prospective husbands rather than as a place of learning. The late teen years were prime mating years, and why should women waste time in college (except to meet men, of course) if they faced a future as a homemaker? This mindset was especially prevalent in the years after World War II, when American women returned (sometimes kicking and screaming) to the kitchen when the mostly male veterans came home and wanted their jobs back. But it doesn't take much searching to find earlier examples of college as a prelude to domesticity. "To the average American girl the two most important events in life are her matriculation in college and her matriculation in wedlock," wrote the dean of women at Oregon State Agricultural College in 1925. According to the dean, both the B.A. and the MRS. were part of a girl's "progress towards complete womanhood."[29]

College was presented by one 1940 advice book not as career training but a mere stop gap before a job and ultimately marriage:

> A girl finishes school at about sixteen, seventeen, or eighteen, and then she is confronted with what she wants to do. She is too young to marry. She is also very young for work. She realizes she has a great deal to learn. So, if she has the opportunity, she will want to go to college.[30]

Of course, many of us went to college because we had nothing better to do at the time. "But what if you're planning—or hoping—to get married as soon as you can?" *Teen World* asked its readers in 1960, before going right ahead and putting some words in their mouths: " 'How well I do in school won't help me cook a pot-roast, or iron a crisp collar when I'm a housewife,' you might say." *Teen World* didn't mention college in its answer—it was trying to get girls to stay in high school, let alone go on— but gave an otherwise pat response: "you know school is vital to helping you enjoy many things—the newspapers, being part of your community, and later, even being a helpful mother."[31]

When marriage and college collided in midcentury advice books for teen girls, college almost always came away the worse for wear. One such book, dating from 1952, listed study as a "dating handicap" to girls who eventually planned on being married: "If one's study is not to be a life-time pursuit and one is expecting eventually to be married, then study must not absorb all one's time during the dating years."[32]

Another guidebook included a chapter titled "I want to get married some day—how far shall I go in school?" The answer here was just far enough to mirror one's future husband's education. It was another case of being "smart enough" rather than fully educated. Another guide praised wives who dropped out of college to put their husbands through school ("a bright new trend"). This gave a woman "the joy of being a part of her husband's preparation for a career."[33]

The specter of old-maid spinsterhood loomed large. A girl who remained single past "the dating years" (an amorphous time frame that advice writers never quite got around to identifying) might never marry. Considering that marriage, motherhood, and homemaking were seen to be the prime female vocations, an unmarried woman rocked the social boat—especially if she was happy and fulfilled. Fortunately, from this point of view, the latter was a rarity, at least in most prescriptive literature and fiction. "Satisfaction and self-sufficiency" might result from a career, according to a 1939 advice book for young women, but that paled when compared to the "full, complete happiness and satisfaction" offered by marriage.[34]

Refugees from the Spinster Factory

Given the mid-twentieth-century emphasis on marriage and mating, it's not surprising that guidebooks and fiction suggested that girls considering college think less about a school's prestige and academic programs than the presence of the opposite sex—or lack thereof. The women's colleges had venerable histories, yet they were often derided as "spinster factories" that regularly graduated classes filled with highly educated old maids. It was a popularly held notion that girls who wanted to find husbands were better served by coed campuses. A scene from a 1948 short story that appeared in *Calling All Girls* magazine perfectly summed up this line of thinking. "And Now Farewell!" is the story of Ellen, a high-school senior whose parents can't afford to send her to college, and of how she learns to accept her fate. Things aren't made any easier for poor Ellen as her friends insist on discussing in front of her the pros and cons of the campuses they'll be attending in the fall. Two of her buddies have chosen coed schools, whereas a third contemplates four years in a single-sex institution:

> "Gosh, Darlene, why go to a girl's college in this day and age?"
> "Why not?" said Darlene.
> Marilyn caricatured a sigh. "Answer her in one word, Virginia."
> "Men!"
> "Lush college men," Marilyn chattered. "Scads of them, Darlene. Simply battalions."[35]

The availability of datable men, lush or not, was the reason why the formidable author of *CO-EDiquette* (1936) noted that "trying to persuade a girl to return to a 'spinster factory' after she has tasted co-ed life is like persuading a kitten to return to milk after it has tasted raw meat."[36] Yet kittens also needed to learn when to sheath their claws— during class, for example, if they were going to get anything of an academic nature accomplished:

> [The co-ed] must be able to work side-by-side with [men], managing an election or getting the paper to press, without letting sentiment interfere, and she must be able to dance and date with them without letting her bluestockings show. Bluestockings in class, and silk hose and silver slippers in the evening. It's a big order, but a girl today must be equal to it if she is to deserve the name of co-ed.[37]

Going to a coeducational school was simply not "a one-way ticket to popularity unlimited," as Elisabeth Ann Hudnut reminded readers of her guidebook *You Can Always Tell a Freshman* (1949). Neither was spinsterhood the inevitable outcome for those taking up residence at a single-sex school:

> You who choose a women's college are apt to be pitied as ones who are about to take a four-year vacation from the bright lights and all things

Hunting College for Girls

In the 1950s, a barroom wag might draw a few chuckles by offering a light from a novelty matchbook featuring a spoof advertisement for "Hunting College for Girls." A "clever" name play on New York's women-only Hunter College, the fictitious Hunting College offered "special courses in the hunting, trapping, care and feeding of men."* The Hunting girl's back-to-school supplies were pictured in a cartoon on the matchbook's cover: among them, a set of falsies, a marriage license, and a rolling pin—presumably for keeping hubby in order as much as for the production of pastry. The facetious first-year curriculum included:

- What the Man [sic] Act can do for you! . . .†
- How to let yourself go (but only to a license bureau)
- How to load a shotgun (when all else fails)

On the bright side, these witticisms probably weren't much funnier back then either. But on whole, the matchbook illustrated a commonly held assumption about college girls—that on either coed or women's campus, they were simply trolling for a man rather than studying for any true academic purpose.

HUNTING COLLEGE FOR GIRLS...

who are hunting for husbands!

SPECIAL COURSES IN THE HUNTING, TRAPPING, CARE AND FEEDING OF MEN

---

* Hunter College's Bronx campus accepted its first male students in 1951; by 1964, all campuses were fully coed.

† Also known as the White Slave Traffic Act, the Mann Act (1910) made it a federal offense to transport women across state lines "for the purpose of prostitution or debauchery, or for any other immoral purpose."

masculine. Needless to say, this is a misconception. A women's college is not a graveyard, so if you are buried there you have no one to blame but yourself.[38]

Much fun could be had at dances and festivities held with boys imported from nearby men's schools—and come Friday, girls lined up at local train stations to head off to weekends at the men's colleges. Even with these opportunities for gals at the fem sems to take advantage of, Hudnut concluded that the coed's opportunities to meet boys on campus were downright "boundless."

Coeducation provided such limitless opportunities for fraternizing with the opposite sex that some "immature-minded girls" went boy crazy, taking nothing from the collegiate experience but "a hectic and unwholesome social training."[39] Hudnut addressed this issue and provided a prudent reminder as to why—at least in theory—girls were at college in the first place: "If you are apt to be the type who goes Crazy Over Numbers [of men], remember to watch yourself. College rhymes with knowledge. Your primary purpose in being here is bigger and better than learning to distinguish fraternity pins at fifty paces."[40]

Academics may have been the primary purpose for some of Hudnut's audience, but for others, given the post–World War II economic boom that allowed a single breadwinner to support a family, and a renewed cultural emphasis on women as homemakers, for many the "primary purpose" of education was indeed to find a husband. In fact, while some disparaged "husband hunters," others considered it an absolutely acceptable reason for going to a coed college—as it had been almost from the start.

In May 1940, *Better Homes & Gardens* magazine published two essays under the umbrella title "If Your Daughter Goes to College." The essayists compared the types of education girls received at women's colleges and coeducational universities. Both arguments, however, were couched in terms of "what sort of homemaker, wife, mother, and useful citizen" the varying institutions would graduate. The issue was of vital importance as it underlay "the whole structure of family life, and the future of the homes of America."[41] It wasn't quite the eugenicists' argument for motherhood, citizenship, and racial purity, nonetheless it was based on an assumption that "homemaker" was the ultimate career for which college fitted middle-class white women. "If you do not care about going to college in order to prepare yourself for a career," stated a midcentury advice book for teenage girls, "at least go, if you can, in order to prepare yourself to be a good mother."[42]

Wainwright Evans (coauthor with Ben Lindsey of *The Revolt of Modern Youth,* a famous 1920s exposé of a younger generation besotted by jazz, gin, and sex) used the example of the quite possibly fictitious Fay Lathrop to discuss why coeducation was a better choice for girls. Red-haired, freckle-faced Fay "wasn't much on looks," according to Evans, but she had "a Figure and lots of Personality." Those positive attributes, plus a pushy mother with sewing skills, were all she needed to land her man. Her mother whips up a wardrobe that "clung in just the right places; . . . Fay had plenty of them," then sees to it that Fay is transferred from her public high school to a prestigious girls' school, where she graduates. Armed with a résumé padded to match her figure, Fay enrolls at the state university. Here she finds "a maximum number of men" and promptly joins "one of the best" sororities: "From then on her energies, except for the modicum of study needed not to flunk out, were devoted to men. Men were her occupation, study and other girls her avocation. Knowing just what she was after, she soon had more dates than any girl in the place."[43]

She also soon accomplishes her man-hunting mission. It's a good thing that Mrs. Lathrop has been busy stitching up Fay's trousseau in the short interim between enrollment and engagement.

To Evans, the moral of Fay's story was clear: separating women from the "normalizing and naturally desired companionship of men . . . during the vital and irreplaceable mating years just [didn't] make sense." Evans wasn't the first one to argue that isolation from the opposite sex led to spinsterhood. Almost forty-five years earlier, in the course of writing about the apparently dismal marriage rates among college women, another observer noted that it was her impression that "four years of early womanhood spent in seclusion from free acquaintance from men" left the woman's college graduate "less fitted afterward for informal friendships and cooperations with men."[44] Spending time with the opposite sex in the classroom benefited both; it helped "callow youth toward the mental maturity of manhood" and led girls "toward the bloom of womanhood."[45]

For women especially, the point of higher education was not purely to gain knowledge in an academic sense (though Evans pointed out that "Fay managed to collect a pretty fair book education, too," even if it sounded like she had precious little time to do so). It was to gain a thorough knowledge of men, even if she didn't find one to marry during her years as an undergraduate. But this was a rarity for girls who planned ahead; a 1940 guidebook suggested that girls who wanted to marry as soon as possible attend a state university and study home economics, dietetics, and interior decoration.[46]

The idea that men were elusive quarry, ever wary of the aggressive husband-hunting female, was a time-honored stereotype. Played out in the campus setting, there was a suggestion that women were less interested in study than their male counterparts, who, after all, were going to be the heads of households: "Men, especially, have a mental set against a serious love affair which may cut into the real business of college, and possibly end it. Girls, on the other hand, even though serious students, realize their chief business is marriage or the promise of marriage."[47]

Matrimony lurked around even the most innocuous of corners. The senior who won Wellesley's traditional hoop rolling race was awarded a bridal bouquet and proclaimed most likely to be the first woman in her class to marry. (In a concession to modern times, she's now said to be the "first person in her class who will achieve success, however she defines it."[48])

Sadie Hawkins Day

Although the strict etiquette preached by the mid-twentieth-century teen guides and etiquette books made it impossible (or at least unladylike) for young women to take the initiative in dating, there was one college tradition that changed all that—if only for one special day in November. Sadie Hawkins Day and its attendant festivities grew out of Al Capp's popular "Li'l Abner" comic strip. On November 15, 1937, a story line debuted featuring Sadie Hawkins, "the homeliest gal in the hills," and her father's desperate measures to marry her off. One of his schemes included instigating a footrace in which eligible (and not-so-eligible) bachelors were chased down by the single women of Dogpatch, with matrimony the consequence for the captured. The story line proved so popular that Capp repeated it annually.

Considering the restrictions placed on young women, not to mention the flow of youthful hormones in both sexes, it's perhaps not surprising that colleges began re-creating Sadie Hawkins's pursuit of the Dogpatch bachelors on their own campuses. In a complete reversal from long-accepted norms, on Sadie Hawkins Day girls asked boys for dates, then planned and paid for the evening's entertainment, sending beet green and radish corsages ("all in a spirit of mock seriousness" noted the 1955 *Your Best Foot Forward*)—a perfect touch for the special hillbilly-themed dances held by many schools in honor of the occasion.[49]

The dances were the genteel end to an action-packed day. Many campuses held Sadie Hawkins races, wherein college men were chased down by their coed counterparts. Morris Harvey College (now the University of Charleston, West Virginia) claims to have sponsored the first Sadie Hawkins Day Race and Dance in 1938, though by the following year *Life* magazine reported that over two hundred colleges held similar festivities.[50] Some students went so far as to dress up Dogpatch-style, with boys in tattered jeans and torn shirts, while girls played Daisy Mae in skimpy skirts or burlap dresses sewed with twine.[51] Whether participants were in costume or street clothes, the race always began with the men taking a head start followed by a bevy of presumably lusty coeds. At San Francisco State University in the late 1940s and early 1950s, the men had an extra advantage: their pursuers were blindfolded.

While Sadie Hawkins Day gave young women, used to a system in which they were considered "forward" if they so much as telephoned the object of their desire, an opportunity to act aggressively without being the brunt of social stigma, it was not the protofeminist ritual some currently suggest.[52] The race was a popular human-interest subject for the local papers—those who carried Capp's strip might tie the campus ritual in with promotion of their comics page. News photos labeled participating coeds "scheming, husband-hungry females" who "dragged [male students] to the slaughter."[53] It was all in good fun, of course, but this was hardly the language of liberation.

There were regional variants of the turnabout dance. For the annual Golddigger's Ball at Ohio State, girls invited boys to the dance, sent corsages "of the vegetable variety," and crowned a "Golddigger's King."[54] Like Sadie Hawkins Day, the Golddigger's Ball gave college girls a chance to take the initiative, but "golddigger" was hardly less pejorative than the barracuda image associated with girls chasing boys.

A coed trees her man. Sadie Hawkins Day at San Francisco State University, 1947.

The College Weekend

Schooled as we are today in scenarios of abduction and date rape, it's hard to imagine a young woman taking a train to an unfamiliar town for a weekend-long rendezvous with a hardly known boy—or even for a blind date. But the college weekend or house party was a popular ritual from the 1920s through the late 1960s and early 1970s, when many of the traditionally single-sex schools went coed or dropped their parietal rules. In the 1940s, Emily Post reassured mothers "inclined to fear that it cannot be proper for their daughters to stay in fraternity houses" that the level of chaperonage provided changed the wolves' den into a veritable bunny's nest. Thanks to a profusion of housemothers and faculty members pressed into supervisory duty, from the moment of arrival to that of departure, "house-party visitors couldn't be more thoroughly chaperoned."[55] (Twenty years later, the chaperons appeared to have fled the scene entirely, when a previously "sheltered" Vassar junior recalled the shock of her first Ivy League weekend: "I walked into this Princeton house party. There in one corner of the floor were a boy and girl making love—and in another corner, a boy and boy. Talk about coming of age in Samoa!" [referencing Margaret Mead's anthropological classic].)[56]

Chaperonage was usually the least of a girl's worries. Those who secured invitations to whatever festivities were happening at the local men's campus on any given weekend descended on the local train station en masse, and chances were good that two or more girls who already knew each other would be sharing a room together. Group activities were the norm at these weekends—even *Esquire Etiquette* (1953), a guide compiled by the editors of the debonair men's magazine for the sophisticated young man, admitted that the "secret of college week-ending" was to plan "so that you and she will never be surrounded by less than fifteen people."[57] This protected both parties from the potential disaster inherent in making small talk with a complete stranger for a period of twenty-four or more hours.

For men and women, the etiquette of the college weekend was complex. According to Post, who included four pages of "Don'ts Which All House Party Visitors Must Remember," one of the first challenges to a pleasant weekend was the state of a young woman's luggage:

DON'T arrive with a shabby down-at-heel suitcase with handle half off or lock broken, or packed with straps carelessly hanging out, which to every fastidious man will discount the effect of your otherwise lovely appearance as completely as though you wore unshined oxfords tied with laces made of knotted together string.[58]

Who would have expected that "neat, compact, good-looking luggage" would please the girl-starved denizens of the Ivy Leagues "much more than the smartest hat ever bought"?

Carrying their smartest suitcases, then, girls usually arrived on a Thursday or Friday evening, just in time for a welcoming dance. "For this," Miss Post advised that Sally wear "the prettiest evening dress she owns":

Her clothes, by the way, must have the effect of simplicity suitable to her age. College faculties do not look with approval at bare backs, dripping earrings and obvious make-up. . . . Moreover, the boy who invited Sally to the house party likes her as he remembered her at home and does not want a blasé woman who looks thirty-five in her place. He has asked a girl—not a blasé woman.[59]

If you believed Emily Post, Ivy League men really went for a sturdy trunk.

But in the estimate of *Esquire Etiquette*, the big dance was exactly the right time for wholesome girls to flash a little bare-backed sophistication—and if it increased their date's status with the boys, so much the better.

> You've asked her for the prime purpose of showing her off—that wholesome-looking girl you really *like* rates only the opening game. So, let her show. If you don't tell her what she has to know, she'll play it safe in a little "basic black" which she can "dress up or down" when she sees what's up. But if you *tell* her: well, you might find out what a red dress in a sea of "little black" look-alikes does for a man's ego.[60]

Despite the intricacies of planning and etiquette, a lot could go wrong in the course of a weekend. In 1959, *Seventeen* ran a story about a college weekend gone bad—almost beyond redemption. In "Blind Date," college junior Virginia goes to visit Jack at law school. She has never met him, but his mother and her aunt used to know each other at school, and his "big bold handwriting, scrawled dashingly across the . . . special delivery letter" intrigued her enough to turn down another date and take the train to his neighboring college. After all, Jack is in graduate school, "a sure sign of maturity and worldliness." Poor Virginia! Her first inkling that things are not going as planned is when he leaves her "humiliated, unclaimed" at the train station. Finally, after all the other girls have met their dates, Jack rushes up, claps her on the back like one of the boys, and greets her with a hearty "Hi, Beaver!"—for her fur coat, of course.[61]

Then Virginia gets shock number two. Like many online dating devotees of the internet era, she discovers she has been snookered by a misleadingly attractive photo of her date. Instead of the expected "boyish grin, tousled hair and open-necked polo shirt," Jack turns out to be short and four-eyed. What's far worse, though, is that he has never read *Esquire Etiquette*, which stressed the importance of telling a visiting date exactly what activities the weekend would include in order for her to dress appropriately. "One walk with High Heels, or one cocktail party with Moccasins, will convince you of the importance of being explicit," the book counseled.[62] Virginia is in clothing hell. First she must borrow his jeans and tennis shoes and submit to a quick horse-back ride ("You wrote you liked the outdoors, remember?" he tells her), then he hauls her off to a dressy cocktail party at the clubhouse with-out allowing her to change into the "exquisite" dress she's brought for the occasion.[63] Virginia keeps her composure when Jack goes off to refill her drink, "nodding her head and forcing a laugh" with his friends. He does his best to keep her entertained, but Virginia is angry and shy in equal measure, unnerved by the large group of people who find Jack "absolutely hilarious" while she is stuck wearing her fur coat over his too-big blue jeans.

Later, Jack allots her fifteen minutes to shower and change into her evening gown before the big dance. Virginia is flooded with relief at finally being properly attired, but when Jack's roommate cuts in during their first dance she learns that she and Jack are the victims of a prank: "I cut out a snapshot of him and wrote you as a joke, and then when it was all sewed up and you answered right away, there was nothing he could do," laughs the roommate. Jack, he tells Virginia, has sworn to never date "another drip recommended by his mother" and thinks dances are a waste of time. Aghast at these revelations, Virginia begins to see Jack with new eyes. He, after all, has done his best to please her despite the awkward situation. Everything is sorted out during a walk in the rain the next morning. Virginia realizes she likes Jack and that he even looks like the extremely flattering picture in the letter. "Just a little."[64]

"Blind Date" ended with Virginia dreaming of fixing Jack's dinner when he came home from the office, but all college weekends didn't end so cozily. Getting dumped by the boy who invited her or being stuck with a dud date were probably a girl's biggest house-party night-mares, barring sexual assault. *Esquire Etiquette* warned men against leaving "your own date to free-lance" with another girl, though it was perfectly acceptable to contact her more appealing classmate after the weekend was over. "Only if your date has gone beyond the pale, and the new girl's date is passed out beyond yon sofa," could a man make a move to "change the order of things" during the weekend itself.[65] It was equally bad form for a girl to ditch her date. Emily Post didn't provide any contingency plans for girls who found themselves in either such awkward position beyond the succinct "DON'T show chagrin or disappointment, ever."[66]

"More Rules Than a Prison"– Football for the Disinterested

Hiding one's emotions was a useful strategy at other points during the college weekend. Wearing a lovely chrysanthemum and waving a team pennant while seated in the chilly fall air of the stadium with a date were all well and good if a girl actually enjoyed the game (and I know plenty of women do). For the rest of us, however, football was "more elaborate than a ballet and [had] more rules than a prison," as one teen magazine described it.[67] For disinterested parties, sitting through a game could certainly seem as long as several life sentences. Articles in magazines like *Co-ed* and *Mademoiselle* explained the game of football (or occasionally basketball, an indication of how far its star had fallen since the turn of the century) to casual spectators who didn't want to look like fools in front of dates. While spontaneous enjoyment might occur with knowledge of the rules, learning them was usually presented as a mere expedient to keeping one's date happy. Before heading off to the big game, it was recommended that a girl bone up on current team information in reference books and sports pages, the better to ask the intelligent questions that would permit her date to display his knowledge—but only during time-outs or halftime. "Never interrupt him for a coke or a bite of your hot dog or depart for the little girls' room at a crucial moment—he'd never forgive you." It was better by far to keep one's mouth shut than risk asking a stupid question while his beloved team was on the field. "Wise women often keep still," counseled *Datebook's Complete Guide to Dating* (1960) in a chapter titled "Spectator Sport Dates."[68]

If the game didn't end the way a boy wanted it to, it was important for

A stylish college girl with a traditional chrysanthemum corsage and football pennant decorates a place card used at a sorority dinner in the early 1930s.

a girl to adjust her mood to his—he wouldn't "appreciate [her] high spir-its" while he suffered the agony of defeat.[69] In such situations, it was important to remember that football wasn't just a game. To think other-wise might mean going dateless until after the play-offs:

> To many men, it's life in miniature, good versus evil fighting it out right
> there in front of him. . . . If you can't get excited about a bunch of big boys
> banging into each other for a couple of hours, conceal your feelings, or you
> may find yourself spending the season alone in the girls' rooting section.[70]

Hiding one's boredom was integral not only to the success of the date itself, but was also a useful strategy for future dates (and marriages) to come. There was an easy alternative for the girl who simply couldn't rouse the enthusiasm necessary to learn the rule book prior to the game—all she had to do was follow her boyfriend's lead. "Cheer when he cheers, cry when he cries" certainly seemed simple enough advice and was a precursor to the mood matching she'd need to do after the game.[71]

Mid-twentieth-century advice books and teen magazines recommended spectator sports as a dating activity because they provided an outlet for pent-up youthful emotions and a wholesome alternative to necking. Girls, after all, were the ones responsible for making sure things didn't go too far. In a 1959 article, for example, girls learned "How to Handle a College Man": "Your college man may well control the arrangements for the date, but the necking bit requires your holding the reins with a light but very firm touch. Try a velvet glove approach—with an iron hand underneath the glove. And, do try to keep everything good natured."[72]

"Is it true," asked another teen magazine from 1960, "that today's coed can't be pure and popular both?"[73] The book and film versions of *Where the Boys Are* (both appeared in 1960, six years before the dating guide of the same name) gave radically different answers.

"Where the Boys Are": Spring Break, Sex, and Its Consequences at Midcentury

Merrit Anderson is an eighteen-year-old coed who attends an unnamed Midwestern university. "Merrit of the U," as she sportingly calls herself, is spending her first spring break on the beach in sunny Fort Lauderdale, Florida. It's a successful trip: in three nights she beds three different boys and has her first orgasm in the process. She doesn't feel particularly bad about any of it, even when she discovers she's "preg. That's right, p.r.e.g." She has no idea which of her lovers is the father or whether "the father and the one I loved would turn out to be identical," or even if she loves any of them at all.[74] She's not losing any sleep over it either.

Is Merrit a contestant for an MTV game show or a cast member of *The Real Life: Fort Lauderdale*? Neither—she's the protagonist of *Where the Boys Are*, a novel by Glendon Swarthout. In 1959, Swarthout read a short article in *Time* magazine about the hoards of college students whose spring-vacation takeover of the beaches at Fort Lauderdale had been an annual occurrence for the past twenty years. After describing the week-long beer-bust bacchanal, the essay summed up with a quote from a coed. When asked why she made the migration, she simply answered: "This is where the boys are." Swarthout, a writer and instructor in the English department at Michigan State University, recognized a killer title when he

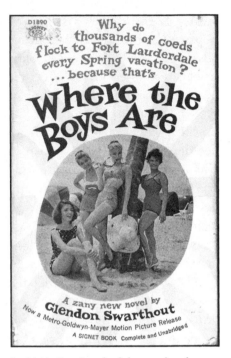

In 1960, Fort Lauderdale was the place to be for spring break.

saw one. He immediately headed south, taking a flock of honors students with him for verisimilitude and/or camouflage.[75]

For the female protagonist of a novel published in 1960 and set just a few years earlier, Merrit shows a stunning lack of remorse for her free-wheeling ways. Nor does the author choose to punish her with a catastrophic event or, at the very least, the wrath of vengeful parents. Instead, as she contemplates her future with a cigarette in hand and visions of a farewell-to-Florida beer dancing in her head (both acceptable vices for pregnant women at the time), she decides to call her father, whose acceptance of her pregnancy she knows will be total.

Of course, some of Merrit's bravura may have resulted from being the creation of a *male* author, who probably didn't feel the social constraints on female sexuality as intensely as a woman. If Glendon had been Glenda, would Merrit have cried tears of sympathy for boyfriend TV Thompson when he told of date raping a girl when "she all at once said no"? It's impossible to know— but I rather doubt it.

In any event, *Where the Boys Are* (the book) is a revelation to anyone who's seen the 1960 movie, which starred future Catholic mother superior Dolores Hart as Merrit Anderson. A line in the syrupy title song (a top ten hit) sets the tone: "Till he holds me I wait impatiently." As the movie opens, it's a snowy day on a Midwestern campus, and Merrit is seated in the "Courtship and Marriage" class

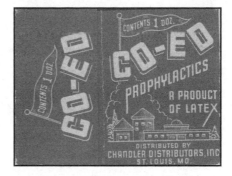

Co-ed Condoms came packaged one dozen to a bright red cardboard sleeve, illustrated with a cheery white line drawing of a university. Distributed by a St. Louis company in roughly the 1950s–1960s, their manufacturer clearly knew its audience: college men on the prowl for college girls. What better name for its condoms, then, than "Co-ed"? It was more than a name—it was a prediction, or so the buyer fervently hoped.

required of all freshman females. When she uses the term "making out" and says she thinks it's all right for couples to "play house" before marriage, the instructor (an older woman winkingly named Dr. Raunch) sends her straight to the dean's office. It seems that Merrit is "overly concerned with the problem of sex," and if she doesn't shape up after spring break, she will be sent back to her parents.

In the movie, sex really is a problem. When Merrit, Tuggle, and Melanie check into their motel room for ten days of fun, sun, and sand, they begin a delicate balancing act. Unlike the novel's playgirl protagonist, these characters are serious students of the midcentury social compact that suggested girls were responsible for controlling their dates' sexuality. They are on the prowl for the opposite sex, but they are also responsible for making sure things don't go too far: Tuggle pledges chastity even if she has to "stop at a blacksmith and buy a belt." To her, spring break is merely an excuse to look for Mr. Right, and if finding him means she won't graduate, it's no big deal: "Girls like me weren't built to be educated, we were made to have children. That's my ambition: to be a walking, talking baby factory. Legal, of course—and with union labor."

The movie also provides a morality play of a good girl gone very bad in her quest for popularity. Ditzy, sweet Melanie longs to meet, date, and marry an Ivy League man. She almost quivers with joy when she discovers a cluster of Leaguers living at their motel. A cute blonde, she has no trouble scoring a date with big man on campus Dill, but storm clouds gather when she ignores the rules of chastity. "You'd never say anything—tell anyone?" she shyly asks when he brings her home from a late date. He smiles like a crocodile. We next see her at "The Sheik" knocking back cocktails with another BMOC type. Dill has passed her off to his frat brother Franklin, and now poor Melanie thinks they're in love. "Don't get caught on some crazy merry-go-round," Merrit warns her when she comes in drunk and disheveled. "I'm not caught!" Melanie cries, but her use of a euphemism for pregnancy lets us know that what she's been riding lately isn't a merry-go-round. When she makes the mistake of telling Franklin about a girl who met and married the man of her dreams on spring break, he dumps her. Slow to catch on, Melanie telephones him later. Franklin says he'll meet her at their special place—the no-tell motel out on the highway. When Melanie, dressed in a flouncy pink party dress, answers the door of the motel room, it's Dill. He pushes his way inside and rapes her. We later see her sitting disheveled and abandoned on the bed as she tries, unsuccessfully, to reach Merrit on the phone. Tuggle takes the call instead, and hurries out the door.

Merrit can't take Melanie's call because she is in the bushes, wrestling with a boy and her conscience. She's just about to give in when Tuggle appears on the scene with news of the assault on Melanie. Just like the cavalry, Tuggle has saved Merrit from a similar if less violent fate in this cinematic world where premarital sex is always punished. Just in case the audience misses the point, we next see Mel taking a suicidal stroll down the center of the highway before she is rescued by her girlfriends. "You want to hear the big joke?" she asks when Merrit visits her hospital room where she is recovering from the rape. "They weren't even Yalies."

In real life, girls did look out for one another. "A Monday-morning report on the weekend's dating disasters is posted near every dormitory phone by coeds at the University of Florida in Gainesville," reported *Seventeen* in 1967. "It lists the names of boys-to-beware-of, with comments ('An octopus!'), but it doesn't always discourage girls from accepting dates ('Curiosity killed the cat, you know!')."[76] *Seventeen* kept its description lighthearted, but it's not hard to imagine girls warning one another about date rapists like Dill.

At the book's end, Merrit merely shrugs at her pregnancy, regretting neither it nor the encounters that landed her in that condition. Hollywood's Merrit decides her virginity is a sacred rose which must be preserved until marriage to the right man. Neither incarnation of Merrit adequately portrayed the real-world consequences of and attitudes toward premarital sex in the mid-twentieth century. In the mid-1960s, birth control pills were on the market but not widely available on college campuses, and many doctors would prescribe diaphragms only to engaged women or those over twenty-one (of course, many girls lied about "upcoming" nuptials). Condoms were fragile, and a girl had to depend on her male partner to supply them. The fact that society condemned sexually active girls at the same time it congratulated sexually active boys led to the most egregious behavior. In the mid-1960s, a male University of Houston student chillingly explained to journalist Gael Greene how this affected contraceptive usage:

> "I figure if she's that kind of girl . . . she will have her own protection, and if not, that's her problem."
>
> "If she becomes pregnant, it could be your problem, too," I suggested.
>
> "Not when my five friends here get finished testifying how they laid her too," he said.[77]

This was the classic double standard in action. By virtue of having sex, a girl became "that kind of girl"—the type who got labeled a "slut" or the "campus punchboard" if she didn't maintain a certain discretion.

College girls had premarital sex—sometimes with contraception and sometimes without—and some got pregnant. Very few of them shrugged it off. A girl who didn't want to marry the baby's father had few options. She could arrange for an illegal abortion, an expensive and often danger- ous prospect if she even knew how to go about procuring one. A Mills alumna remembered how a classmate in the 1940s took a ski trip during Christmas vacation hoping to bring on a miscarriage. It didn't work, and the girl later went into labor in the residence halls.[78] A Radcliffe senior in the 1950s who discovered she was pregnant remembered a housemother who told students to call her if they ever got into trouble; she did and was given the name of a doctor who performed safe and sanitary abortions. Unfortunately, he was jailed at the moment, and after visiting a less rep- utable practitioner who took her money but did not end her pregnancy, she gave the baby up for adoption. She attended classes in a loose rain- coat and took her final exams a few days beforehand; nobody noticed her advanced state of pregnancy.[79]

A young woman who found herself "in trouble" knew that a burgeoning belly marked her as a pariah in school and community, and sometimes even in her family. Maternity homes run by charitable agencies like the Salvation Army gave unmarried women a place to spend the waning months of their pregnancies concealed from public view as they contemplated the error of their ways. Historian Rickie Solinger described the postwar American maternity home as "a gothic attic obscured from the community by closed curtains . . . and high spiked fences," its predominantly white, middle-class inmates considered "part criminal, part patient."[80] (Not that society was very fond either of married women who displayed their pregnancies— maternity girdles safely hid an early trimester bump.)

Sex Kittens Go to College

By the time *Where the Boys Are* hit the bookstores and movie theaters, the idea of sexy coeds was nothing new—though one still guaranteed to titillate. The college girl had almost from the start been granted a quickly commercialized aura of eroticism.

"I am past fifty years of age, (no matter how much,) am President of a small college for women, and love my work." So begins the confession of Cyrus Walcott, D.D., LL.D., the head administrator (and because of a limited endowment, teacher), at the fictitious Hypatia College, as documented in the lighthearted short story "A Case of Discipline" (1896). Its author, Charles Van Norden, D.D., LL.D., was in fact a fifty-three-year-old businessman, Congregational minister, and past president of Elmira, a small college for women in New York. Perhaps Dr. Van Norden wrote from his personal experience with the tempting damsels at Elmira—or perhaps he made up his story from whole cloth. In any case, the fictional Dr. Walcott is a kind and affectionate man who is oh-so-aware of the temptation that surrounds him. "The reader must not misunderstand me," he explains. "My love for the girls is Platonic and paternal." He finds his young charges "a perpetual delight":

> Their sweet all too pale, young faces and flashing, thoughtful eyes fascinate me. . . . I seldom see them in dress adapted to display to the utmost advantage the physical graces they really possess; as a rule, I meet them book in hand in simple gowns a little negligée. But they please me beyond description.[81]

His pleasure is not entirely beyond description in the post-Freudian world of Humbert Humbert and *Girls Gone Wild*. With the benefit of twenty-first-century

The forbidden love of student and teacher was the basis for countless stories, novels, and films—some dirty, some not. Campus Scandal (1962) definitely fell in the first category.

hindsight, it's obvious that the president gets an erotic kick when he finds himself sandwiched "between the Devil and the deep sea,— naughty girls on the one side and a grim faculty, mostly of elderly unmarried ladies, on the other" over the matter of student discipline, for which he is responsible. Hypatia's students aren't truly unmanageable, but "they are human and have red blood, aye and sometimes hot blood; and there are young men in Cedar City," the closest fictitious city to the faux college.[82]

One night, well after the 10:00 bell signaling lights-out has rung, the president steps out of his office for a fresh breath of evening air—then watches, stunned, as Miss Evelyn Wood ("a natural leader, of excellent family" and one of Hypatia's best students) kisses her beau good night before sneaking back into her dormitory via a basement window.

All in all, it's the worst breach of deportment to hit the Hypatia campus since an incident wherein a "wild girl from Arkansas . . . threw a crust of bread in playfulness, at a no less frivolous roommate" one evening at dinner. Given the rigid etiquette that prevails at this "stately and portentous meal," where even Dr. Walcott's "naturally festive disposition" is dampened by the dignity of the occasion, it's apparent that the Arkansas bread-tosser didn't stand a chance. The president banished her "at once and forever." What, then, can be the consequences of an out-of-bounds kiss?

When the kiss itself as well as the identity of one of the kissers are ratted out to the strict lady principal by the night watchman, Dr. Walcott is forced to call Miss Wood before him. Despite the gravity of the occasion, one look at Evelyn's radiant face as she confesses her deep love for her boyfriend makes Dr. Walcott want "to go down before her in a Louis Quatorze salaam—my French blood, again," he notes by way of apology to the reader. Unfortunately, it doesn't change the fact that Evelyn's indiscretion has "tarnished" the reputation of Hypatia College. She must leave, but Dr. Walcott resolves that she will be able to hold her head up when the gates close behind her. He calls for the young man in question, the son of "one of the best citizens and most solid men in Cedar City," and brokers his marriage to Evelyn. The wedding takes place immediately after the commencement ceremony. The college is avenged, but

Evelyn leaves in glory instead of disgrace. In short, everyone lives happily ever after.

While "A Case of Discipline" isn't in the same league with the hot-cha fiction and movies that appeared in the twentieth century, it is an early example of the college girl used as a popular-culture sex object. The story is far from prurient, but it's clear from the start that Hypatia College is a voyeur's delight—and that the voyeur in question is Dr. Walcott. While he would "cut off my right hand ere it should rest in unholy touch upon one of" his girls, he holds his eyes to a different standard, marveling at the "mere extemporized gowns of delicately tinted cheesecloth" they wear for a holiday pageant. He claims to never "play the spy," but he is an inveterate lurker: he catches his ten-year-old son kissing Evelyn under the mistletoe, and later watches from the shadows when she busses her beau in the moonlight. Evelyn is the great grandmother of all sexy innocent college girls to come, while Dr. Walcott is the prototype for the well-meaning older man, pure in deed though maybe not quite so in heart.

At the turn of the twentieth century, the college girl was as much an object of public interest as Civil War battlefields or the natural wonders of Yosemite. So it's not surprising that stereographs of college girls participating in dormitory life were sold alongside other, perhaps more august, subjects. In the distant time before DVDs, television, or even radio, the stereoscope was a cutting-edge home entertainment technology, not to mention a forerunner of the boomer-beloved Viewmaster. No middle-class parlor of the 1850s or 1860s would have been without one of these wood and metal viewing devices and a goodly selection of stereographs to go with it. These were special cardboard-backed slides bearing a double set of photographic images that, when viewed through the stereoscope, appeared three-dimensional. Although the stereoscope reached its peak of popularity as a parlor entertainment in the mid-nineteenth century, it had a long fade out: new stereographs were still being produced as late as the 1930s. Stereographs depicted all manner of things: people and places from around the word, historical events, allegorical images. Many told ministories in a series of three or four images and captions before ending with a frequently hideous pun. Some were mildly risqué, such as the one titled "Favorites of the Harem": a grouping of smiling corn-fed white girls dressed in "oriental" outfits lolled about on floor pillows while a turbaned and bearded man in equally outlandish dress acted the role of sultan (or eunuch—it's hard to tell).

One such slide from 1902 depicted the celebrated spread. Here, five girls peek into a pan filled with Welsh rarebit. Banners from Yale and Harvard hang on the walls of the ornately draped room alongside photographs of family members and celebrities. "A Rare Group making a Rarebit" was the caption. It's a not particularly racy card, though the adjective "rare" calls some attention to the girls' physical charms. Rather it showed the folks back home the wholesome way in which high-spirited college girls had a little harmless fun by bending strict dormitory rules— just as they raided the icebox in their own homes.

The spread was also depicted in a series of four cards released the same year by the same manufacturer. The subject may have been the same, as were the crowded dorm-room background and even some of the models, but all in all, these cards were quite different from the get go. This get-together takes place under cover of darkest night, and the girls are shown in various states of dishabille, in robes and nightgowns, some with hair flowing past their shoulders. Gone is the innocent teapot, replaced by a

"College Girls—A Rare Group making a Rarebit" (1902).

"The Midnight Spread—'Girls, what if Miss Grey should come!'" (1902).

naughty bottle of wine placed conspicuously at the bottom center of the first picture. "The Midnight Spread," read the caption. " 'Girls, what if Miss Grey should come!' "

What indeed? We soon find out: the next card is titled "Approaching Footsteps—'Hurry Girls! The Old Cat's nearly here.' " In anticipation of the chaperon's arrival, the girls scurry to hide evidence: the tablecloth is

"Approaching Footsteps—'Hurry Girls! The Old Cat's nearly here'" (1902).

"The Finale—A Chapter in Revelations" (1902).

picked up, the chafing dish removed, the wine bottle is nowhere to be seen, and one out-of-bounds friend hides under the bed while another pair seeks shelter in a cushioned trunk. Curiously, though, between the first and second views, two girls seem to have become overheated. What other explanation could there be for the way their gowns have slipped so far off their shoulders? The third card in the set is missing, but "The Finale—A Chapter in Revelations" shows another pair of comely shoulders as well as a finely turned ankle exposed to view. The party comes to an abrupt end as the two bare-shouldered girls and their friend under the bed helplessly watch "the old cat" discover the pair hiding in the trunk (one of whom displays some impressive décolletage).

These days, when a bare ankle rates all the erotic oomph of an old sweat sock, it's hard to look at these as titillating. Yet they were clearly meant to be: viewers became Peeping Toms or Tom-ettes as they gazed at young women cosseted in their bedroom, nightgowns falling from their shoulders, prim hairdos undone, and not a man in sight (though the classic scenario of "boy crashing girls' slumber party" was also a popular stereograph subject). Even so, these cards retained an essential innocence that allowed Great Aunt Mabel to comfortably view them in the front parlor.

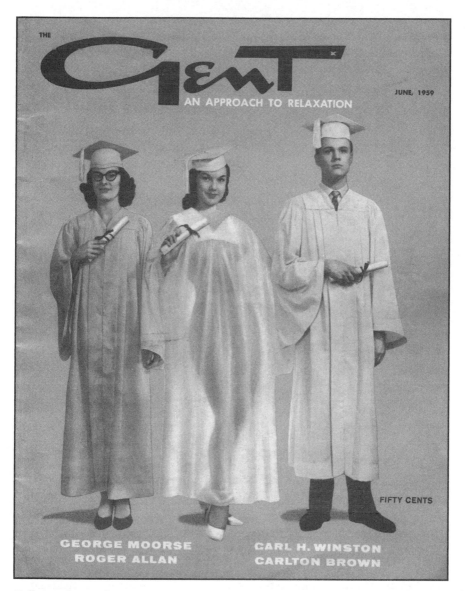

College girl as sex kitten. Gent, 1959.

This was not the case by the time the men's magazines discovered the college girl in the 1940s and 1950s. Whereas illustrations of sweetly sexy college girls frequently graced the covers of magazines like *College Life* and *College Humor* in the 1920s and 1930s, by the mid to late 1950s *Playboy* and a host of its imitators regularly visited campuses and photographed coeds for photo spreads. Before the late 1960s, these rarely featured full nudity or even frontal views at all. They were nonetheless racy, and usually appeared in "back to campus" issues that presented scantily clad coeds as one of the delights of college life. In 1959, *Rogue* followed "The Lush Life of a Miami Co-ed" named Carrie Price. It might have seemed almost academic ("Moderation and balance in study or play mark her collegiate career," noted the text) except for the fact that Price seemed to spend a lot of time in low-cut evening gowns and swimsuits, before she bared almost all to pose in transparent underpants with college pennant, books, and a stuffed animal. In addition to the spicy pictures, some of the men's magazines initiated college boys into a certain type of rugged masculinity, with articles on how to dress, what stereo equipment to buy, and which new jazz records were the coolest. Sometimes the information was of a more personal nature. *Esquire*, for example, sketched out the "pilgrim's progress on the road to sex freedom" at college in 1962: "Freshman year, girls tend to be idealistic and to believe in premarital chastity. Sophomore year is the season to go steady, and sexual urgencies increase. Junior is often the time when the breakout from the cage of virginity is likely to take place."[83]

Esquire didn't explain what happened senior year.

Ultimately, men's magazine pictorials and pulp novels like *Campus Scandal* (1962; "What can a college professor do when a young co-ed wants extra-curricular lessons in love" read the back cover) and *Co-eds Three* (1964; "They violated all the campus rules in their search for excitement") helped cement a popular culture image of the college girl as a sexpot who could barely keep her skirt on. Portraying the college girl as an eroticized playmate defused the threatening image of a man-hating intellectual harpy by reducing her to a sexy submissive pussycat.

This stereotype perhaps reached its big screen apotheosis in the amazing *Sex Kittens Go to College* (1960). Collins College's resident humanoid computer, Thinko the Robot, chooses Dr. Mathilda West to head its science department. Dr. West is eminently qualified: she holds thirteen degrees and speaks seventeen foreign languages. A welcoming committee is already at the train station when Thinko spits out a more unsettling set of statistics about Dr. West: her measurements are 40-20-32. This becomes apparent to the welcoming committee when, after turning first to a matronly passenger in a case of mistaken identity, they discover Dr. West in the person of platinum bombshell actress, Mamie van Doren. "But Dr. West is a genius!" sputters the disbelieving dowdy, horn-rimmed-glasses-wearing female college dean. Herein lies the crux of the movie: Mathilda West *is* a genius with a photographic memory, but no one will take her seriously because of the way she looks. "One glance at that wiggle and no foundation in the world will give us money for research," remarks an administrator. But dressed in a lab coat and requisite Clark Kent glasses, West doesn't act like a sex kitten; she respects herself, her students, and her profession.

It's all over when the faculty discovers that the new science department head worked her way through college as "The Tallahassee Tassel Tosser"—a stripper in Vegas. "It's nothing personal," the college's press agent tells Dr. West. "You may be the greatest genius in the world, but you just don't look the part."

"That's my tragedy," she sighs before capitulating. "I'm not meant to be a professor of science. I must accept myself as I am." In the mid-twentieth century, this meant that instead of slapping Collins College with a lawsuit, Dr. West does what cultural mores dictated be done with dangerous female sexuality: as the movie ends, she accepts the press agent's proposal of marriage as well as a baby-care book penned by Collins's chimpanzee mascot, Abraham Q. Voltaire.

The moral seems to be that secondary sex characteristics will always trump intelligence. There's simply no room for a sex bomb with brains on the Collins campus.

Hark! Is that the future I hear? Graduates poised to enter the wider world, ca. 1900.

Graduation and After

No man wants to come home at night and find his wife testing some new process for manufacturing oleomargarine . . .

A TURN-OF-THE-CENTURY VANDERBILT STUDENT,
THE AMERICAN COLLEGE AND UNIVERSITY: A HISTORY (1962)

You don't need a college degree to stir up a box of cake mix.

A "FORMER SOCIAL WORKER WITH A GRADUATE DEGREE,"
LADIES HOME JOURNAL (NOVEMBER 1958)

For most early college girls, graduation day came almost before they knew it. A last step sing, the final hoop roll, and it was time to step into a frothy white dress, walk across a platform, and collect one's diploma. Missing from the picture, you may have noticed, are a mortarboard and academic gown. Well into the twentieth century, the "traditional" commencement outfit for girls was a white dress, whether she was graduating from college or high school. "The first effect of the graduating frock must be simplicity," reported the *New York Times* in 1894. "The sheerest of lawn, the finest of lace, the most diaphanous of petticoats floating over the lightest of silk foundation—it takes all these with the freshest of ribbons and the most immaculate gloves to produce

An 1898 advertisement for graduation caps and gowns featured a comely college girl.

the finish of simple purity and unadorned beauty."[1] Simplicity, purity, and beauty all added up to one thing: the virginal femininity of the bride or first communicant.

The cap and gown didn't enter the picture for men or women until the late nineteenth century, when American academics returning from study at European universities brought the tradition back with them—and then it took years to become established as the outfit for commencement. For example, at Oberlin, students adopted the mortarboard for daily wear in 1881 (the various classes distinguished themselves with different colored tassels). The faculty objected, particularly to women wearing the headgear. "It is rumored that the Faculty propose to interfere to prevent the Classical ladies from wearing the mortar board uniform," reported the *Oberlin Review* in early 1882, ". . . on the ground that the cap would not be suitable head covering for both ladies and gentlemen. Surely the Faculty would not go so far as to say the caps MUST NOT be worn. Such an attitude would doubtless cause a rebellious spirit among the students which it would be unwise to awaken." Despite the threat, by October most students had of their own accord given up wearing the awkward hats anyway. Caps and gowns were thereafter an intermittent fad at Oberlin, and didn't become the recommended commencement wear until 1908. Sixty-two years later, the class of 1970 did away with what they called the "elitist symbol" of cap and gown.[2]

By the 1890s, at most women's colleges the cap and gown were worn over the traditional white dress at commencement. A notable exception was Vassar, where girls did not wear the cap and gown until after the retirement of its conservative president, James Monroe Taylor, in early 1914 (though it was rumored in 1887 that 275 students were "displeased" by his refusal to let them adopt it).[3] The white gown remained indispensable as late as the mid-1930s, when *CO-EDiquette* suggested girls headed off to college take their "white graduation dress from high school" for use at sorority or other initiation services.[4]

Home to Stay

For many college girls, a larger problem than what to wear at graduation was what to do with their newly minted degrees. "Of what use degrees are to be to girls I don't see, unless they addict themselves to professional life," was the opinion of Yale's president in 1857.[5] In fact, at the time he made this statement women were beginning to do just that, led by such pioneers as Elizabeth Blackwell (who received her M.D. in 1849) and E. R. Jones (who obtained her D.D.S. in 1855). To the majority of Americans, who remained ensconced in a strictly gendered worldview that understood women to be "angels of the hearth," to use a popular contemporary description, the thought of female attorneys, architects, or other professionals was beyond the pale for years to come. "Young women could not build the houses that would line eight streets from New York to San Francisco, but, rightly educated, they could convert each one of these houses into a home," wrote the author of *What a Young Woman Ought to Know* (1905), expressing her belief that homemaking, not architecture, was what girls were best suited for.[6]

Most nineteenth-century college graduates went back to their parents' home, sometimes for an interval before marriage, or if no husband loomed on the horizon, for good. To many of these young women, the bosom of the family felt smothering and restrictive after the intellectual stimulation of the classroom and companionable pranks and spreads of the dormitory. *After College, What? For Girls* was the title of a slim volume published in 1896. In it, author and college graduate Helen E. Starrett recounted a "pathetic figure" from her childhood, a young woman newly returned from "a famous female seminary" to her father's farm. Seated at dinner, the daughter faced her family's barrage of questions about her seminary years, "all of which she answered kindly and seriously" until the end of the meal:

At last the good old farmer, her father, pushed back his chair from the table and said, "Well, Amanda, I reckon ye've just got home in time. Har-

The Vassar farmerettes raised vegetables for the home front during World War I. Here one of them demonstrates her skill behind the wheel of a tractor at the Eastern States Exhibition and Dairy Show in 1917.

vest begins next week, and there'll be a lot of hands to cook for; and I reckon now you're through school and home to stay, we won't need to keep any extra hired girl any more. I s'pose your seminary learnin' hain't made ye forget how to bake and cook and wash and iron. . . ."[7]

This would be the moment for Amanda to admit that Greek and Latin had in fact crowded the intricacies of ironing right out of her head, and to remind her father that hired help was money well spent before kissing him good-bye in a rush to catch the next buggy to the big city. In the real world, however, her story was a common one. In fact, the argument that housework stifled college-educated women would be a prime component of Betty Friedan's *The Feminine Mystique* (1963). Luckily for Amanda, there was a happy ending. She married a clergyman and the two of them traveled west, where they founded a successful academy. "Truly Amanda's education had proven 'worth while'!"[8]

An underlying message of Amanda's story was that college changed daughters, and not always for the better in the eyes of their parents. "When the College Girl Comes Home to Stay" was the subject of an article in the *New York Times* in 1913. It was not a pretty sight. The problem started in a girl's freshman year, much of which was spent "in becoming as different as possible in appearance and manner to the life and to the people who are and should be nearest and dearest to her." The next three years only intensified the gap between parent and child, until the "dear daughter upon whom has been lavished so much love and care" was completely "unable to fit . . . into her mother's and father's existence."[9] In short, the writer suggested that college made a girl too high-toned to appreciate the simple goodness of her parents. It took a while for this to become apparent, however. Upon her arrival home after graduation, a girl and her parents were genuinely happy to see one another, but soon the daughter began to find fault with everything from the furniture to her parents' grammar and dress. Little by little both parties realized the change that had occurred: the parents understood that their way of doing things did not make their daughter happy, while daughter understood that her parents were not going to change. "It is a tragedy that is hard to put into words," concluded the writer, who advocated that colleges "train our girls to return home happily to take real joy to the parents."[10]

All of this sounds suspiciously like the normal push and shove on the path from late adolescence to adulthood. While the pressure of large student debts and high urban rents means chances are good that today's Jane Doe (and/or her brother) may move back in with Mom and Dad for a period of time after graduation, eventually she will go off to make an independent life for herself.[11] At some point in the next decade or so, she may even begin to see, if not that everything her parents did in raising her was right, then at least how hard they tried. But for the first generations of college girls, the question of what to do after college was pretty much limited to staying home, getting married, or teaching.

The "Ubiquitous" Spinster

Marriage and a husband sympathetic to her education rescued Amanda. But what of women who didn't marry, whether by choice or circumstance? Many commentators pointed to the lack of opportunities for these women. One of the more original voices of the mid-nineteenth century belonged to John Cowan, M.D., a supporter of both woman suffrage and married women's right to hold property. He was also an ardent believer in phrenology, the nineteenth-century craze for divining character by feeling the bumps on one's head; he urged every man to have his sweetheart's personality read. He was also an early proponent of what would come to be called personal ads. He advised bachelors unhappy with the crop of local girls to "draw up an advertisement, stating in as few words as possible your idiosyncrasies, and [that you] desire replies from only those who imagine they approach your standard of character." This would be inserted in newspapers of large circulation, there to be read "by thousands of marriageable women," though he advocated a thorough phrenological assessment of any likely candidates before meeting. [12]

Cowan expounded on these and other theories in *The Science of a New Life* (1869), a sex-education guide that went through multiple printings before the turn of the century. Regarding women who weren't able to marry (here Cowan pointed out the grim statistics that in post–Civil War Massachusetts women outnumbered men by thirty thousand, by forty thousand in New York), he believed they should be fitted for work—and not just service, sewing, teaching, or writing. Women, in Cowan's opinion, could "do light work on the farm, keep books, become tellers in the banks, agents for the insurance companies, engage in various kinds of businesses, enter the professions" if only they received the proper education. Even taking into account "the genetic differences of sex," a woman could be trained for "every avocation for which she possesses a decided talent." Cowan broadmindedly believed women's work needed to be "determined by trial . . . not by false theories" that suggested women were incapable of doing anything other than raising children and keeping house, a theory that condemned spinsters to a life of dependence on relatives for their keep.[13]

In other ways, however, Cowan was a product of his times. He urged bachelors to choose for wives those women who were competent in household arts:

> See to it that the woman of your choice be educated in the practical details of every household duty; that she be as capable of cooking a relish-able meal as she is of playing a gem from the last new opera on the piano; that she is as competent to mend her stockings as to dance the quadrilles; that she is as qualified to make a bed, a shirt, or dress, as she is to speak the French, German or Italian languages.[14]

In short, wives needed domestic skills instead of the business ones Cowan proposed for spinsters because he did not anticipate married women working outside the home. Cowan made man the corporate head of the household shipyard in a curious extended metaphor: "What would a merchant, possessing a ship and valuable cargo, want with a captain who did not know the practical use and application of every rope and yard in a vessel?"[15] Cowan didn't say it, but it was implicit that Cap'n Wifey knew her way around the galley.

Cowan wrote just as Vassar was awarding its first baccalaureate degrees. Thirty years later, at the turn of the twentieth century, the college girl was an accepted if not always understood fixture in the American landscape. A college education and the profitable work it trained women for meant that for the first time, marriage became a choice, not a necessity. Editor and writer Margaret E. Sangster tied together education, economics, and an argument for companionate marriage in *Winsome Womanhood* (1900). Thanks to the "more extended and liberal education" given to girls, who were formerly "sufficiently prepared for life in their parents view if they could read and write," marriage had "dropped into the background":

> A girl need not marry for support or for a home. A girl no longer dreads old maidhood. No opprobrium attaches to the single woman. A young

lady marries because she has found some one who fills her ideals, some one of congenial disposition, similar social condition, and agreeable qualities; some one she loves, some one who loves her.[16]

Sangster was optimistic in her belief that "no opprobrium" attached to single women. It did when she wrote, and it still does—or a vast component of the self-help industry wouldn't exist, and neither would *Sex and the City*. Nevertheless, the fact that college-educated women could indeed choose career over marriage made observers increasingly nervous, as surveys of the first generations of college women seemed to indicate that that was exactly what they were doing. Between 1889 and 1908, 53 percent of Bryn Mawr's graduates remained single. During the same period, 43 percent of Wellesley grads and 47 percent of those from the University of Michigan remained unwed. The percentage of single women among those who held advanced degrees was higher still: three-quarters of those who received Ph.D.s between 1877 and 1924 never married.[17] The marriage rate of college women ignited a firestorm almost the size of the conflagration caused by *Sex in Education*.

Some thought the marriage rate was situational. For example, if a female college graduate went on to a profession, it was most likely that of schoolteacher. As one female observer trenchantly noted in 1895, there was "no station in life (save that of a nun) so inimical to marriage as that of resident teacher in a girls' school." The same writer had "no doubt" that the low marriage rate was due in part to the fact that "many men dislike[d] intellectual women—whether because such women are really disagreeable or because men's taste is at fault" she would "not try to determine."[18]

Others faulted the college girl herself. In a letter to *The Century* in 1899, a correspondent who professed to find the oft-discussed subject of the college girl "shopworn" wondered "Has it really never occurred to those interested that the real explanation [for the low marriage rate] lies back of all of these suggestions?" According to M.T. (the writer identified him- or herself only by initials), college girls were a self-selected lot of "predestined spinsters": studious elder daughters who wished to support their families instead of seeking husbands, quiet girls who preferred "books to personal companionship," and "unattractive girls" who resorted "to study and college interests as compensation for social unpopularity." Rather than "vainly seeking to discover why black sheep are not white," M.T. concluded it was better to rejoice that these misfits had found a means of self-support and the potential for happy, useful, and satisfy-ing—albeit single—lives.[19]

Assuming the college girl in general was quite as attractive as any other, finding a beau who was smart enough to appreciate her education could be difficult. *After College, What? For Girls* quoted the concerned father of four Vassar-educated daughters, all of whom were back on the family farm in Illinois after graduation. The young storekeepers and rich farmers who otherwise might have interested "ordinary girls" as potential husbands, "why, they have nothing in common with a girl that's spent four years studying Latin and Greek and history and literature and the sciences":

> The girls don't take any pleasure in their company, and the boys are afraid of them; and, as a consequence, I guess I'll have a lot of college-educated old maids on my hands. But still . . . that would not make so much difference if only the girls themselves were happy and contented; but I see they are not, and that is the puzzle. I declare, it's all a muddle![20]

The unhappy father touched on what became a leitmotiv in the public perception of female college graduates: that they remained unmarried because they were "too smart" for men—hence all those articles about hiding one's Phi Beta Kappa key lest its golden glint scare a man off.

A twist on the argument came from Rev. Daniel A. Lord, chairman of the Catholic women's group Sodality. At the organization's convention in 1929, he addressed the membership on that old standby "college women and marriage." But instead of taking college girls to task for being "too erudite," Father Lord blamed men who slighted the humanities in favor of commercial and professional studies. This made it difficult for women to find partners "whose conversation and companionship interest[ed] them." Or as a *New York Times* headline writer succinctly summed up Father Lord's talk, "College Girl Prefers Singleness to Dumb College Boy."[21] Who could argue with that?

"It may be that college women are simply too choosy to compete successfully in the competition for husbands," posited the authors of *They Went to College* (1952), a study based on a *Time* magazine survey of 9,064 American college graduates. As part of their analysis, Ernest Havemann and Patricia Salter West employed a seven-point rating system of their own device to judge the matrimonial success of college graduates over the age of forty. Even they admitted it was extremely subjective: points were assigned for marriage (the highest number for being currently married to one's first spouse), children, and home ownership, with a maximum of seven attainable. Women graduates ranked lowest, with a whopping 34 percent scoring two or less (only 6 percent of the men scored so low). "The very best that any of the 2-points-and-under people have done is to marry, divorce, and remarry—without having children or buying a home," Havemann and West noted disparagingly, equating a lack of children and real estate with total failure and unhappiness.

Next, they channeled the *Century* letter writer from half a century earlier who thought college girls were a self-selected lot of spinsters, except Havemann and West blamed Mom and Dad:

> In fact today's parents, sensing that one of their daughters is less attractive by conventional standards than the other, may actually be more inclined to help her through college and into a career than they would in the case of her more marriageable sister. In many instances, the mere fact that a girl obtained a college degree may mean that her parents have already earmarked her for spinsterhood.[22]

College thus became a sort of refuse heap for the unattractive girl— the poorly dressed, glasses-wearing, makeup-shunning stereotype of the women's colleges, perhaps.

Race Suicide

Even if a college girl managed to find and marry a man who appreciated her education, she still wasn't off the hook as regards her obligations to society at large. As immigration swelled in the early twentieth century, middle-class white women were reminded of their obligation to "the race," i.e., they were urged to bear lots of healthy babies, the better to counter the rising tide of Italians, Poles, Czechs, Slavs, and Slovenians, among other immigrants from Europe, as well as African and other Americans of color. In the 1910s and 1920s, these arguments were increasingly based on eugenics: a branch of pseudoscience devoted to breeding racially "superior" human beings. Eugenicist arguments slipped into most marriage manuals and sex-education books of the era. Margaret Sangster suggested that a girl be educated for motherhood from infancy, "not because she may marry and become a mother, but rather for the reason that the upbringing of the race in its earliest and most impressionable years is in the molding hands of woman."[23] Some even went so far as to describe the appropriate conditions under which the conception of superior children could occur.

Anxiety ran high: in 1922, the *Ladies Home Journal* published articles on "College Women and Race Suicide" and the "Alarming Decrease in American Babies." "If New York conditions were to prevail for one hundred years, the 'native American' would have black hair, black eyes and be of swarthy complexion," the latter direly predicted, its author blithely unaware of the irony in describing most Native Americans to a T.[24] This was the frequently mentioned "race suicide," the result in part of college women who married late or not at all, and tended to have small families, if any. Only if mothers gave birth to four or more children would the "old-fashioned family," i.e., lily white and middle-class, be saved.[25]

Eugenics fell out of mainstream favor in the wake of Nazi Germany's experiments in racial purity, but the idea that college-educated women shirked their duty to reproduce took a while to die out. In August 1940, *Mademoiselle* surveyed the attitudes and future plans of the most recently graduated class of college women in an article called "College Maid to Measure." All of them wanted—or professed to want—huge herds of children, a fact *Mademoiselle* happily emphasized:

> All of them, too, want children, and those eugenicists who are concerned over the failure of the college graduates to replace themselves should be heartened by the *number* of children these seniors hope to have—there are a few cautious young women who want one or two children but the great majority wish to have three or more.[26]

Even though the Depression wasn't completely over until after the United States entered World War II (still over a year away at the time of *Mademoiselle*'s article), economics were clearly such that people felt comfortable having large families, or in the case of *Mademoiselle*'s respondents, at least thinking about having large families. Furthermore, they did not anticipate having to work to support those children: most 1940 graduates expected to quit their jobs after marriage or, at the latest, after the birth of their first child, a luxury of which most of today's parents can only dream.

As further proof of just how different both economics and attitudes toward work were some sixty years ago, the article noted that these young women were "prepared to treat marriage and home-making as jobs from which no 'escapist' activities will be needed."[27] Equating work outside the home with "escapist activity" indicates that few college-educated, middle-class women anticipated the need to supplement a household income. A job was just another hobby, like gardening or playing bridge with the girls.

Working mothers came in for the deepest scrutiny. "They say a woman can't have a profession and take care of a family well, and I'd like to show that she can if it is possible," says Will Elliott in *An American Girl and Her Four Years in a Boys' College* (1878).[28] Alas, the reader never finds out if Will ever gets a chance to try, for at the novel's end, Will faces an uncertain future: she's off to a teaching job in Wisconsin, while a reconciliation with her beau looms on the horizon.

Lillian Moller Gilbreth was a real-life college girl who quietly set an example against stereotypes of working mothers in the early years of the twentieth century. Between 1905 and 1922—prime years for public fears of race suicide and eugenicist arguments for better breeding—the time and motion study innovator and *Cheaper by the Dozen* (1948) matriarch gave birth to twelve children, eleven of whom survived to adulthood. A 1900 graduate of the University of California, Gilbreth was denied a place on the Phi Beta Kappa list because, she was told, "when it came to finding a good job, men needed the help of this honor more than women did."[29] Urged on by her husband, she received her Ph.D. in industrial psychology from Brown University in 1915, when she was already the mother of six small children. But when Frank Gilbreth died in 1924, leaving his wife with eleven children aged eighteen and under, the public was unwilling to accept her as a woman engineer—despite the fact that she had been a full partner in their engineering consulting firm from its incorporation. Undaunted, Lillian Moller Gilbreth was eventually recognized as an industrial efficiency expert in her own right (though she had to focus on the more ladylike arena of household efficiency first), but even then her ability to earn a living and raise her children properly was questioned by family members and others.

In *Belles on Their Toes* (1950), Frank B. Gilbreth, Jr., and Ernestine Gilbreth Carey remembered how their young brother Jack was pumped for the intimate details of their home life by a nosy kindergarten teacher in the late 1920s. When Jack enumerated the sorts of things his busy mother did (from mending his stockings to serving at dinner to playing the piano so the family could sing together), the teacher was immediately doubtful:

> "But she can't do all that, John."
>> "Why can't she?" Jack asked suspiciously.
>> "Doesn't she have a career, John?"
>> "I don't think so."
>> "Why you know perfectly well she does," the teacher said accusingly.
>> "Well if she does," Jack shouted, "she never showed it to me."[30]

Observers may not have appreciated how hard Gilbreth worked both outside and inside her home in the years after she was widowed, but her children certainly did. Even with help of a combination cook/handyman, not to mention an extremely organized household in which older children were responsible for younger ones and assigned chores were marked off on daily progress charts, Gilbreth was remembered by her son and daughter as "slow and fumbling" at night, as sure a sign of her exhaustion as the circles under her eyes.[31]

In 1958, the *Ladies Home Journal* visited Hugh and Frances Olsen and their four children as part of its "How America Lives" series, in which families of different economic, social, and geographic backgrounds were given the once-over for the benefit of *Journal* readers. What made the Olsens different from their neighbors in Philadelphia was that after thirteen years of marriage, thirty-five-year-old Frances entered medical school. When the *Journal* caught up with the Olsen family, Dr. Frances Olsen was only a few months away from starting private practice. Husband Hugh (who also worked) and the children, aged twelve to seventeen, all shared in household chores and cooking. Her friends and coworkers ("even professional people") sometimes asked her how she could bear to leave her children at home. Dr. Olsen wryly observed that she didn't "think they've been *too* badly damaged by my career." The *Journal* rejoined, "They do not *look* damaged," its use of italics leaving some room for question even as it noted the good looks and health of the Olsen children. The article also made sure to mention that at home Frances Olsen's title was " 'mother,' not 'doctor.' "[32]

Five months later, the *Journal* explored the life of Sally Shannon, a happily married mother of two who worked outside the home not from economic need but, as she made clear, because she enjoyed it. "Does that mean I'm not a good mother?" she asked in the article, defensively titled "My Working Doesn't Hurt Anyone."[33] The following month, a female Jungian analyst participated in a roundtable discussion ("Should Mothers of Young Children Work?") where she blamed a college education for making women "masculine": "When a girl is in college and cultivates her mind, this may stimulate, even inflate, the masculine side, and she can become aridly intellectual, with a strong power drive, and then it is easy to become a doctor or a lawyer who is hardly feminine at all."[34]

No one directly responded to the articles about working women (though around the same time the letters to the editor column exploded with reader reaction, pro and con, to an exposé on whether maternity-room procedures were "cruel"), but *Journal* readers didn't remain entirely mute. The following letter appeared in June 1958, under the title "Career at Home":

> *Dear Editors*: I just finished making an apple pie. It's baking now and smells wonderful, and that's very satisfying. Because I'm a housewife, and I'm glad.
>
> I used to complain a lot, as many women do. I wanted an exciting, glamorous job—any kind. Instead I have a house to keep clean and two children to feed and a husband to get off to work in the mornings. . . .[35]

She estimated she did "about $140 worth of work a week, with no tangible pay" but that it was balanced out by the occasional opportunity to "leave the beds unmade and read." When the children were older, she could have a paying job and finish college "if I want to." For the present, she was "getting the greatest possible return" for her labor. "And I'll get dividends the rest of my life," she concluded. One thing was clear: both the working women portrayed in the articles and the stay-at-home letter writer felt the need to defend the choices they made.

Career Opportunities

If women were best suited to housewifery, as much of the debate seemed to indicate, then what of women who wanted—or in many cases needed —to work outside the home? (Of course, lower class white and women of color left their homes every day, and there was no hue and outcry regarding their abilities to both keep house and hold a job.) Discussions of middle-class women and work often stressed training for "womanly" careers that emphasized "innate" feminine traits. The dean of women at the Oregon State Agricultural College described the importance of these traits in 1925: "The one who brings to her task those qualities which have in the past been termed feminine—the qualities of womanliness—will be really contributing a new factor to the solution of the world's problems."[36]

The dean defined these qualities as the "old-fashioned virtues" of sympathy, kindness, and high moral standards. By bringing them into the workplace, women feminized it, made it a kinder, gentler place for their fellow workers, much as a wife and mother made home a pleasant refuge for husband and children.

Women actually "preferred" those professions with "large carry-over values for the home," reported the head of Simmons College in the mid-1950s, occupations such as teaching, nursing, librarianship, and social work—all of which provided "opportunities for developing understanding and abilities that are of value also in homemaking."[37] They were best suited for occupations that combined "intellectual content and a concern for people," such as work in churches, schools, libraries, social and health agencies, and business establishments (as personnel workers and secretaries—not executives).[38]

Teaching, in particular, was a profession that cried out for early generations of college-trained women. It had been an acceptable way for single women to earn money since the days of the female seminaries, in part because it conformed with social standards that suggested women had the responsibility for molding children into citizens—not to mention what a 1920 brochure describing women's programs at the University of Oregon called an "instinctive fondness for children." Teaching was far and away the most popular profession for early college girls. Of the forty-three female members of the University of California's class of 1905 who sent in update letters on the occasion of their first reunion (held a mere three years after graduation), thirty were teachers, five didn't mention an occupation, four were housewives, two were secretaries, one was a school administrator, and one was a third-year student at the Women's Medical College in Philadelphia. "I believe it is commonly conceded that a girl, upon her graduation from college does one of three things: She gets married, she teaches or—she dies," quipped class member Lois Kohn. She was, of course, a teacher. Of 119 members of Mount Holyoke's class of 1913 who answered questionnaires prior to their twenty-fifth anniversary, 94 of them reported that they had taught high school, "and several more had done other types of teaching."[39]

It was still a popular choice in 1950, when the dean of the New York University School of Education recommended that the would-be teacher ask herself, "Am I willing to teach for less money than I might get as a doctor or lawyer?"—a question notable both for its honesty as well as the assumption that readers might in fact consider the professions.[40]

Nursing, too, was "womanly and professional" and, as *Seventeen* magazine told readers in 1948, it offered girls good preparation for marriage:

> Right now, in your teens and twenties, it offers you sound scientific training and exciting work. Then the One Man, Love and Lohengrin come along. . . . You can have your wedding cake and your job, too, if you like. Or you may decide to bid your work good-bye. In either case, you discover that nursing was the best preparation you could have had for marriage and motherhood. Later on, as a member of the P.T.A . . . and a leader in community clubs, you'll find your professional training a social and civic asset.[41]

The same article pointed out that the percentage of women who married was higher among nurses than any other group of professional women. (Another popular choice that promised quick matrimonial results was a career in the air: "Stewardesses are so desirable as wives that they usually don't last longer than 18 months on the job before they marry.")[42]

In the mid-twentieth century, it was as if all paths led to homemaking, no matter how circuitous the path. Consider architecture, for

Nursing was considered "a woman's career," but some women fought sexism and gender stereotypes to become doctors. Here, female medical students watch as women surgeons perform an operation at the turn of the twentieth century.

example. A 1958 article in *McCall's* described how twenty-three art and home-economics majors at the Woman's College of the University of North Carolina designed a three-bedroom house, which was then constructed at a local site. It was less an exercise in the traditionally male realm of architectural design than in the specialized, presumably female, knowledge of "problems they would face in making homes for themselves and their families" as well as "exactly what they, as average homemakers, wanted—and how to get it." The result? "A real honey of a home."[43]

Articles about women working in the sciences were often couched in terms that were equally applicable to home economics. Dr. Gladys Hobby was a Vassar graduate who received her M.D. at Columbia. In 1952, *Woman's Home Companion* described her contribution to early penicillin trials in appropriately feminized terms: "Gladys Hobby tended thousands of flasks—as solicitous about her molds as an anxious mother might be about a sick infant." The same article also described how chemicals were compounded during drug company research "in the hope that they will have valuable properties—just as an experimental cook will invent a new cake in the hope it will taste good."[44] Apparently, science didn't conflict with a woman's cooking ability the way the dead languages did, because the comparison was a popular one in the 1950s. A *Seventeen* magazine exploration of careers in science asked interested readers to first consider "How do you make out in the kitchen? A good chemist needs the kind of imagination, ingenuity and patience that makes a good cook."[45] "Cosmic rays and cake baking are both lots of fun" was the caption under a photo of a "research physicist—and homemaker," Dr. Mary Summerfield, that accompanied an *American Girl* (the Girl Scouts magazine) article on women scientists.[46]

Science was also the focus of one installment of an ongoing series of articles on career training that intermittently appeared in *Seventeen* in the 1950s: "One scientist (male) said to us, 'Women in science? Yes, I think they're fine. You should see the deft way those girls handle animals in the laboratory.' Another one (also male) assured us women's ability for minute work came in handy on many an experiment."[47]

Women didn't actually run those experiments, of course, but they were whizzes when it came to juggling lab rats and their little tiny fingers conveniently fit into spaces where big clumsy males just couldn't reach. *Seventeen* didn't seem to notice that these women scientists were being praised for handiwork—not unlike needlepoint—instead of intellectual investigation.

Soft Pedaling

There was a danger, though, in becoming too satisfied with one's job. The normally procollege, prowork (either as a lifelong path or as a pleasant interval before marriage) *Mademoiselle* magazine spelled out the danger of ignoring matrimonial prospects for office ambitions in an article called "Soft Pedal That Career." Ironically, this virulently anti-working-girl article kicked off the 1940 "Careers" issue:

> If you must have a career, or if you do have one, you'd better keep it on the good old q.t. That is, of course, if you have the halcyon idea in mind of eventually bagging a mythical Mr. Right. On the other hand, if it's honestly the single course for you, play up your job and, sister, you won't have any offers to give it up.[48]

Just as the intelligent woman who didn't hide her IQ ran the risk of becoming an old maid, so too did the career girl jeopardize her prospects with men. Not that she couldn't every once in a while, through skill or blind luck, trap one of the "bores with baggy eyes and large-sized hangovers," which were the only men willing to date career girls. Even then, she might have to buy her own corsage.[49]

It was not so much the business world per se that ruined the career girl's appeal, but her ambition, otherwise known as "that confounded inner desire to oppose her natural makeup." Taking her job seriously was a masculine attribute, and robbed a woman of her feminine charm—the lure by which she might ensnare a loving husband and good provider. It wasn't necessary for a career girl to give up her ambitions, just to keep them under cover: "You can make a killing at the office and yet be big enough to admit that woman's place is still in the home . . . This may give him the idea that you're 'like mother' after all and in spite of everything. And that's what you want, isn't it?"[50]

In other words, career women only thought they knew what they wanted. What's worse, many didn't realize that working outside the home had serious psychological consequences, at least according to pop-psych pundits Ferdinand Lundberg and Marynia F. Farnham, M.D., whose influential *Modern Woman: The Lost Sex* (1947) was later indicted by Betty Freidan as an agent of the feminine mystique. In it, they explained that work outside the home (just like college, in the eyes of other commentators) "masculinized" women and made them men's "rivals." As such, women "insensibly" developed "the characteristics of aggression, dominance, independence and power," a role reversal that was "driving women steadily deeper into personal conflict soluble only by psychotherapy."

Luckily, the problem was nothing that a little spin couldn't solve. To help women regain their mental health, "public recognition" needed to be made of "the fact that the psychically balanced woman finds greatest satisfaction for her ego in nurturing activities. Teaching, nursing, doctoring, social service work, guidance, catering, decorating, play direction, furnishing are all entirely feminine nurturing functions . . . ," as was of course Farnham's own field, psychology.[51] Women who nevertheless wanted to "enter fields belonging to the male area of exploit or authority—law, mathematics, physics, business, industry and technology," would "certainly be allowed to do so," but make no mistake about the level of social engineering that Lundberg and Farnham proposed:

> Government and socially-minded organizations should, however, through propaganda, make it clear that such pursuits are not generally desirable for women. Solely in the public interest, the disordered fantasies of the masculine-complex women should be combated in so far as those fantasies are advanced as the proper basis for public policy toward women as a whole. The emphasis of prestige, honor, subsidy and public respect should be shifted emphatically to those women recognized as serving society most fully as women.[52]

Women could work as scientists or engineers, but in the world envisioned by Lundberg and Farnham they'd get no respect—a situation unknown today . . . oh, wait a minute . . . never mind.

But Nonetheless Satisfied

As a *New York Times* reporter phrased it in her "Middle-Life Portrait of the Woman Graduate" (a peek at the Class of 1913 twenty-five years after graduation), although the college girl "may not have done exactly as she had planned with her life, she is in the main content with her present lot and with her college preparation for it." College gave her " 'background,' 'wider culture,' 'a lift above the level of the day-by-day drudgery of after-life' " as well as an economic advantage.[53]

Despite the experts who called them disordered or masculine, who questioned their attractiveness and marriageability, or declared them high-toned, many college girls did not regret their education for a red-hot minute. In the midst of the 1958 *Ladies Home Journal* roundtable on whether not mothers of young children should work, for example, a participating sociologist announced that in response to a recent poll of male and female college graduates, "seven out of ten of the full-time home-makers said [of their years on campus], 'It helped a lot.' "[54]

They Went to College (1952) suggested that female college graduates were most often spinsters and quoted disgruntled "former coeds" on how higher education left them unprepared for the drudgery of house-work. But it also included the opinions of many women graduates who were pleased with their education and their lives—it just buried them in back chapters. "I cannot conceive that a college education could be a disappointment to anyone," marveled a high-school administrator in Pennsylvania. A woman who had earned an M.D. but chose to stay home and raise her children instead of practicing medicine (could any-one carrying the student loans necessary for a medical-school education today afford to do this?) found that college gave her "a sense of accom-plishment, a broadening of viewpoint, a feeling of being able to evaluate situations that arise . . . I don't know how college could have helped me more."[55]

By the time their twenty-fifth reunion rolled around, even Smith's class of 1942 had mellowed. Ten years earlier, in responding to question-naires from fellow alumna Betty Friedan, they had revealed themselves to be frustrated housewives plagued by the "problem that has no name." Speaking to the *New York Times* in 1967, they seemed to suggest that Friedan had merely caught them at a bad time. "Surrounded by dirty dishes and diapers, with your husband on the rise and very busy, and not enough finances to do what you want to, you are in the middle of wondering why you ever went to college," recalled one of the former Smithies. Now, with their children almost grown, half of them were taking courses to help them establish or advance careers. "On the whole," the *Times* reported, "the reunion-goers gave a resounding endorsement to the liberal arts education they received."[56]

EPILOGUE

Since Then

In 2003, a group of women who had graduated from Wellesley some fifty years before gathered together with reporter/alumna Marian Burros to discuss *Mona Lisa Smile,* a movie set at their alma mater in 1953. They recognized the campus with its hoop rolling, Maypole, and dormitory curfew lockout all right, but they didn't recognize the students. "If I were 18 and I saw this movie I'd never want to go there," said one member of the class of 1954. The movie made Wellesley look like a finishing school, with etiquette classes attended by Stepford wives-to-be in crisp organza aprons, a bunch of snooty upper-class girls who wore skirts and pearls to class instead of jeans and sweatshirts. The movie focused on a bohemian art history teacher from California who comes to Wellesley to "make a difference" by teaching modern art—only, as one of the alums pointed out, the subject had been taught there since the 1920s. And while the movie describes Wellesley as "the most conservative college in the nation," a black sociology professor, William Cousins, was a faculty member from 1949 to 1952.[1]

Of course, anyone who expects Hollywood to tell the truth is bound to be disappointed. But what if a college girl from the past found herself, in the best Grade Z sci-fi tradition, on a college campus in 2005? Would she recognize anything? Forget the obvious things like technology and clothing ("Well, you see, Molly Beth of 1875, this little gadget hooked to my thong underwear is called a cell phone"). The answers change depending on where and when our girl of the past comes from. (For example, College Girl 1905 and College Girl 1955, used to the rules of in loco parentis, perhaps had more in common with each other than with the parietal-rule-busting, coed-dorm-dwelling College Girl 1975.) But for many of them the most monumental, never-thought-it-would-happen change would be the demise of the women's colleges.

Better Dead Than Coed

Wellesley remains devoted to the higher education of women only, but it is one of an ever-shrinking number of schools to do so. In 1961, Vassar president Sarah Gibson Blanding predicted that "no more than ten [women's colleges] will be functioning in 2061."[2] She was off the mark only in her assessment of how long the extinction would take. When she made the statement, there were approximately 298 women's colleges; as of 2005, there were 60.[3] If they continue to close or go coed at this rate, there will be none left long before 2061. Blanding hinted that Vassar itself might consider partnering with a men's school in a coordinate relationship like that of Radcliffe to Harvard. Here she was wrong—Vassar went coed in 1969.

The signs had been there for a long time: according to the *Encyclope-*

dia of Women's Studies, attendance at the women's colleges peaked in 1890. Given a choice, most girls chose proximity to the opposite sex rather than face down stereotypes of women's colleges as spinster factories or bastions of lesbianism. Straight and gay students at Barnard were shocked to discover in 1998 that a brochure intended for the parents of prospective applicants seemed to countenance these long-standing insinuations with the reassuring information that nowadays women's college students were more likely to become wives and mothers than those graduating from coed schools. After students complained, the offending sentence was removed.[4]

Supporters of women's colleges point to the opportunities for leadership and the sense of empowerment conferred by the all-female classroom. It's been long recognized that when both sexes share a classroom, men wind up doing most of the talking. "You go to any intercollegiate convention and co-eds don't raise their voices," a Seven Sisters student government president told the *New York Times* back in 1933. "They wait for the men in their delegations to speak. On the other hand, we of the women's colleges . . . have plenty of ideas and we're not afraid to express them."[5]

When Mills College's board of trustees, facing a severe monetary shortfall, voted in May 1990 to admit men the following academic year, the campus erupted in protest from students who were loath to give up the affirmation and empowerment they found at the single-sex campus. "Within hours of the announcement," the 1991 yearbook recalled, "hundreds of serious women had gathered in the student union to organize a massive student strike and campus takeover."[6] Students stopped going to class. They blockaded administrative offices and presented their demands—the most important of which was that the decision to go coed be reversed—to college officials, including the chairman of the board of trustees, Warren Hellman. Then they shaved their heads, taped their mouths shut, and hung "Warren Go-to-Hell-man" in effigy. The national media took notice. A cartoon in a San Diego newspaper portrayed the strikers as a bunch of spoiled brats who compared unfavorably with the martyred students at Kent State.[7] Others accused them of hypocrisy and reverse discrimination, in light of recent efforts by female applicants to crack the ranks at two military schools. (What these latter critics ignored was that Mills, unlike the military schools in question, had not rejected male applicants. In fact, men were already accepted at the graduate level.)

On May 9, 1990, two weeks after they had voted to admit men to Mills, the board of trustees via chairman Hellman announced that the decision had been reversed. The financial crisis was averted when, in the wake of the strike, alumni donations went up, as did student applications. Fifteen years after the strike, Mills College remains women only.

Cigarettes, Booze, and Mental Health Issues

One of the things *Mona Lisa Smile* accurately portrayed was the frequency with which college girls smoked in the 1950s. Although no longer the symbol of female independence it had been in the 1920s, cigarette smoking retained a certain chic—especially since its status as an agent of ill-health had yet to be fully revealed.

In decades to come, awareness of its dangers stopped some, but far from all, people from smoking. By 1999, a survey of college freshman showed that women smoked more than men (16.5 percent reported they "smoked frequently," compared with 15 percent of the men).[8] Depending on where she went to school, however, a smoker may have had a harder time finding a place to light up without risking a fine. Beginning in the late 1980s, many campuses banned smoking from classrooms and non-residential buildings, or limited it to just a few designated zones. More recently, a few colleges went so far as to declare their entire campuses (except perhaps the parking lots) or all of their residence halls smoke free, but others tried to balance rights of smokers and nonsmokers—

allowing students to smoke in their dormitory rooms if roommates and neighbors agreed, for example.

No self-respecting college guidebook author today would slight the dangers of alcohol. A Columbia University study released in the mid-1990s revealed that the number of college women who reported they drank with the intent to get drunk had tripled in the past twenty years (from 10 to 35 percent). A poll taken by the Alcohol Studies Program at the Harvard School of Public Health in 1994 showed that nearly half of college students were binge drinkers, defined for women as having four or more drinks in a row in a two-hour period. In practice, though, consumption could be much, much higher: a nineteen-year-old sophomore woman at Colorado State University died of alcohol poisoning in 2004, after ingesting the equivalent of thirty to forty beers and shots. There were nonfatal consequences as well. By wide margins, binge drinkers were more likely to get behind a steering wheel while drunk, have unprotected sex, or fall behind in their studies. Even where binging wasn't involved, alcohol played a role in 90 percent of reported campus rapes (used by victim, assailant, or both), and 60 percent of college women with STDs or HIV infection got them while intoxicated. As it had for so many previous generations of college women and men, peer pressure and the desire to fit in remained a reason why students drank, the Columbia study reported, but it also pointed to something new: college students, especially women, turned to alcohol to relieve stress.[9]

In fact, college women were more likely to suffer from stress than their male counterparts. In 1999, 38 percent of the young women who took part in the nationwide Annual Freshman Survey said they were "overwhelmed by all I have to do" as compared with a mere 7.3 percent of men. Women are more likely than men to report their feelings, but questions about student lifestyle seemed to indicate deeper differences. The survey of 383,815 first-year students found that the men spent more time doing relaxing things such as exercising, playing video games, and watching TV, whereas the women juggled studying, household chores, and child care—a trickledown version of the stress some adult women felt to be "super moms," pursuing careers while raising children.[10]

Stress could also lead to depression. A 2004 survey by the American College Mental Health Association showed that close to half of all students were at some point so depressed they had trouble functioning; another 15 percent could be classified as clinically depressed. Across the country, campus mental-health counselors reported a rise in the number of students seeking care. Seeking help for depression and other mental-health issues is more acceptable than it once was and may account for some of the increased visits, but some professionals pointed to the uncertainty of life under threat of terrorist attack—though a survey taken before September 11, 2001, showed that freshmen's "self-reported emotional well-being" had already hit a "record low" at the beginning of that academic year.[11]

One thing is sadly certain: students still commit suicide with perplexing regularity, and colleges struggle over the best way to prevent future deaths. After nineteen suicides over a period of eight years, the University of Illinois implemented a highly successful prevention program in 1983. Students who are known to be suicidal undergo four mandatory counseling sessions during which their "current suicidal intentions" are assessed and they are invited to take part in further counseling. The school also makes it clear that "suicide threats and attempts are unacceptable on our campus," according to the program founder and director, psychologist Paul Joffe. Students who don't attend the four required sessions are not allowed to remain enrolled. It's tough love, but it works: none of the eighteen hundred students who have gone through the program in the past twenty years has committed suicide, and the overall suicide rate at UI has dropped by half.[12]

At New York University, access to dormitory balconies was restricted after a string of student suicides in 2004. An editorial in the student newspaper called the efforts "infantilizing" and suggested the school was more concerned with liability than reaching out to suicidal students. A consultant hired by the university countered that barring access to the balconies made it "less easy for someone to take impulsive action."[13]

Both approaches reflect current trends: greater willingness on the part of colleges to take a paternalistic role in their students' lives, and the ever increasing fear of litigation.

Welcome Back, In Loco Parentis

The issue of in loco parentis returned to the public spotlight with the $27 million lawsuit filed in 2002 against four MIT psychiatrists, a housemaster, and a student life dean (neither of the latter two were mental-health professionals) by the parents of Elizabeth Shin, a highly driven nineteen-year-old who had committed suicide in her dorm room two years previously. Her parents contended that they should have been told about Shin's depression and trips to the campus counseling center, and that a psychiatrist there considered hospitalizing her. Their suit specifically claimed that the MIT employees failed to act as *"in loco parentis* to the deceased."[14]

In July 2005, a Massachusetts Superior Court judge dismissed the Shins' claims against MIT. But the judge also ruled that the case against the four psychiatrists and two administrators could proceed to a jury trial, as their knowledge of Elizabeth Shin's mental state constituted a "special relationship" with her and thus required them to protect her from her suicidal behavior. It was not an outright vindication of in loco parentis, but as the *Education Law Update* noted, *Shin v. MIT* was "yet another example of a growing trend in courts across the country to chip away" at the notion that colleges and universities had no duty to keep their students safe while on campus.[15]

Long before Elizabeth Shin's tragic death, in loco parentis—or a modified form of it—was making a slow but steady return. On some campuses in the early 1980s (about the time the students who manned the barricades in the late 1960s or 1970s started to think about their eldest children going to high school), administrators began trying to rein in student behavior, especially where substance abuse was concerned. Predictably, this didn't go over well with students for whom in loco parentis

had never been anything but an obscure Latin phrase, but this generation of young people did little more than grouse. When the State University of New York at Stony Brook announced in 1982 that it would be
enforcing long-neglected sections of the Student Conduct Code concerning public pot smoking and underage drinking, critical editorials
appeared in the student paper—but nobody barricaded the administration building.[16]

By the late 1990s, stricter rules were not only becoming the norm,
they were actually a selling point. After decades of baby-boom children waiting in line for admissions, colleges saw a decline in applications beginning in the late 1970s. Combined with skyrocketing tuition
and housing costs, higher education became a buyer's market. Students and their parents quickly developed a consumer mentality and
demanded added value when it came to selecting a college. Along with
better food and up-to-date computer labs, a commitment to mental-
heath counseling, student safety, and clearly defined, well-enforced
rules of behavior were something a college could point to with pride in
its application packet.

There was also a change in how students were viewed. Back in the
1970s, college students demanded to be treated like adults; eighteen-
year-old boys, after all, could be and were drafted to Vietnam. Two
decades later, parents who had been there and done it all at the laissez-
faire campuses of the 1970s and 1980s got cold feet when it came to
their own offspring and urged more rules. Others saw the return to rules
as an outcome of overinvolved, coddling parenting whereby college
became an extension of summer camp. "I see this all as coming out of
baby-boomer guilt," reflected a Dartmouth student in 1999. "I've had
many wonderful times at college but they have largely been outside of
the college-sponsored, group-bonding events which I consider somewhere between absurd and offensive."[17]

For some, only a return to the strict parietal rules of the 1960s would
do. In 2005, Vigen Guroian, a professor of theology at Baltimore's Loyola
College, claimed that colleges have "forfeited the responsibilities and
rights of in loco parentis and have gone into the pimping and brothel

business," a conclusion he reached after reading essays written by his female students. The culprit, yet again, was the coed dorm. Peer pressure led to promiscuity, and women had no place to retreat (though Loyola's residence halls were in fact single sex by floor and subject to restricted visiting hours). Instead of protecting female students, colleges shoveled out "self-serving rhetoric about respecting . . . students as adults," but to Guroian's mind and those of other parents advocating the return to in loco parentis, they clearly weren't.[18]

News Flash: College Girls Have Sex

Cleanliness, quietude, and the chance to walk around casually dressed are frequently mentioned by young women as advantages of single-sex housing; the opportunity to hide out from sex-crazed males is not. These males, however, may be exactly what coeds are seeking when it's time for spring break.

Even the sexually aware Merrit Anderson of the novel *Where the Boys Are* might be shocked by the anything-goes mentality that rules spring break in the twenty-first century. In an attempt to put the brakes on, Fort Lauderdale's mayor officially pronounced students unwelcome during a 1985 appearance on *Good Morning America*. Daytona Beach strengthened its public nudity laws in 2003, requiring that "that portion of the buttocks which lies between the top and bottom of the buttocks, and between two imaginary straight lines" must be covered (effectively banning the thong bikini), and banned open containers of alcohol within 100 feet of its main thoroughfare.[19]

Even with the new restrictions, Daytona Beach expected 150,000 students to show up that year. And there were plenty of other welcoming environs for the college girl who needed to unwind after a semester of hard work: Panama City, Florida (450,000 expected), South Padre Island, Texas (150,000), Lake Havasu City, Arizona (40,000), or Cancun, Mexico (40,000).[20] Once there, the combination of too many Jell-O shots, beer bongs, and the proximity of a *Girls Gone Wild* tour bus has led more than one college girl to do something she regrets in the morning. Unlike a hangover, however, baring her breasts or making out with a sorority sister in front of a video camera might have future consequences in the Web age.

In a possible cautionary tale, a female news anchor from Ohio was forced to resign in 2004 after a videotape of her dancing naked in a Key West, Florida, bar surfaced on the Internet. A decade of professional integrity was instantly destroyed (though one has to wonder why a thirty-seven-year-old professional woman didn't realize that participating in a wet T-shirt contest was probably a bad idea to begin with). She might have learned from an editorial in the Elon University (Elon, North Carolina) student newspaper: "Think of the consequences. You do not want to be that person who ends up on one of those 'wild' spring break videos, do you?" Or as student editors at the University of Central Florida put it, "Will your boyfriend, husband, or parents buy the excuse, 'It was spring break'?"[21]

Of course, there's more than a little of the old double standard afoot here, when girls who go wild face "consequences" while the boys who egg them on are seen as exercising a bacchanalian right of passage. (The ethics of adult men who make money by obtaining drunken "consent" to get girls to act out sexually on video in exchange for a T-shirt or a trucker hat are something else entirely.) In other words, despite claims that "it was fun" or "it was a very freeing feeling," as two video-vixens told a journalist in 2004 (the second also admitted she was "pretty drunk" and was "pretty sure I'll see a downside tomorrow morning"), a girl's reputation is still a fragile thing.[22] It may, however, be more resilient than it was even fifteen years ago, given today's highly sexualized culture where appearing in an amateur sex video is no longer an immediate kiss of career death—if you're an heiress, model, or starlet that is, as opposed to an anchorwoman.

Adults inevitably get their granny-sized panties in a bunch when it comes to the sexcapades of the younger generation. Still, some aspects of the current "hookup" (definition for fogies: a "new" type of one-night stand with presumably no strings attached for either sex) culture sound disturbingly familiar. Two *Chicago Sun-Times* reporters investigating the phenomenon found that even though it is generally accepted for a college woman to want and even initiate sex, it isn't OK for her to want it too often—in which case she will be labeled a skank, slut, or ho. "If I go all the way with her on the first night, this isn't a girl I want to date," said a University of Chicago senior, sounding as if he'd been reading mid-twentieth-century dating guides all his life.[23] To avoid being labeled a slut, women have to make sex look like it is unplanned. Getting drunk first is key, and then it's best not to carry condoms. This, of course, is a recipe for disaster.

In 2001 the conservative Independent Women's Forum (the same people who contend that women's studies "miseducates" women) commissioned a report called "Hooking Up, Hanging Out, and Hoping for Mr. Right: College Women on Dating and Mating Today" which concluded that current relationship styles did not allow college women to "explore the marriage worthiness of a variety of men before settling into a long-term commitment with one of them," i.e., they didn't go on dates, so they couldn't get their MRS. degree. This was because there had been a "reduction in male initiative" when it came to dating (hint: cow, milk, free). The answer was to create "socially prescribed rules and norms" and involve "older adults, including parents, college administrators, and other social leaders" in guiding young people "toward the marriages they seek"—and, of course, to get rid of coed dorms, which "clearly help to facilitate the hook up culture."[24] In short, it was time for wise elders to revive old-fashioned prefeminist dating, where men took the lead, and women knew their place was . . . prone (but only after the wedding).

∽

Perhaps you're wondering what happened to me when my college-girl days were over. Six months after I graduated (only three semesters late), I moved to San Francisco, where I actually put my B.A. in Art History to work at a gallery space in the South of Market neighborhood. I made lots of wonderful friends and met the man I would marry. And, rather ironically given the angst of my freshman year (and while we're at it, that of my sophomore, junior, and senior years), I went to graduate school. Perhaps because I was all grown up and living a comfortable 1,800 miles from home, it was another experience entirely. I attended classes regularly, did assignments and turned them in on time, and frighteningly, became one of those older students who has their hand up in the air the instant the professor asks a question. This time around, I was a straight-A student.

Sometimes I wonder how different my undergraduate years would have been if I had gone to a small, out-of-state, liberal arts college instead of a big commuter university half an hour away from my parents' house. Would I have been happier—or at least gotten better grades? I don't waste a lot of time thinking about it, because twenty-some years down the road, I wouldn't change a thing.

NOTES

Introduction: From Bluestocking to Sex Kittens

1. Rachel Metz, "Web Sites Satisfy Late-Night Campus Snack Attacks," *New York Times*, December 2, 2004.
2. Joe Garofoli, "On College Campuses, It's a Woman's World," *San Francisco Chronicle*, August 26, 2002 (http://sfgate.com/article.cgi?file=/chronicle/archive/2002/08/26/BA176264.DTL [accessed January 18, 2004]).
3. http://www.lawrence.edu/about/trads/mdc.shtml (accessed August 1, 2004).
4. "If Your Daughter Goes to College," *Better Homes & Gardens*, May 1940, 20.
5. Wainwright Evans, "Coeducation Is the American Way," *Better Homes & Gardens*, May 1940, 21.
6. William A. McKeever, "Is Your Daughter Safe at College?" *New York Times Magazine*, March 20, 1910, 10; Elizabeth Eldridge, *CO-EDiquette: Poise and Popularity for Every Girl* (New York: E. P. Dutton, 1936), 220; Rita Halle Kleeman, "What About College?," *Calling All Girls*, April 1945, 53.
7. "The College Scene," *Teens Today*, February 1961, 51.
8. Mary C. McComb, "Rate Your Date: Young Women and Commodification of Depression-Era Courtship," in *Delinquents & Debutantes: Twentieth-Century American Girls' Cultures*, ed. Sherrie A. Inness (New York: New York University Press, 1998), 43. McComb was discussing the relationship between youth and prescriptive literature in the 1930s and 1940s, but her phrasing is just as relevant here.
9. Garofoli, "On College Campuses."
10. 60 Minutes, "The Biological Clock," August 17, 2003.
11. Sam Dillon, "Harvard Chief Defends His Talk on Women," *New York*

Times, January 18, 2005; Daniel J. Hemel and Zachary M. Seward, "Summers: 'I Made a Big Mistake,' " *The Harvard Crimson*, January 21, 2005; Sara Rimer, "Professors, in Close Vote, Censure Harvard Leader," *New York Times*, March 16, 2005.

Chapter One: The Birth of the College Girl

1. Paula Findlen, "Science as a Career in Enlightenment Italy: The Strategies of Laura Bassi," *Isis*, vol. 84, no. 3 (September 1993), 441.
2. Phyllis Stock, *Better Than Rubies: A History of Women's Education* (New York: G. P. Putnam's Sons, 1978), 25.
3. Barbara Miller Solomon, *In the Company of Educated Women: A History of Women and Higher Education in America* (New Haven, Conn.: Yale University Press, 1985), 3–4.
4. Christopher J. Lucas, *American Higher Education: A History* (New York: St. Martin's Press, 1994), 105.
5. Solomon, *In the Company of Educated Women*, 2.
6. Stock, *Better Than Rubies*, 75.
7. Christie Anne Farnham, *The Education of the Southern Belle: Higher Education and Student Socialization in the Antebellum South* (New York: New York University Press, 1994), 36.
8. Monseigneur Dupanloup, "Learned Women and Studious Women," *Catholic World* (1867), 209.
9. Linda Kerber, "The Republican Mother: Women and the Enlightenment— An American Perspective," *American Quarterly*, vol. 28, no. 2 (Summer 1976), 187–205.
10. Jennifer Manion, "The Young Ladies' Academy of Philadelphia: Attitudes Toward the Formal Education of Women in America, 1790–1800," *Penn History Review*, Spring 1997, accessed online at www.history.upenn.edu /phr/archives/97/manion.html (accessed April 5, 2004).
11. Ibid.

12. Frederick Rudolph, *The American College and University: A History* (New York: Alfred A. Knopf, 1962), 307.

13. Kate Gannett Wells, "A Family Bookcase," *New England Magazine*, April 1896, 187.

14. Farnham, *Education of the Southern Belle*, 31.

15. Solomon, *In the Company of Educated Women*, 1.

16. Alma Lutz, *Emma Willard: Daughter of Democracy* (Boston: Houghton Mifflin, 1929), 56.

17. Helen Lefkowitz Horowitz, *Alma Mater: Design and Experience in the Women's Colleges from Their Nineteenth-Century Beginnings to the 1930s* (2d ed.; Amherst: University of Massachusetts Press, 1993), 11; Stock, *Better Than Rubies*, 184; Lutz, *Emma Willard*, 86, 82, 84.

18. Lutz, *Emma Willard*, 96.

19. Ibid., 92, 88, 99.

20. Ibid., 88–89, 96.

21. Ibid., 100–1, 70.

22. Catharine Beecher, *Suggestions Respecting Improvement in Education* (n.p., 1829), quoted at http://www.britannica.com/women/pri/Q00177.html (accessed April 8, 2004).

23. Barbara M. Cross, ed., *The Educated Woman in America: Selected Writings of Catharine Beecher, Margaret Fuller, and M. Carey Thomas* (New York: Teachers College Press, 1965), 6.

24. Horowitz, *Alma Mater*, 4, 11, 20, 17, 24, 25.

25. Henrietta Edgecomb Hooker, "Mount Holyoke College," *New England Magazine*, January 1897, 551, 550.

26. Lutz, *Emma Willard*, 196.

27. Farnham, *Education of the Southern Belle*, 18.

28. Lutz, *Emma Willard*, 196, 121; Beecher's letter to Lyon can be viewed online at http://www.newman.baruch.cuny.edu/digital/2001/beecher/catherine.htm (accessed March 1, 2005).

29. Solomon, *In the Company of Educated Women*, 24, 21; A. L. Shumway and C. DeW. Brower, *Oberliniana* (n.p., 1883), 83, 86.

30. Farnham, *Education of the Southern Belle*, 13.

31. *Connecticut Journal*, February 24, 1835, and Springfield Republican, March 14, 1835, quoted in Vera M. Butler, *Education as Revealed by New England Newspapers Prior to 1850* (Philadelphia, n.p., 1935), 147.

32. Alexander Hyde, "The Co-Education of the Sexes," *Scribner's Monthly*, September 1871, 523. "A.B" stood for *Artium Baccalaureus*, Latin for "Bachelor of Arts"—our modern B.A. degree.

33. Rudolph, *American College and University: A History*, 325.

34. A Young Wife, "Men and Women," *Harper's New Monthly Magazine*, vol. 1, issue 1 (June 1850), 89.

35. In *The Cambridge History of English and American Literature*, ed. A. W. Ward, A. R. Waller, W. P. Trent, et al. (New York: G. P. Putnam's Sons, 1907–21), cited at Bartleby.com, 2000 (www.bartleby.com/Cambridge/ [accessed July 24, 2003]).

36. Ibid.

37. Rev. A. J. Battle, *Piety, the True Ornament and Dignity of Woman* (Marion, Ala.: Dennis Dykous, 1857), quoted in Farnham, *Education of the Southern Belle*, 177.

38. Frances Lieber, ed., *Encyclopædia Americana* (Boston: Mussey & Co., 1851), 144.

39. "Editor's Easy Chair," *Harper's New Monthly Magazine*, March 1884, 640; Mary Clemmer Ames, *A Memorial of Alice and Phoebe Cary, with Some of Their Later Poems* (New York: Hurd & Houghton, 1875), 59.

40. Ames, *Memorial of Alice and Phoebe Cary*, 59.

41. Young Wife, "Men and Women," 89; William Aikman, *Life at Home, or, the Family and Its Members* (New York: Samuel R. Wells, 1870), 105.

42. "Old Maids," *The Living Age*, August 3, 1872, 292.

43. Mrs. Amelia E. Barr, "Good and Bad Mothers," *North American Review*, April 1893, 410.

44. Cornell University, "Proceedings at the Laying of the Cornerstone of the Sage College of the Cornell University" (Ithaca, N.Y.: University Press, 1873), 54.

45. "Gowns for Commencement," *New York Times*, May 6, 1894, 18.

46. L. T. Meade, *A Sweet Girl Graduate* (New York: New York Book Company, n.d.), 143.

47. Ibid., 164.

48. Farnham, *Education of the Southern Belle*, 12.

49. Lucas, *American Higher Education*, 132–34.

50. Farnham, *Education of the Southern Belle*, 24–25.

51. http://www.wesleyancollege.edu/firstforwomen/history (accessed September 1, 2004); Solomon, *In the Company of Educated Women*, 24.

52. *The Tennessee Encyclopedia of History and Culture* (http://160.36.208.47 /FMPro?-db=tnencyc&-format=tdetail.htm&-lay=web&entryid=M023&find = [accessed September 1, 2004]); Farnham, *Education of the Southern Belle*, 20–21.

53. "The Family Conference," *Good Housekeeping*, September 1909, 110.

54. Horowitz, *Alma Mater*, 34.

55. Moses Tyler, "Vassar Female College," *New Englander and Yale Review*, October 1862, 732.

56. Ruth E. Finley, *The Lady of Godey's, Sarah Josepha Hale* (Philadelphia: J. B. Lippincott, 1931), 29.

57. Ibid., 209.

58. Ibid., 57; Eleanor Wolf Thompson, *Education for Ladies, 1830–1860: Ideas on Education in Magazines for Women* (Morningside Heights, N.Y.: King's Crown Press, 1947), 1; Horowitz, *Alma Mater*, 37.

59. Finley, *The Lady of Godey's*, 216.

60. Ibid., 206.

61. "Vassar College," *New York Times*, June 24, 1868, 4.

62. Ernest Earnest, *Academic Procession: An Informal History of the American College 1636 to 1953* (Indianapolis, Ind.: Bobbs-Merrill, 1953), 182.

63. Susan L. Poulson and Leslie Miller-Bernal, "Two Unique Histories of Coeducation: Catholic and Historically Black Institutions," in *Going Coed: Women's Experiences in Formerly Men's Colleges and Universities, 1950–2000*, ed. Leslie Miller-Bernal and Susan L. Poulson (Nashville, Tenn.: Vanderbilt University Press, 2004), 35.

64. Lucas, *American Higher Education*, 158; Poulson and Miller-Bernal, "Two Unique Histories," 35.

65. Poulson and Miller-Bernal, "Two Unique Histories," 38; "African-American Appointments in Higher Education Continue to Favor Men,"

Journal of Blacks in Higher Education, Summer 1995, 23. Harvard's first black, tenured, woman professor was Eileen Southern in the department of Afro-American Studies.

66. Ibid., 36.

67. Quoted in Raymond Wolters, *The New Negro on Campus: Black College Rebellions of the 1920s* (Princeton, N.J.: Princeton University Press, 1975), 5.

68. Poulson and Miller-Bernal, "Two Unique Histories," 35.

69. Diary of Sophia Packard, quoted in Florence M. Read, *The Story of Spelman College* (Atlanta, Ga., n.p., 1961), 50.

70. Diabolus, "Educational Matters," *New York Times*, June 28, 1866, 5; Read, *Story of Spelman College*, 72–73.

71. http://www.spelman.edu/about_us/facts/ (accessed March 3, 2005).

72. Mary Caroline Crawford, *The College Girl of America and the Institutions Which Make Her What She Is* (Boston: L. C. Page & Co., 1905), 276.

73. William A. McKeever, "Is Your Daughter Safe at College?" *New York Times Magazine*, March 20, 1910, 10.

74. Solomon, *In the Company of Educated Women*, 53; Reuben Gold Thwaites, *History of the University of Wisconsin* (n.p., c1900), accessed online at http://www.library.wisc.edu/etext/WIReader/Thwaites/Chapter06.html#Section03 (accessed May 24, 2004); David B. Frankenburger, "University of Wisconsin," *New England Magazine*, March 1893, 18.

75. Orrin Leslie Elliott, *Stanford University: The First Twenty-Five Years* (Stanford, Calif.: Stanford University Press, 1937), 133.

76. Ibid., 133–34.

77. Ibid., 134–36; Solomon, *In the Company of Educated Women*, 242 note 4.

78. Alexander Hyde, "The Co-Education of the Sexes," *Scribners Monthly*, September 1871, 520–21.

79. Dorothy Gies McGuigan, *A Dangerous Experiment: 100 Years of Women at the University of Michigan* (Ann Arbor, Mich.: Center for Continuing Education of Women, 1970), 1–2.

80. Olive San Louie Anderson, *An American Girl and Her Four Years in a Boys' College* (New York: D. Appleton and Co., 1878), 52, 49.

81. Ibid., 129.

82. Edward J. Power, *Catholic Higher Education in America: A History* (New York: Appleton-Century-Crofts, 1972), 301.

83. Ibid., 297.

84. Ibid., 273.

85. Solomon, *In the Company of Educated Women,* 50; Power, *Catholic Higher Education,* 303.

86. Power, *Catholic Higher Education,* 304.

87. Ibid., 304–5.

88: Ibid., 306.

89. Ibid., 275, 277.

90. Figures quoted in Solomon, *In the Company of Educated Women,* 44, 63, 64. As Solomon points out, these percentages shrink dramatically when compared with the general population: in 1920, the 283,000 college girls made up only 7.6 percent of all women aged 18 to 21.

Chapter Two: New Girl on Campus

1. Calvin B. T. Lee, *The Campus Scene, 1900–1970: Changing Styles in Undergraduate Life* (New York: David McKay, 1970), 45.

2. Elisabeth Ann Hudnut, *You Can Always Tell a Freshman: How to Get the Most Out of Your College Years* (New York: E. P. Dutton, 1949), 97.

3. Harriet C. Seelye, "Festivals at American Colleges for Women. At Smith," *The Century,* January 1895, 433.

4. Mrs. Clark Johnson, *Her College Days* (Philadelphia: Penn Publishing Co., 1896), 21–22.

5. Ibid., 23.

6. Susan G. Walker, "Festivals at American Colleges for Women. At Bryn Mawr," *The Century,* January 1895, 429.

7. Helen Lefkowitz Horowitz, *Alma Mater: Design and Experience in the Women's Colleges from Their Nineteenth-Century Beginnings to the 1930s* (2d ed., Amherst: University of Massachusetts Press, 1993), 172.

8. *Mills College Year Book* 1933, 70–71, 60–61, 50–51, 38–39.

9. "Open Forum," *Blue and Grey*, October 14, 1927, 2.

10. Doris Hillman Hutchings and Jane Cudlip King, interview by Kathleen McCrea, August 6, 1995, Mills College Fires of Wisdom Oral History Project.

11. Helen Lefkowitz Horowitz, *The Power and Passion of M. Carey Thomas* (New York: Alfred A. Knopf, 1994), 37.

12. Kate W. Jameson and Frank C. Lockwood, eds., *The Freshman Girl: A Guide to College Life* (Boston: D. C. Heath, 1925), iii.

13. Sarah H. Gordon, "Smith College Students: The First Ten Classes, 1879–1888," *History of Education Quarterly*, vol. 15, no. 2 (Summer 1975), 155–56; Nellie Ballou, *Etiquette at College* (also called *The Campus Blue Book*) (Harrisburg, Pa.: Handy Book Corp., 1925), 19.

14. B.F. "First Aid to Homesick Freshman," *New York Times*, October 16, 1955, 9; Jeanne Phillips, "Visiting Mom Has Become Coeds' Fifth Roommate," *The Record* [Bergen County, N.J.], December 1, 2002, F6. Abby told the girls to "stick to your guns and insist the mother" honor her promise to stay elsewhere.

15. Hudnut, *You Can Always Tell a Freshman*, 30, 32.

16. Ibid., 22

17. Agatha Townsend, *College Freshmen Speak Out* (New York: Harper & Brothers, 1956), 45–46.

18. "Have You Any Spare Parts?" *Florida Flambeau*, March 27, 1942, 1.

19. Elizabeth Eldridge, *CO-EDiquette: Poise and Popularity for Every Girl* (New York: E. P. Dutton, 1936), 150; "Educators Chided as Poor Leaders," *New York Times*, February 21, 1935, 21.

20. James H. Fairchild, "Oberlin. Its origin, progress and results. An address, prepared for the alumni of Oberlin College, assembled August 22, 1860. By Pres. J. H. Fairchild" (Oberlin, Ohio: R. Butler, Printer, 1871), 24.

21. Ibid., 24; W. E. Bigglestone, "Oberlin College and the Negro Student, 1865–1940," *Journal of Negro History*, vol. 56, no. 3 (July 1971), 198.

22. Bigglestone, "Oberlin College," 200.

23. "Race Issue at Cornell," *New York Times*, March 28, 1911, 7; "Colored Coeds Explain," *New York Times*, April 3, 1911, 3.

24. Olivia Mancini, "Vassar's First Black Graduate: She Passed for White,"

Journal of Blacks in Higher Education, no. 34 (Winter 2001–2002), 108. Beatrix (Betty) McCleary entered Vassar in 1940 as its first "openly acknowledged" black student.

25. Horowitz, *Alma Mater*, 155–56.

26. Barbara Miller Solomon, *In the Company of Educated Women: A History of Women and Higher Education in America* (New Haven, Conn.: Yale University Press, 1985), 143.

27. Horowitz, *Alma Mater*, 155.

28. Horowitz, *Power and Passion*, 340–41.

29. "Jews See Race Ban in Harvard Questions," *New York Times*, September 20, 1922, 18; "Anti-Semitism and the Colleges," *The Nation*, July 12, 1922, 46.

30. Solomon, *In the Company of Educated Women*, 144; "Dr. Taylor Assails College Barriers," *New York Times*, January 16, 1949, 38; Richard Bernstein, "Anti-Semitism in an Old File Stirs a College," *New York Times*, May 20, 1983, B1.

31. "Tolerance Practiced," *Florida Flambeau*, January 30, 1942, 4.

32. Connecticut Literary Institution catalog, quoted in Florence M. Read, *The Story of Spelman College* (Atlanta, Ga., n.p., 1961), 17.

33. Edward H. Clarke, M.D., *Sex in Education, or, A Fair Chance for the Girls* (2d ed., 1873; reprint, New York: Arno Press, 1972), 40.

34. Francis Cummins Lockwood, "How to Study," in *The Freshman Girl*, ed. Kate W. Jameson and Frank C. Lockwood, 53.

35. Mrs. S. T. Rorer, "Why I Am Opposed to Pies," *Ladies Home Journal*, August 1900, 28.

36. Ernest Earnest, *Academic Procession: An Informal History of the American College 1636 to 1953* (Indianapolis, Ind.: Bobbs-Merrill, 1953), 186.

37. Catalogue of Mills College for Women. Alameda County, California. 1907–1908, 68.

38. May E. Southworth, *Midnight Feasts: Two Hundred and Two Salads and Chafing Dish Recipes* (San Francisco: Paul Elder & Co., 1914), iii.

39. Elizabeth Howard Westwood, "College Girls at Play," *New York Times Magazine*, April 19, 1903, 11.

40. Southworth, *Midnight Feasts*, iv, iii.

41. "College Girls' Larks and Pranks," *Ladies Home Journal*, March 1900, 8.

42. "Christmas Pranks of College Girls," *Ladies Home Journal*, December 1906, 17.

43. Ballou, *Etiquette at College*, 301–2.

44. Margaret A. Lowe, *Looking Good: College Women and Body Image, 1875–1930* (Baltimore: Johns Hopkins University Press, 2003), 108–9; 183 note 21.

45. "Eat and Run," *Mademoiselle*, August 1940, 82.

46. *Within the Ivy: A Handbook for New Students at Stephens College* (Columbia, Mo.: Civic Association of Stephens College, 1947), 136.

47. Olive San Louie Anderson, *An American Girl and Her Four Years in a Boys' College* (New York: D. Appleton and Co., 1878), 36, 87.

48. L. Clark Seelye, "The Influence of Sororities," *Ladies Home Journal*, September 1907, 12.

49. Diana B. Turk, *Bound by a Mighty Vow: Sisterhood and Women's Fraternities, 1870–1920* (New York: New York University Press, 2004), 165 note 1; L. C. Seelye, "Sororities," 12.

50. Shirley Kreasan Strout, *The History of Zeta Tau Alpha, 1898–1948* (Zeta Tau Alpha Fraternity [Menasha, Wis.: Collegiate Press], 1956), 12. Georgia Female College became Wesleyan Female College in 1843, and finally, Wesleyan College in 1917.

51. L. C. Seelye, "Sororities," p. 12.

52. Ibid.; Horowitz, *Alma Mater*, 154.

53. Frances Louise Nardin, "The Social Life of the Campus," in *The Freshman Girl*, ed. Kate W. Jameson and Frank C. Lockwood, 87.

54. "Sorority Linked to Girl's Suicide," *New York Times*, February 18, 1942, 21.

55. "College Sororities: They Pose a Social Problem," *Life*, December 17, 1945, 97.

56. "Thank You for Your Letters," *Seventeen*, December 1953, 4.

57. "Thank You for Your Letters," *Seventeen*, January 1951, 4.

58. Eldridge, *CO-EDiquette*, 53–4.

59. "Sorority Bans Co-ed for Dating a Negro," *New York Times*, May 22, 1951, 33.

60. Lawrence Otis Graham, *Our Kind of People: Inside America's Black Upper*

Class (New York: HarperCollins, 1999), 87; "Negroes Pledged, Sororities Ousted," *New York Times*, August 2, 1956, 27.

61. Jeanne Contini, "Sororities—Do They Still Swing?" *Seventeen*, August 1966, 297.

62. Ibid.

63. Gulielma Fell Alsop, M.D., and Mary F. McBride, M.A., *She's Off to College: A Girls' Guide to College Life* (New York: Vanguard Press, 1940), 160.

64. James W. Putnam, ed., *Lady Lore* (Lawrence, Kans.: The Witan, 1939), 40.

65. "Chicago Co-eds Drop Man-Haters' Club Idea," *New York Times*, March 13, 1924, 14; "Here and There," *Blue and Grey*, December 2, 1927, 6.

66. "Senior Members of Mortified Tap 13 Girls for Membership," *Florida Flambeau*, April 17, 1942, 1.

67. Rona M. Wilk, " 'What's a Crush?' A Study of Crushes and Romantic Friendships at Barnard College, 1900–1920," OAH *Magazine of History*, July 2004, 20.

68. Lillian Faderman, *Odd Girls and Twilight Lovers* (New York: Columbia University Press, 1991), 19.

69. Alice Stone Blackwell, quoted in Wilk, " 'What's a Crush?' ", 21.

70. Horowitz, *Alma Mater*, 167.

71. Hudnut, *You Can Always Tell a Freshman*, 119.

72. "College Girls' Larks and Pranks," *Ladies Home Journal*, March 1900, 8.

73. Carroll Smith-Rosenberg, *Disorderly Conduct: Visions of Gender in Victorian America* (New York: Oxford University Press, 1986), 60.

74. Horowitz, *Power and Passion*, 46.

75. Faderman, *Odd Girls*, 20–21.

76. Read, *Story of Spelman College*, 4.

77. Ibid., 23.

78. Ibid., 16, 162.

79. Faderman, *Odd Girls*, 30.

80. Mrs. Mary Wood-Allen, M.D., *What a Young Woman Ought to Know* (Philadelphia: VIR Publishing, rev. ed., 1905), 177–78.

81. Faderman, *Odd Girls*, 35, 49.

82. Wanda Fraiken Neff, *We Sing Diana* (Boston: Houghton Mifflin, 1928), quoted in Faderman, *Odd Girls*, 35.

83. Faderman, *Odd Girls*, 52.

84. *The Touchstone* [Hood College yearbook] 1931, 104.

85. Helen D. Bragdon, Ed. D., *Counseling the College Student* (Cambridge: Harvard University Press, 1929), 90.

86. Alsop and McBride, *She's Off to College*, 30.

87. Westmoorland *Wand* 1928, 114.

88. Paula S. Fass, *The Damned and the Beautiful: American Youth in the 1920s* (New York: Oxford University Press, 1977), 124.

89. Mary A. Jordan, "The College for Women," *Atlantic Monthly*, October 1892, 545.

90. Beth L. Bailey, *From Front Porch to Back Seat: Courtship in Twentieth-Century America* (Baltimore: Johns Hopkins University Press, 1988), 26.

91. Ibid., 28.

92. Alsop and McBride, *She's Off to College*, 19, 29.

93. Ibid., 29.

94. Janet Halliday, "The Freshman You Want to Be," *Mademoiselle*, August 1945, 191.

95. Florence Howe Hall, *The Correct Thing in Good Society* (Boston: Dana Estes & Company, 1902), 312–13.

96. Ballou, *Etiquette at College*, 10.

97. Charles D. Lockwood, M.D., "Good Health: Letter from a Medical Man to His Niece," in *The Freshman Girl*, ed. Kate W. Jameson and Frank C. Lockwood, 137.

98. Le Baron Russell Briggs, "To Schoolgirls at Graduation," in *The Freshman Girl*, ed. Kate W. Jameson and Frank C. Lockwood, 68–9.

99. Eldridge, *CO-EDiquette*, 17–8.

100. Student Religious Council, Freshman Handbook of the Massachusetts State College 1935–1936, 88.

101. Mary Caroline Crawford, *The College Girl of America and the Institutions Which Make Her What She Is* (Boston: L. C. Page & Co., 1905), 43.

102. Ibid., 44.

103. Lowe, *Looking Good*, 40–41.

104. Read, *Story of Spelman College*, 143.

105. Student Religious Council, Freshman Handbook of the Massachusetts State College 1935–1936, 20.

106. "Maryland Coeds Demonstrate the Do's and Don't's of Campus Etiquet," *Life*, February 17, 1940, 40.

107. Irene Pierson, *Campus Cues* (3d ed.; Danville, Ill.: Interstate Printers & Publishers, 1962), 188.

Chapter Three: The Collegiate Look

1. Laura Ingalls Wilder, *Little Town on the Prairie* (New York: Harper & Row, 1941), 92.

2. "The College Girl's Wardrobe—What Should Go in the Freshman Trunk," *New York Times*, September 9, 1906, 26.

3. Ibid.

4. "Gowns for Commencement," *New York Times*, May 6, 1894, 18.

5. Margaret A. Lowe, *Looking Good: College Women and Body Image, 1875–1930* (Baltimore: Johns Hopkins University Press), 89–90, 91.

6. Ibid., 89.

7. A Mother, "Some College Girl Follies," *Good Housekeeping*, September 1909, 238.

8. Ibid., 239.

9. "Old Clothes and Remnants Combine to Frock the College Girl," *Ladies Home Journal*, August 1922, 56.

10. James Monroe Taylor, *Vassar* (New York: Oxford University Press, 1915), 88. Italics in original.

11. Edith M. Burtis, "What a Girl Should Take to College," *Ladies Home Journal*, September 1912, 88.

12. Edward J. Power, *Catholic Higher Education in America: A History* (New York: Appleton-Century-Crofts, 1972), 318.

13. Florence M. Read, *The Story of Spelman College* (Atlanta, Ga., n.p., 1961), 188.

14. Lowe, *Looking Good*, 126–27.

15. Martha Pike Conant, *A Girl of the Eighties: At Home and at College* (Boston: Houghton Mifflin, 1931), 113.

16. Diana Crane, *Fashion and Its Social Agendas: Class, Gender, and Identity in Clothing* (Chicago: University of Chicago Press, 2000), 100–1.

17. Sharon O' Brien, *Willa Cather: The Emerging Voice* (New York: Oxford University Press, 1987), 119–21.

18. "College Girls' Larks and Pranks," *Ladies Home Journal*, March 1900, 7.

19. Ibid. Despite the gender-bending nature of the story, the word "queer" as used here simply means "odd." Using the word as a slur against homosexuals didn't come into fashion until the 1930s.

20. Ibid.

21. Crane, *Fashion and Its Social Agendas*, 106–7.

22. *Flaming Youth* (1923) was penned by Warner Fabian, whose 1928 novel *Unforbidden Fruit* is the subject of a sidebar in chapter 2.

23. Paula S. Fass, *The Damned and the Beautiful: American Youth in the 1920s* (New York: Oxford University Press, 1977), 126–27.

24. Ibid.

25. All price comparisons are made using American Institute for Economic Research's Cost-of-Living Calculator (http://www.aier.org/cgi-aier/colcalculator.cgi [accessed November 20, 2005]).

26. *Mademoiselle*, August 1940, 127.

27. *Mademoiselle*, August 1940, 3, 2, 80.

28. Jane Cobb, "Girls Will Be Boys," *New York Times*, November 3, 1940, 123.

29. Patricia Blake, "Why College Girls Dress That Way," *New York Times*, April 7, 1946, 104.

30. Janet Halliday, "The Freshman You Want to Be," *Mademoiselle*, August 1945, 191. Emphasis in original.

31. Mina Curtiss, "The World We Wanted, 1918," *Mademoiselle*, August 1945, 253, 255.

32. "Wellesley Lacks Prinking," *New York Times*, February 10, 1911.

33. "College Girls Criticised," *New York Times*, March 9, 1914.

34. Fass, *The Damned and the Beautiful*, 286; "Sport Costume Barred," *New*

York Times, February 25, 1921, 11; Associated Students of Mills College, Students' Handbook, Mills College, 1927–1928, 27.

35. Eunice Fuller Barnard, "Our Colleges for Women: Co-ed or Not?" *New York Times Magazine,* March 26, 1933, 4.

36. Marilyn Moreland, "I Chose an Eastern 'Dream' College," *Seventeen,* January 1961, 16.

37. Gulielma Fell Alsop, M.D., and Mary F. McBride, M.A., *She's Off to College: A Girls' Guide to College Life* (New York: Vanguard Press, 1940), 30, 50.

38. Estelle Safier McBride, "Why College Girls Dress That Way," *New York Times,* December 10, 1944, 28.

39. Patricia Blake, "Why College Girls Dress That Way," *New York Times,* April 7, 1946, 104.

40. Helen Quien Stewart, *Some Social Aspects of Residence Halls for College Women* (New York: Professional & Technical Press, 1942), Appendix E, 165–66.

41. *Within the Ivy: A Handbook for New Students at Stephens College* (Columbia, Mo.: Civic Association of Stephens College, 1947), 154–55.

42. Elizabeth Ann Hudnut, *You Can Always Tell a Freshman: How to Get the Most Out of Your College Years* (New York: E. P. Dutton, 1949), 129.

43. Irene Pierson, *Campus Cues* (3d. ed.; Danville, Ill.: Interstate Printers & Publishers, 1962), 25.

44. Marilyn Bender, "Another Blow to *In Loco Parentis*—Housemothers Fading from College," *New York Times,* October 17, 1969, 55.

45. "Successful Campaign," *Mademoiselle,* August 1940, 292. Skidmore went fully coed in 1971.

46. Elinor Boyes, "Lily-Gilding," *Mademoiselle,* August 1940, 254, 253.

47. John C. Crighton, *Stephens: A Story of Educational Innovation* (Columbia, Mo.: American Press, 1970), 285.

48. Victoria K. Reynolds, "Your College Interview—How to Make a Good Impression," *Seventeen,* January 1961, 41.

49. Alsop and McBride, *She's Off to College,* 18.

50. Jimmy Wescott, "Any Christmas Miss-Takes?" *Seventeen,* December 1958, 8.

51. Mary Ellin Barrett, "Brains Are Not Enough," *Glamour*, August 1961, 108–9.

52. *Seventeen*, May 1946, 37.

53. "By Using Their Heads: Four Girls Defeat the Boys on a Quiz Show," *Seventeen*, August 1959, 239.

54. *Seventeen*, May 1946, 33.

55. *Seventeen*, August 1948, 226.

56. *Seventeen*, April 1956, 167.

57. *American Girl*, August 1957, 49.

58. *Seventeen*, August 1948, 198, 87.

59. Paul H. Landis, *So This Is College* (New York: McGraw-Hill, 1954), 33.

60. Alice Beaton, "The Pond Grows Bigger," *Seventeen*, May 1946, 53.

61. Alsop and McBride, *She's Off to College*, 20, 23.

62. Bernadette Carey, "Collegiate Shoppers Will Be Majoring in Classics This Year," *New York Times*, July 25, 1967, 26.

63. "College Shops," *Life*, September 8, 1941, 64, 63. In 2005 dollars, that was just over $53,000 in collegiate fashions.

64. Advertisement, *New York Times*, August 26, 1970, 21.

65. *Mademoiselle*, August 1948, 325.

66. *Mademoiselle*, August 1953, 54, 235, 252.

67. "Mlle's Last Word on College, '53," *Mademoiselle*, August 1953, 235.

68. Virginia Hanson, "N.B.—They Made the Grade," *Mademoiselle*, May 1942, 138–39.

69. Ellen Melinkoff, *What We Wore: An Offbeat Social History of Women's Clothing, 1950 to 1980* (New York: Quill, 1984), 203.

70. *Mademoiselle*, August 1947, 209.

71. David Cross, "OSU Students Use Smarts, Not Looks, for Victoria's Secret," *The Lantern*, October 4, 2004 (http://www.thelantern.com/news /2004/10/04/Campus/Osu-Students.Use.Smarts.Not.Looks.For.Victorias .Secret-740980.shtml [accessed December 2, 2004]); Jake Coyle, "Victoria's Secret Targets Women in College," *Salon*, July 30, 2004 (http://www.salon .com/news/wire/2004/07/30/victoria/index.html [accessed July 30, 2004]).

72. "Issue of the Week: Underpants Mascot Invades Campus," *Arizona Daily Wildcat*, September 15, 2004 (http://www.wildcat.arizona.edu/papers /98/17/text/03_1.html [accessed December 2, 2004]).

Chapter Four: In Loco Parentis and Other Campus Rules

1. Gulielma Fell Alsop, M.D., and Mary F. McBride, M.A, *She's Off to College: A Girl's Guide to College Life* (New York: Vanguard Press, 1940), 53.

2. Ibid., cover flap text.

3. Frederick Rudolph, *The American College and University: A History* (New York: Alfred A. Knopf, 1962), 97; Helen Lefkowitz Horowitz, *Campus Life: Undergraduate Cultures from the End of the Eighteenth Century to the Present* (New York: Alfred A. Knopf, 1987), 24–25, 32–23, 42.

4. Hank Nuwer, *Wrongs of Passage: Fraternities, Sororities, Hazing, and Binge Drinking* (Bloomington: Indiana University Press, 1999), 239.

5. James Orton, ed., *The Liberal Education of Women: The Demand and the Method* (New York: A. S. Barnes & Co., 1873), 270, quoted in John Rury and Glenn Harper, "The Trouble with Coeducation: Mann and Women at Antioch, 1853–1860," *History of Education Quarterly*, vol. 26, no. 4 (Winter 1986), 488.

6. Rev. Samuel Harris, "The Complete Academic Education of Females," *New Englander and Yale Review*, May 1853, 312.

7. Edward J. Power, *Catholic Higher Education in America: A History* (New York: Appleton-Century-Crofts, 1972), 305.

8. Moses Tyler, "Vassar Female College," *New Englander and Yale Review*, October 1862, 736.

9. Rury and Harper, "The Trouble with Coeducation," 488.

10. William A. McKeever, "Is Your Daughter Safe at College?" *New York Times Magazine*, March 20, 1910, 10.

11. Helen Lefkowitz Horowitz, *Alma Mater: Design and Experience in the Women's Colleges from Their Nineteenth-Century Beginnings to the 1930s* (2d ed.; Amherst: University of Massachusetts Press, 1993), 38.

12. Mary Caroline Crawford, *The College Girl of America and the Institutions Which Make Her What She Is* (Boston: L. C. Page & Co., 1905), 165; Catalogue of the State College for Women, Tallahassee, Florida, 1908–1909, 91; "The University and the Woman," University of Oregon Leaflet Series, vol. 5, no. 12 (July 1920), unpaginated.

13. McKeever, "Is Your Daughter Safe?" 10.

14. Ernest Earnest, *Academic Procession: An Informal History of the American College 1636 to 1953* (Indianapolis, Ind.: Bobbs-Merrill, 1953), 109.

15. Horowitz, *Alma Mater*, 39.

16. Peg Deane interview, August 8, 1994, Mills College Fires of Wisdom Oral History Project, 11.

17. Lawrence Otis Graham, *Our Kind of People: Inside America's Black Upper Class* (New York: HarperCollins, 1999), 73.

18. Crawford, *College Girl of America*, 41.

19. Graham, *Our Kind of People*, 73.

20. Leslie Miller-Bernal, "Coeducation: An Uneven Progression," in *Going Coed: Women's Experiences in Formerly Men's Colleges and Universities, 1950–2000*, ed. Leslie Miller-Bernal and Susan L. Poulson (Nashville, Tenn.: Vanderbilt University Press, 2004), 19 note 36.

21. "Lack of Rules Characterize Senior Hall," *Florida Flambeau*, November 28, 1941, 5.

22. Graham, *Our Kind of People*, 73.

23. Horowitz, *Alma Mater*, 15.

24. "Smoking Co-eds Penalized," *New York Times*, March 15, 1930, 10.

25. Horowitz, *Alma Mater*, 74–75.

26. A Physician, *Satan in Society* (Cincinnati, Ohio: Edward F. Hovey, 1880), 70, 74.

27. Horowitz, *Alma Mater*, 74–75, 77–78, 228.

28. Power, *Catholic Higher Education*, 306.

29. Earnest, *Academic Procession*, 39.

30. Ibid., 41.

31. Ibid., 40.

32. "The Topic of the Day," *Blue and Grey*, December 2, 1927, 2.

33. Earnest, *Academic Procession*, 40.

34. Catalogue of the State College for Women, Tallahassee, Florida, 1908–1909, 91.

35. "Mount Holyoke forever will be, Mount Holyoke forever will be, For Women Only," *New York Times*, April 9, 1972.

36. Jean Webster, *When Patty Went to College* (New York: Grosset & Dunlap, 1903), 276, 269, 260, 268, 270–71, 279.

37. "Drops Compulsory Chapel," *New York Times*, November 13, 1926.

38. Mary Lee, "The College Girl Starts a Revolution," *New York Times*, May 13, 1928.

39. Anne Eloise Pierce, *Deans and Advisors of Women and Girls* (New York: Professional & Technical Press, 1928, 56.

40. Ibid., 51.

41. Dorothy A. Plub and George B. Dowell, eds., *The Magnificent Enterprise: A Chronicle of Vassar College* (Poughkeepsie, N.Y.: Vassar College, 1961), quoted in Anne Firor Scott, *The American Woman: Who Was She?* (Englewood Cliffs, N.J.: Prentice-Hall, 1971), 80. In 1871, founder Otis Bisbee also acted as principal of Poughkeepsie's Riverview Military Academy.

42. Jane Addams, *Twenty Years at Hull House* (New York: MacMillan Company, 1912), 46.

43. While some locales, such as San Francisco, outlawed the smoking of opium as early as the 1870s, it wasn't until ratification of the Harrison Narcotics Act in 1914 that opium was restricted to medical use only.

44. Catalogue of the State College for Women, Tallahassee, Florida, 1908–1909, 90.

45. Lynne H. Kleinman, *The Milwaukee-Downer Woman* (Appleton, Wis.: Lawrence University Press, 1997), (http://www.lawrence.edu/news/pubs/mdwoman/daily.shtml [accessed August 1, 2004]).

46. Ibid.

47. Ibid.

48. Ibid.

49. Ibid.

50. "Smith College Girl Arrested for Theft," *New York Times*, June 7, 1901, 1; "Theft in College, Girls Searched," *New York Times*, June 3, 1909, 18.

51. "College Girl Slain, Suitor a Suicide," *New York Times*, April 30, 1909, 1.

52. Ibid; "Brooded Over Lost Love," *New York Times*, April 30, 1909, 2. Built in 1903, the Students' Building was torn down in the late 1960s.

53. Horowitz, *Alma Mater*, 24.

54. Samuel Haig Johnson, "Adjustment Problems of University Girls in Collective Living," *Social Forces*, vol. 17, no. 4 (May 1939), 504.

55. Rury and Harper, "The Trouble with Coeducation," 494.

56. Maryland College for Women, *Oriole* 1898 (unpaginated).

57. "College Girls' Larks and Pranks," *Ladies Home Journal*, January, March, April, August 1900; "Christmas Pranks of College Girls," *Ladies Home Journal*, December 1906, 17.

58. Lynn D. Gordon, "The Gibson Girl Goes to College: Popular Culture and Women's Higher Education in the Progressive Era, 1890–1920," *American Quarterly*, vol. 39, no. 2 (Summer 1987), 215.

59. "College Girls' Larks and Pranks," *Ladies Home Journal*, March 1900, 7.

60. Rury and Harper, "The Trouble with Coeducation," 494–98.

61. Ibid., 496, 498.

62. Maxine D. Jones, "Student Unrest at Talladega College, 1887–1914," *Journal of Negro History*, vol. 70, no. 3/4 (Summer–Autumn 1985), 73.

63. Ibid., 75.

64. Ibid., 76.

65. Ibid., 76–77.

66. Raymond Wolters, *The New Negro on Campus: Black College Rebellions of the 1920s* (Princeton, N.J.: Princeton University Press, 1975), 17.

67. Ibid., 31, 46, 37.

68. Ibid., 37.

69. Ibid., 34.

70. Ibid., 45, 47–48, 50, 64.

71. "College Students Strike over 6 P.M. Coed Curfew," *New York Times*, October 1, 1926, 1; "Students Strike at St. Lawrence," *New York Times*, May 3, 1931, 2.

72. "Vassar and Virginity," *Newsweek*, May 21, 1962, 86.

73. Gael Greene, *Sex and the College Girl* (New York: Dell Publishing, 1964), 201–22.

74. Jonathan Randal, "Relaxed Campus Rules Reflect Liberalized Attitudes on Sex," *New York Times*, April 25, 1966, 28; "Coeds Vote to Ban Curfew," *New York Times*, December 15, 1966, 56.

75. "Georgia Students Call Off Protests on Women's Rules," *New York Times*, April 13, 1968, 11; "College Sleep-In Ended," *New York Times*, March 18,

1969, 42; Robert M. Smith, "Girls at Barnard Defy Dorm Rule," *New York Times*, October 24, 1968, 57.

76. Marilyn Bender, "Another Blow to *In Loco Parentis*—Housemothers Fading from College," *New York Times*, October 17, 1969, 55.

77. Fran Schumer, *Most Likely to Succeed: Six Women from Harvard and What Became of Them* (New York: Random House, 1986), 41–42.

78. Nan Robertson, "A Father's Charge of Campus Promiscuity Upsets Wellesley," *New York Times*, May 1, 1976, 36; Nan Robertson, "Wellesley: Tempest in a Dormitory Abates," *New York Times*, November 13, 1976, 36.

Chapter Five: Book Smart or House Wise? What to Study

1. Frederick Rudolph, *The American College and University: A History* (New York: Alfred A. Knopf, 1962), 326.

2. Sophia Jex-Blake, *A Visit to Some American Schools and Colleges* (1867; reprint, Westport, Conn.: Hyperion Press, 1976), 57.

3. Ibid., 50.

4. James Monroe Taylor, *Vassar* (New York: Oxford University Press, 1915), 63–64.

5. Helen Lefkowitz Horowitz, *Alma Mater: Design and Experience in the Women's Colleges from Their Nineteenth-Century Beginnings to the 1930s* (2d ed.; Amherst: University of Massachusetts Press, 1993), 41.

6. Preparatory departments weren't restricted to women's colleges. Antioch's first class in 1853 had a total of six students (four men, two women), but there were more than two hundred students (including ninety-six women) enrolled in its preparatory department; John Rury and Glenn Harper, "The Trouble With Coeducation: Mann and Women at Antioch, 1853–1860," *History of Education Quarterly*, vol. 26, no. 4 (Winter 1986), 485.

7. Vera M. Butler, *Education as Revealed by New England Newspapers Prior to 1850* (Philadelphia, n.p., 1935), 459.

8. Ibid.
9. An American Mother, "Is a College Education the Best for Our Girls?," *Ladies Home Journal*, July 1900, 15.
10. Sue W. Hetherington, "Mental Culture," *The Ladies' Repository*, vol. 11, issue 3 (March 1873), 217–18.
11. G. G. Buckler, "The Lesser Man," *North American Review*, September 1897, 295.
12. This section draws primarily on research presented in Cynthia Eagle Russett's *Sexual Science: The Victorian Construction of Womanhood* (Cambridge: Harvard University Press, 1991).
13. Russett, *Sexual Science*, 36.
14. Ibid.
15. Ibid., 36–37.
16. Ibid., 37.
17. Paul Topinard, *Anthropology* (London: Chapman and Hall, 1878), quoted in Russett, *Sexual Science*, 54; Edward Drinker Cope, *The Origin of the Fittest* (1887; reprint, New York: Arno Press, 1974), quoted in Russett, *Sexual Science*, 55.
18. Cesare Lombroso, *The Man of Genius* (London: Walter Scott, 1894), quoted in Russett, *Sexual Science*, 95; Russett, *Sexual Science*, 95.
19. William A. Hammond, "Woman and Politics," *North American Review*, August 1883, 142.
20. Edward Thorndike, "Sex in Education," *Bookman* 23 (1906), 212–13, quoted in Russett, *Sexual Science*, 100.
21. Hammond, "Woman and Politics," 142.
22. Helene Deutsch, M.D., *The Psychology of Women*, vol. I, *Girlhood* (New York: Grune & Stratton, 1944), 142, 290–91.
23. Ibid., 143.
24. Edwin F. Healy, *Marriage Guidance* (Chicago: Loyola University Press, 1948), 23, 21, 25.
25. Ibid., 30.
26. Anne Firor Scott, *The American Woman: Who Was She?* (Englewood Cliffs, N.J.: Prentice-Hall, 1971), 62.
27. Taylor, *Vassar*, 86. Emphasis in original.

28. Horowitz, *Alma Mater,* 60.

29. Mary Caroline Crawford, *The College Girl of America and the Institutions Which Make Her What She Is* (Boston: L. C. Page & Co., 1905), 145, 144.

30. "The real purpose of the story," Gilman said, "was to reach Dr. S. Weir Mitchell, and convince him of the error of his ways. I sent him a copy as soon as it came out, but got no response. However many years later, I met someone who knew close friends of Dr. Mitchell's who said he had told them that he had changed his treatment of nervous prostration since reading 'The Yellow Wallpaper.' If that is a fact, I have not lived in vain." Quoted in Julie B. Dock, *Charlotte Perkins Gilman's "The Yellow Wallpaper," and the History of Its Publication and Reception* (University Park: Pennsylvania State University Press, 1998), 89 (http://www-unix.oit.umass.edu /~clit121/AmesYel/weir.html [accessed October 12, 2004]).

31. Dr. S. Weir Mitchell, M.D., LL.D., "When the College Is Hurtful to a Girl," *Ladies Home Journal,* June 1900, 14.

32. Ibid.

33. Anne Randolph, "Is the American Girl Being Miseducated?" *Ladies Home Journal*, September 1, 1910, 9.

34. Ibid.

35. Margaret E. Sangster, *Winsome Womanhood* (New York: Fleming H. Revell Co., 1900), 125, 102–3.

36. Ernest Havemann and Patricia Salter West, *They Went to College: The College Graduate in America Today* (New York: Harcourt, Brace & Co., 1952), 64.

37. Sarah Stage, "Ellen Richards and the Social Significance of the Home Economics Movement," in *Rethinking Home Economics: Women and the History of a Profession*, ed. Sarah Stage and Virginia B. Vincenti (Ithaca, N.Y.: Cornell University Press, 1997), 21–22.

38. Ibid., 22–24.

39. Ibid., 25.

40. Barbara Miller Solomon, *In the Company of Educated Women: A History of Women and Higher Education in America* (New Haven, Conn.: Yale University Press, 1985), 79–80.

41. Rudolph, *American College and University*, 250.

42. "The University and the Woman," University of Oregon Leaflet Series, vol. 5, no. 12 (July 1920), unpaginated.

43. Edward J. Power, *Catholic Higher Education in America: A History* (New York: Appleton-Century-Crofts, 1972), 311.

44. Spelman catalog and Morgan quoted in Johnetta Cross Brazzell, "Bricks without Straw: Missionary-Sponsored Black Higher Education in the Post-Emancipation Era," *Journal of Higher Education*, vol. 63, no. 1 (January/February 1992), 37–38.

45. Florence M. Read, *The Story of Spelman College* (Atlanta, Ga., n.p., 1961), 192.

46. Brazzell, "Bricks without Straw," 42, 44.

47. *Teachers College Record*, vol. 10, no. 3 (1909), 68–95 (http://www.tcrecord.org ID Number:10038, [accessed July 28, 2005]).

48. "Laundry Work as Part of Regular College Course," *New York Times Magazine*, January 11, 1914, 6.

49. Ibid.

50. Mary W. Woolley, "The College Woman as a Home-Maker," *Ladies Home Journal*, October 1, 1910, 16; "Modern College Not the Place to Train Housewives," *New York Times Magazine*, May 10, 1914, 2.

51. "Miss Gildersleeve Now Heads Barnard," *New York Times*, February 17, 1911, 6.

52. Horowitz, *Alma Mater*, 297.

53. Rose C. Feld, "Vassar Girls to Study Home-Making as Career," *New York Times*, May 23, 1916, 8.

54. Horowitz, *Alma Mater*, 297.

55. *The Saturday Evening Post*, September 11, 1948. Emphasis in original.

56. Dorothy D. Lee, "What Shall We Teach Women?" *Mademoiselle*, August 1947, 213.

57. Ibid., 354.

58. Ibid., 213, 354.

59. Brett Harvey, *The Fifties: A Women's Oral History* (New York: Harper-Collins, 1993), 46.

60. Lynn White, Jr., *Educating Our Daughters: A Challenge to the Colleges* (New York: Harper & Brothers, 1950), 84.

61. "Courses to Stress Homes, Family," *New York Times*, June 28, 1942, D5.

62. "Prom Visits Stephens College," *Senior Prom*, September 1950, 46.

63. *Within the Ivy: A Handbook for New Students at Stephens College* (Columbia, Mo.: Civic Association of Stephens College, 1947), 187; "Stephens Studies for Marriage," *Senior Prom*, September 1950, 48.

64. "Stephens Studies for Marriage," 82.

65. Stephens became a fully accredited four-year institution in 1968.

66. "College Girls: If They Could Only Cook," *Quick*, September 8, 1952, 26.

67. Ibid., 23–24.

68. Bancroft Beatley, *Another Look at Women's Education* (Boston: Simmons College, 1955), 5.

69. George D. Stoddard, quoted in Beatley, *Another Look at Women's Education*, ix.

70. Betty Friedan, *The Feminist Mystique* (New York: W. W. Norton, 1963), 156.

71. Simone de Beauvoir, *America Day by Day* (New York: Grove Press, 1953), 50.

72. Gay Head, "Resolved: A Happy New Year!" *Co-ed*, December 1958, 22.

73. "Is Your Sub-Deb Slang Up-to-Date?" *Ladies Home Journal*, December 1944, 153. "Sub-debutantes" or "sub-debs" were too young to be debutantes—in other words, girls under eighteen.

74. B. H. Hall, *A Collection of College Words and Customs* (1856; reprint, Detroit, Mich.: Gale Research Co., 1968), 241–42.

75. Crawford, *College Girl of America*, 28–29.

76. Ibid., 150.

77. Havemann and West, *They Went to College*, 59.

78. Marion K. Stocker, "College on a Shoestring," *Calling All Girls*, September 1948, 71.

79. "You and Your Teacher," *Teen World*, April 1960, 44–45.

80. Alice Lent Covert, "Brains Are for the Birds!," *Redbook*, August 1957, 79, 81–82.

81. John E. Gibson, "What Men Really Think of Women!" *Redbook*, January 1953, 35.

82. Ibid., 70.

83. Quoted in Amelie Rives, "Innocence versus Ignorance," *North American Review*, September 1892, 287–92

84. "Wives and Daughters," *The Living Age*, August 19, 1865, 302–3.

85. Alice-Leone Moats, *No Nice Girl Swears* (New York: Blue Ribbon Books, 1933), 65–66.

86. Frances Bruce Strain, *Love at the Threshold: A Book on Social Dating, Romance, and Marriage* (New York: Appleton-Century-Crofts, 1952), 115.

87. Diana Trilling, "Are Women's Colleges Really Necessary?" in *Women Today: Their Conflicts, Their Frustrations, and Their Fulfillments*, ed. Elizabeth Bragdon (Indianapolis, Ind.: Bobbs-Merrill, 1953), 260.

88. Strain, *Love at the Threshold*, 114–15.

89. "College Boys Agree: We Date to Love and Learn," *Teens Today*, September 1959, 7.

90. "I'm Sick of Acting Like a Moron!," *Teens Today*, September 1959, 58.

91. Ibid., 59.

92. Ibid.

93. Helen Tierney, ed., "Women's Colleges," *Women's Studies Encyclopedia, vol. 2, Literature, Arts, and Learning* (New York: Greenwood Press, 1990), 352.

94. Rury and Harper, "The Trouble with Coeducation," 497–98.

95. Olive San Louie Anderson, *An American Girl and Her Four Years in a Boys' College* (New York: D. Appleton and Co., 1878), 91–93.

96. Sharon Hartman Strom, "Leadership and Tactics in the American Woman Suffrage Movement: A New Perspective from Massachusetts," *Journal of American History*, vol. 62, no. 2 (September 1975), 302.

97. Helen Lefkowitz Horowitz, *The Power and Passion of M. Carey Thomas* (New York: Alfred A. Knopf, 1994), 401.

98. "Vassar's Head Indignant," *New York Times*, January 10, 1908, 7.

99. Annie Nathan Meyer, "Barnard Girls and Suffrage," *New York Times*, December 18, 1910, 12.

100. "Suffragism and Colleges," *New York Times*, December 27, 1910, 8.

101. Solomon, *In the Company of Educated Women*, 112.

102. E. K. R., "College Suffragettes," *New York Times*, January 5, 1911, 8.

103. Solomon, *In the Company of Educated Women*, 87; Alan Sica, "A Century

of Sociology at Kansas," American Sociological Association *Footnotes*, March 1991 (http://www.ku.edu/~socdept/centuryofsoc.pdf [accessed August 4, 2005]).

104. "Mrs. Beard Decries Dominance of Men," *New York Times*, June 7, 1936, 45.

105. "Neglect of Women in History Is Denounced by Mary Beard," *New York Times*, February 11, 1936, 25; Catherine Mackenzie, "Putting Women 'On Record,' The World Center for Women's Archives Begins Gathering Elusive Documents," *New York Times*, June 26, 1938, 30; "Women's Archives Given to Colleges," *New York Times*, November 24, 1940, 55.

106. "Women's Interest Seen in Economics," *New York Times*, April 20, 1940, 17; Doris Greenberg, "Asks Women Avoid Martyr Complex," *New York Times*, May 30, 1948, 22.

107. Linda Greenhouse, "A Graduate Program Sets Out to Find History's Women," *New York Times*, March 20, 1973, 34; *Newsweek* article quoted in Marilyn J. Boxer, *When Women Ask the Questions: Creating Women's Studies in America* (Baltimore: Johns Hopkins University Press, 2001), 8.

108. Sara Evans, *Personal Politics: The Roots of Women's Liberation in the Civil Rights Movement & the New Left* (New York: Vintage Books, 1980), 87.

109. Florence Howe, *Myths of Coeducation: Selected Essays, 1964–1983* (Bloomington: Indiana University Press, 1984), 83.

110. Ibid., 39–40, 44–45.

111. All quoted in "New College Trend: Women Studies," *New York Times*, January 7, 1971, 37.

112. Christine Stolba, "Lying in a Room of One's Own: How Women's Studies Textbooks Miseducate Women" (Arlington, Va.: Independent Women's Forum, 2002), 16, 28, 30; Boxer, *When Women Ask*, 10.

113. Susan Chira, "An Ohio College Says Women Learn Differently, So It Teaches That Way," *New York Times*, May 13, 1992, B7.

114. Ibid. According to the college's Web site, the Ursuline Studies Program remains "the heart of an Ursuline education" as of 2005.

Chapter Six: Fit in Mind and Body

1. Elizabeth Missing Sewell, *Principles of Education, Drawn from Nature and Revelation, and Applied to Female Education in the Upper Classes* (1866), quoted in *Victorian Women: A Documentary Account of Women's Lives in Nineteenth-Century England, France, and the United States*, ed. Erna Olafson Hellerstein, Leslie Parker Hume, and Karen M. Offen (Stanford, Calif.: Stanford University Press, 1981), 69–70.

2. Edward H. Clarke, M.D., *Sex in Education, or, A Fair Chance for the Girls* (2d ed., 1873; reprint, New York: Arno Press, 1972), 38.

3. George H. Napheys, A.M., M.D., *The Physical Life of Woman: Advice to the Maiden, Wife and Mother* (Philadelphia: David McKay, 1894), 59–60; Vern Bullough and Martha Voght, "Women, Menstruation, and Nineteenth-Century Medicine," in *Women and Health in America: Historical Readings*, ed. Judith Walzer Leavitt (Madison: University of Wisconsin Press, 1984), 29.

4. Napheys, *Physical Life of Women*, 63. Italics in original.

5. Ibid., 52–53. Historian Joan Jacobs Brumberg has pointed out that chlorosis was an illness particular to a certain population (teenage girls) at a particular time (the end of the nineteenth century), with both physical and sociocultural origins.

6. Clarke, *Sex in Education*, 157.

7. Ibid., 39.

8. Ibid., 93.

9. Ibid., 80–82.

10. Ibid., 85–87.

11. Ibid., 105–6, 98–100.

12. Clarke, preface.

13. Dorothy Gies McGuigan, *A Dangerous Experiment: 100 Years of Women at the University of Michigan* (Ann Arbor, Mich.: Center for Continuing Education of Women, 1970), 56.

14. "Current Literature," *The Galaxy*, vol. 17, issue 5, May 1874, 717.

15. Hellerstein et al., *Victorian Women*, 70.

16. Ibid., 70–71.

17. Julia Ward Howe, ed., *Sex and Education: A Reply to Dr. E. H. Clarke's "Sex in Education"* (1874; reprint, New York: Arno Press, 1972), 15.

18. Shirley Marchalonis, *College Girls: A Century in Fiction* (New Brunswick, N.J.: Rutgers University Press, 1995), 10.

19. Olive San Louie Anderson, *An American Girl and Her Four Years in a Boys' College* (New York: D. Appleton and Co., 1878), 96, 98.

20. Clarke, *Sex in Education*, 119–20.

21. Carroll Smith-Rosenberg and Charles Rosenberg, "The Female Animal: Medical and Biological Views of Woman and Her Role in Nineteenth-Century America," in *Women and Health in America: Historical Readings*, ed. Judith Walzer Leavitt (Madison: University of Wisconsin Press, 1984), 16; Reuben Gold Thwaites, *The University of Wisconsin* (1900), http://www.library.wisc.edu/etext/WIReader/Thwaites/Chapter08.html Section 12 [accessed July 30, 2003].

22. William Lee Howard, M.D., *Confidential Chats with Girls* (New York: Edward J. Clode, 1911), 28.

23. A Mother, "Some College Girl Follies," *Good Housekeeping*, September 1909, 239–40.

24. Harvey Green, *Fit for America: Health, Fitness, Sport, and American Society* (New York: Pantheon Books, 1986), 12, 87; P. A. Fitzgerald, Esq., *The Exhibition Speaker* (New York: Sheldon, Lamport & Blakeman, 1856), 247.

25. Green, *Fit for America*, 191.

26. Fitzgerald, *Exhibition Speaker*, 247.

27. Green, *Fit for America*, 96.

28. Catharine Beecher, *Educational Reminiscences and Suggestions* (New York: J. B. Ford and Co., 1874), 85. Italics in original.

29. Ernest Earnest, *Academic Procession: An Informal History of the American College 1636 to 1953* (Indianapolis, Ind.: Bobbs-Merrill, 1953), 177.

30. Helen Lefkowitz Horowitz, *Alma Mater: Design and Experience in the Women's Colleges from Their Nineteenth-Century Beginnings to the 1930s* (2d ed., Amherst: University of Massachusetts Press, 1993), 36.

31. *Ladies Home Calisthenics* (Boston: Educational Publishing, 1890), 1, quoted in Green, *Fit for America*, 225.

32. Frances M. Abbott, "A Comparative View of the Woman Suffrage Movement," *North American Review*, February 1898, 145.

33. Barbara A. Schreier, "Sporting Wear," in *Men and Women: Dressing the Part*, ed. Claudia Brush Kidwell and Valerie Steel (Washington, D.C.: Smithsonian Institution Press, 1989), 100.

34. Ibid., 98–99.

35. Howard, *Confidential Chats*, 25.

36. Ibid., 16, 19.

37. Ibid., 25.

38. Ibid., 43.

39. Ibid., 43, 84.

40. Martha H. Verbrugge, *Able-Bodied Womanhood: Personal Health and Social Change in Nineteenth-Century Boston* (New York: Oxford University Press, 1988), 150.

41. Dudley A. Sargent, M.D., "Are Athletics Making Girls Masculine?" *Ladies Home Journal*, March 1912, 72, 11, 71.

42. Ibid., 73.

43. Ibid., 11.

44. Alice W. Frymir, *Basket Ball for Women* (New York: A. S. Barnes & Co., 1928), 8.

45. Schreier, "Sporting Wear," 101; Frymir, *Basket Ball*, 9.

46. Frymir, *Basket Ball*, 8.

47. Schreier, "Sporting Wear," 101.

48. Susan K. Cahn, *Coming on Strong: Gender and Sexuality in Twentieth-Century Women's Sport* (New York: Free Press, 1994), 85–86.

49. Harriet C. Seelye, "Festivals at American Colleges for Women. At Smith," *The Century*, January 1895, 434; Verbrugge, *Able-Bodied Womanhood*, 182.

50. H. Seelye, "Festivals," 434.

51. Gulielma Fell Alsop, M.D., and Mary F. McBride, M.A., *She's Off to College: A Girl's Guide to College Life* (New York: Vanguard Press, 1940), 140.

52. Elizabeth Eldridge, *CO-EDiquette: Poise and Popularity for Every Girl* (New York: E. P. Dutton, 1936), 232.

53. Schreier, "Sporting Wear," 101.

54. Green, *Fit for America*, 228.

55. Mary Caroline Crawford, *The College Girl of America and the Institutions Which Make Her What She Is* (Boston: L. C. Page & Co., 1905), 12.

56. Frymir, *Basket Ball*, 245.

57. Ibid., 13–14.

58. Ibid., 20, 25.

59. Green, *Fit for America*, 228. Green reports that the practice of mixing teams before interschool play continued into the 1970s in some private schools.

60. "Play Day," *Blue and Grey*, February 6, 1931, 2.

61. Helen Eustis, "Smith College," *Holiday*, May 1950, 65.

62. Eunice Fuller Barnard, "The New Freedom of the College Girl," *New York Times Magazine*, March 19, 1933, 9.

63. Margot Berol, "Athletics for Life," *Mademoiselle*, August 1940, 310.

64. Abigail Wood, "What Would You Do?" *Seventeen*, September 1959, 42.

65. Berol, "Athletics for Life," 186.

66. Mrs. S. T. Rorer, "What College Girls Eat," *Ladies Home Journal*, November 1905, 13.

67. Martha Pike Conant, *A Girl of the Eighties: At Home and at College* (Boston: Houghton Mifflin, 1931), 99.

68. Margaret A. Lowe, *Looking Good: College Women and Body Image, 1875–1930* (Baltimore: Johns Hopkins University Press, 2003), 31. Much of this section is based on Lowe's research.

69. Quoted in Lowe, *Looking Good*, 30–31.

70. Catalogue of the State College for Women, Tallahassee, Florida, 1908–1909, 13.

71. Elizabeth Howard Westwood, "College Girls at Play," *New York Times*, April 19, 1903, SM11.

72. Ibid.

73. Lowe, *Looking Good*, 31.

74. Cornell University's special collections librarian could not find an Elsie Scheel listed in either alumni or student directories for the appropriate year in question, and wonders whether the story could have been a student

hoax picked up and reported by the *New York Times*. However, I found a 1933 *New York Times* obituary for the husband of an Elsie Scheel Hirsh, who would have been about the correct age of the Cornell Venus.

75. "Flapper Lines Oust Venus de Milo Plan," *New York Times*, April 16, 1923, 12.

76. *Smith College Weekly*, quoted in Lowe, *Looking Good*, 145; H. I. Phillips, "It Is Never Too Late to Shrink," *American Magazine*, December 1925, quoted in Hillel Schwartz, *Never Satisfied: A Cultural History of Diets, Fantasies & Fat* (New York: Anchor Books, 1986), 183; "Finds Girls Starving to Keep Underweight," New York Times, October 12, 1926, 13.

77. "Gained 105 Pounds, N.Y.U. Girl Ends Life," *New York Times*, January 31, 1930, 18.

78. "Effects of Overstudy," *New York Times*, September 21, 1884, 9; "A Detective Who Didn't Detect," *New York Times*, November 27, 1884, 2.

79. "Mt. Holyoke Student Gone," *New York Times*, November 21, 1897, 1; "Search for Bertha Mellish," *New York Times*, November 24, 1897, 1; "Woman's Foot in Meadow," *New York Times*, August 30, 1898, 5.

80. Alan Bodnar, Ph.D., "Can Too Much Studying Cause Mental Illness?" MassPsy.com, June 2000 (http://www.masspsy.com/columnists/bodnar_0006.html [accessed December 16, 2004]); Henry Smith Williams, M.D., "A Modern Form of Insanity," *North American Review*, June 1892, 721.

81. E. M. Hale, *Materia Medica and Special Therapeutics of the New Remedies* (New York: Boericke & Taefel, 1875), 493.

82. "Girl Student Arrested," *New York Times*, March 21, 1903, 1.

83. "Think Death Due to Hazing," *New York Times*, November 16, 1910, 1; "Student Dies Insane," *New York Times*, November 17, 1910, 1.

84. "Called Professor Daddy," *New York Times*, March 20, 1927, 4.

85. "Wellesley Speeds Bigger Infirmary," *New York Times*, September 7, 1941, 58. Simpson Cottage became Simpson Infirmary in 1908.

86. "Student a Suicide, 26th Since Jan. 1," *New York Times*, March 9, 1927, 27.

87. Charles D. Lockwood, M.D., "Good Health: Letter from a Medical Man to His Niece," in *The Freshman Girl: A Guide to College Life*, ed. Kate W. Jameson and Frank C. Lockwood (Boston: D. C. Heath, 1925), 136.

88. Alsop and McBride, *She's Off to College*, 194.

89. Ibid., 195.

90. Ibid.

91. Elisabeth Ann Hudnut, *You Can Always Tell a Freshman: How to Get the Most Out of Your College Years* (New York: E. P. Dutton, 1949), 121–22.

92. Jean Glidden Henderson and Algo D. Henderson, *Ms. Goes to College* (Carbondale: Southern Illinois University Press, 1975), 77.

93. A Woman of Fashion, *Etiquette for Americans* (Chicago: Herbert S. Stone & Co., 1898), 179–80.

94. "Women Smokers," *New York Times*, February 29, 1920, in George E. Mowry, ed., *The Twenties: Fords, Flappers, and Fanatics* (Englewood Cliffs, N.J.: Prentice Hall, 1963), 179.

95. Paula S. Fass, *The Damned and the Beautiful: American Youth in the 1920s* (New York: Oxford University Press, 1977), 294.

96. "Smoking in Public Barred for Women; Police Enforce Law," *New York Times*, March 28, 1922, 1.

97. Harry Burke, "Women Cigarette Fiends," *Ladies Home Journal*, June 1922, 20.

98. Larry Tye, *The Father of Spin: Edward L. Bernays and the Birth of Public Relations* (New York: Crown Publishers, 1998), 28, 30–31.

99. Ibid., 24.

100. Eldridge, *CO-EDiquette*, 138.

101. "Michigan College Sends 17 Girls Home," *New York Times*, April 13, 1922, 16; "Suspends Two Co-Eds for Smoking at Dance," *New York Times*, April 17, 1923, 19.

102. Fass, *The Damned and the Beautiful*, 295; "Frown on Smoking by Co-Eds in West," *New York Times*, February 14, 1922, 8.

103. "Frown on Smoking by Co-eds in West," 8.

104. "Goucher College Girls Put Taboo on Tobacco," *New York Times*, May 18, 1924, 22.

105. Barbara Miller Solomon, *In the Company of Educated Women: A History of Women and Higher Education in America* (New Haven, Conn.: Yale University Press, 1985), 162; Tye, *Father of Spin*, 34.

106. Fass, *The Damned and the Beautiful*, 295–96.

107. "Smoking for Women," *New York Times*, March 1, 1922, 18.

108. Solomon, *In the Company of Educated Women*, 161.

109. "Stanford Girls Smoke in Dorms," *Blue and Grey*, May 13, 1927, 2.

110. Calvin B. T. Lee, *The Campus Scene: 1900–1970* (New York: David McKay, 1970), 28–29.

111. Solomon, *In the Company of Educated Women*, 161.

112. *Daily Illini*, April 14, 1920, quoted in Fass, *The Damned and the Beautiful*, 299; "Ask Girls' Smoking Room," *New York Times*, January 19, 1930, 36.

113. Doris Webster and Mary Alden Hopkins, eds., *Mrs. Grundy Is Dead: A Code of Etiquette for Young People, Written by Themselves* (New York: Century Co., 1930), 77.

114. Eunice Fuller Barnard, "The New Freedom of the College Girl," *New York Times Magazine*, March 19, 1933, 8.

115. "We're Telling You!" *Ladies Home Journal*, December 1944, 20.

116. *Within the Ivy: A Handbook for New Students at Stephens College* (Columbia, Mo: Civic Association of Stephens College, 1947), 150.

117. "Is Smoking Thing of Past?" *Mills Stream*, October 3, 1963, 2; Peter Bar, "Advertising: College Media to Miss Cigarette Accounts," *New York Times*, June 21, 1963, 36.

118. Fass, *The Damned and the Beautiful*, 311.

119. Daily Princetonian, January 15, 1926, quoted in Fass, *The Damned and the Beautiful*, 313.

120. Andrew Barr, *Drink: A Social History of America* (New York: Carroll & Graf, 1999), 135.

121. "Says College Girls Are Given to Drink," *New York Times*, January 10, 1924, 7.

122. "College Looseness Blamed on Co-eds," *New York Times*, September 15, 1926, 10.

123. "Co-eds Are Defended by Heads of Colleges," *New York Times*, September 16, 1926, 44.

124. C. D. Lockwood, "Good Health," 137.

125. "Mary Harris Armor Speaks in Chapel," *Blue and Grey*, October 14, 1927, 6.

126. "Says College Girls Oppose Prohibition," *New York Times*, March 20, 1930, 2.

127. Eldridge, *CO-EDiquette*, 148–49.

128. Ibid., 149–50.

129. Dorothy C. Stratton and Helen B. Schleman, *Your Best Foot Forward: Social Usage for Young Moderns*, rev. ed. (New York: McGraw-Hill, 1955), 112.

130. Eldridge, *CO-EDiquette*, 149–50; "Morals at College," *Teens Today*, November 1960, 59.

Chapter Seven: Sex Ed and Husband Hunting

1. Helen Lefkowitz Horowitz, *The Power and Passion of M. Carey Thomas* (New York: Alfred A. Knopf, 1994), 387.

2. Patricia J. Campbell, *Sex Education Books for Young Adults 1892–1979* (New York: R. R. Bowker Co., 1979), 8.

3. Quoted in Jeffrey P. Moran, *Teaching Sex: The Shaping of Adolescence in the 20th Century* (Cambridge: Harvard University Press, 2000), 163.

4. Edith Rickert, "What Has the College Done for Girls? III: Where the College Has Failed with Girls," *Ladies Home Journal*, March 12, 1912, 16.

5. Moran, *Teaching Sex*, 73–74.

6. Paula S. Fass, *The Damned and the Beautiful: American Youth in the 1920s* (New York: Oxford University Press, 1977), 261.

7. Frances Louise Nardin, "The Social Life of the Campus" in *The Freshman Girl: A Guide to College Life*, ed. Kate W. Jameson and Frank C. Lockwood (Boston: D. C. Heath, 1925), 95.

8. Fass, *The Damned and the Beautiful*, 264–66.

9. Moran, *Teaching Sex*, 101.

10. Ibid., 126; "Marriage Courses Urged in Colleges," *New York Times*, February 14, 1933, 13.

11. Eunice Fuller Barnard, "Teaching Them How to Live Happily Ever After," *New York Times*, October 2, 1938, 11.

12. James H. Jones, *Alfred C. Kinsey: A Public/Private Life* (New York: W. W. Norton, 1997), 322, 324–25.

13. Ibid., 330.

14. Ibid., 337.

15. Beth L. Bailey, *From Front Porch to Back Seat: Courtship in Twentieth-Century America* (Baltimore: Johns Hopkins University Press, 1988), 131.

16. A. L. Shumway and C. Dew. Brower, *Oberliniana* (n.p., 1883), 91.

17. Ibid., 86–87.

18. "New Cash Rule Worries Whittier Hall Girls," *New York Times*, March 14, 1906, 9.

19. Florence M. Read, *The Story of Spelman College* (Atlanta, Ga., n.p., 1961), 211.

20. Eldridge, *CO-EDiquette: Poise and Popularity for Every Girl* (New York: E. P. Dutton, 1936), 135–36.

21. Ibid., 134–35.

22. Jeane Westin, *Making Do: How Women Survived the '30s* (Chicago: Follett Publishing, 1976), 117. Emphasis in original.

23. Gael Greene, *Sex and the College Girl* (New York: Dell Publishing, 1964), 45.

24. "Princetonians Sell Girl-Hunters Guide," *New York Times*, October 9, 1965, 1.

25. Peter M. Sandman and the staff of the *Daily Princetonian, Where the Girls Are* (New York: Dial Press, 1967), 89–90.

26. Ibid., 200, 217.

27. "What Every Girl Should Know," *Time*, April 15, 1966, 22.

28. J. A. Latham and T. G. Plate, *Where the Boys Are* (Amherst, Mass.: Amherst Publishing, 1966), 20, 32.

29. Kate W. Jameson, "Getting Adjusted to the Campus," in Jameson and Lockwood, *The Freshman Girl*, 8.

30. Gulielma Fell Alsop, M.D., and Mary F. McBride, M.A., *She's Off to College: A Girl's Guide to Campus Life* (New York: Vanguard Press, 1940), 12.

31. "You and Your Teacher," *Teen World*, April 1960, 17.

32. Francis Bruce Strain, *Love at the Threshold: A Book on Social Dating, Romance, and Marriage* (New York: Appleton-Century-Crofts, 1952), 30–31.

33. Joyce Jackson [Helen Louise Crounse], *Joyce Jackson's Guide to Dating* (Eau Claire, Wis.: E. M. Hale, 1957), 125.

34. James W. Putnam, ed., *Lady Lore* (Lawrence, Kans.: The Witan, 1939), 52–53.

35. James L. Summers, "And Now Farewell!" *Calling All Girls*, June 1948, 55.

36. Eldridge, *CO-EDiquette*, 26.

37. Ibid., 28.

38. Elisabeth Ann Hudnut, *You Can Always Tell a Freshman: How to Get the Most Out of Your College Years* (New York: E. P. Dutton, 1949), 103.

39. Wainwright Evans, "Coeducation Is the American Way," *Better Homes & Gardens*, May 1940, 87.

40. Hudnut, *You Can Always Tell a Freshman*, 98.

41. "If Your Daughter Goes to College," *Better Homes & Gardens*, May 1940, 20.

42. Jackson, *Guide to Dating*, 129.

43. Evans, "Coeducation," 20–21.

44. Milicent Washburn Shinn, "The Marriage Rate of College Women," *The Century*, October 1895, 947.

45. Evans, "Coeducation," 21.

46. Ibid.; Alsop and McBride, *She's Off to College*, 16.

47. Strain, *Love at the Threshold*, 15.

48. http://www.wellesley.edu/Welcome/Traditions/hooprolling.html (accessed September 19, 2002).

49. Dorothy C. Stratton and Helen B. Schleman, *Your Best Foot Forward: Social Usage for Young Moderns*, rev. ed. (New York: McGraw-Hill, 1955), 122.

50. "Sadie Hawkins Day," http://www.uchaswv.edu/library/sadie.html (accessed September 21, 2003).

51. Maureen Daly, ed., *Profile of Youth* (Philadelphia: J. B. Lippincott, 1951), 240.

52. See the authorized Al Capp Web site: http://www.lil-abrev.com/sadiehawk. html.

53. San Francisco Historical Photograph Collection #aad-7896 (November 19, 1947); #aad-7907 (November 14, 1947).

54. Peggy Brandstrom, "Campus Correspondence," *Mademoiselle*, August 1948, 12.

55. Emily Post, *Etiquette* (New York: Funk & Wagnalls, 1942), 339.

56. Greene, *Sex and the College Girl*, 203.

57. Editors of *Esquire* Magazine, *Esquire Etiquette: A Guide to Business, Sports, and Social Conduct* (Philadelphia: J. B. Lippincott, 1953), 366.

58. Post, *Etiquette*, 342.

59. Ibid., 340.

60. Editors of *Esquire* Magazine, *Esquire Etiquette*, 365–66.

61. Alice Low, "Blind Date," *Seventeen*, September 1959, 158.

62. Editors of *Esquire* Magazine, *Esquire Etiquette*, 365.

63. Low, "Blind Date," 158, 223.

64. Ibid., 227, 229.

65. Editors of *Esquire* Magazine, *Esquire Etiquette*, 367.

66. Post, *Etiquette*, 345.

67. "So You Want to Be a Football Expert?" *Co-ed*, October 1969, 37.

68. Art Unger, ed., *Datebook's Complete Guide to Dating* (Englewood Cliffs, N.J.: Prentice-Hall, 1960), 144–45.

69. Ibid., 145.

70. "So You Want to Be a Football Expert?" 37.

71. Unger, *Datebook's Complete Guide to Dating*, 145.

72. "How to Handle a College Man," *Datebook*, September 1959, 48.

73. "Morals at College," *Teens Today*, November 1960, 9.

74. Glendon Swarthout, *Where the Boys Are* (New York: Signet Books, 1960), 157.

75. "Beer & the Beach," Time, April 13, 1959, 54; www.glendonswarthout .com/novels/wheretheboysare.htm [accessed March 16, 2004].

76. "The Teen Scene," *Seventeen*, April 1967, 159.

77. Greene, *Sex and the College Girl*, 171.

78. Aimee Wolfe Minkin, interviewed by Katherine Sanderson, October 19, 1993, Mills College Fires of Wisdom Oral History Project, 5.

79. Brett Harvey, *The Fifties: A Women's Oral History* (New York: Harper-Collins, 1993), 33–34.

80. Rickie Solinger, *Wake Up Little Susie: Single Pregnancy and Race before Roe v. Wade* (New York: Routledge, 1992), 103.

81. Charles Van Norden, "A Case of Discipline," *Overland Monthly and Out West Magazine*, March 1896, 282–83.

82. Ibid., 283.

83. Editors of *Esquire* Magazine, *What Every Young Man Should Know* (New York: Bernard Geis Associates, 1962), 147.

Chapter Eight: Graduation and After

1. "Gowns for Commencement," *New York Times*, May 6, 1894, 18.

2. Robert A. Haslun, "Commencement and Tradition at Oberlin," *Oberlin Alumni Magazine* 69, July/August 1973, 12–14.

3. Helen Lefkowitz Horowitz, *Alma Mater: Design and Experience in the Women's Colleges from Their Nineteenth-Century Beginnings to the 1930s* (2d ed.; Amherst: University of Massachusetts Press, 1993), 296; "No Trouble at Vassar," *New York Times*, March 31, 1887, 1.

4. Elizabeth Eldridge, *Co-Ediquette: Poise and Popularity for Every Girl* (New York: E. P. Dutton, 1936), 39.

5. Quoted in Jean Glidden Henderson and Algo D. Henderson, *Ms. Goes to College* (Carbondale: Southern Illinois University Press, 1975), 8.

6. Mrs. Mary Wood-Allen, M.D., *What a Young Woman Ought to Know* (Philadelphia, VIR Publishing, rev. ed., 1905), 24.

7. Helen E. Starrett, *After College, What? For Girls* (Boston: Thomas Y. Corwell, 1896), 10.

8. Ibid., 12 note 1.

9. Mary Fanton Roberts, "When the College Girl Comes Home to Stay," *New York Times*, January 26, 1913, 8.

10. Ibid., 8.

11. According to 2002 U.S. Census Bureau statistics, 46 percent of women ages eighteen to twenty-four lived at home, as did 55 percent of men. Deb-

bie Geiger, "For Adult Children Living at Home—and Their Parents—Here Are Ways to Smooth the Road," *Newsday*, February 23, 2004, 44.

12. John Cowan, M.D., *The Science of a New Life* (New York: Cowan & Co., 1869), 59–61.

13. Ibid., 382–83.

14. Ibid., 53.

15. Ibid.

16. Margaret E. Sangster, *Winsome Womanhood* (New York: Fleming H. Revell Co., 1900), 80–81.

17. John D'Emilio and Estelle B. Freedman, *Intimate Matters: A History of Sexuality in America* (New York: Harper & Row, 1988), 190.

18. Milicent Washburn Shinn, "The Marriage Rate of College Women," *The Century*, October 1895, 948.

19. M.T., "College Women and Matrimony," *The Century*, June 1899, 325.

20. Starrett, After College, 8.

21. "Calls Girls of Today Too Erudite for Men," *New York Times*, July 7, 1929, 21.

22. Ernest Havemann and Patricia Salter West, *They Went to College: The College Graduate in America Today* (New York: Harcourt, Brace & Co., 1952), 55.

23. Sangster, *Winsome Womanhood*, 125.

24. Royal S. Copeland, M.D., "Alarming Decrease in American Babies," *Ladies Home Journal*, July 1922, 37.

25. William S. Sadler, M.D., "College Women and Race Suicide," *Ladies Home Journal*, April 1922, 29.

26. "College Maid to Measure," *Mademoiselle*, August 1940, 225.

27. Ibid., 226.

28. Olive San Louie Anderson, *An American Girl and Her Four Years in a Boys' College* (New York: D. Appleton and Co., 1878), 113.

29. Irving Stone, ed., *There Was Light: Autobiography of a University, Berkeley: 1868–1968* (Garden City, N.Y.: Doubleday, 1970), 78, 84–85.

30. Frank B. Gilbreth, Jr., and Ernestine Gilbreth Carey, *Belles on Their Toes* (New York: Thomas Y. Crowell, 1950), 141.

31. Ibid., 95.

32. Neal Gilkyson Stuart, "Mother Is a Doctor Now!" *Ladies Home Journal*, May 1958, 138.

33. J. T. Freeman, "My Working Doesn't Hurt Anyone," *Ladies Home Journal*, October 1958, 161.

34. "Should Mothers of Young Children Work?" *Ladies Home Journal*, November 1958, 158.

35. Judy Rogers, "Career at Home," *Ladies Home Journal*, June 1958, 6.

36. Kate W. Jameson, "Getting Adjusted to the Campus," in *The Freshman Girl: A Guide to College Life*, ed. Kate W. Jameson and Frank C. Lockwood (Boston: D. C. Heath, 1925), 30.

37. Bancroft Beatley, *Another Look at Women's Education* (Boston: Simmons College, 1955), ix, 11.

38. Ibid., 8.

39. "The University and the Woman," University of Oregon Leaflet Series, vol. 5, no. 12 (July 1920), unpaginated; University of California Class of 1905, *Record of the Class of 1905. University of California, Volume I* (Berkeley, Calif.: Berkeley Press, 1908), 32; Eunice Fuller Barnard, "Middle-Life Portrait of the Woman Graduate," *New York Times*, June 19, 1938, 7.

40. "Break in This Summer," *Senior Prom*, May 1950, 25, 24.

41. Eileen Murphy, "Nurse . . . Someone Needs You," *Seventeen*, August 1948, 113.

42. "You and Your Career: The Sky's the Limit!" *Co-ed*, October 1956, 19.

43. "Designed by 23 College Girls," *McCall's*, November 1958, 139.

44. J. D. Ratcliff, "Careers in Saving Lives," *Women's Home Companion*, April 1952, 40, 109.

45. Margot MacDonald, "So You Want to Be a Scientist," *Seventeen*, September 1951, 150.

46. Bil Gilbert, "Science, the Future Career," *American Girl*, January 1956, 15.

47. "Training for Your Career," *Seventeen*, September 1951, 190.

48. Marion Odmark, "Soft Pedal That Career," *Mademoiselle*, May 1940, 91.

49. Ibid.

50. Ibid., 91, 172.

51. Ferdinand Lundberg and Marynia F. Farnham, M.D., *Modern Woman: The Lost Sex* (New York: Harper & Brothers, 1947), 366.

52. Ibid., 370.

53. Barnard, "Middle-Life Portrait," 7, 20.

54. "Should Mothers of Young Children Work?" 156.

55. Havemann and West, *They Went to College*, 134, 136.

56. Marilyn Bender, "The Class of 1942: What Happened to Those Girls in Saddle Shoes?" *New York Times*, June 10, 1967, 24.

Epilogue: Since Then

1. All quoted in Marian Burros, "Critique from 50's Wellesley Grads," *New York Times*, December 29, 2003, E.1; http://www.wellesley.edu/PublicAffairs/WellesleyWeek/Archive/2004/ww021604.html#five (accessed August 10, 2005).

2. Fred M. Hechinger, "Women's College Seen in Decline," *New York Times*, March 19, 1961, 69.

3. Jonathan Miller, "Is There a Role Today for a Women's College?" *New York Times*, July 24, 2005, 14NJ.1.

4. Karen W. Arenson, "Barnard Students Will Stick with Ms.," *New York Times*, December 8, 1998, B.3.

5. Eunice Fuller Barnard, "Our Colleges for Women: Co-ed or Not?" *New York Times Magazine*, March 26, 1933, 4.

6. Mills College, *Mills Crest* 1991, 17.

7. Cartoon by Corky, *San Diego Star-Bulletin*, May 7, 1990.

8. "Stress Worse for Freshman Women," *Madison Capital Times* [Madison, Wis.], January 25, 1999, 1A.

9. William Cellis 3d, "More College Women Drinking to Get Drunk," *New York Times*, June 8, 1994, B7; "44% of College Students Are Binge Drinkers, Poll Says," *New York Times*, December 7, 1994, B12; Mindy

Sink, "Drinking Deaths Draw Attention to Old Campus Problem," *New York Times*, November 9, 2004, A16.

10. "Stress Worse for Freshman Women," 1A.

11. Mary Duenwald, "The Dorms May Be Great, But How's the Counseling?" *New York Times*, October 26, 2004, F1; Deborah Sontag, "Who Was Responsible for Elizabeth Shin?" *New York Times Magazine*, April 28, 2002, 58.

12. Jody Temkin, "Q&A/Paul Joffe; U. of I. Takes No-Nonsense Stance on Curbing Suicides," *Chicago Tribune*, January 9, 2005, 3.

13. Karen W. Arenson, "After Suicides, N.Y.U. Will Limit Access to Balconies," *New York Times*, March 30, 2005, B2.

14. Sontag, "Who Was Responsible for Elizabeth Shin?" 58.

15. Jeffrey R. Armstrong, ed., *Education Law Update*, vol. 4, no. 1, October 2005, accessed online at http://www.psgglaw.com/Education%20LAw%20Up date%20October%202005%20FINAL.htm (accessed November 27, 2005).

16. "College Tightens Its Behavior Code," *New York Times*, October 10, 1982, 57.

17. Ethan Bronner, "In a Revolution of Rules, Campuses Go Full Circle," *New York Times*, March 3, 1999, A1.

18. Susan Reimer, "In Essay, Loyola Professor Likens Coed Dorms to Brothels," *The Sun* [Baltimore, Md.], March 8, 2005, 1D.

19. Jayne Clark, "Some Resorts Throwing Cold Water on Spring Break," *USA Today*, February 14, 2003, D1.

20. Ibid.

21. Marco R. Della Cava, "Girls on Film—What Happens on Spring Break May Not Stay There as Partiers Pack Video Cameras," *Chicago Sun-Times*, April 4, 2005, 50.

22. Students quoted in Mireya Navarro, "The Very Long Legs of 'Girls Gone Wild,'" *New York Times*, April 4, 2004, 6.

23. Lori Rackl and Andrew Hermann, "Women trekking back to their dorm in the morning after a hookup take the 'walk of shame.' For guys, it's the 'stride of pride.' College women today are more sexually liberated, but double standards remain. Series: SEX ON CAMPUS: HANGING OUT AND HOOKING UP," *Chicago Sun-Times*, March 21, 2005.

24. Peggy O'Crowley, "Study Says a Good Man Is Hard to Date: Family File," *The Star-Ledger* [Newark, N.J.], July 29, 2001, 1; Norval Glenn and Elizabeth Marquardt, "Hooking Up, Hanging Out, and Hoping for Mr. Right: College Women on Dating and Mating Today," (New York: Institute for American Values, 2001), 4.

SELECTED BIBLIOGRAPHY

Alsop, Gulielma Fell, M.D., and Mary F. McBride, M.A. *She's Off to College: A Girl's Guide to College Life.* New York: Vanguard Press, 1940.

An American Mother. "Is a College Education the Best for Our Girls?" *Ladies Home Journal*, July 1900.

Anderson, Olive San Louie. *An American Girl and Her Four Years in a Boys' College.* New York: D. Appleton and Co., 1878.

Bailey, Beth L. *From Front Porch to Back Seat: Courtship in Twentieth-Century America.* Baltimore: Johns Hopkins University Press, 1988.

Ballou, Nellie. *Etiquette at College [The Campus Blue Book].* Harrisburg, Pa.: Handy Book Corp., 1925.

Bigglestone, W. E. "Oberlin College and the Negro Student, 1865–1940." *Journal of Negro History*, vol. 56, no. 3 (July 1971), 198–219.

Brazzell, Johnetta Cross. "Bricks without Straw: Missionary-Sponsored Black Higher Education in the Post-Emancipation Era." *Journal of Higher Education*, vol. 63, no. 1 (January/February 1992), 26–49.

Butler, Vera M. *Education as Revealed by New England Newspapers Prior to 1850.* Philadelphia [n.p.], 1935.

Cahn, Susan K. *Coming On Strong: Gender and Sexuality in Twentieth-Century Women's Sport.* New York: Free Press, 1994.

"Christmas Pranks of College Girls." *Ladies Home Journal*, December 1906, 17.

Clarke, Edward H., M.D. *Sex in Education, or, A Fair Chance for the Girls.* Boston: James R. Osgood and Co., 2d ed., 1873. Reprint, New York: Arno Press, 1972.

"College Girls: If They Could Only Cook." *Quick*, September 8, 1952.

"College Girls' Larks and Pranks." *Ladies Home Journal*, January 1900; March 1900; April 1900; August 1900.

"College Sororities: They Pose a Social Problem," *Life*, December 17, 1945.

Covert, Alice Lent. "Brains Are for the Birds!" *Redbook*, August 1957.

Crane, Diana. *Fashion and Its Social Agendas: Class, Gender, and Identity in Clothing*. Chicago: University of Chicago Press, 2000.

Crawford, Mary Caroline. *The College Girl of America and the Institutions Which Make Her What She Is*. Boston: L.C. Page & Co., 1905.

Cross, Barbara M., ed. *The Educated Woman in America: Selected Writings of Catharine Beecher, Margaret Fuller, and M. Carey Thomas*. New York: Teachers College Press, 1965.

Deane, Peg. August 8, 1994. Interview by Mills College Fires of Wisdom Oral History Project.

Earnest, Ernest. *Academic Procession: An Informal History of the American College 1636 to 1953*. Indianapolis, Ind.: Bobbs-Merrill Co., 1953.

Eldrige, Elizabeth. *CO-EDiquette: Poise and Popularity for Every Girl*. New York: E. P. Dutton, 1936.

Elliott, Orrin Leslie. *Stanford University: The First Twenty-Five Years*. Stanford, Calif.: Stanford University Press, 1937.

Esquire Magazine, editors. *Esquire Etiquette: A Guide to Business, Sports and Social Conduct*. Philadelphia: J. B. Lippincott, 1953.

Farnham, Christie Anne. *The Education of the Southern Belle: Higher Education and Student Socialization in the Antebellum South*. New York: New York University Press, 1994.

Fass, Paula S. *The Damned and the Beautiful: American Youth in the 1920s*. New York: Oxford University Press, 1977.

Finley, Ruth E. *The Lady of Godey's, Sarah Josepha Hale*. Philadelphia: J. B. Lippincott, 1931.

Friedan, Betty. *The Feminine Mystique*. New York: W. W. Norton, 1963.

Garofoli, Joe. "On College Campuses, It's a Woman's World. Females Outnumber Males—and Diploma Gap Will Widen." *San Francisco Chronicle*, August 26, 2002.

Going Places: A Guidebook to Eastern Women's Colleges from Virginia to New Hampshire. New York: Yale Banner Publications [Kelly Publishing], 1956.

Gordon, Lynn D. "The Gibson Girl Goes to College: Popular Culture and

Women's Higher Education in the Progressive Era, 1890–1920," *American Quarterly*, vol. 39, no. 2 (Summer 1987), 211–30.

Greene, Gael. *Sex and the College Girl*. New York: Dell Publishing, 1964.

Hall, Florence Howe. *The Correct Thing in Good Society*. Boston: Dana Estes & Co., 1902.

Havemann, Ernest, and Patricia Salter West. *They Went to College: The College Graduate in America Today*. New York: Harcourt, Brace & Co., 1952.

Henderson, Jean Glidden, and Algo D. Henderson. *Ms. Goes to College*. Carbondale: Southern Illinois University Press, 1975.

Holzinger, Jean. "What's in a Name?" *Hollins*, Spring 2004, 24.

Horowitz, Helen Lefkowitz. *Campus Life: Undergraduate Cultures from the End of the Eighteenth Century to the Present*. New York: Alfred A. Knopf, 1987.

———. *Alma Mater: Design and Experience in the Women's Colleges from Their Nineteenth-Century Beginnings to the 1930s*. 2nd ed. Amherst: University of Massachusetts Press, 1993.

———. *The Power and Passion of M. Carey Thomas*. New York: Alfred A. Knopf, 1994.

"How to Handle a College Man." *Datebook*, September 1959.

Howard, William Lee, M.D. *Confidential Chats with Girls*. New York: Edward J. Clode, Publisher, 1911.

Hudnut, Elisabeth Ann. *You Can Always Tell a Freshman: How to Get the Most Out of Your College Years*. New York: E. P. Dutton, 1949.

Hutchings, Doris Hillman, and Jane Cudlip King. Interview by Kathleen McCrea. August 6, 1995, Mills College Fires of Wisdom Oral History Project.

"If Your Daughter Goes to College." *Better Homes & Gardens*, May 1940, 20.

"I'm Sick of Acting Like a Moron!" *Teens Today*, September 1959.

Jameson, Kate W., and Frank C. Lockwood, eds. *The Freshman Girl: A Guide to College Life*. Boston: D. C. Heath and Co., 1925.

Jones, Maxine D. "Student Unrest at Talladega College, 1887–1914." *Journal of Negro History*, vol. 70, no. 3/4 (Summer–Autumn 1985), 73–81.

Kleinman, Lynne H. *The Milwaukee-Downer Woman*. Appleton, Wisc.: Lawrence University Press, 1997. http://www.lawrence.edu/news/pubs/md woman/daily.shtml (accessed August 1, 2004).

Latham, J. A., and T. G. Plate. *Where the Boys Are*. Amherst, Mass.: Amherst Publishing Corp., 1966.

Lee, Calvin B. T. *The Campus Scene, 1900–1970: Changing Styles in Undergraduate Life*. New York: David McKay Co., 1970.

Lee, Dorothy D. "What Shall We Teach Women?" *Mademoiselle*, August 1947.

Lowe, Margaret A. *Looking Good: College Women and Body Image, 1875–1930*. Baltimore: Johns Hopkins University Press, 2003.

Lucas, Christopher J. *American Higher Education: A History*. New York: St. Martin's Press, 1994.

Lundberg, Ferdinand, and Marynia F. Farnham, M.D. *Modern Woman: The Lost Sex*. New York: Harper & Brothers, 1947.

Lutz, Alma. *Emma Willard: Daughter of Democracy*. Boston: Houghton Mifflin, 1929.

Mancini, Olivia. "Vassar's First Black Graduate: She Passed for White." *Journal of Blacks in Higher Education*, no. 34 (Winter 2001–2002), 108–9.

Marchalonis, Shirley. *College Girls: A Century in Fiction*. New Brunswick, N.J.: Rutgers University Press, 1995.

McGuigan, Dorothy Gies. *A Dangerous Experiment: 100 Years of Women at the University of Michigan*. Ann Arbor, Mich.: Center for Continuing Education of Women, 1970.

Meade, L. T. *A Sweet Girl Graduate*. New York: New York Book Co., n.d.

Minkin, Aimee Wolfe. Interview by Katherine Sanderson. October 19, 1993. Mills College Fires of Wisdom Oral History Project.

Mitchell, S. Weir. "When College Is Hurtful to a Girl," *Ladies Home Journal*, June 1900.

Moats, Alice-Leone. *No Nice Girl Swears*. New York: Blue Ribbon Books, 1933.

A Mother. "Some College Girl Follies," *Good Housekeeping*, September 1909.

"New College Trend: Women Studies." *New York Times*, January 7, 1971, 37.

Pierce, Anna Eloise. *Deans and Advisors of Women and Girls*. New York: Professional & Technical Press, 1928.

Pierson, Irene. *Campus Cues*. 3d ed. Danville, Illinois: Interstate Publishers & Printers, 1962.

Pouslon, Susan L., and Leslie Miller-Bernal. "Two Unique Histories of Coeducation: Catholic and Historically Black Institutions." Pp. 22–51 in *Going*

Coed: Women's Experiences in Formerly Men's Colleges and Universities 1950–2000, ed. Leslie Miller-Bernal and Susan L. Poulson. Nashville, Tenn.: Vanderbilt University Press, 2004.

Power, Edward J. *Catholic Higher Education in America: A History*. New York: Appleton-Century-Crofts, 1972.

Read, Florence M. *The Story of Spelman College*. Atlanta, Ga. [n.p.], 1961.

University of California, Class of 1905. *Record of the Class of 1905. University of California, Volume I*. Berkeley, Calif.: Berkeley Press, 1908.

Rorer, Mrs. S. T. "Why I Am Opposed to Pies." *Ladies Home Journal*, August 1900.

———. "What College Girls Eat." *Ladies Home Journal*, November 1905.

Rowland, Helen. *Reflections of a Bachelor Girl*. New York: Dodge Publishing, 1909.

Rudolph, Frederick. *The American College and University: A History*. New York: Alfred A. Knopf, 1962.

Rury, John, and Glenn Harper. "The Trouble with Coeducation: Mann and Women at Antioch, 1853–1860," *History of Education Quarterly*, vol. 26, no. 4 (Winter 1986), 481–502.

Russett, Cynthia Eagle. *Sexual Science: The Victorian Construction of Womanhood*. Cambridge: Harvard University Press, 1991.

Sandman, Peter M., and the staff of the *Daily Princetonian. Where the Girls Are*. New York: Dell Publishing, 1967.

Sangster, Margaret E. *Winsome Womanhood*. New York: Fleming H. Revell Co., 1900.

Schreier, Barbara. "Sporting Wear." Pp. 92–123 in *Men and Women: Dressing the Part*, ed. by Claudia Brush Kidwell and Valerie Steele. Washington, D.C.: Smithsonian Institution Press, 1989.

Schumer, Fran. *Most Likely to Succeed: Six Women from Harvard and What Became of Them*. New York: Random House, 1986.

Scott, Anne Firor. *The American Woman: Who Was She?* Englewood Cliffs, N.J.: Prentice-Hall, 1971.

Seelye, L. Clark. "The Influence of Sororities." *Ladies Home Journal*, September 1907, 12.

Solomon, Barbara Miller. *In the Company of Educated Women: A History of*

Women and Higher Education in America. New Haven, Conn.: Yale University Press, 1985.

Sontag, Deborah. "Who Was Responsible for Elizabeth Shin?" *New York Times Magazine*, April 28, 2002.

"Stephens Studies for Marriage." *Senior Prom*, September 1950, 48.

Stock, Phyllis. *Better Than Rubies: A History of Women's Education*. New York: G. P. Putnam's Sons, 1978.

Strain, Frances Bruce. *Love at the Threshold: A Book on Social Dating, Romance, and Marriage*. New York: Appleton-Century-Crofts, 1952.

Student Religious Council. Freshman Handbook of the Massachusetts State College 1935–1936.

Swarthout, Glendon. *Where the Boys Are*. New York: Signet Books, 1960.

Thompson, Eleanor Wolf. *Education for Ladies, 1830–1860: Ideas on Education in Magazines for Women*. Morningside Heights, N.Y.: King's Crown Press, 1947.

Trilling, Diana. "Are Women's Colleges Really Necessary?" Pp. 255–62 in *Women Today: Their Conflicts, Their Frustrations, and Their Fulfillments*, ed. Elizabeth Bragdon. Indianapolis, Ind.: Bobbs-Merrill Co., 1953.

Tye, Larry. *The Father of Spin: Edward L. Bernays and the Birth of Public Relations*. New York: Crown Publishers, 1998.

Webster, Jean. *When Patty Went to College*. New York: Grosset & Dunlap, 1903.

Wilk, Rona M. " 'What's a Crush?' A Study of Crushes and Romantic Friendships at Barnard College, 1900–1920." OAH *Magazine of History*, July 2004, 20–22.

Wolters, Raymond. *The New Negro on Campus: Black College Rebellions of the 1920s*. Princeton, N.J.: Princeton University Press, 1975.

"You and Your Teacher." *Teen World*, April 1960.

Zagarri, Rosemarie. "The Rights of Man and Woman in Post-Revolutionary America." *William and Mary Quarterly*, 3d ser., vol. 55, no. 2 (April 1998), 203–30.

PERMISSIONS/ILLUSTRATION CREDITS

Page 2 Chapter head: College women balancing books on heads. © Bettmann/CORBIS.

Page 7 Lynn's college I.D. Collection of the author.

Page 9 Co-ed 1904, from *The College Girl of America*, by Mary Caroline Crawford (Boston: L.C. Page & Company, 1905).

Page 11 Front cover, *The College Female*, by William E. Miles (Derby, Connecticut: Monarch Books, Inc., 1963). Cover Kodachrome from Three Lions Studios, Inc.

Page 14 Chapter head: Young women sketching nearly naked man in art class. © FPG/Getty Images.

Page 22 Emma Willard. Library of Congress, Rare Book and Special Collections Division.

Page 37 Matthew Vassar. Special Collections, Vassar College Libraries.

Page 38 Vassar College. Library of Congress, Prints and Photographs Division [LC-USZ62-4194].

Page 52 Chapter head: Women in white skirts rolling hoops. © Bettmann/CORBIS.

Page 59 Homesick college girl at Florida State, from *Flastacowo* (1941), Florida State College for Women, Tallahassee, Florida.

Page 64 Students at Bethune-Cookman College. Library of Congress, Prints and Photographs Division, FSA/OWI Collection [LC-USW3-016867-C].

Page 75   Chafing dish party, from *The College Girl of America*, by Mary Caroline Crawford (Boston: L.C. Page & Company, 1905).

Page 80   Car packing sorority girls. © Bettmann/CORBIS.

Page 98   Front cover, *CO-EDiquette*, by Elizabeth Eldridge (New York: E.P. Dutton & Company, Inc., 1936).

Page 104   Chapter head: Four girls abreast. Women standing in shorts, skirts. © Bettmann/CORBIS.

Page 114   Girls in ties, from *The Oriole* (1898), Maryland College, Lutherville, Maryland.

Page 116   Co-ed frocks. Co-ed dresses catalog, circa 1920s.

Page 117   College Girl hairnets, circa 1920s.

Page 118   Advertisement for Campus Make-up, 1944.

Page 119   Co-Ed Citrus Fruit label, circa 1950s.

Page 120   "Betty Co-Ed Script Girl." Betty Co-Ed of Hollywood catalog, circa 1940s.

Page 129   Advertisement for Singer Sewing Machines, 1946. Used with permission from Singer Sewing Company.

Page 130   Advertisement for Hanes Stockings, 1959. Courtesy of Sara Lee Corporation.

Page 132   Advertisement for Laco Shampoo, 1946.

Page 142   Chapter head: Wall climbing. © Kurt Hutton/Getty Images.

Page 147   Students relaxing in the smoking room of Grace Dodge Hall. Courtesy of Teachers College, Columbia University.

Page 155   Fisk students in chapel. Library of Congress, Prints and Photographs Division [LC-USZ62-38623].

Page 161   College women having pillow fight. © Bettmann/CORBIS.

Page 176   Chapter head: Sewing students at Howard University. © CORBIS.

Page 182   Man, woman, elephant. Montage of nineteenth-century advertising cuts by the author.

Page 195   Students in laundry lab. Courtesy of Teachers College, Columbia University.

Page 199   Advertisement for Borden products, 1948. Borden, Elsie, and "Elsie the Cow" used with permission from BDS Two, Inc.

Page 201   Cornell University home economics students learning the different

elements of various irons and the proper maintenance of the tool. ©
Nina Leen/Getty Images.

Page 203 *Quick* magazine cover photo by John Vachon, 1952.

Page 205 Front cover of *Waverly*, by Amelia Elizabeth Walden (Berkley Highland Books, 1963).

Page 208 Front cover of *College Knits* (Bernhard Ulmann Co., Inc., 1958).

Page 211 Advertisement for Dura-Gloss Nail-Polish, circa 1940s.

Page 214 PBK baby. Illustration by Lucille Corcos, by permission of David C.
Levy.

Page 219 College suffragists. Library of Congress, Prints and Photographs
Division [LC-USZ62-31799 DLC].

Page 226 Chapter head: Women practicing fencing. © Bettmann/CORBIS.

Page 232 Oklahoma State University students jogging. © Bettmann/CORBIS.

Page 240 Maryland College class of 1899 basketball team, from *The Oriole*
(1898), Maryland College, Lutherville, Maryland.

Page 241 Maryland College class of 1900 basketball team, from *The Oriole*
(1898), Maryland College, Lutherville, Maryland.

Page 245 Advertisement for Tomboy middy blouses, 1922.

Page 248 Portrait of Gladys Scherer. © Bettmann/CORBIS.

Page 276 Chapter head: Sadie Hawkins Day Race at San Francisco State
(blindfolded girl). San Francisco History Center, San Francisco Public Library.

Page 280 Front cover of *Sex Life of the College Girl*, by M. D. Nevins (The
Genell Corporation, 1964).

Page 286 Front cover of *Going Places* (Yale Banner Publications, 1956). Illustration by Phelps Berdan.

Page 291 Hunting College. Tip 'n' Twinkle brand novelty matchbook (1957).

Page 296 "Sadie Hawkins Race" (girl grabs guy climbing away). Sadie Hawkins
Day Race. San Francisco History Center, San Francisco Public
Library.

Page 298 Big Trunk On Campus. Advertisement for Horn Luggage, circa 1940s.

Page 302 Football favor. Party favor, circa 1930s.

Page 304 Front cover of *Where the Boys Are*, by Glendon Swarthout (New York:
Signet Books, 1960).